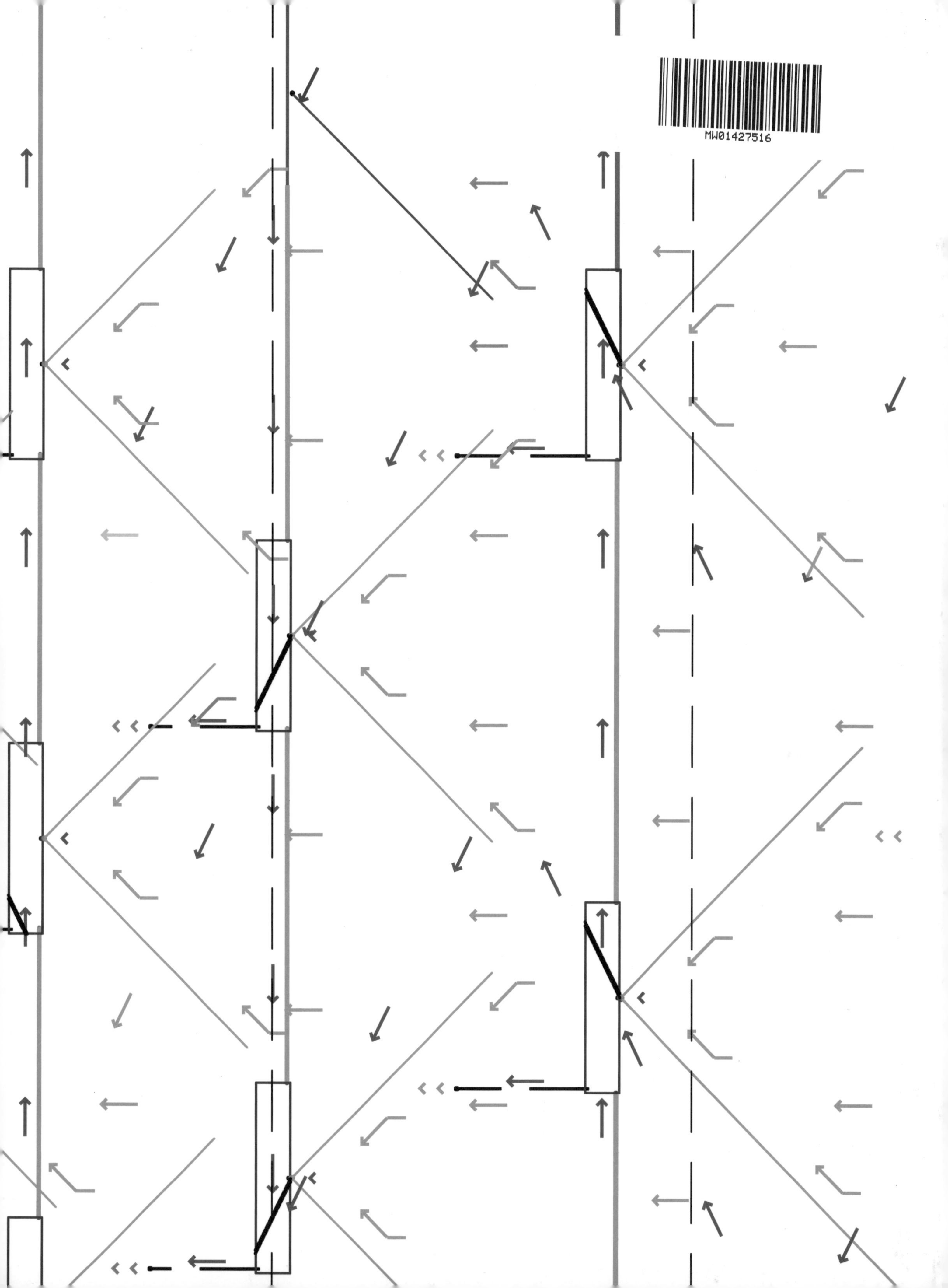

LIAT MARGOLIS
AZIZA CHAOUNI

**OUT
OF
WATER
Design Solutions
for Arid Regions**

With a Foreword by Herbert Dreiseitl

Birkhäuser
Basel

This research and publication was kindly supported by:
SSHRC (Social Sciences and Humanities Research Council), Canada
Holcim (Canada) Inc.
John H. Daniels Faculty of Architecture, Landscape, and Design, University of Toronto
Connaught New Researcher Award, University of Toronto
OALA (Ontario Association of Landscape Architects)
LACF (Landscape Architecture Canada Foundation)

Layout, cover design, and typography:
Anita Matusevics, Wonder incorporated, Toronto

Copy editing: Robin Paxton-Beesley

Library of Congress Cataloging-in-Publication data
A CIP catalog record for this book has been applied for at the Library of Congress.

Bibliographic information published by the German National Library
The German National Library lists this publication in the
Deutsche Nationalbibliografie; detailed bibliographic data are available on the Internet at
http://dnb.dnb.de.

This work is subject to copyright. All rights are reserved, whether the whole or part of the material is concerned, specifically the rights of translation, reprinting, re-use of illustrations, recitation, broadcasting, reproduction on microfilms or in other ways, and storage in databases. For any kind of use, permission of the copyright owner must be obtained.

This publication is also available
as an e-book pdf (ISBN 978-3-03821-006-1) and
EPUB (ISBN 978-3-03821-970-5).

© 2015 Birkhäuser Verlag GmbH, Basel
P.O. Box 44, 4009 Basel, Switzerland
Part of Walter de Gruyter GmbH, Berlin/Boston

Printed on acid-free paper produced from chlorine-free pulp. TCF ∞

Printed in Germany

ISBN 978-3-03821-541-7

9 8 7 6 5 4 3 2 1
www.birkhauser.com

Foreword *Herbert Dreiseitl* 7
Preface 8
How to Read the Case Studies 12

Introduction: Are We Out of Water? 14

Water, Technology, and Society: A Historical Overview *Antoine Picon* 28

PART 1
WATER FOR DOMESTIC USE

INTRODUCTION Beyond Low-Flush Toilets 41

ESSAYS

Technical Optimism as an Antidote to Water Scarcity:
Desalination Systems in Israel, Australia, and Spain *Alon Tal* 46

A New Model for Water Technology Dissemination:
Reaching 20 Million People by 2020 with Better Water and Sanitation
Camille Dow Baker and Tommy Ka Kit Ngai 60

CASE STUDIES

Kanchan Arsenic Filter 70

Liquid Wrap 74

Vena Water Condenser 78

Isla Urbana 82

Down to Earth 86

PART 2
WATER FOR AGRICULTURAL PRODUCTION

INTRODUCTION Water Equals Food 91

ESSAYS

Bridging the Gap between Available Water and Water Demand:
Water Technologies for Agricultural Production in Israel *Eilon M. Adar* 96

The African Market Garden: Introduction of Drip Irrigation
to the Sudano Sahel Region *Dov Pasternak and Lennart Woltering* 104

The Role of Design in Hydrological Modeling of River Basins:
The Drâa Oasis Valley *Aziza Chaouni* 112

A Model for Integrated Agrarian Urbanism:
Water Management in the Jordan River Basin *Fadi Masoud* 128

CASE STUDY

Wastewater Treatment and Reclamation in Israel 142

PART 3
WATER FOR ECOSYSTEM SERVICES

INTRODUCTION Urban Aquatic Ecosystems 147

ESSAYS

Micro-Urban Communities and Water-Made Landscapes: Critical Refugia,
Technologies, and Coexistence in the Arid Lands *Gini Lee* 152

Water-Conserving Design Solutions: Contributions of Water Budget Analysis
in Arid and Semi-Arid Regions *James L. Wescoat Jr.* 162

CASE STUDIES

Hiriya Landfill Recycling Park 174

Taragalte Ecolodge 178

Wadi Hanifah Restoration Project 182

Wadi Hanifah Bioremediation Facility 186

Bibliography and References 192   *Illustration Credits* 200

About the Authors 202   *Project Index* 207   *Acknowledgements* 208

Foreword

Water has always been one of the strongest driving influences for structures in both the natural and urban environments. Societies in arid and desert regions maintain powerful and deep-rooted cultural narratives about water. It is such a significant resource that people in some desert regions actually use numerous words for each of the various manifestations of water—perhaps unsurprisingly, since every drop counts.

Water events can effect dramatic changes to such fragile landscapes. Although a prolonged period of aridity ultimately creates a desert landscape, the character of desert morphology is nonetheless influenced by the flow of water. Water reshapes topography through erosion and sedimentation, digs new *wadis*, carves out rock formations, and alters the structure of plains. What is considered an ordinary rain shower in a temperate climate may temporarily transform a barren desertscape into a flowering paradise. Seemingly overnight, the dryland turns into a bustling hub of animals, insects, and plants, brightly colored and emitting exotic scents and fantastical chirping sounds. This transformation is among the most magical that one can experience in the desert.

There are critical questions at hand about climate change and other man-made alterations to natural water systems. Increasing urbanization of arid regions and the gradual desertification of formerly non-arid regions urge us to ask the questions: How should water be understood in relation to human habitation? What relationship should exist between natural water systems and urban water infrastructure in arid regions?

To explore these questions effectively, we must consider the social and technological aspects of human habitation as intertwined systems. All cultural values, practices, rituals, and beliefs, including those that influence food production, trade, and craft, have an impact on how water is perceived and managed. In order to evaluate the relationship between human habitation and water, we need to understand the priorities behind the regulation of water quantity via storage and supply systems, as well as how water quality is improved by way of filtration. A lack of appropriate water management systems and practices reflects a failure of sustainable human development and of any related design agenda.

Water research and development today focuses primarily on water engineering, such as development of mathematical models for hydraulics, flood risk analysis, and energy efficiency. Although we have acquired a sophisticated array of engineering tools and planning instruments to modify and modulate water, we have done very little research into how urban communities in arid zones can co-evolve with their fragile environments, and with ongoing water shortages. The main challenge, in my view, is *not* a lack of technological know-how, but a lack of integration between technology and urban design, and a shortage of multi-functional design strategies that can address a variety of often conflicting requirements.

Based on my 30 years of experience studying and working with water in a diversity of regions and climate zones across the globe, I have come to realize that traditional engineering solutions often fail to address the issue of extreme water variability in arid regions. Therefore, we need to develop a new approach, in the form of a multi-disciplinary conversation which includes the perspectives of city planning, urban design, landscape architecture, architecture, material technologies, engineering, policy, and community capacity building. Perhaps most importantly, we would benefit from the creation of a stronger emotional and spiritual connection to water. This could be done with artworks that celebrate the value of water and designs that emphasize its boundless properties.

Out of Water: Design Solutions for Arid Regions showcases essays from a diverse group of experts, and features projects by innovative designers. These studies are strong contributions to key topics, such as the sustainable city, water conservation design, and best water management practices. By analyzing different case studies through drawings, diagrams, and text, the book brings theory into the realm of practice, and reaches a wide audience within the design world and beyond. This book presents new insights about water scarcity, and new strategies for keeping water-sensitive regions liveable.

Professor Herbert Dreiseitl

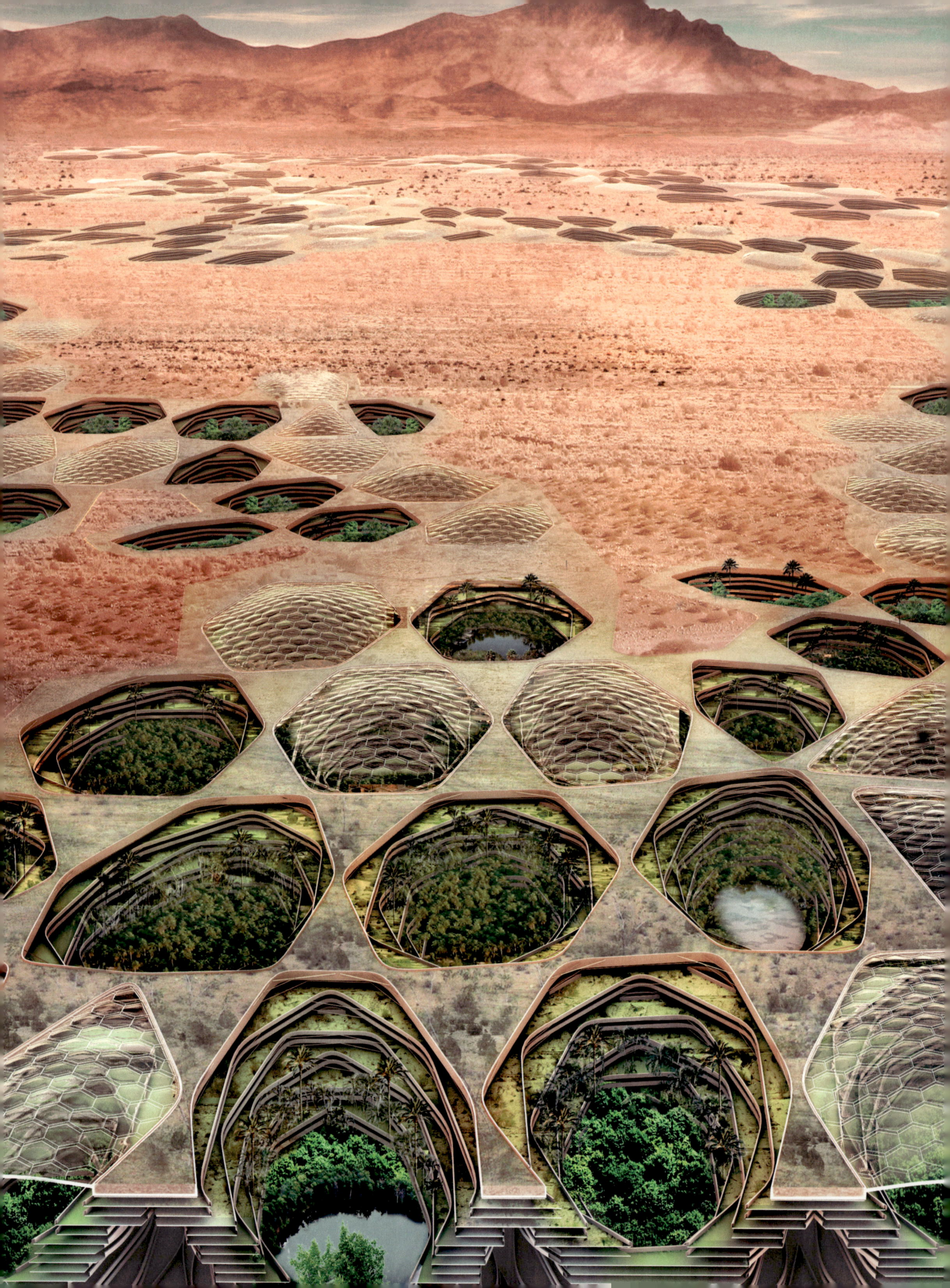

Preface

Based on five years of research, the preparation of and feedback from a traveling exhibition, and the output of a major conference, the results of the *Out of Water* project are represented here in a series of case studies and essays by international experts, including analytical drawings of both projected and implemented solutions. It may be helpful, in the case of this rather complex topic, to describe some of the project's background.

In 2008, architecture professor Aziza Chaouni invited me to collaborate on a design project in the Moroccan Sahara. Born and raised in Fez, Morocco, Aziza had cultivated an interest and expertise in desert tourism and rural developments. She had been working with the Moroccan Ministry of Tourism to develop design models for "eco-tourism" as a way to protect the delicate desert ecology and ethnic culture, prone as they are to the damage and stress associated with a booming tourism industry. We focused on the Drâa Valley, located at the edge of one of the largest oases in Morocco, which has been the home of nomadic and sedentary tribes throughout many centuries.

The Drâa Valley is 1,000km long, reaches from the Atlas Mountains to the edge of the Sahara, and is known as Morocco's "date basket." In the last 40 years, the Drâa Valley's oasian ecology and economy have been threatened by the rapid advancement of the desert dunes in the south, and ongoing desiccation of vast agricultural areas. This transformation is the result of two processes: climate change and man-made alterations to the natural flow of the Drâa River. The agriculture-based economy in the southern reaches of the Drâa began to shrink, defenseless in the face of ongoing desertification, and tourism began to take its place. Our charge was to develop new architectural and landscape models for tourism that would promote water conservation and reforestation as a means to reinforce the oasis edge.

As part of our continuing research, I attended the 2008 International Conference on Drylands, Deserts, and Desertification at Ben Gurion University of the Negev, Israel. The conference was a global gathering of scientists, industry and government representatives, international development aid agencies, and other stakeholders from over 60 countries, concerned about land degradation, sustainable use, and development in the drylands. Lecture topics ranged from agriculture and biotechnology to hydrology, desalination and water treatment, climate change, policy, and desert ecology. Over the four days of the conference, I took the opportunity to introduce myself to a number of presenters, all of whom were absolutely perplexed by my attendance: "What does landscape architecture have to do with water scarcity, land degradation, and climate change?" they would ask.

It immediately dawned on me that the gap between science, politics, and design with respect to water conservation and sustainable development still poses a great challenge to deeper understanding of these issues. I also noted that research efforts in architecture with respect to arid climates are largely concerned with thermal insulation and energy efficiency, while water is considered a given resource to be configured by science and engineering and governed by municipal and regional entities. Architecture, landscape, and urban design were not part of the conversation to discuss mitigating water scarcity and land degradation in drylands. This lack of communication and exchange meant that innovations in water engineering and agricultural science were not being carried over to architecture, landscape, and urban design. That struck both Aziza and myself as untenable, so we decided to address this lack.

Back in Toronto, we created the exhibition "Out of Water: Innovative Technologies in Arid Climates," intended to highlight the vital mechanisms of water flow and sanitation in arid climates. It featured a range of design proposals and built projects, and questioned their roles in contemporary design. In particular, we asked ourselves whether today's environmental preoccupation with water scarcity is actually discernible in the design of urban form. In the exhibition, 24 built and unbuilt case studies were visually analyzed for their approaches to the integration of three water processes: collection, treatment, and/or distribution. The drawings focused on how water management is embedded into design form, environmental function, and experience, while the case studies were selected to represent a diversity of scales and geographical contexts (Figure 1).

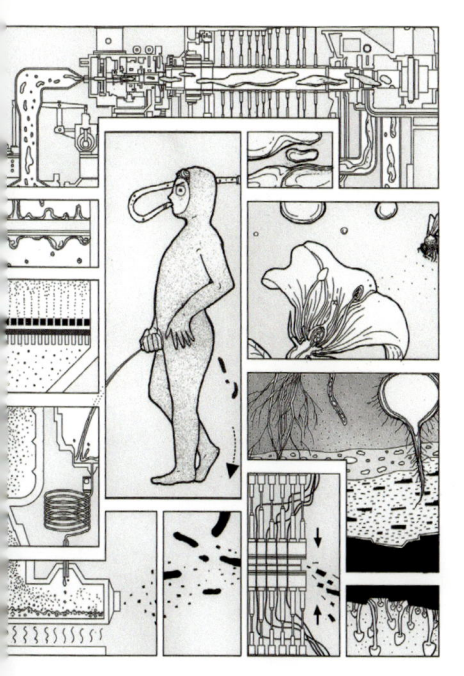

Figure 1: The "Out of Water" exhibition featured five mobile "toilet thrones;" viewers were required to occupy the toilet seat when reading the case studies. Self-conscious and slightly embarrassed by the invasion of privacy, the viewer was invited to reflect upon his or her individual relationship to water and accountability to wastewater cycling (top)

Figure 5: Inspired by David Lynch's 1984 movie *Dune*, architect Jimenez Lai's illustrated narrative "Super Earth" investigates the future of a water-less world (bottom)

Figure 3: Architect Andrew Kudless' "Sietch Nevada" proposes a new typology of underground communities to form around subterranean water storage canals in Nevada (opposite)

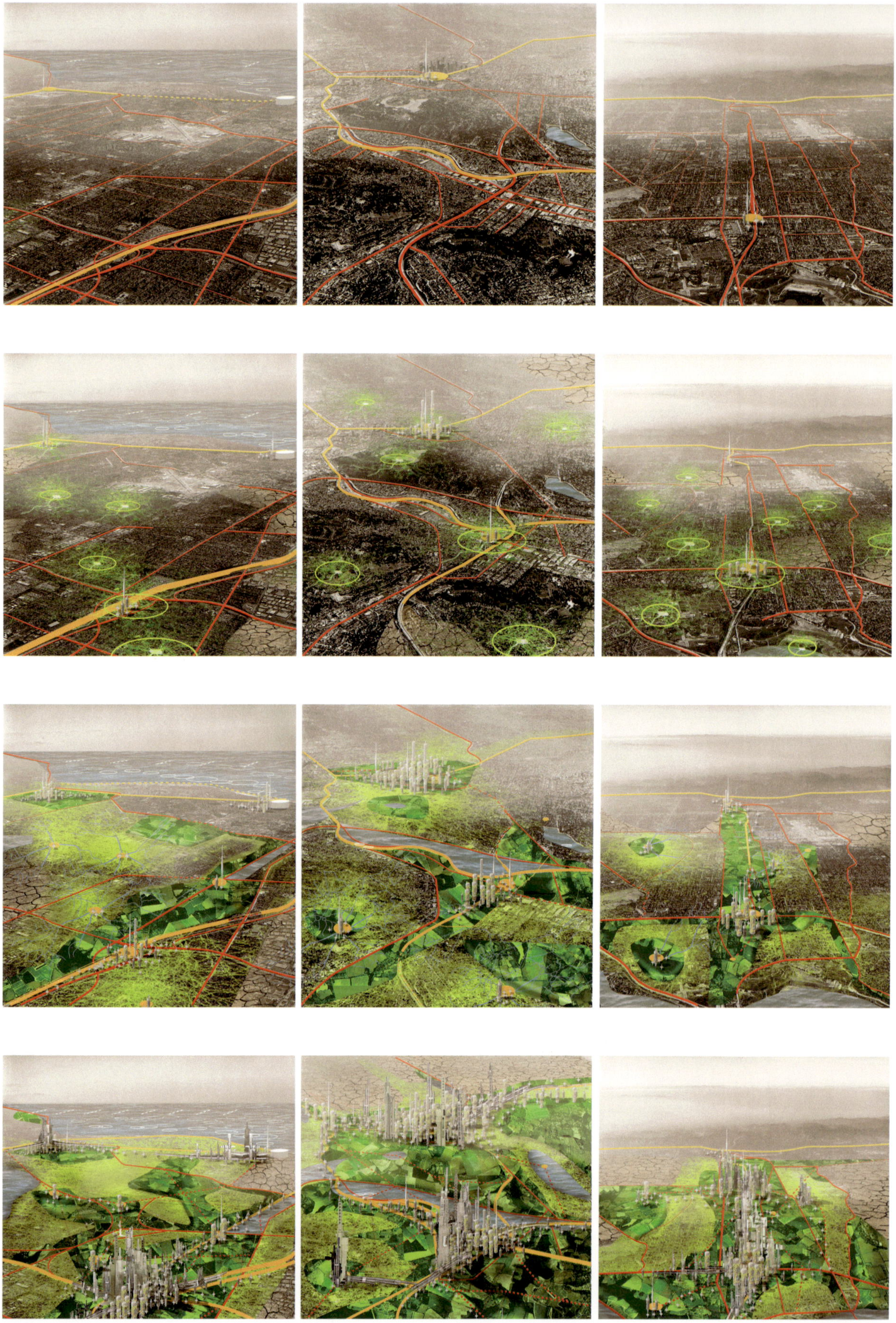

The exhibition also invited ten designers to imagine the future of arid cities, 100 years from now. David Fletcher, for example, imagined the incremental urban densification of Los Angeles, which in turn opens up vast areas for wastewater reclamation via reservoirs and wetlands. As sea levels rise, tidal energy is harnessed to operate desalination, as well as the distribution of reclaimed water (Figure 2). Andrew Kudless inverted the typical urban pattern found in Nevada, imagining an underground community structured around a network of subterranean water storage canals (Figure 3). N-1 turned the house and garden relationship inside out; they employed a biological system for the recycling of grey water in situ that would, in turn, provide interior cooling (Figure 4). And Jimenez Lai told a story of spaceship travelers who fled a parched Earth in search of fresh water, but who, in the meantime, depended on a mechanism that processed their bodily waste into potable water (Figure 5).

The exhibition attempted to speculate upon the relation between water technology and design and to reassert the designer's role in synthesizing the environmental and technical aspects of water systems in arid regions. The "Out of Water" exhibition generated enough interest to travel to six architecture programs across the U.S., so we felt the time was right to go a step further. We wanted to extend our conversations to specific fields of study beyond our own, and so open up a broader dialogue with other disciplines about the sustainable development of arid regions, in particular the natural and social sciences.

The result was the two-day conference "Out of Water: Sustaining Development in Arid Climates," a forum to discuss water scarcity and management in arid regions. The conference encouraged knowledge transfer among a diversity of disciplines with regard to methods and priorities.

The attendees consisted of 22 established and emergent designers, scholars, and scientists, brought together to evaluate currently implemented solutions with regard to their efficiency and geographic relevance. The disciplines represented included environmental law and water policy, public health, agronomy, hydrology, geography, building science, business strategies, civil engineering, landscape architecture, architecture, and urban design. Our primary objectives were, first, to identify applied and theoretical intersections among distinct areas of expertise; and second, to discuss the diverse definitions of water scarcity, technology, and transdisciplinarity. The speakers were selected to represent an array of arid and semi-arid regions, including Australia, Nepal, India, United Arab Emirates, Saudi Arabia, Jordan, Israel, Egypt, the Sudano Sahel, Morocco, Arizona, and Southern California. Despite regional similarities in climate, each project was unique both in the scale of the intervention and in the cultural, economic, and political contexts. The opportunity to transfer lessons learned across regions and disciplines was augmented by the opportunity to compare geographic specificities of arid regions.

- **You may ask: Why focus on arid regions?**
 The answer is clear; arid regions have had no choice but to mandate, innovate, and fully integrate water conservation modalities. From city planning to investment in engineering and infrastructure, to the redesign of building facades, societies in arid climates are faster to embrace a retrofit of their entire operations.

- **You may also ask: Why study water scarcity in non-arid regions?**
 Water scarcity is a symptom of a variety of factors, not only climatological but also anthropogenic, such as water diversion, over-consumption, deforestation, unsustainable agriculture, contamination, and failing or non-existent infrastructure. In fact, some of the world's wettest, most water-rich countries continuously rank highest in water scarcity due to the lack of infrastructure. Other water-rich areas that have reliable access to water and sanitation may be characterized by a general perception of abundance, often resulting in high water usage, and a lack of urgency to rethink water systems in order to make them more efficient and multi-functional.

Arid climates are where necessity begets inventions that may serve as examples for action across a multitude of climate zones and geographies, examples that may soon be even more directly relevant in light of population growth, peak resources, and climate change projections.

We hope that this publication will create new insight about the development of sustainable cities, and inspire designers to exchange ideas and expertise with a broader set of academic and professional fields. The goal, as we see it, is to learn about new concepts, technologies, and materials, as well as to gain exposure to different methods and tools as derived from such exchanges. We are optimistic that this publication will engender new discussions within architectural schools and professional practices, and that these discussions will feature a greater range of approaches that landscape, urban, and architectural designers can apply in conjunction with their own specific professional skills and expertise.

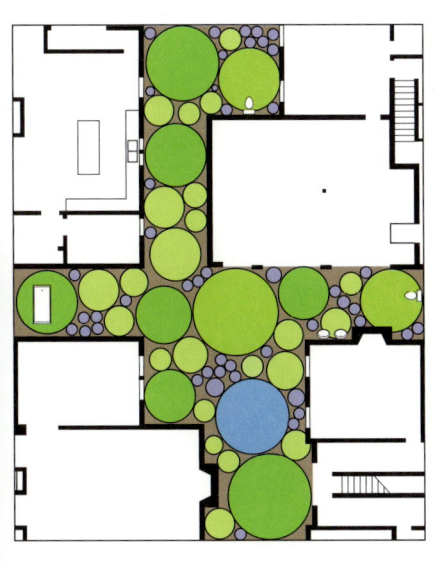

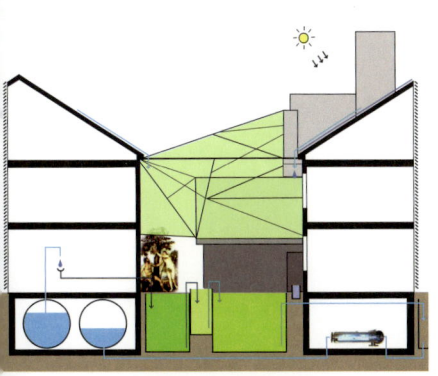

○ Open Aerobic Reactors
(Living System Vegetation)

○ EFB (Ecological Fluidized Beds, Crushed Rocks)

● Filter
(Sand)

● Aromatic Plants
(Lavender, Mint, Lemon Verbenna)

Figure 4: N-1 Architects and their team propose to invert the McMansion such that it ingests its own front- and backyard. Titled the Out-House, its ingested interior yard becomes an activated organic machine for the harvesting and recycling of water. The newly ingested yard is sustained by the bathroom—the site of human waste disposal becomes the site of production, providing the necessary nutrients for plant and organisms, which in turn clean the water. What was once the exterior of the house is now the most private zone

Figure 2: Landscape architect David Fletcher's "Age of Waste" envisions Los Angeles to transition from a watershed to a waste-watershed (opposite)

How to Read the Case Studies

The case studies in this book are meant to support the essay contributions with built and speculative design project examples. The projects range in scale and geographical context. These are explored through an original set of architectural drawings and diagrams, generated by Margolis and Chaouni. The drawings are based on materials sourced from the respective design firms or institutions.

To support the main premise of the book, a legend of water quality and flows are represented in each project's drawings using a color legend. Each project can be read in terms of five gradients of blue; for example, the lightest blue represents potable water and the darkest blue represents contaminated/saline water. The case studies are also explored through an evaluation matrix, which ranks from high to low energy use and quantity of water flowing through the project, and identifies the level of connectivity (e.g., regional, site, object) and scale (e.g., small, medium, large). Using icons, this ranking system is overlaid with additional information about the water input (i.e. the original source of the water) and water output usage (e.g., drinking, irrigation). The water output icons are marked by an additional blue ring according to the water quality legend (i.e. gradient).

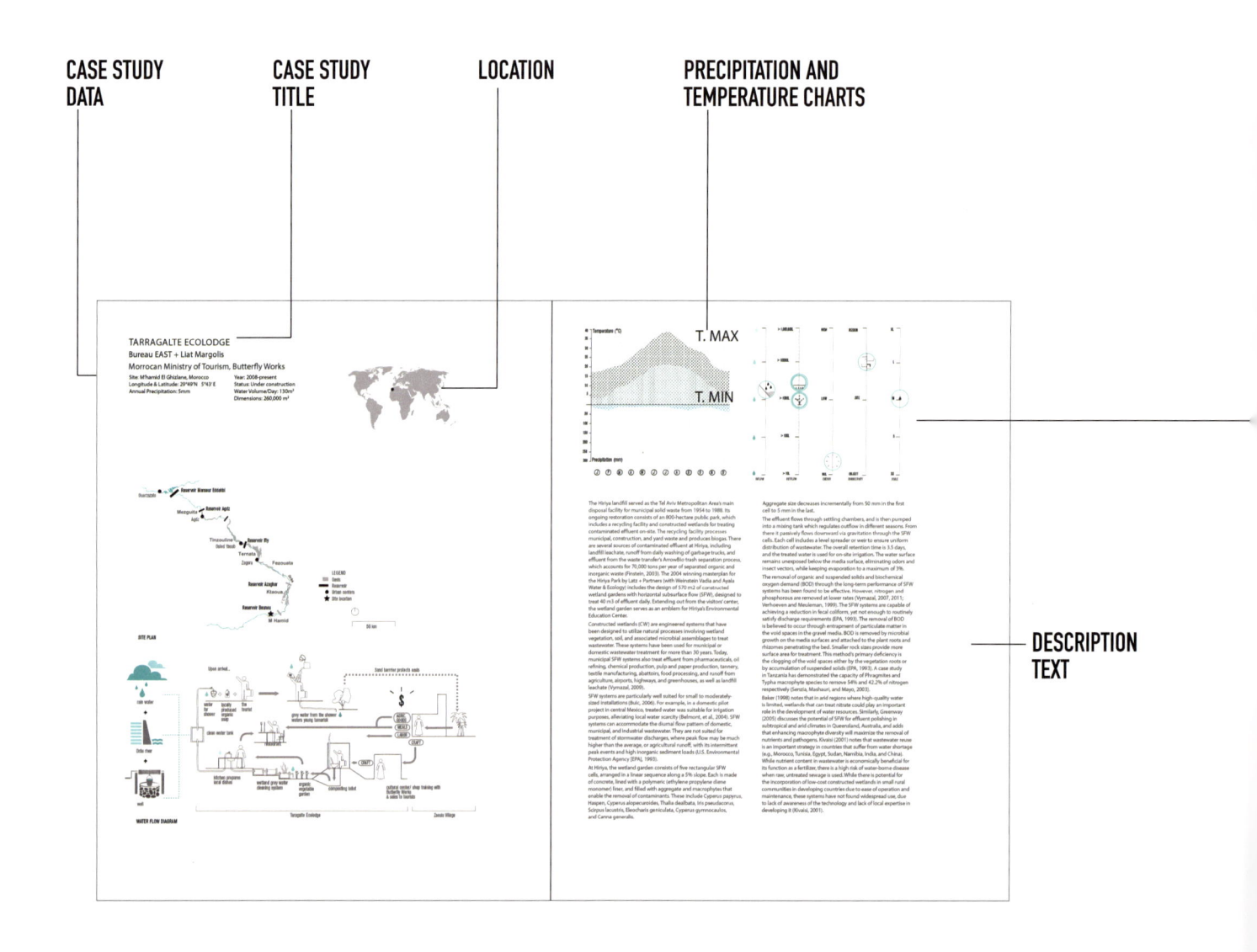

PERFORMANCE MATRIX

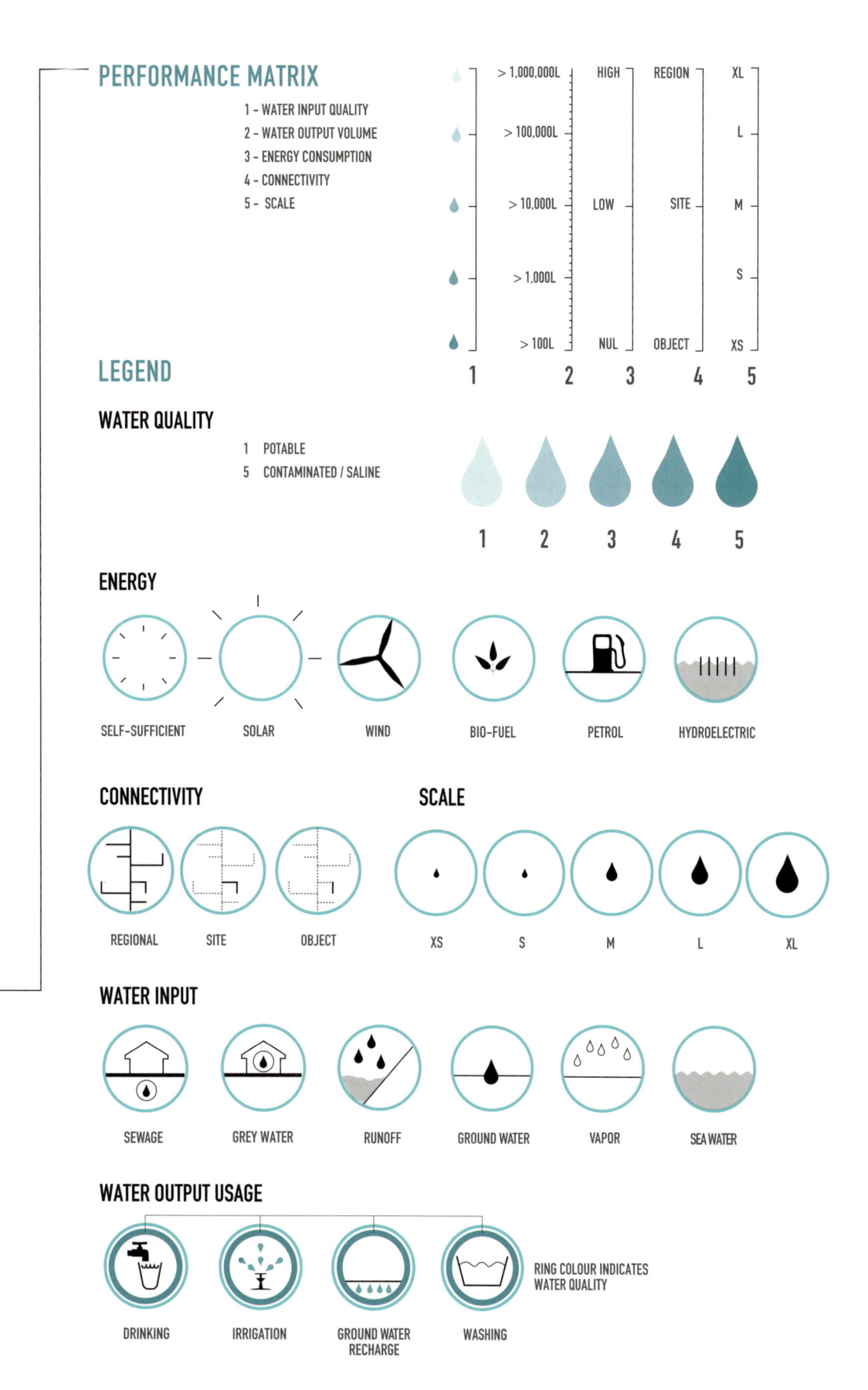

1 – WATER INPUT QUALITY
2 – WATER OUTPUT VOLUME
3 – ENERGY CONSUMPTION
4 – CONNECTIVITY
5 – SCALE

1	2	3	4	5
	> 1,000,000L	HIGH	REGION	XL
	> 100,000L			L
	> 10,000L	LOW	SITE	M
	> 1,000L			S
	> 100L	NUL	OBJECT	XS

LEGEND

WATER QUALITY

1 POTABLE
5 CONTAMINATED / SALINE

1 2 3 4 5

ENERGY

SELF-SUFFICIENT   SOLAR   WIND   BIO-FUEL   PETROL   HYDROELECTRIC

CONNECTIVITY

REGIONAL   SITE   OBJECT

SCALE

XS   S   M   L   XL

WATER INPUT

SEWAGE   GREY WATER   RUNOFF   GROUND WATER   VAPOR   SEA WATER

WATER OUTPUT USAGE

DRINKING   IRRIGATION   GROUND WATER RECHARGE   WASHING

RING COLOUR INDICATES WATER QUALITY

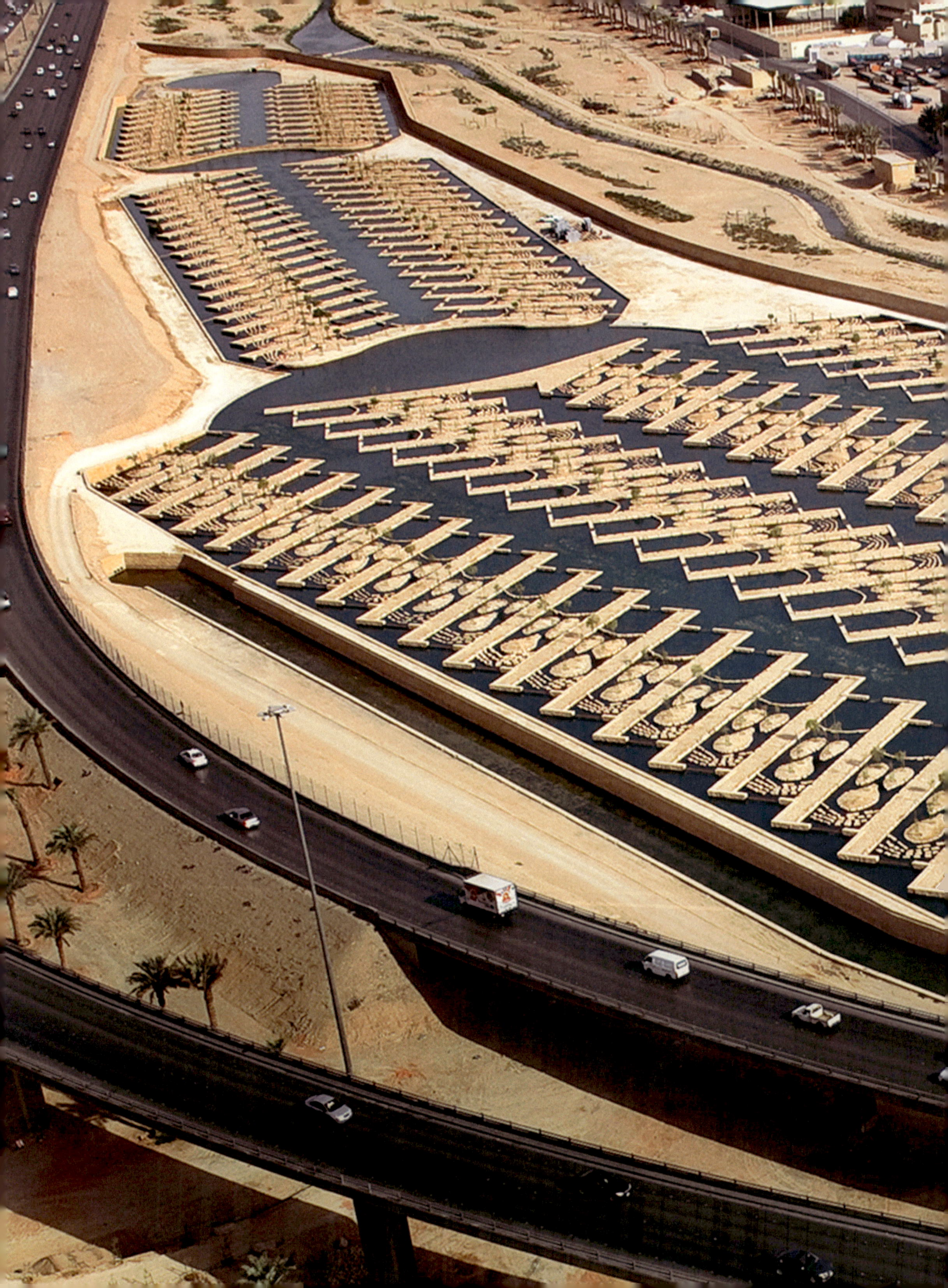

Introduction: Are We Out of Water?

On one level, this book is focused on contemporary technologies and design solutions to problems associated with water scarcity and fragile aquatic ecosystems in urbanized arid regions. The issues and projects discussed in the essays and case studies address the limited and unpredictable water availability—alternating from drought to flood, scarcity to surplus—and offering a window into the technological ingenuity that emerges from arid regions.

Yet the book's title, *Out of Water*, is meant as a provocation. Although the book highlights a growing crisis, its collection of essays and case studies actually demonstrates that water scarcity is a relative term—a condition that is contingent upon the interrelation between humans and water, and upon water management and technology. Therefore, the book is intended to provoke a new perception of water. Instead of framing water as a given and inert resource, and as a backdrop to habitation and development, it asks us to imagine new relations between availability (quantity and quality) and allocation, use and reuse; it asks us to imagine new relations between human habitation and aquatic ecosystems over variable time (daily, seasonally, annually) and spatial scales (site, neighborhood, watershed).

Water scarcity is becoming increasingly familiar to us, and it is no longer limited to arid regions. The 2014 U.S. Drought Monitor reported that more than 80% of California is now in a state of extreme or exceptional drought. In 2012, nearly two-thirds of the continental United States was in a state of drought, the most severe and extensive drought in at least 25 years, prompting the U.S. Department of Agriculture (USDA) to declare a disaster (USDA, 2012). Central and eastern Canada experienced equally catastrophic economic and environmental ramifications, also threatening food security (CBC News, 2012). Although arid and semi-arid regions have always struggled with prolonged periods of drought, now regions that were historically "wet" are experiencing record droughts. The arid belt is expanding. Some predict that drier and drier seasons are on the horizon. But it is the increase in demand due to population growth and mismanagement of water that is making the situation more controversial. Waterlessness is not only defined according to its climatic context, but also by its socio-technological milieu. In fact, water should be reframed as a factor of natural-social-technological dynamics (Bakker, 2012).

Along the same lines, water technology requires a broader definition that goes beyond its association with engineered or mechanical solutions. Water technology must be considered as a set of strategies that value the benefits of natural system functions, such as the capacity of aquatic and vegetal ecosystems to regulate water flow, cool ambient air, and provide green open spaces for public recreation within cities (Larson, et al., 2013). At the same time, technology should be understood in the context of a social dimension, for example, the ways in which technology can be mobilized under varying centralized or distributed social structures. In that regard, technology encompasses a range of expert (high-tech) and non-expert (low-tech) solutions.

The essays and case studies represent perspectives from several science, engineering, and social science fields. We believe that it is the designer's role to mediate, translate, and synthesize the range of approaches and priorities of the natural, social, and engineering sciences. Moreover, it is the designer's role to communicate to a broader public and to decision-makers the possibilities of implementing, or integrating new solutions. Finally, it is also the designer's role to engage the public in imagining new societies, new communities, and new ways of defining water, both culturally and physically (Nassauer, 2013).

Water Scarcity and Desertification

Two terms, water scarcity and desertification, merit a brief description, as the approach taken in this book differs from the standard approach to water management and urban planning. In the standard approach, municipal potable water supply is distinct from the environmental management of streams, rivers, and lakes, and also distinct from agricultural irrigation, which typically takes place outside of cities. By contrast, the essays and case studies in this book take as a starting point an interest in "integrated urban water cycle planning and management,"

FIGURE 3: An aerial view of the Wadi Hanifah bioremediation facility

FIGURE 1: The Wadi Hanifah's naturalized channels employ check dams to attenuate water flow (bottom)

FIGURE 2: Wadi Hanifah has become a poplular public park and a civic destination (top)

which is defined as an integrated management of waterways, groundwater, stormwater, wastewater, and potable water supply, a comprehensive urban and regional strategy (Wong and Brown, 2009).

Water scarcity is the outcome of a complex set of factors, and is therefore defined through different models and priorities. One of the most common models, which is known as the "Falkenmark indicator" or "water stress index," measures the amount of renewable fresh water availability per person, per year (Falkenmark, 1989). Although straightforward, this method fails to recognize differences in water availability and water use habits from region to region within one country, or accessibility to water resources (e.g., deep aquifers), or man-made sources (e.g., desalination; Rijsberman, 2006). Another model defines water scarcity according to a criticality ratio, which is based on demand and supply, or annual water withdrawal relative to available water resources (Raskin, 1997). Yet, again, this model does not consider a range of water technologies such as desalination, or water treatment and recycling (Rijsberman, 2006).

Others maintain a wider assessment of water management, taking into consideration both physical and economic factors. For example, the International Water Management Institute (IWMI) defines water scarcity according to each country's water infrastructure and technologies (e.g., desalination, water recycling) as well as its adaptive capacity, the potential for infrastructure development and improvement (Seckler, 1998). This enables an assessment of economic investment relative to water demand (Molden, 2007). Water scarcity is also measured according to the "water poverty index," which is better suited for analysis at a local level, since it takes into account income and wealth in relation to water access, quantity, quality, and variability, as well as water uses for domestic, food, and productive purposes, the capacity for water management, and environmental conditions (Sullivan, 2003).

There is no single definition for water scarcity. Water scarcity in hot arid regions is largely affected by low rainfall and prolonged droughts (see essays by Lee and Wescoat). Water-intensive agricultural and over-extraction of ground water are also common factors (see essays by Chaouni and Masoud), as well as environmental degradation (see Wadi Hanifah case study), contamination (see essay by Baker and Ngai), damming, and diversion of surface water (see essays by Chaouni and Masoud). Economic water scarcity typically manifests in an absence of water and sanitation infrastructure (see essay by Baker and Ngai), failure to upgrade aging infrastructure (see Isla Urbana case study), or inappropriate water management practices (see essay by Pasternak and Woltering), all of which are directly correlated to poverty and hunger.

The term "desertification" is defined as land degradation in arid, semi-arid, and dry sub-humid areas resulting from various factors, including climatic variations and human activities (United Nations Convention to Combat Desertification [UNCCD], 2014). It is interrelated with water scarcity, as the same factors that contribute to water scarcity (e.g., water diversion, deforestation, soil erosion, climate change, unsustainable agricultural practices, etc.) result in land degradation. Regardless of the semantics, what is pertinent here is that water systems must be understood in the context of their broader ecological systems, both natural and constructed, specifically in relation to plant ecology and soil.

Water for What?

Globally, we are not out of water. In fact, there is enough water for present and future needs for drinking and food. But as Antoine Picon notes in his opening essay, water is not where, or when, we want it to be. Nor is it in the quality state that we always want it to be, but instead salty or contaminated. The first paradigm shift suggested by this book is that attention should shift from availability to quality of water. As Eilon Adar states in his essay: "There is no water deficit, but a deficit in high water quality." By reframing the questions—what is water used for, what is the required quality state, and when is it needed?—water can be perceived in a much more nuanced way, a valuable resource in all of its quality states.

The main thematic thread running through the essays and case studies in this book articulates a new, or expanded water vocabulary: there is not just one water, but a gradient of water qualities. In other words, in addition to conventional fresh water resources (lakes, rivers, aquifers), non-potable water sources (seawater, contaminated surface runoff, grey water, vapor) have become viable by means of a variety of treatment processes, including the relatively new reverse osmosis (see essay by Tal), but also the traditional sand filter (see Kanchan Arsenic Filter case study) and the well-known principle of vapor condensation (see Vena Water Condenser case study). Consequently, total available water has increased.

The vocabulary of water ought to exceed the binary mode of water and sanitation at either end of the pipe, which is still the primary model that dictates the relationship between water and city in the developed world. In most cities today, stormwater runoff is not collected for reuse. Furthermore, in cities with water and sanitation infrastructure, greywater reuse is commonly disallowed rather than mandated or incentivized. Non-potable quality water should be allocated to various uses such as toilet flushing and irrigation in urban and rural areas, utilizing a dual water supply system with parallel potable and non-potable pipe networks. As a result, the pressure on diminishing potable water resources would be minimized, while wastewater discharge would be diverted away from natural water systems, reducing their environmental degradation.

Framing water in terms of chemical and biological quality requires not only a new organizational scheme to link a range of water qualities and use requirements, but also a comprehensive water calendar that takes into account natural water cycles in conjunction with non-potable water streams. In other words, what is the quality and quantity needed, and when? As James Wescoat describes in his essay, the design of arid land habitation has been traditionally structured around the variability between scarcity and surplus. The legacy of this design approach is rooted in water budget analysis and water conserving design, and in methods of regulating the presence of water according to temporality—frequency, intensity, and duration of weather events—as well as the spatial scale and physical attributes of a site—volume of water relative to topography, surface porosity, vegetation, and built structures. While having no water or too much water is often seen as a vulnerability, it can also be thought of as an opportunity to develop joint strategies for water management that mediate the two extremes.

Modifying the presence of water offers vast possibilities for design and for shaping both social and ecological systems. At the regional scale, for instance, municipal sewage offers a continuous source of water that can bridge the seasonal and annual gaps caused by drought with respect to both irrigation and hydro-ecological needs, including stream restoration and aquifer recharge (see Wastewater Treatment and Reclamation in Israel, Hiriya Landfill Recycling Park, and Taragalte Ecolodge case studies). The detention and attenuation of water flow on-site or within a riverbed via reservoirs, check dams, micro-catchments (see essay by Masoud as well as Wadi Hanifah and Wastewater Treatment and Reclamation in Israel case studies; Figure 1), and inflatable dams, as well as the mechanical distribution of water via pumps and channels, can be utilized to dissipate or attenuate water (see essays by Chaouni and Wescoat), and conversely, to intensify or concentrate water in specific areas.

Lastly, all the examples featured in this book point to spatial configurations and aesthetic potentials based in an understanding of the temporal and spatial scales of various water sources. At the urban scale, the regulation of an ephemeral river transforms a barren landscape into a civic destination (see Wadi Hanifah case study; Figure 2). At the site scale, a network of sunken courtyards or constructed open and covered reservoirs, in combination with planting geometries and materials selection, come to reveal the fluctuating levels of water, and the seasonal transformation of space becomes its aesthetic expression (see essay by Wescoat).

Design with Water: Integrated Water Cycles

The second paradigm shift that emerges from this collection of essays and case studies is a transition from an extremely utilitarian, single-purpose system to integrated or hybrid systems that are multi-functional—a kind of opportunism by a large number of interactions at multiple and nested scales (material, building, site, area, region, inter-region; Nassauer, 2013), which prioritizes a range of values (natural, social, technological) as follows:

- Effectiveness vs. efficiency
- Interconnectedness is more important than self-sufficiency
- Multi-objective optimization
- Diverse and redundant solutions generate resilience
- Adaptive and flexible water management

Effectiveness vs. Efficiency

Open-loop water and sanitation systems are indeed efficient. Potable water is delivered to a variety of end users, and sanitation infrastructure removes wastewater as quickly as possible, ensuring that there is no overlap with drinking water supplies. By contrast, a water management model that best exemplifies "effectiveness" is Integrated Water Cycle Management (IWCM). The central idea of IWCM is that the value of all natural waterways, groundwater, stormwater, wastewater, and potable water supply is assessed and managed as part of a comprehensive urban design strategy. A key component of this strategy is incorporation of closed-loop systems in which excess water or effluent becomes an input for new processes (Khouri, 2006).

One such closed-loop system, called Water Sensitive Urban Design (WSUD), is intended to manage the impacts of stormwater from development by integrating water cycle management into urban planning and design. WSUD considers, among other things, urban design, infrastructure design, streetscapes, roads, and drainage systems, and aims to protect and improve waterway health by working with the natural water cycle as closely as possible (Wong and Eadie, 2000).

In Australia, where IWCM is well established, the national water recycling guidelines include regulations for stormwater and wastewater reuse and have consequently reduced domestic potable water consumption significantly. The cycling of non-potable water resources is implemented through a dual water supply system: two parallel systems of which one supplies potable water for household uses such as drinking, cooking, and washing, and the other supplies recycled wastewater and/or stormwater runoff for toilet flushing and outdoor uses such as garden watering (Lazarova, et al., 2013).

Interconnectedness is More Important than Self-Sufficiency

Eilon Adar, in his essay contribution, offers an exemplary closed-loop model in the agricultural sector in Israel. At a business-to-business scale, networks of end-users synergistically exchange surplus low-quality water and residue. In effect, multiple end users utilize the same unit of water for their crops and operations. In parallel, 75% of all municipal wastewater across the country is treated and reused for irrigation in agriculture and parks, as well as stream restoration and aquifer recharge (see Wastewater Treatment and Reclamation case study). The unconventional idea here is that while urbanization can alter and degrade aquatic ecosystems and exacerbate water scarcity, urban effluent maintains a constant flow into otherwise dry river systems. The result is not only significant with respect to water conservation, but also to combined economic and ecological productivity, which arguably could not be realized at this scale without the interconnectedness of public and private entities.

These closed-loop agricultural models could equally serve as a reference for design thinking. Through the interconnection of end users in the city and beyond, new and unconventional pairings of urban land uses could emerge, which in turn could generate new architectural typologies, cultural or commercial programs, and amenities. This idea invokes a proposal by the architecture firm BIG (Bjarke Ingels Group) for a new way of thinking about a sustainable energy future for Denmark. Of course, the deployment of renewable energy technology, such as solar arrays or windmills, might be the first idea to come up and may be the most efficient. However, this proposal takes the position that rather than maintaining the idea of cities as consumers of energy, cities can be designed to be zero net energy. The BIG proposal offers a new approach to urban design that is based on interconnected energy users. For instance, they imagine new pairings of end users who produce excess heat with end users who require energy for heating. They couple supermarkets, which generate excess heat from refrigeration, with indoor swimming pools, which require heating. The new urban architectural typology could produce a scenario in which a parent is grocery shopping while their child enjoys a swim lesson at the pool. This level of synergy and opportunism can be extrapolated for water cycling in the city and the ways in which new programs and experiences could develop.

In addition to interconnectedness among end users, closed-loop systems at the urban and regional scales can also pertain to the interaction between urban water systems and hydrological flows or natural aquatic ecosystems. This type of interaction is defined by the term "ecosystem services"—physical, economic, and cultural benefits gained from the functions of ecosystems. Urban aquatic ecosystems can provide a range of such ecosystem services: as flood

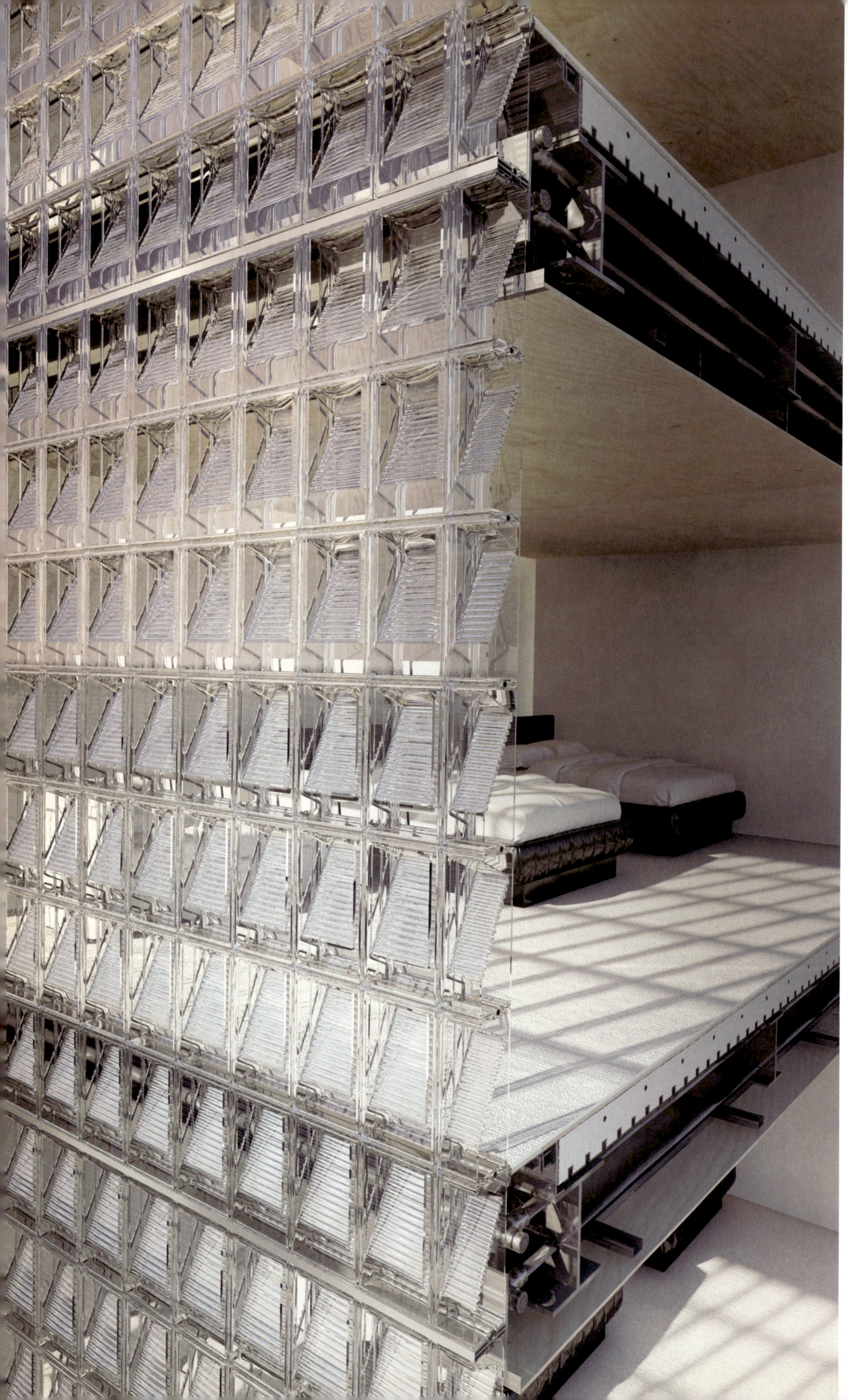

mitigation, erosion control, or the protection of property and human life, as well as water quality improvement and conservation, wastewater treatment, the creation of habitat, and provision of education, recreation, and aesthetic value (Larson, et al., 2013). Furthermore, the management of urban aquatic ecosystems also has a direct relation to urban energy management, as the presence of water within the urban landscape is imperative for such functions as evaporative cooling and subsequent reduction in energy consumption.

Multi-Objective Optimization

Integrated water cycle management is also characterized by solutions that are multi-functional. The Wadi Hanifah restoration project, for instance, diverts urban wastewater to a bioremediation facility, which also functions as a public park and a landmark for the city. This project demonstrates that although regional water cycling programs are typically legislated and operated by water authorities and affiliated engineering services, the shift toward multi-objective optimization at the regional and metropolitan scales offers designers and planner the opportunity to rethink emergent infrastructural landscapes as a socio-cultural, economic, and ecological extension of the city (Figure 3).

For instance, the network of wastewater treatment reservoirs in Israel that span vast agricultural valleys can integrate wildlife sanctuaries, recreational parks, and agro-tourism destinations, learning from case study examples such as Emscher Landschaftspark and Peter Latz's Duisburg-Nord Landscape Park (Weilacher, 2008). In fact, it is Latz's design at the Hiriya Landfill Recycling Park which gives context to the subsurface wetland garden featured in this book (see Hiriya Landfill Recycling Park case study). At a much smaller scale, this bioremediation facility serves as an extension of the park's environmental education center by meeting not only ecological objectives—water conservation, pollution reduction, and habitat forming—but also educational and aesthetic objectives (Figures 4a and 4b).

Masoud's proposal for the Jordan Valley, as described in his essay, blurs the line between urban and rural by conceiving of a new urban code for systematic integration of agricultural production and recycling of non-potable sources. His proposal visualizes water systems as a framework around which urban development, public space, water-sanitation infrastructure, ecological systems, and agriculture are organized. Here, natural, social, and technological systems converge as multi-use spaces that operate in a mutually beneficial manner.

Two projects under development that were presented as part of the "Out of Water" conference at the University of Toronto are evidence of similar trends in the field of architecture, with experimental building façades that utilize atmospheric elements to collect or recycle water. The Solar Enclosures for Water Reuse (SEWR) by the Center for Architecture Science and Ecology (CASE) are exterior building façade modules that decontaminate grey water via ultraviolet exposure for reuse within the building (Figures 5a, 5b, and 5c). Water out of Air Device (WOA) by Transsolar and Foster + Partners is a vapor condensation façade that incorporates a desiccant material to absorb humidity for reuse in irrigation (Figure 6).

Here, we may recall that the integrative model is not new, but in fact has been a part of recurring 20th century architectural debates about whether to camouflage or celebrate the innards of a building. One recalls LeCorbusier's famous hatred of tubes and his regretful conceit to hide them within his buildings; Reyner Banham's extreme embrace of the building's mechanical systems to the detriment of the rest (Banham, 1969); as well as the high-tech, postmodern, water-carrying green pipes exposed on the façade of the Centre Pompidou. These approaches never questioned the very necessity or functioning of these systems, but they did question their aesthetic expression and their position within theoretical discourses. In both SEWR and WOA, as well as in many of the essays and case studies featured in this book, focus on the interaction between environmental dynamics and architectural or landscape structure represents an interest in integrated and hybrid systems, requiring multidisciplinary collaboration across the fields of design, engineering, and the natural and social sciences.

Figure 4a: The bioremediation wetland garden and adjacent environmental education center with the Hiriya Landfill "mountain" in the distance (top)

Figure 4b: The wetland garden and environmental education center seen from the top of the Hiriya Landfill "mountain" during construction, Israel, 2007. The bioremediation garden is part of a complex of waste recycling and demonstration projects (bottom)

FIGURE 5a: The Solar Enclosures for Water Reuse (SEWR) are exterior building façade modules that decontaminate grey water via ultraviolet exposure for reuse within the building (opposite)

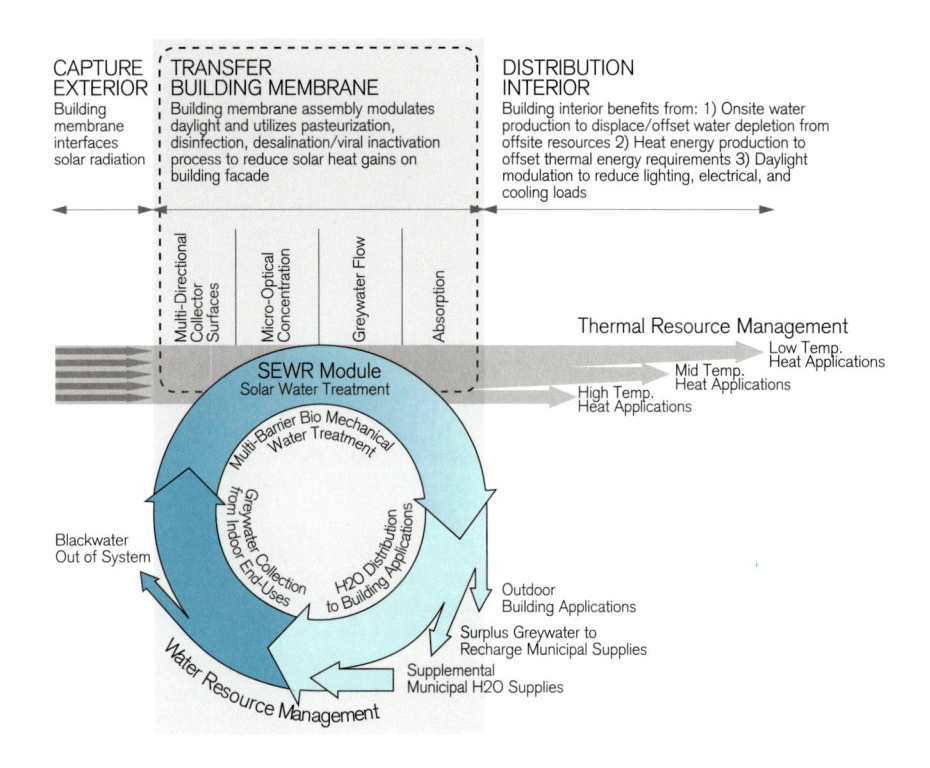

FIGURE 5b: Diagram of the Solar Enclosure for Water Reuse (SEWR) system's water and thermal resource management (top)

FIGURE 5c: Section-diagram of SEWR (bottom)

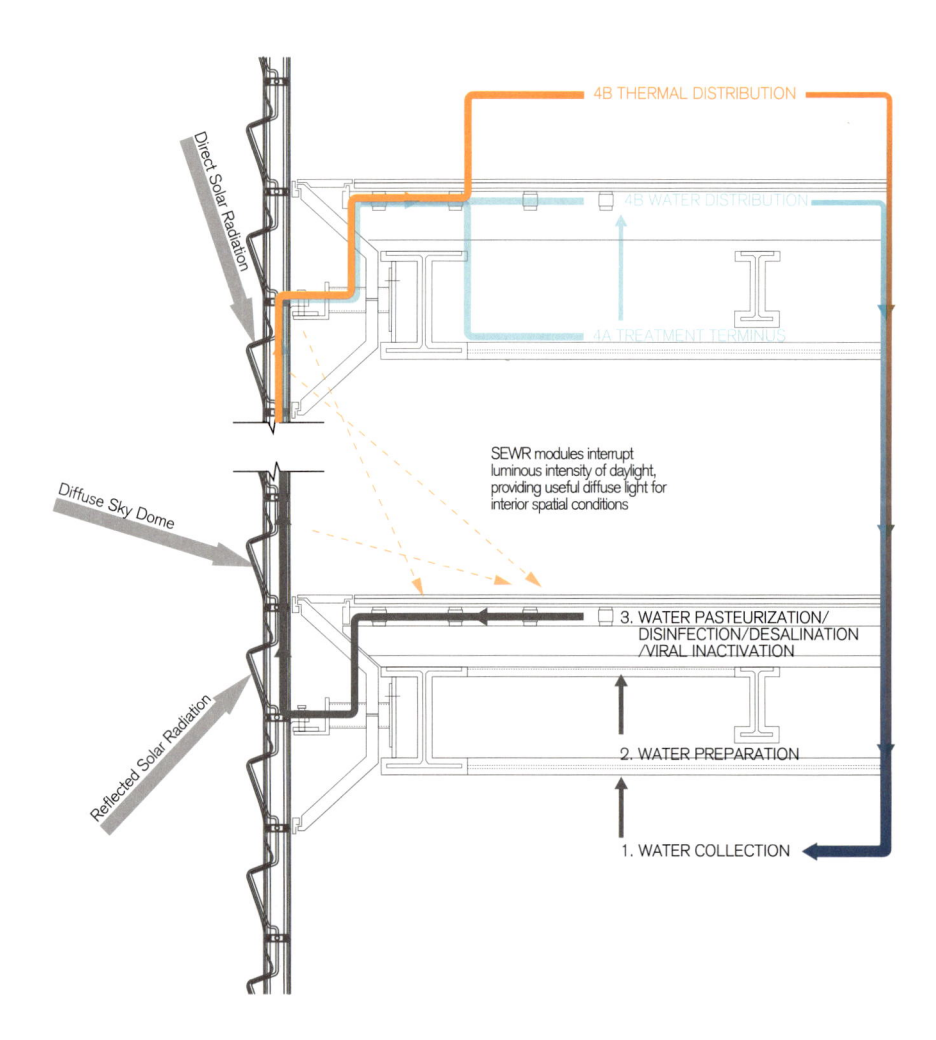

FIGURE 6: A diagram of the principle of absorption and desorption of the Water out of Air Device (WOA)

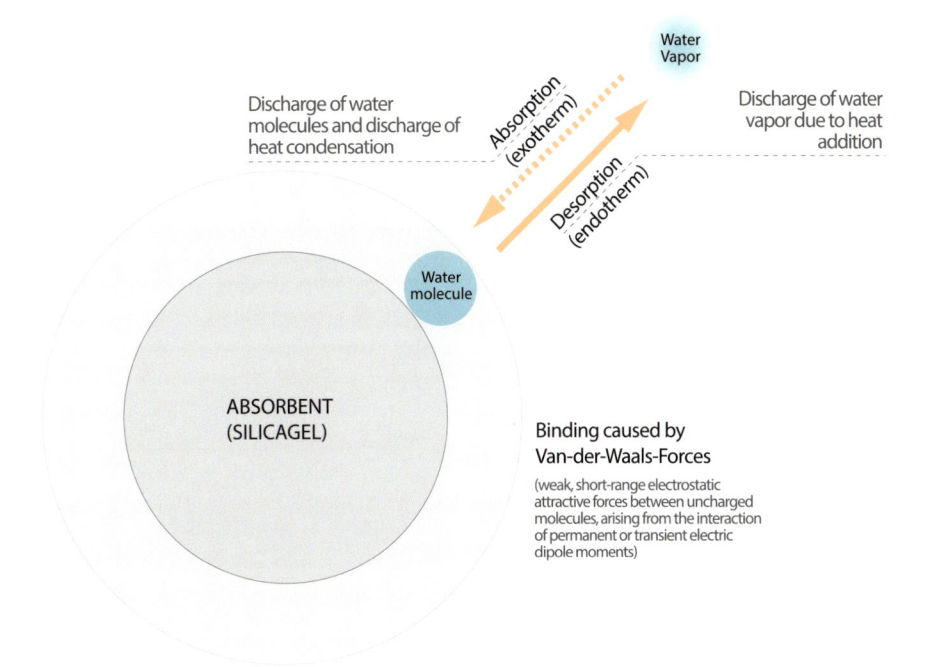

Diverse and Redundant Solutions Generate Resilience

A collaborative approach is key to achieving effectiveness, interconnectedness, and multi-objective optimization, as well as resilience to environmental or socio-economic changes. A collaborative approach, which includes a range of expertise, methods, and perspectives, implies the facility to develop a diverse set of solutions. Diversity could be manifest in terms of implementing multiple solutions at the various scales of region, city, street, and building. It could also manifest itself in different typologies, including mechanical-hydraulic solutions, ecosystem services, and social engineering strategies. Deploying a range of solutions also produces redundancy, in the sense of a duplication of various components or functions of xa system with the intention of increasing reliability.

The role of the designer is not only to glean information from the natural and social sciences, but also to communicate how design methods may offer new approaches to scientific research and practice. It is possible and important to embed design into the scientific lexicon in order to make use of every aspect and component of the urban realm—from streetscapes to buildings, gardens, and parks—in order to reconcile ecological and urban systems. For instance, the essays by Chaouni and Masoud highlight the important roles that landscape, urban, and architectural design can play in hydrologic analysis and projective modeling of water management (whose algorithms often include data from the fields of political science, economics, sociology, and geography, as well as hydrology, geology, ecology, climatology, and agronomy) in relation to sustainable urban development. These analyses are concerned with how water cycling could be made more effective with respect to ecosystem services, in terms of urban form (e.g., density, built vs. open and vegetated space) and construction (e.g., pervious vs. impervious surfaces).

Chaouni and Masoud also remind us that the designers have the capacity to envision new and unconventional scenarios and produce multi-functional solutions that meet both technical and cultural needs, and they are also able to identify forgotten or abandoned vernacular building practices that not only have high performance attributes, but also cultural significance.

Adaptive and Flexible Water Management

Inherent to diversity and resilience is the ability to adapt to changing conditions, or to easily compensate for gaps between supply and demand. For instance, mass migration into city regions often exceeds the speed at which water-sanitation services are implemented. According to the essay by Baker and Ngai, 780 million people in both urban and rural areas around the world still lack access to improved water, and 2.5 billion lack sanitation (World Health Organization and United Nations Children's Fund [WHO/UNICEF], 2012). Therefore, we must adapt water-sanitation technology and infrastructure to suit a variety of geopolitical conditions. This may result in independent or networked systems that are able to balance the gap in public infrastructure. These may be non-governmental strategies for in situ implementation of simple, non-expert, and low-cost technologies, whereby the individual is responsible to construct, operate, and maintain their water-sanitation needs (see essay by Pasternak and Woltering, as well as Kanchan Arsenic Filter, Liquid Wrap, Vena Water Condenser, Isla Urbana, Down to Earth, Hiriya Landfill Recycling Park, and Taragalte Ecolodge case studies).

The term "technology" is understood as "Technology" (upper-case)—expert, advanced, mechanical, intensive, and large-scale; but also as "technology" (lower-case)—non-expert, individual, community-based, grassroots, and small-scale. It is important to note that the two approaches to technology are not mutually exclusive and certainly not strictly associated with specific political scenarios. In other words, lower-case technology can be integrated in parallel to upper-case Technology as a means to increase resilience and redundancy. Likewise, Technology can be implemented at a small scale and modified from expert to non-expert practices. For example, Pasternak and Woltering describe how the informal (private) small-scale irrigation sector, which operates in a more market-driven fashion, has proven to be more profitable than more expensive formal-sector irrigation initiatives.

Also pertaining to the idea of flexible water management is the ability to customize the chemical-biological composition of water for each farmer according to specific crop requirements, discussed in Eilon Adar's essay. Although the economic and political contexts do not necessitate complete self-reliance, the example here demonstrates the possibility of evolving beyond the standard approach to the provision and cycling of water.

A theme that emerges here highlights the social dimension of lower-case technology. For instance, Baker and Ngai discuss methods of community capacity building through education and training. Both Lee and Chaouni emphasize the significance of local know-how of the landscapes and ecosystems within which they have lived for centuries. Wescoat also discusses the adaptation of reference materials with input from local expertise and site-specific data and proposes that vernacular water budgeting and crop cultivation could offer both technical and spatial models for contemporary design schemes. Lee and Chaouni lament the loss of memory with respect to water in the landscape, which affects the way urban development encroaches upon flood plains. Both argue that solutions must be comprehensive and engage the social and cultural dimension. Otherwise they are limited in their effectiveness; without being embedded within cultural and economic practices, lifestyles, and people's perception and understanding of the landscape they inhabit, they would be merely technical solutions (see also Nassauer, 2013). The Wadi Hanifah Restoration is a case in point as to how the transformation of a landscape can alter public perception, and vice versa. In fact, all the design projects featured in this book seek to either reintroduce a historical relationship with the landscape that was lost, or generate a new narrative.

Structure of the Book—An Overview

This book is organized into three parts that are specific to the relationship between water and human habitation, namely access to clean drinking water in the domestic environment (Part 1), agricultural production (Part 2), and ecosystem services (Part 3). These subjects are recognized as the most basic and fundamental requirements to human and environmental health and to the sustainable development of urbanized regions. Each part is meant as an assembly of diverse perspectives, socio-geographical contexts, and prevalent trends in progressive water management solutions.

Building upon recent publications such as *Resilience in Ecology and Urban Design: Linking Theory and Practice for Sustainable Cities* (Pickett, et al., 2013), *Water Centric Sustainable Communities: Planning Retrofitting, and Building the Next Urban Environment* (Novotny, Ahern, and Brown, 2010), *Water Sensitive Cities* (Howe and Mitchell, 2012), and *Resilient Sustainable Cities* (Pearson, Newton, and Roberts, 2014), this book is ultimately interested in the design and planning of sustainable cities—whereby the extreme problems that arid regions and regions lacking water-sanitation infrastructure face serve as a model for out-of-the-box solutions—and in the roles that architectural, landscape, and urban design can assume with respect to water management.

- **Part 1—Water For Domestic Use**
  The first part is primarily focused on two questions: 1) How can design integrate water collection, treatment, and cycling into the home or building? and 2) What components of the building structure or materiality can facilitate these functions? This part first challenges designers to move beyond the complacent position of accepting conventional water infrastructure and merely specifying water-conserving devices. The part encourages designers to take into consideration the quality of water needed for different uses (with reference to dual water systems in Israel and Australia), as well as the different governance and social structures under which water is managed. Environmental policy expert Alon Tal makes the case for the manufacturing of "new water" via desalination technologies. He uses the cases of Israel, Australia, and Spain to deliberate on the political and economic settings and changes in public opinion that made this technological shift possible. Camille Dow Baker and Tommy Ngai, of the non-governmental organization Centre for Affordable Water and Sanitation Technology, represent political and economic circumstances that necessitate self-reliance. In this context, water technology is defined as expert and non-expert, public or private, and multi-scale. The case studies in this part showcase built and proposed designs for water collection and treatment that could be implemented by non-expert individuals in conjunction with new or existing structures.

- **Part 2—Water for Agricultural Production**
  The second part focuses on the relationship between water and food in the context of contemporary design interest in urban food production and the integration of crop cultivation within the urban environment. In particular, it asks, what can the designer learn from the ways in which the agricultural sector has overcome water shortages? And can city regions develop a water management strategy that meets the synergistically unified agriculture, urban design, and aquatic ecosystems? Here, designers are challenged to focus their efforts on the transition to closed-loop urban water-sanitation systems, as well as to the systemization of new productive landscape typologies within the built environment.

  Hydrologist Eilon Adar opens the part with a call to reframe water as commodity, not a resource as a means to incentivize a zero-waste approach to water use in agriculture. He delivers a fascinating account of how one unit of water can be used by multiple end users, with high economic returns. Agronomists Dov Pasternak and Lennart Woltering describe the introduction of efficient irrigation technologies along with the optimization of crop selection for smallholder farms in the Sahel as a means to increase productivity and reduce labor. They demonstrate the advantages of the informal (private) small-scale irrigation sector over more expensive formal sector irrigation initiatives. Architect Aziza Chaouni contemplates possible future scenarios of a designated cultural heritage oasis in southern Morocco, with emphasis on the influence of urban development and tourism on water management. And finally, landscape architect Fadi Masoud offers a landscape urbanism approach for the integration of housing, open spaces, water-sanitation infrastructure, and agriculture along the Jordan River basin.

- **Part 3—Water For Ecosystem Services**
  The third part focuses on design strategies for water management that regulate and benefit from the limited and unpredictable availability of water—from drought to flood. In particular, the essays and case studies are interested in the mutually beneficial outcomes of integrating urban and ecological systems. The themes that emerge include the fragility of ecosystems and their interdependent culture and economy, the importance of local and vernacular knowledge of the landscape for present and future design and development, and the transformation of public perception of water in the city. Landscape architect Gini Lee discusses the significance of ephemeral water holes in the barren lands of Central Australia for a diversity of species habitats and the ways in which human communities have evolved. She argues that contemporary design and planning should be informed by an interdisciplinary understanding of the history of water and human habitation in the region. Landscape architect and geographer James L. Wescoat outlines the history of methods and tools for regulating the presence of water, from earthworks to sensor technologies. Drawing conclusions from case studies in India and the United Arab Emirates, Wescoat demonstrates how historical concepts can be adapted to modern water supply systems, and how these can generate the aesthetic and experiential characteristics of a site. The case studies provide examples of landscape design strategies that incorporate bioremediation and bioengineering techniques at various scales.

Water, Technology, and Society

The three parts inform an emerging design dialogue around water, technology, and society. As Antoine Picon notes, water technologies and management have a systemic character as well as a sociopolitical dimension as they force people to redefine theirrelationship to nature and technology. Hence, this dialogue is of a transdisciplinary character, which necessitates the inclusion of diverse perspectives, the development of a shared reference, and a broadening of definitions and concepts (Nassauer, 2013).

The roles of the architect, landscape architect, and urban designer are as mediators, by virtue of design, between political and social agendas at one end and the technological and organizational means at the other end. Landscapes, buildings and urban spaces offer visual and material evidence of the natural and cultural processes that produce and change dynamic environments. Their inherently integrative character enables the synthesis among different disciplines, decision makers, and stakeholders that is needed to affect change. As well, landscapes and urban spaces not only link everyday experience with other environmental phenomena that are invisible or not widely understood, but also mediate diverse environmental and technological functions and human perspectives (Nassauer, 2013). As such, design has the capacity to shape individual behavior and perception, and bring about a cultural adaptation that has the potential to propel political action.

REFERENCES

Bakker, K. (2012). "Water: Political, Biopolitical, Material." *Social Studies of Science* 42(4): 616–623.

Banham, R. (1969). *Architecture of the Well-Tempered Environment*. Chicago: University of Chicago Press.

CBC News (2012). "Drought in Central, Eastern Canada baking crops." *CBC News*, July 15, 2012.

Falkenmark, M., Lundquist, J., and Widstrand, C. (1989). "Macro-scale Water Scarcity Requires Micro-scale Approaches: Aspects of Vulnerability in Semi-arid Development." *Natural Resources Forum* 13(4): 258–267.

Howe, C., and Mitchell, C., eds. (2012). *Water Sensitive Cities*. IWA Publishing.

Khouri, G. (2006). "Integrated Water Cycle Management: An Australian Perspective." *European Water* 15/16: 23–32.

Larson, E. K., Earl, S., Hagen, E. M., Hale, R., Hartnett, H., McCrackin, M., McHale, M., and Grimm, N. B. (2013). "Beyond Restoration and into Design: Hydrologic Alterations in Aridland Cities." in S.T.A. Pickett et al. (eds.), *Resilience in Ecology and Urban Design: Linking Theory and Practice for Sustainable Cities, Future City 3*. Springer Science+Business Media Dordrecht. 183–210.

Lazarova, V., Asano, T., Bahri, A., and Anderson J., eds. (2013). *Milestones in Water Reuse: The Best Success Stories*. IWA Publishing.

Molden, D., ed. (2007). *Water for Food, Water for Life: A Comprehensive Assessment of Water Management in Agriculture*. London: Earthscan/International Water Management Institute.

Nassauer, J. I. (2013). "Landscape as Method and Medium for the Ecological Design of Cities" in S.T.A. Pickett, et al. (eds.), *Resilience in Ecology and Urban Design: Linking Theory and Practice for Sustainable Cities, Future City 3*. Springer Science+Business Media Dordrecht. 79–98.

Novotny, V., Ahern, J., and Brown, P. (2010). *Water Centric Sustainable Communities: Planning, Retrofitting and Building the Next Urban Environment*. Hoboken, NJ: Wiley.

Pearson, L. J., Newton, P. W., and Roberts, P., eds. (2014). *Resilient Sustainable Cities*. Routledge.

Pickett, S.T.A., Cadenasso, M. L., and McGrath, B., eds. (2013). *Resilience in Ecology and Urban Design: Linking Theory and Practice for Sustainable Cities, Future City 3*. Springer Science+Business Media Dordrecht.

Raskin, P., Gleick, P., Kirshen, P., Pontius, R. G., and Strzepek, K. (1997). *Water Futures: Assessment of Long-range Patterns and Prospects*. Stockholm: Stockholm Environment Institute.

Rijsberman, F. R. (2006). "Water Scarcity: Fact or Fiction?" *Agricultural Water Management* 80: 5–22.

Seckler, D., Amarasinghe, U., Molden, D., de Silva, R., and Barker, R. (1998). *World Water Demand and Supply, 1990 to 2025: Scenarios and Issues*. Colombo, Sri Lanka: International Water Management Institute (IWMI).

Sullivan, C.A., Meigh, J. R., Giacomello, A. M., Fediw, T., Lawrence, P., Samad, M., Mlote, S., Hutton, C., Allan, J. A., Schulze, R. E., Dlamini, D.J.M., Cosgrove, W., Delli Priscoli, J., Gleick, P., Smout, I., Cobbing, J., Calow, R., Hunt, C., Hussain, A., Acreman, M. C., King, J., Malomo, S., Tate, E. L., O'Regan, D., Milner, S., and Steyl, I. (2003). "The Water Poverty Index: Development and Application at the Community Scale." *Natural Resources Forum* 27: 189–199.

United Nations Convention to Combat Desertification (2012). "Glossary." *United Nations Convention to Combat Desertification*. www.unccd.int/en/resources/Library/Pages/Glossary.aspx

USDA. "U.S. Drought 2012: Farm and Food Impacts." *United States Department of Agriculture Research Service*. www.ers.usda.gov/topics/in-the-news/us-drought-2012-farm-and-food-impacts.aspx#.U-KaxagdW2Q

Weilacher, U. (2008). *Syntax of Landscape: The Landscape Architecture of Peter Latz and Partners*. Basel, Berlin, Boston: Birkhäuser.

WHO and UNICEF (2012). *Progress on Sanitation and Drinking-Water: 2012 Update*. Geneva: WHO/UNICEF. http://www.unicef.org/media/files/JMPreport2012.pdf

Wong, T.H.F., and Brown, R. R. (2009). "The Water Sensitive City: Principles for Practice." *Water Science & Technology* 60(3): 673–682.

Wong, T.H.F. and Eadie, M. L. (2000). "Water Sensitive Urban Design: A Paradigm Shift in Urban Design." In International Water Resources Association, *10th World Water Congress: Water, the World's Most Important Resource*. Melbourne, Australia: International Water Resources Association. 1281–1288.

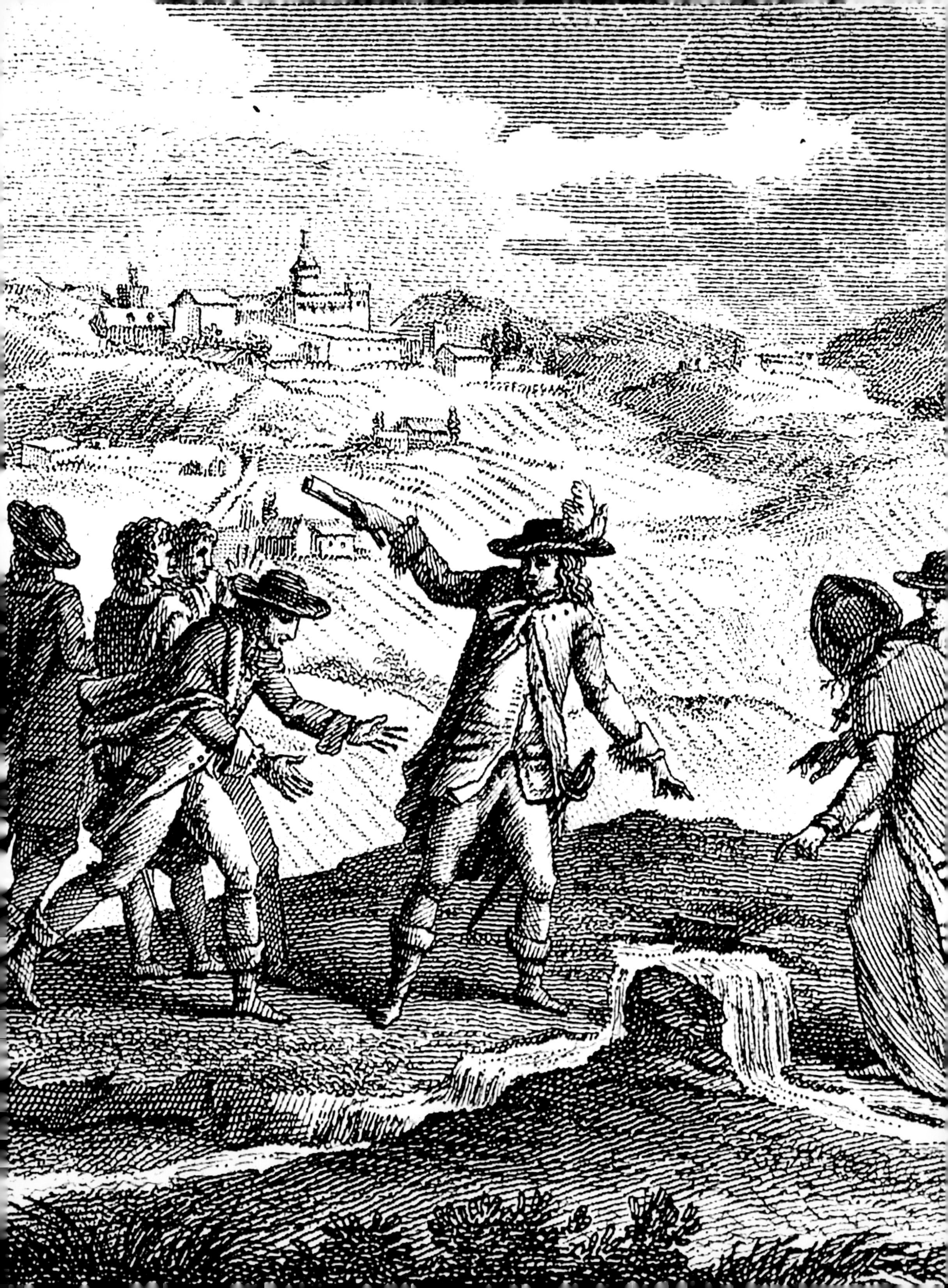

Water, Technology, and Society: A Historical Overview

Antoine Picon

The following is an edited transcript of Antoine Picon's keynote lecture delivered at the "Out of Water" conference, Thursday, April 1, 2011.

The management of water is among the oldest technological challenges to confront humankind. Its terms have been strikingly variable from one region of the globe to another. Whereas the abundance of water was often a problem for Northern Europeans in past centuries, it was its scarcity that represented the major obstacle to development in countries belonging to the dry belt, such as those in the Middle East. In any given region in the world, water could be at once abundant in certain conditions and for certain uses, and scarce in others.

What can we learn by looking at the relationship between water and technology from a broad historical perspective? Given the diversity of conditions, the topic is inexhaustible. Certain themes and perspectives must be privileged, and so two major historical threads are outlined in this essay.

The first concerns the systemic character of water management. From very ancient times onwards, water has been associated with technologies that possessed a decidedly systemic dimension. Until the 18th century, the European technological system as a whole could even be described as water-centered. History shows that, at times, profound crises disrupted these systems and technologies and forced them to evolve. From this perspective, our present-day incertitude is perhaps an early sign of a transition from current types of systems to new ones, the characteristics of which have barely begun to appear. One of the ambitions of this book may be to contribute to a better comprehension of these emerging features.

Yet, technology is only part of the problem. The second historical thread concerns the intricate links between technology's societal and political influences. Dating back to the most ancient periods, hydraulic systems have been the products and mechanisms of society and politics as much as of technology in a narrow sense. These social and political aspects are among the greatest challenges that we are facing today. Obstacles to technology and technological innovation are, of course, part of the problem, but the most pressing issues have to do with technology's socio-political implications. Following science and technology scholars such as Bruno Latour, the term "politics" here is used in a broader-than-usual sense. Water possesses a political dimension because it is a public resource and a public affair, and above all because its management and use force people to redefine their relations. We are definitely in need of a new politics of water.

Among the Oldest Technological Challenges

Management of water plays a seminal role in the development of technological expertise. In Europe, for instance, water management was among the key domains of early engineering. Besides the design and realization of waterways—the true high-tech enterprises of the Renaissance and 17th century—engineers also mobilized the power of water for fortification purposes. We tend to forget today how defense was, in many cases, based as much on water as on earthworks and masonry walls. Such was the case with the voluntary floods of the

FIGURE 1: Pierre-Paul Riquet presenting to the King's envoys his project for the Canal du Midi at the watershed between the Mediterranean and the Atlantic, after a 19th-century engraving

FIGURE 2: Pierre-Denis Martin, *Vue de la Machine Marly*, view of the Marly hydraulic engine, 1783

FIGURE 3: Turbulences created by bridge piers (opposite)

Netherlands, employed to resist the invasion of the French troops of Louis XIV in 1672—a tactic that epitomizes the defensive importance of water.

Until the mid-18th century, engineering was often presented as a discipline which was primarily focused on hydraulic problems; in fact, it was commonly known as "architecture hydraulique"(hydraulic architecture). In Charles D'Aviler's influential late-17th century dictionary of architectural terms, engineering appears under this denomination, as a sub-branch of architecture. Architecture Hydraulique is also the title of the 18th century's most important engineering treatise, by Bélidor, which was concerned with the art of conveying, distributing, and managing water for all of life's needs.

In the context of Northern Europe, one would readily suppose that the main problem was the abundance of water, rather than its scarcity. Traditional engineering design, such as that of Dutch polders and masonry bridges, seemed to evince a pressing need to resist the abundant flow of water. However, even in Europe, water was neither abundant nor scarce; rather, the issue was if it was where, and when, it was needed.

Take, for example, water canalization in Europe; for many years, the sole, rather ineffective, method to maintain water availability year-round was to waterproof the canals with clay. In northern France, for instance, canals were often dry throughout the summer and fall months. Moreover, the most strategic canals linked different river basins and watersheds, which meant that canals had to circumvent the ridges that separated them. Consequently, canals had to be designed to reach high elevations. Yet the higher the canal section, the more difficult it was to locate a water source. This was the main difficulty for the Canal du Midi of 17th-century France, which was considered at the time to be one of the masterpieces of French engineering (Figure 1). At one of its highest elevations, the canal passes through a plateau, where water supply is very limited.

The most spectacular expression of this relative scarcity of water is perhaps Versailles, where Louis XIV had envisioned a spectacular display of waterworks. One of the major works built to supply water to Versailles was the Marly machine. Considered one of the most impressive hydraulic engines built in early modern Europe, the machine had 14 paddlewheels, each about 38ft in diameter, turned by the Seine to power more than 250 pumps, all in order to send water uphill (Figure 2). Another massive waterworks, a giant aqueduct, was never completed, although construction involved the death of a few thousand workers. Despite the colossal works, which also included pumps, reservoirs, channels, and an aqueduct, the Sun King was never able to achieve his ultimate goal.

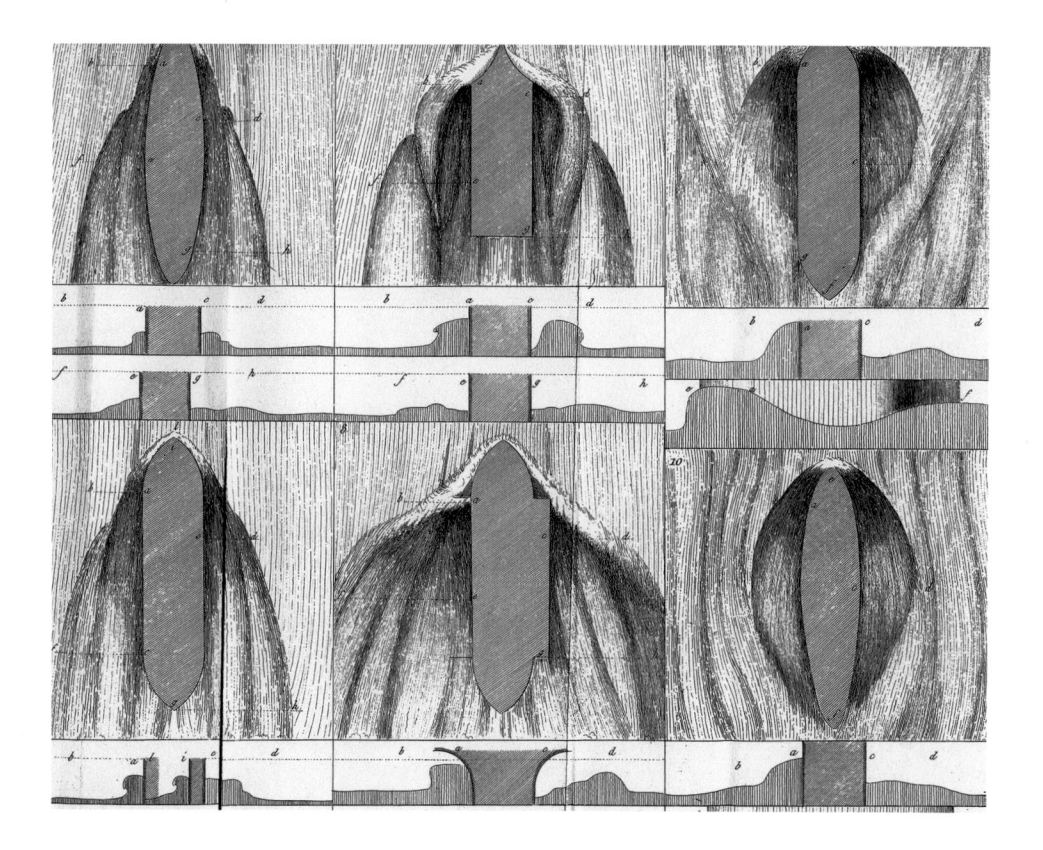

These two cases reveal that waterworks are seldom simple and linear. Even a canal requires multiple reservoirs and channels in order to supply it with water, reinforcing the systemic character of water management. The problems raised by water can seldom be apprehended in simple terms, such as overabundance or scarcity. The most common condition is actually that the right kind of water is not where it should be, which seems to be more the case today than ever before.

On the other hand, Middle Eastern engineers, whether Arab or Persian, were always confronted with scarcity. It is worth noting that in the Muslim world, water management was also at the core of emerging engineering competence, and for centuries was more advanced than its western counterpart. The realizations of the Cairo Nilometer and the Corduan Noria bear testimony to the level of sophistication, far before the technological rise of Western Europe.

Past these early moments, it is important to note the long-term influence of hydraulic considerations and models on the engineering field, far beyond hydraulics and water management proper. This includes the conception of flow within modern and contemporary engineering thought. This influence emerged during the 18th century and onward, when the laws of hydrodynamics were beginning to be better understood at both the theoretical and practical levels. For example, a relatively new idea at the time concerned the study of turbulence generated by bridge piers (Figure 3).

Modern engineering generalized the notion of flow, applying it to many elements both natural and human—from water in canals, to goods in the circulation systems of nations (Figure 4). Simultaneously, stagnation and stagnating water became synonymous with decay and unhealthy conditions. This was a spectacular inversion from the classical notion of optimum, which was static in essence; this is seen in medieval theology, where God is immobile and mobility is associated with imperfection. Dynamics became the norm, and with modern hydraulic models, strange ideas arose, such as the claim by Parmentier that the water that flows out of Paris is cleaner than when it entered the city—in direct proportion, paradoxically, to all the garbage thrown into it. As he explains in his 1787 dissertation "Sur la Nature des Eaux de la Seine", water is purified by the movement given to it by what is thrown into it.

From the 18th century on, fluidic models have been found in all types of domains, from material engineering to network management. They are at the core of modern material physics, which is based on the assumption that forces literally flow in structures, and that strains are analogous to pressures. This is among the reasons for the rediscovery in the 18th century of the Gothic, where constructive techniques are based on fluidic conceptions of effort. This, too, remains characteristic of engineering thought. In the French case, this fluidic model permeates the general layout of the Haussmannian city, as well as the design of its gardens. Such is the case with Parc des Buttes-Chaumont, which was designed by engineers in a way that clearly bears the mark of a fluidic conception of the garden.

Today, however, one of the main challenges has to do with a very different notion: flows are not infinite. Thus, new conservation imperatives have arisen. To progress from a monomania with flow to a more complex understanding of hydraulic models, we may need to recapture a sense of the meditative character that was associated with water in so many traditional cultures. We must think about how we can reconceive water circulation while also rediscovering the lure of unproductive stagnation, which was not of interest to the rational, industrial mind.

FIGURE 4: Abraham-Louis-Rodolphe Ducros, *Cascata delle Marmore*, Marmore's Fall, Terni, Italy, circa 1785 (opposite)

Hydraulic Systems

The most important aspect of water management is its strong systemic turn; in other words, water technologies are strongly interdependent on each other. They constitute a coherent whole, linked by numerous feedback loops. This is especially evident in the case of irrigation, one of the first large-scale technologies ever invented, with origins that can be traced back to the sixth millennium B.C. in Mesopotamia and Egypt. Irrigation, and hydraulic works more generally, are principally about preserving water, which largely accounts for the systemic character of the technologies involved. In the case of irrigation, its relevance throughout history is also striking. A classic example is that of the shaduf, a mechanism for raising water, consisting of a pivoted pole with a bucket at one end and a counterweight at the other. Though it first appeared around 1700 B.C. in Egypt, it was still in use when the French invaded the country in 1798.

For centuries, water management techniques represented the core of the technologies in use by most societies; one could say that most traditional technological systems were, in fact, water-based. This is quite clear in the Middle East, but it also became the case in Western Europe, in a number of decisive steps. The Middle Ages in Western Europe were marked by a decisive water moment: the invention of the watermill to power the engine. Until at least the end of the 18th century, watermills remained the fundamental source of energy for all types of artisanal and proto-industrial fabrications. The importance of water as a source of power led to a very different manufacturing geography than the one that would prevail after the first industrial revolution; mountainous regions, such as the Alps, were often highly industrial because of the presence of numerous fast-flowing streams. Yet, this geography would again be radically altered by the development of the steam engine and railway (Figure 5).

Since the start of their discipline, historians of technology have been very aware of the systemic dimension of hydraulic technologies. It played an essential role in their early attempts to define precisely what a technological system was. In his 1934 *Technics and Civilization*, Lewis Mumford famously divided the evolution of technology into three distinct phases: "eotechnical," "paleotechnical," and "neotechnical." The eotechnical phase is marked largely by early attempts at rational uses of water, particularly of its energetic power.

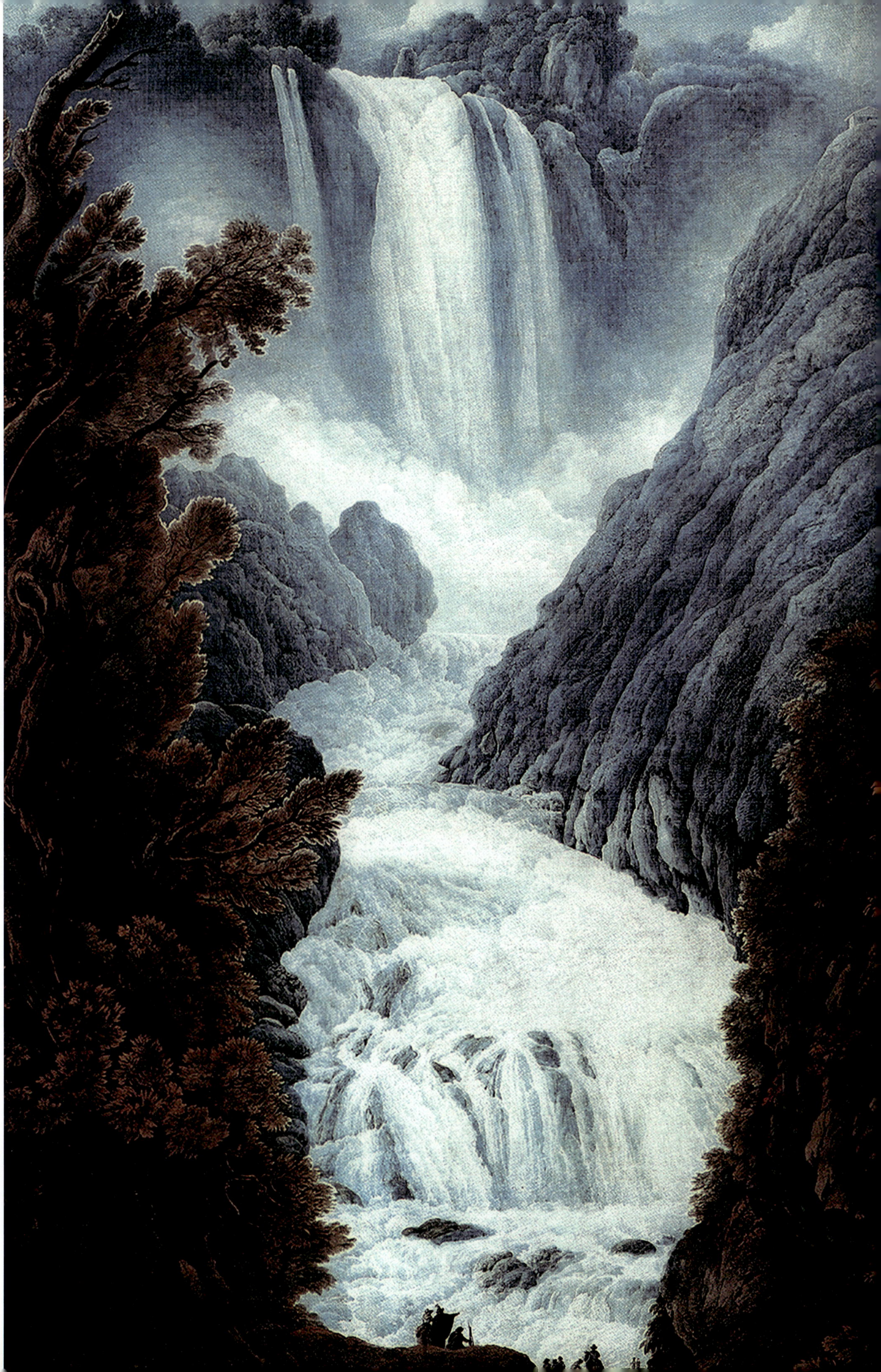

FIGURE 5: Watt steam engine, after the drawings made in England by Augustin de Betancourt y Molina, circa 1788

FIGURE 6: Nicolas and Jean-Baptiste Raguenet, *Joust of Sailors Between the Bridge of Notre-Dame and the Bridge au Change in Paris*, 1752 (opposite)

A few decades later, the founding father of modern French history of technology, Bertrand Gille, framed this evolution in terms of two different periods. He characterized the first as the period of classical and traditional technological systems, marked by the predominance of water, and the second as the period of the industrial system, beginning with the first industrial revolution of the 19th century. For Gille, the two essential components of the classical technological systems were water and wood. Water was the main source of energy, and its presence or absence determined the possibility of large-scale production and its geography. Water also acted as the main means of transportation, as there were very few roads until the 18th century, and navigation through Europe was mainly on water. The other element, wood, was by far the most important construction material, before brick or stone, and was also the main combustible. This meant that the productive geography of Europe was drawn at the intersection of water and wood resources. For Gille, water and wood technologies were constitutive of a system, because they were also highly interdependent and interconnected.

Ultimately, this water-wood system reached a limit towards the beginning of the 18th century, for a series of reasons. The main one was that its inputs and outputs were limited. There was only so much hydraulic power one could harness using waterwheels, and wood was also becoming depleted. For Gille, the first industrial revolution saw this fundamental water-wood coupling replaced by a triadic coal-iron-steam structure. This triad functioned in a series of feedback loops: coal fed the steam engines, which enabled the production of iron, from which steam engines were made, and they, in turn, made extensive coal mining possible by enabling deep underground water pumping. These three elements brought with them a whole new series of feedback loops and ultimately led to a totally different system, for which the geography was also very different. Coal, iron, and the steam engine were also responsible for the two major technological transformations of the time: the great textile mills of the Midlands, and the railway, leading to what has often been characterized as the transportation revolution.

This shift appeared to be the starting point of a massive change that would deprive water of its central technological role. However, in recent decades, historians of technology have become more nuanced in their assessment of how rapid the change was. First, water still continued to play an essential role in production and transportation for a very long time. It is worth noting that the industrial revolution itself was a revolution first linked to canal building rather than railways. This was, for instance, the case in England where, prior to the development of railways, a dense network of waterways and canals was developed from the mid-18th century onwards. This English waterway network included some remarkable engineering works, like the Pontcysyllte navigable aqueduct, completed in 1805. Waterways were just as important in North America, where canals were key to the development of the cotton economy in the South and played a crucial role in the growth and development of the northeast, as in the case of the Erie Canal.

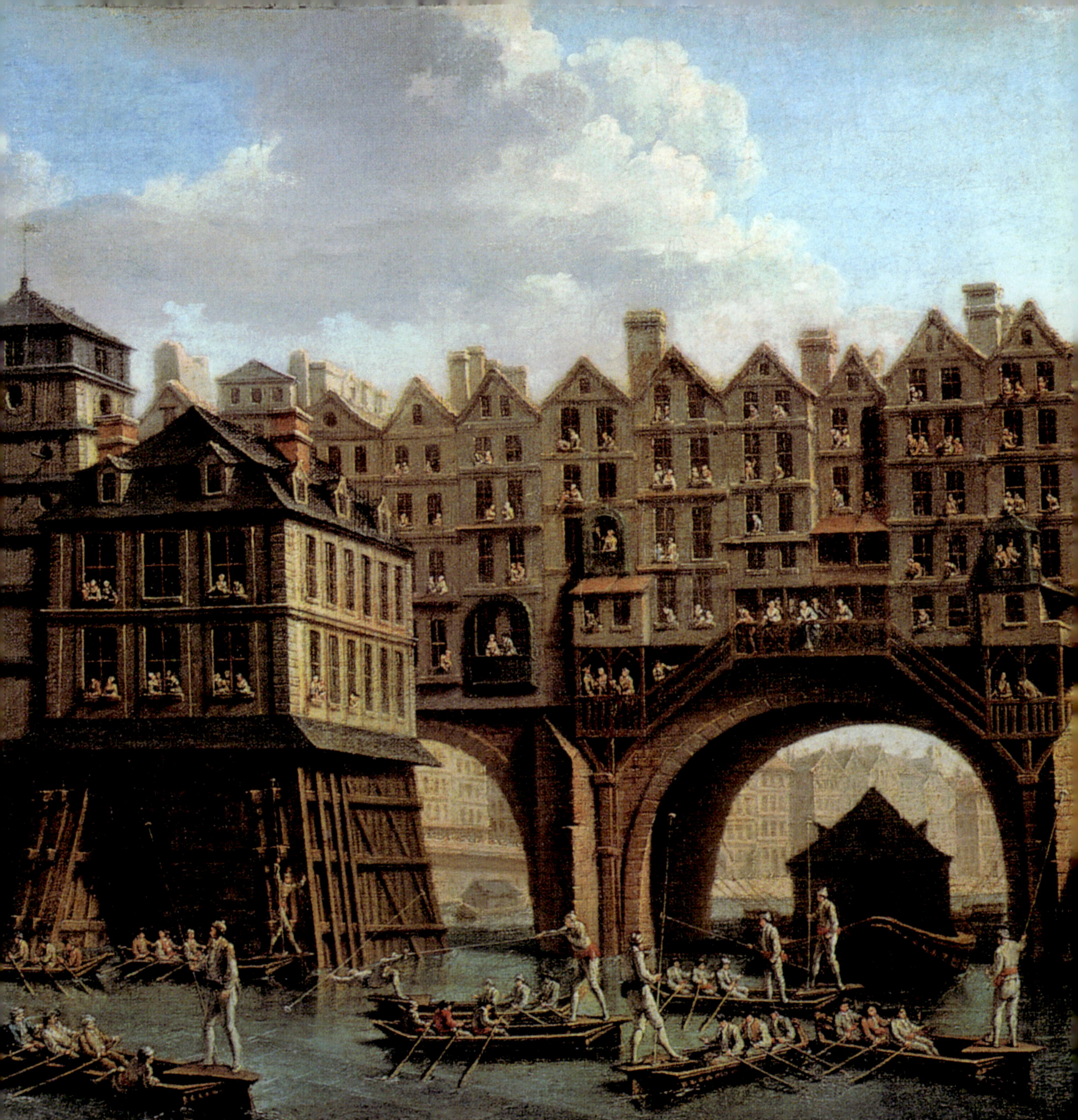

More generally, the transition between systems was far more gradual than what either Mumford or Gille had in mind. In France for instance, steam engine power exceeded hydraulic power relatively late, in the 1860s. While the transition between systems took a long time, it is what happened during this transition that is important. Water began to lose its centrality in the 19th century, but it did not yet lose its importance. Furthermore, spectacular progresses and innovations were still made, making hydraulic energy far more efficient than in the past. For instance, with the 19th century came the invention of the turbine, which came to play a major role in the development of electricity. The turbine also led to one of the major uses of water in the 20th century: the production of electricity with hydro-powered dams.

The turbine, then, provides a good transition towards the return of major hydraulic work, led by the development of electricity. Examples of such large-scale hydraulic works were to be found everywhere throughout the 20th century, from France's Barrage du Sautet on the River Drac, built in the 1930s, to incomparable achievements like the Tennessee Valley Authority and the Hoover Dam. In some ways, water itself became less important, but dealing with it was still an absolutely essential problem.

If we consider waterworks in the context of landscape architecture, we can address the overall systemic character of what Bertrand Gille called the classical period and how it connected intimately with landscape. For centuries, hydraulic works had shaped landscape in a slow and methodical way. Irrigation techniques were emblematic of this patient remodeling, applied in a constant negotiation with the natural elements. In cases such as that of the famous Balinese terracing culture, the overall remodeling could involve extensive, massive reshaping, but nevertheless its methods are respectful of a certain equilibrium between man's constructs and nature, outlining a strong landscape dimension. This equilibrium had been maintained despite the development of engineering during the Renaissance and the desire to overcome the limitation of nature. Eighteenth-century engineers often saw themselves as gardeners of the territory. At the time, engineering students studying at the Ecole des Ponts et Chaussées continued to employ a pervasive presence of water and waterworks, from garden canals and fountains to harbors. Interestingly, 18th-century Ponts et Chaussées engineers were taught landscape drawing. Later, with industrialization, this equilibrium was broken, and it has disappeared completely in the brutality of the current relationship between infrastructure and landscape. This approach to infrastructural building can, of course, evoke sublime effects, yet ultimately it results in unresolved problems. Today's hydraulic works still shape the landscape, but, as is evident in projects such as the Three Gorges Dam in China, they do so with sublimity rather than with the traditional negotiation between nature and man-made work. Negotiation is certainly among the skills that we may have to learn again. Water management in arid climates could serve as a laboratory for this rediscovery.

Water and Cities

In cities also, water was, from early on, managed in systemic ways. A striking example of this was studied by French historian of technology André Guillerme, who showed how overwhelmingly present water was in the medieval and classical-age cities of northern France. Guillerme describes a multiplicity of "little Venices." In a series of plans, he compares the center of Venice to those of various northern French cities to illustrate how hydraulic systems were not only important for transportation, but also for industry and production, like that of tanning. Water was truly a complex urban system, situated at the locus where public and private realms met. The 18th-century Seine in Paris is a good example; houses sat on public bridges, so that the Seine was in a certain respect their backyard (Figure 6). This is a relationship that is likely to seem contradictory today.

At the dawn of industrialization, a series of changes occurred in Europe. First, water was made less immediately accessible, less familiar, more monumental and public. In Paris, this was a process that began with the destruction of houses on bridges, followed by the construction of embankments along the river. Water was also increasingly assimilated into technical resources and harnessed through technologies. Simultaneously, new challenges arose, such as the need to deliver more and better-quality water. This led to constructions such as the Ourcq canal, completed during the Napoleonic period. In essence, the old system was completely destroyed and gradually replaced by a very different one. This process of change in Paris lasted for 20 – 30 years, and quickly became emblematic of European cities in general. It also marked the emergence of a key notion in contemporary engineering and infrastructure thought: the network.

To return to the influence of hydraulic systems in modern and contemporary engineering thought, the notion of network is among the ways in which this influence has exerted itself. The notion has a definite hydraulic origin, relating to the idea of circulation in the body. At the onset, urban networks were literally supposed to irrigate the body of the city. This new regime went hand in hand with a series of new problems, such as water quality control and epidemic prevention. The cholera epidemics of the 19th century played an essential role in triggering this trend. In his famous map of London, Doctor John Snow illustrated a cholera attack in the Broad Street and Golden Square area in 1854. Snow mapped the houses struck by the disease and suggested that the contamination of a specific public pump was responsible for its spread. Accordingly, the pump was removed, and the plague stopped. Snow's discoveries about cholera led to a radical redesign of wastewater management in London. The new networked urban system for water functioned well for a large part of the 19th and 20th centuries. Today, however, we are likely on the eve of its demise, or at least of a major transformation for water in the city.

We can identify a few crucial factors related to the transformation of the networked water model discussed here. First, we have a growing desire to live in close contact with water, which challenges the place to which it was typically assigned at the dawn of the industrial era. The contemporary obsession with waterways is evident all over the world; for example, in people's tendency to migrate to the world's coasts, which raises difficult questions concerning flooding and sea level rise.

Second, traditional networks tend toward dysfunction. For example, a large amount of water is lost due to poor state of pipes and the difficulty of maintenance and repair. In France, which is far from the worst case, the loss of water averages around 25% in most urban water networks, reaching levels as high as 41% in cities like Nîmes. All kinds of catastrophes are generated and amplified by factors linked to waterproofing and network management. These issues have called into question the viability of large, integrated urban networks as the sole model and have spurred the emergence of smaller feedback loops, which work at a lesser distance and with a higher degree of interaction between urban and technological processes. For example, in the Hammarby Sjöstad district of Stockholm, tests are being done on a new model, which includes small-scale, interactive feedback loops among various types of networks. We may, once again, be on the eve of a major mutation in the way water is managed in cities.

A Political and Cultural Problem

The use of water has a clear political character. The politics of water exists beyond the narrow confines of ordinary political life. Its politics is what tends to generate social relations. Its politics is what may be a subject of concern and even disagreement between people. Its politics is also what tends to define and redefine individuals and their relation to the collective. Here, "political" is taken in the sense given to it by contemporary thinkers like Ulrich Beck or Bruno Latour. The impact of risk and catastrophe is an integral part of this.

Why does water have a political dimension? Throughout its history, the management of water has generated social relations. First of all, water is often rare, difficult to access, or erratic, and this entails coordination among different groups regarding its use. For instance, in 19th-century France, the function of water use coordination was given to the "police des cours d'eau" (water flow police), as well as to the bridge and highway administrations. Water is political, not only in moments of scarcity but also in moments of abundance and inundation, when land must be protected. The Dutch were seen as a political model because of their strong collective hydraulic management. This became one of the sources of inspiration for the 19th-century French reformer Frédéric Le Play. Having studied the polder flood-protection system, Le Play was convinced that this was the model to follow in order to reconcile modern technology with the collective spirit of ancient times. Hydraulics would remain an important subject for Le Play throughout his days as a social reformer. Later in his career, his philosophy became instrumental in promoting social geography, in which factors like the abundance and scarcity of water played a definite role.

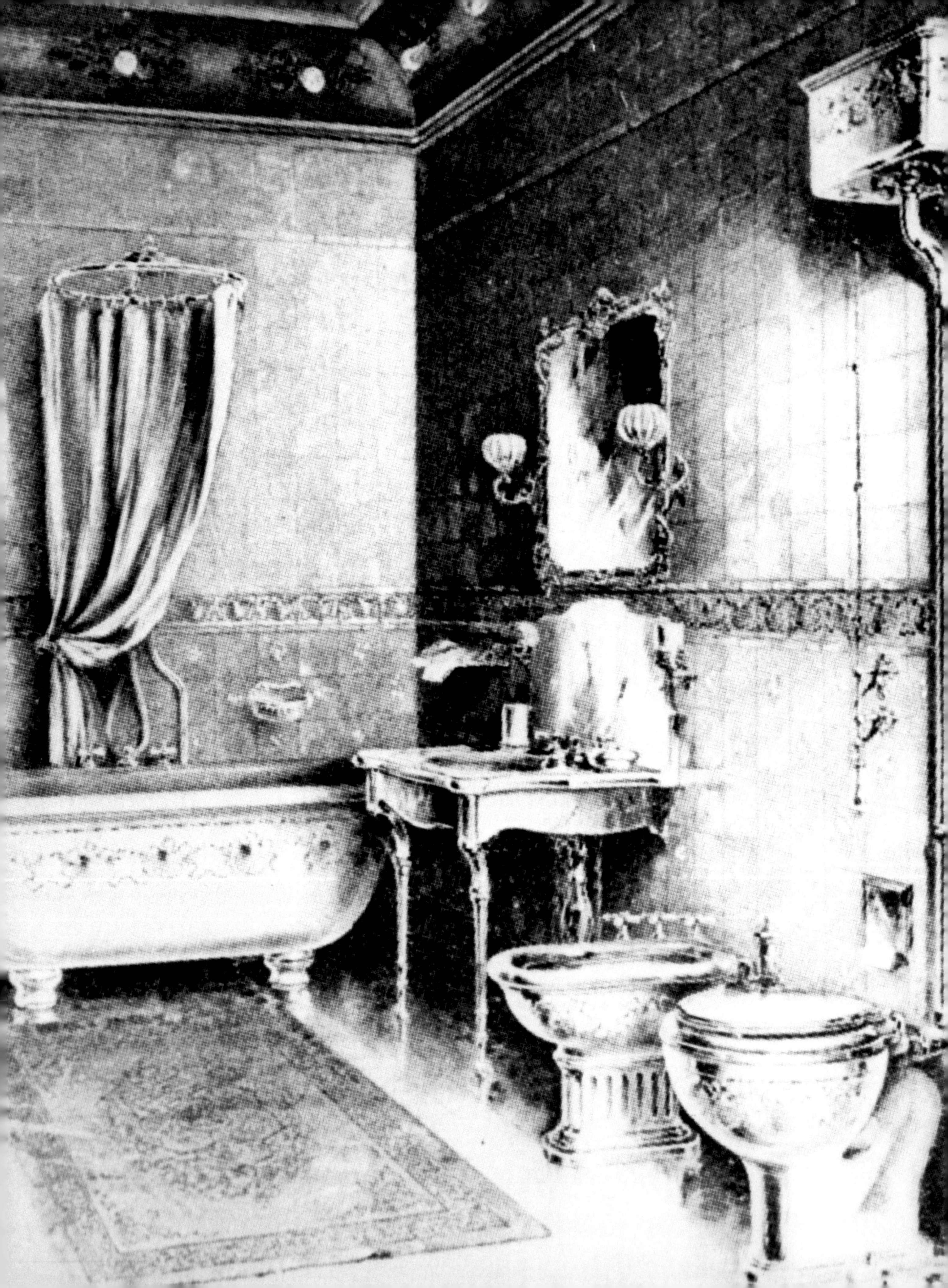

Figure 7: Bathroom of the well-to-do in the United States, early 20th century

Le Play's approach is in striking contrast with one of the most famous attempts to connect hydraulics with politics: the notion of hydraulic empire, also known as hydraulic despotism. The terms were introduced by German-American historian Karl August Wittfogel in his 1957 book *Oriental Despotism* to characterize regimes whose strict control over access to water was their key to power. One of Wittfogel's most popular assertions is that several societies, including Ancient Egypt and Mesopotamia, established monopolies over water control in order to overcome water scarcity. This notion is still found in writings today, but like any oversimplifying thesis, it has been challenged. For example, Joseph Needham has argued that such political practices were not in fact adopted in China, as Wittfogel claimed. Nevertheless, the notion suggests an intersection between hydraulic technology and hydraulic management. One could even argue that technology and management are one and the same in the case of hydraulics. The diversity of perspectives outlined above suggests that technology is not deterministic, but that it raises issues that are political and need to be addressed as such. Regardless, one thing is certain: water management is typically aligned with a certain degree of centralization, whether despotic in nature or not. Hydraulic works are often linked to the existence of a powerful bureaucracy.

Emerging Challenges

Three pressing issues arise in relation to this centralized control of water. The first pertains to the ongoing tendency to privatize the management of water, including the provision of water services and sanitation. Bureaucracy used to be an instrument of the state, whether despotic or democratic; it is unclear what the state of water management would be following the increasing privatization of resources and services across the world. Would we see a new kind of hydraulic despotism in the name of global capitalism?

The second issue relates to the internationalization of water issues, a process that has been underway since the realization of giant infrastructural-scale works such as the Suez and Panama canals. Dealing with projects at the scale of the watershed increasingly requires the resolution of cross-border conflicts by policy makers, diplomats, and planners.

The last, and perhaps most insidious, issue has to do with the increasing individualism of today's lifestyles and the ensuing challenges. One aspect of globalization is that it has created a short circuit between individual behaviors and collective problems; the issue of water is a representative facet of this situation. Traditionally, water was seen as a large-scale and collective challenge; however, today, we are starting to see it as the object of a new dialectic between the individual and the collective. Toilets, for example, constantly remind us of how individualized and personal the question of water is today. The bathroom is fascinating, since it is the first technological room, far surpassing the computer room or kitchen in seniority (Figure 7). It is the first room where one's naked body encounters a large network of the city as a whole. The bathroom is in a strange place, at the direct interface between the individual and collective faces of water. This is also where our individuality and subjectivity in society has been shaped and reshaped. We are probably again on the eve of a new reshaping. As Ulrich Beck and others have pointed out, many contemporary issues can be effectively dealt with only if one takes into account individual behaviors. This is perhaps a true challenge for hydraulic technologies that used to rely heavily on bureaucratic coordination.

Beyond the realm of collective action, water technologies have always possessed a cultural character. Various historians of technology have drawn connections between the pervasive presence of slow and continuous hydraulic movement and a cyclical vision of time and human history. For these historians, the rapid, nervous, linear movement of modern steam engines marked the advent of a totally different system of cultural representations. Another set of cultural determinations has to do with the everyday use of water and how it has shaped our modern identity, from the possibility of running water in the kitchen to the use of domestic swimming pools, and from the Victorian bathroom to today's Jacuzzi. This is part of what is at stake today; we face not only a political but also a cultural adaptation.

1
WATER
FOR
DOMESTIC USE

Introduction: Beyond Low-Flush Toilets

Despite the staggering figures of water shortage worldwide, the provision of water within the domestic environment is a problem that is not nearly addressed enough in architecture, landscape architecture, and urban design. Whereas the topics of food security and environmental management, addressed in the following chapters, have become integral to design practice, the technical aspects of collecting, treating, and delivering water still remain within the purview of science and engineering, while issues of water governance fall under policy and economics.

At the building scale, projects attempting to address water scarcity in arid climates typically focus on water use and conservation standards (e.g., LEED, BREEAM). These performance benchmarks center primarily on the specification of water-saving devices, such as low-flush toilets, toilet dams, low-flow showers and appliances, combined toilet and sink systems, smart meters, and real-time water consumption feedback devices. The implementation of water conservation devices within the home has proven to decrease domestic water use by 30% (U.S. Environmental Protection Agency, 2014). That said, in many cities the reuse of wastewater, rain, or surface runoff within buildings is disallowed due to health concerns. Reuse in irrigation is somewhat more acceptable, particularly in agriculture, but still not a routine practice within the urban environment. The main question that this chapter raises is what the role of design could be in shaping water technology and management as it relates to the domestic environment and the individual user, beyond merely specifying water-conserving products.

It is important to first recognize the political context within which water flows through the urban environment. As such, the two essays and five case studies in this chapter depict two opposite, rather extreme, ends of water management. One is set within a context where the supply of water is deemed a human right and a public service and, thus, water and sanitation infrastructure is centrally governed and its quality controlled. The other is where water and sanitation infrastructure is non-existent. The latter context is typically found in the developing world, where tenuous economic and socio-political conditions frequently form the backdrop to a broad absence of public infrastructure, necessitating alternative approaches such as self-reliance and building capacity of local institutions and communities. Despite the contrast, both positions are first and foremost motivated by human health and survival at the most fundamental level. Water is life.

Two Water Scarcity Scenarios

Hot, arid regions that have water-sanitation infrastructure no longer rely on water conservation as the single answer to increasing demand caused by population growth and persistent droughts. As Tal describes in his essay "Technical Optimism as an Antidote to Water Scarcity," over the last 20 years arid nations such as Israel, Australia, and Spain have been taking bolder steps to actually "produce" or "manufacture" drinking-quality water with technologies for desalination of seawater and brackish groundwater. Critiques of these countries' approaches focus on sole reliance on a single mechanical technology, failure to diversify solutions and build in redundancy, emphasis on supply-side solutions that encourage wasteful consumption habits, and the valid concern around the adverse environmental impacts on marine biology, carbon emissions, and high energy dependency. However, the economics behind desalination outshine what are deemed as "surmountable obstacles."

Tal's essay, as its title suggests, represents a growing confidence in "upper-case" Technology's capacity to overcome water scarcity (see Introduction for a discussion of "lower-case" technology vs. "upper-case" Technology). In all cases, the political, economic, and technological setting has allowed for the robust growth of the desalination industry. Despite public debates around associated environmental issues, Tal states that "recent experience in several countries offers an empirical basis for assessing the potential of desalination, which, along with wastewater reuse, might obviate the projected water shortages of the future." Therefore, with today's advanced technology, water is in fact "a renewable resource more than ever before."

The opposite scenario is a complete lack of water-sanitation infrastructure, a scenario that, as Baker and Ngai discuss in their essay, currently affects over 780 million people. This condition is not exclusively associated with arid climates, but describes more broadly a prolonged state of water scarcity due to contamination. In such conditions, most evident is the unclear distinction between drinking water and wastewater. Typically, if water infrastructure is missing, so is sanitation, and vice versa. Two and a half million people have no access to sanitation services. Two point two million deaths every year, mostly children under 5, are attributed to diarrheal diseases due to ingestion of contaminated water. The collection and treatment of wastewater is therefore paramount to the improvement of drinking water quality and cannot be considered an independent problem. Importantly, the lack of both water and sanitation services has a direct corollary to underdevelopment and poverty (Side Note 1).

Baker and Ngai's essay discusses non-governmental strategies for in situ implementation of simple, non-expert, and low-cost "lower-case" technologies. The key principle is empowerment of local population and organizations through education and training, and encouragement of self-reliance, ownership, and leadership. While this may seem an insurmountable task, the essay cites the example of CAWST (which Baker co-founded), a non-governmental organization (NGO) which projects to help 20 million people with better water and sanitation by 2020.

Baker and Ngai describe a process of disseminating ideas and inventions that would otherwise remain strictly within academic institutions. They do so by acting as a two-way bridge between universities and research labs on one hand and with local NGOs and community leaders on the other. The local groups ensure widespread adoption of new solutions and practices, which in turn provides product testing and feedback to the universities.

Several case studies characterize the type of decentralized/distributed solutions that could address the lack or failure of water infrastructure. The Kanchan Arsenic Filter and Liquid Wrap technologies offer affordable and simple solutions to remove contaminants from unregulated water supplies. The former is typically built within a home; the latter is a portable and wearable vessel. Another small-scale device, the Vena Water Condenser, produces water from vapor through condensation. Isla Urbana and Down to Earth both collect rainwater and surface runoff, in barrels and underground cisterns respectively. These small-scale interventions, ranging in size from human- to household-scale devices, can be multiplied across a community, ultimately creating health or social impacts well beyond the individual appliance, as conveyed in the Isla Urbana and Down to Earth case studies.

The common drawbacks associated with such distributed, off-the-grid, do-it-yourself solutions concern lack of quality control, inability to regulate the level of contaminants in the sourced water, and unreliable commitment of individuals over the long-term. Nonetheless, despite their unquestionable benefits, centralized water infrastructure systems are also criticized today for 1) their lack of capacity to withstand and adapt to extreme weather events and environmental crises, 2) the prerequisite of functioning governance, 3) negative impacts on existing ecological systems, 4) lack of integration with public, or civic space, and 5) the fact that where water infrastructure is a public service, built projects habitually rely on the assumption that faucets, showerheads, hoses, and sprinklers are connected to a limitless piped supply of water.

A Gradient of Water Qualities

The two scenarios are generally representative of the predominant conditions and approaches to water management and technology around the world today. But rather than perceive them in opposition, perhaps a more productive approach would concurrently employ multi-scale solutions that comprise both expert "Technology" and non-expert "technology" as a multifaceted and redundant (fail-safe) urban design strategy.

The common thread between the essays and case studies points to two key design principles: diversifying water sources, and allocating diverse water qualities to a variety of use requirements. In other words, in addition to conventional fresh water resources (e.g., lakes, rivers, and aquifers), non-potable water sources (e.g., seawater, contaminated surface runoff, greywater, and vapor) have become viable by means of a variety of treatment processes, including the relatively new reverse osmosis, but also the traditional sand filter and technologies

1. According to a 2006 United Nations survey carried out in 177 countries, women and girls spend as much as five or six hours per day fetching water (a total of 40 billion hours collecting water each year), keeping girls out of school. The lack of working toilets in schools also deters girls from attending school, thus greatly limiting opportunities to improve their circumstances (Barlow, 2010).

2. The use of water for outdoor irrigation accounts for most of the potable water used in North America, while the largest amount of water indoors is used for toilet flushing (Mayer, et al., 1999). According to the U.S. Environmental Protection Agency, irrigation of residential landscapes accounts for more than a third of residential water use—more than nine billion gallons per day (U.S. Environmental Protection Agency, 2013)—while households located in arid regions such as Arizona use up to 70% of potable water for irrigation (Arizona Department of Water Resources, 2014).

employing the well-known principle of vapor condensation. Consequently, the total available water is increased. The second principle involves the allocation of non-potable quality water to various household uses, such as toilet flushing or irrigation (Side Note 2) through a dual water supply system, thus reserving potable water for only such uses as necessitate drinking-quality water. Consequently, the pressure on diminishing potable water resources is minimized, and at the same time, the adverse effects of wastewater discharge are mitigated.

The idea that there is not just one water but a gradient of water qualities opens up new opportunities and trajectories for design. We would like to point to several case study examples that offer integrated design strategies to link regional water management and large-scale water technology with opportunities for design development at the building, site, or material systems scale.

Dual Water-Supply Systems

Israel and Australia represent the most progressive examples of an implemented dual water system at both regional and neighborhood scales. Israel recycles more than 75% of all municipal wastewater across the country for reuse in agriculture (see pp.142–145). In addition to a long-standing culture of water savings (e.g., use of low-flush toilets) and restrictions (e.g., prohibiting lawn irrigation during droughts), as well as desalination of 500 million m^3 of seawater per year, this has resulted in massive savings of potable water. The purple-colored treated wastewater pipes, distinct from the blue potable water pipes, are often seen in use also in municipal parks and gardens.

Such advances in water engineering and agriculture have yet to influence the ways in which architecture, landscape, and urban design are conceived, regulated, and practiced in Israel. New projects, let alone existing ones, do not frequently incorporate surface runoff collection for irrigation in park systems and urban gardens, nor do most buildings incorporate the reuse of treated wastewater for toilet flushing and other such uses where potable water is not required.

In Australia, Water Sensitive Urban Design (WSUD), part of an overarching concept called whole-of-water-cycle management, is intended to integrate the management of waterways, groundwater, stormwater, wastewater, and potable water supply as a comprehensive urban design strategy. The national water recycling guidelines include regulations for stormwater and wastewater reuse and have consequently reduced domestic potable water consumption by 40%. For example, Australia's Rouse Hill Recycled Water Network System Plan (Lazarova, et al., 2013) serves as a pioneering example for new developments. A suburb of Sydney, the Rouse Hill Project Area has implemented a dual water supply system. Two parallel systems are provided, a potable supply for household uses such as drinking, cooking, and washing, and a recycled supply for toilet flushing and outdoor uses like garden watering.

These groundbreaking projects, however, still only operate within the realm of hydraulic infrastructure such as the pipe network, and miss the opportunity to rethink the potential that the building and landscape could contribute at a site scale to increasing the overall water portfolio. The subsequent parts offer a range of design strategies for capturing and reusing water.

Increasing the Overall Water Portfolio

With nearly 15,000 facilities worldwide, often located along coastlines, desalination plants have an enormous footprint in the landscape. Public pressure around environmental mitigation and coastal integration has changed the approach to the design of desalination plants in recent years. Landscape and architecture play a key role. The Victoria Desalination Project (Australian National Construction Review, 2013), the largest project in Australia, produces 150 billion liters of water per year, and provides an exemplary precedent for a multidisciplinary collaboration between engineering, design, and ecology.

Driven by goals to minimize the ecological footprint and maintain the integrity of Victoria's prime nature tourism, the project's ambition was to seamlessly integrate the desalination plant into the landscape. Thus, the project team included green roof designers, architects, ecologists, and structural, hydrologic, and civil engineers. The roof of the biggest building on site (28,900m^2) is the key aspect of the design. Made up of 438 individual panels installed at 23 different angles, the roof is designed to mimic the undulating sand dunes in the surrounding environment. The green roof vegetation comprises around 100,000 plants of 25 different species of indigenous ground covers, tussocks, and low-lying shrubs (Growing Green Guide). The project is also one of the largest ecological restoration projects undertaken in Victoria. The 263-ha site includes a 38-ha area dedicated to the buildings of the desalination plant, and a 225-ha area dedicated to ecological restoration. This ecological restoration area includes constructed dunes intended to provide visual and acoustic insulation, as well as wetlands, coastal and swampy woodlands, and new habitat for local fauna. Millions of trees, shrubs, grasses, and other endemic coastal scrubland species are being replanted across the site's open spaces.

An emerging area in the fields of architecture and building science involves the engineering of building façade systems to utilize their modular framework and interface with air and sunlight in order to collect or recycle water. The Center for Architecture Science and Ecology (CASE) at Rensselaer Polytechnic Institute (RPI) is currently developing a new façade system called Solar Enclosures for Water Reuse (SEWR). SEWR aims to conserve water through the development of a solar-collecting building envelope that transforms both solar irradiation and greywater into functional resources for reuse. The SEWR building envelope includes arrays of interconnected solar-driven greywater treatment modules. These modules provide both interior shading and passive daylighting through their optical surfacing. On-site water and thermal resource management intersect at the point of tertiary water treatment; ultraviolet light initiates photocatalytic activity to decontaminate and heat greywater for reuse within the building. End uses range from drinking and bathing to toilet flushing, irrigation, cooling, and heating. The SEWR system exemplifies the architectural integration of conventional and isolated plumbing with mechanical and electrical building components (Dyson, et al., 2012). Greywater treatment is made visible through a highly articulated and aestheticized design. The foregrounding of contaminated water reuse is also meant to provoke a new public perception of wastewater as resource, not waste.

Transsolar Klima Engineering is currently developing a vapor condensation façade called the Water out of Air Device (WOA). The façade is part of the Zayed National Museum in Abu Dhabi, designed by Foster + Partners, and demonstrates a collaboration between architecture and engineering. The coastal location of Abu Dhabi presents viable opportunities to augment water availability by drawing water from the air, which has high humidity levels (20–25g/kg).
At nighttime, a desiccant material (small silica gel pellets) absorbs humidity. The absorbent material dries during the day using solar radiation, resulting in condensation of the absorbed water on a cooler surface. The condensed water is then collected in a tank. The water is not potable, but suitable for irrigating the site's garden. With a total surface area of 16,000m², and with a relative humidity above 80% (22g/kg absolute humidity at 30°C air temperature), the façade is estimated to produce 32,000 liters per day. The water collected from the WOA device is completely decoupled from the interior water system of the building, but fully integrated into the façade's design.

Like net zero energy for buildings or sites where the total amount of energy used is equal to the amount of renewable energy created on site, net zero water is a standard intended to close the loop of water consumption. Net zero water means that the water consumed by a building or landscape does not exceed the water captured and produced on site. The above examples offer a middle ground between large infrastructural projects (e.g., desalination plants, dual water networks) and plug-in devices (e.g., low-flush toilets) that can allow designers expand their participation in urban water management, thereby giving agency to building structures and site design in the collection, treatment, and distribution of water.

REFERENCES

Arizona Department of Water Resources. (2014). "Residential Home." www.azwater.gov/AzDWR/StatewidePlanning/Conservation2/Residential/Residential_Home2.htm

Australian National Construction Review. (2013). *Victorian Desalination Project*. www.ancr.com.au/victorian_desalination_project.pdf

Barlow, Maude. *Our Right to Water: A People's Guide to Implementing the United Nations' Recognition of the Right to Water and Sanitation*. The Council of Canadians. http://www.canadians.org/sites/default/files/publications/RTW-intl-web.pdf

Dyson, A, Vollen, J., Mistur, M., Stark, P., Malone, K., and Gindlesparger, M. (2012). U.S. Patent Application No. 0234471: *Solar Enclosure for Water Reuse*. Washington, DC: United States Patent Office.

Growing Green Guide. "Victorian Desalination Project Green Roof." www.growinggreenguide.org/victorian-case-studies/victorian-desalination-project-green-roof/

Lazarova, V., Asano, T., Bahri, A., and Anderson J., eds. (2013). *Milestones in Water Reuse: The Best Success Stories*. IWA Publishing.

Mayer, P. W., DeOreo, W. B., Opitz, E. M., Kiefer, J. C., Davis, W. Y., Dziegielewski, B., and Nelson, J. O. (1999). *Residential End Uses of Water*. Denver, CO: AWWA Research Foundation and American Water Works Association. www.waterrf.org/PublicReportLibrary/RFR90781_1999_241A.pdf

U.S. Environmental Protection Agency. (2013). *Reduce Your Outdoor Water Use*. www.epa.gov/WaterSense/docs/factsheet_outdoor_water_use_508.pdf

U.S. Environmental Protection Agency. (2014). "Conserving Water." http://www.epa.gov/greenhomes/ConserveWater.htm

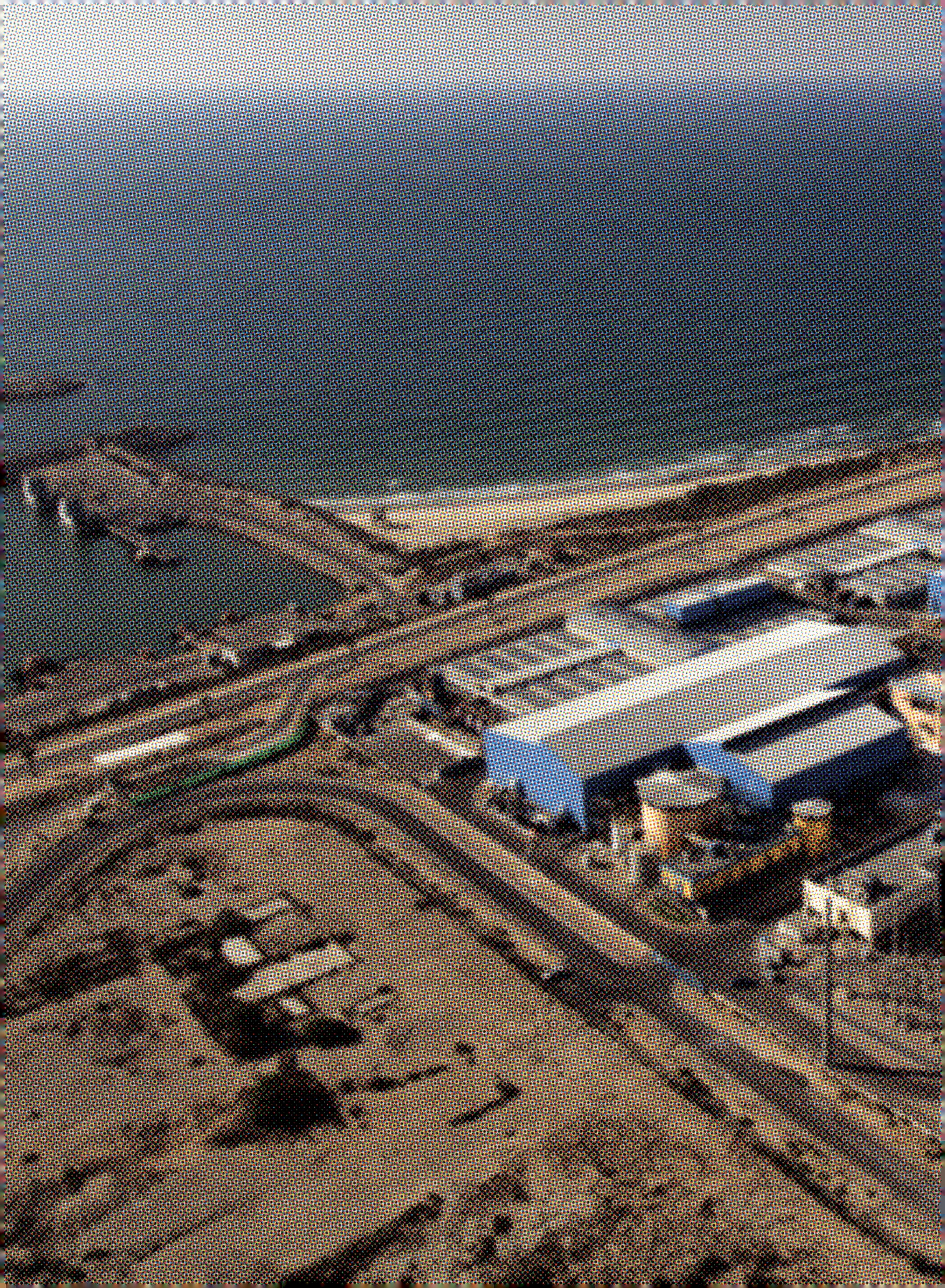

Technical Optimism as an Antidote to Water Scarcity: Desalination Systems in Israel, Australia, and Spain

Alon Tal

For some time the world's environmental movement has tried to mediate the competing claims of two rival schools regarding planetary limitations. On the one hand, there are neo-Malthusians, acutely aware of the constraints that a finite planet places on human development. The earth's resources are limited, and in the face of geometric growth in population and consumption, famine and misery are deemed to be ineluctable. Sustainable growth is an oxymoron (Ehrlich, 1968). At the heart of any environmentally sound strategy for the future are self-restraint and sacrifice.

This view is challenged by a diverse group of advocates on the other extreme who are variously referred to as Prometheans or "cornucopians" (Wapner, 2010). These technological optimists are confident that human ingenuity will be able to overcome any pollution problems (McDonough and Braungart, 2002) or projected shortages and produce the necessary supply of resources or substitutes to expand global prosperity (Myers and Simon, 1994).

Water scarcity constitutes a defining issue in this ongoing debate. On the one hand, the neo-Malthusian pessimists foresee increased shortages leading to massive deprivation, starvation, and the proliferation of water conflicts due to competition over hydrological assets (Ward, 2002). Promethean hydrological optimists, on the other hand, are confident about future water supply (Homer-Dixon, 1999; Selby, 2003). Water is a more renewable resource than ever before and many societies today enjoy the ability to produce as much of it as they need or want. Opposing views on the merits of seawater desalination offer a characteristic manifestation of this ideological divide.

Whether "desal" constitutes a panacea for perennial scarcity, or merely a greenhouse-gas-intensive Band-Aid for wealthy nations, is a debate that hitherto has largely been conducted on a theoretical plane. Yet recent experience in several countries offers an empirical basis for assessing the potential of desalination, which, along with wastewater reuse, might obviate the projected water shortages of the future.

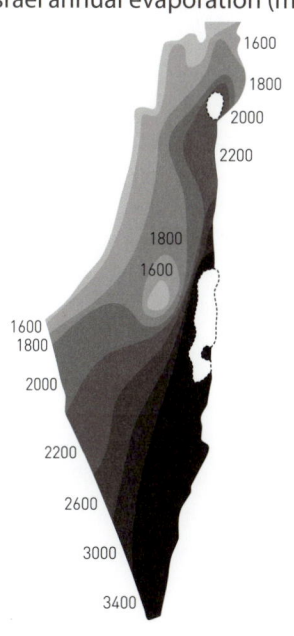

FIGURE 6: Ashkelon Desalination Plant, Israel (opposite)

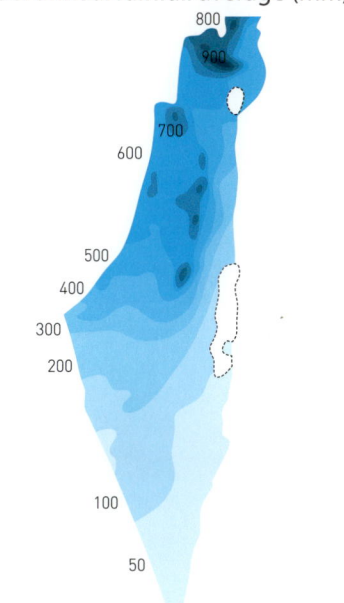

Figure 1: Israel, Annual Precipitation and Evaporation

In particular, Israel, Australia, and Spain have taken different policy approaches to this aspect of water management. While the desalination of seawater frequently offers considerable environmental benefits for nations with access to seawater or with large reservoirs of brackish ground water, the major obstacle to virtually unlimited water supply is energy. Massive reverse osmosis desalination is an experiment that is still fairly young. But for many, the score is already in on a few of the questions facing the planet's newest water-supply technology. And it appears that the cornucopians are going to win this round.

Over the past decade, desalination has at long last emerged as an ostensibly cost-effective solution for dryland nations, such as Israel (Figure 1), who suffer from a shortage of natural hydro resources. Prior to this, several island countries, like Bermuda, Malta, and the Virgin Islands, utilized desalination to produce relatively costly drinking water. In the Middle East, a diverse array of countries—from Gulf States such as Kuwait, Saudi Arabia, and Oman, to, more recently, Mediterranean countries like Israel, Spain, and Egypt—built massive desalination plants.

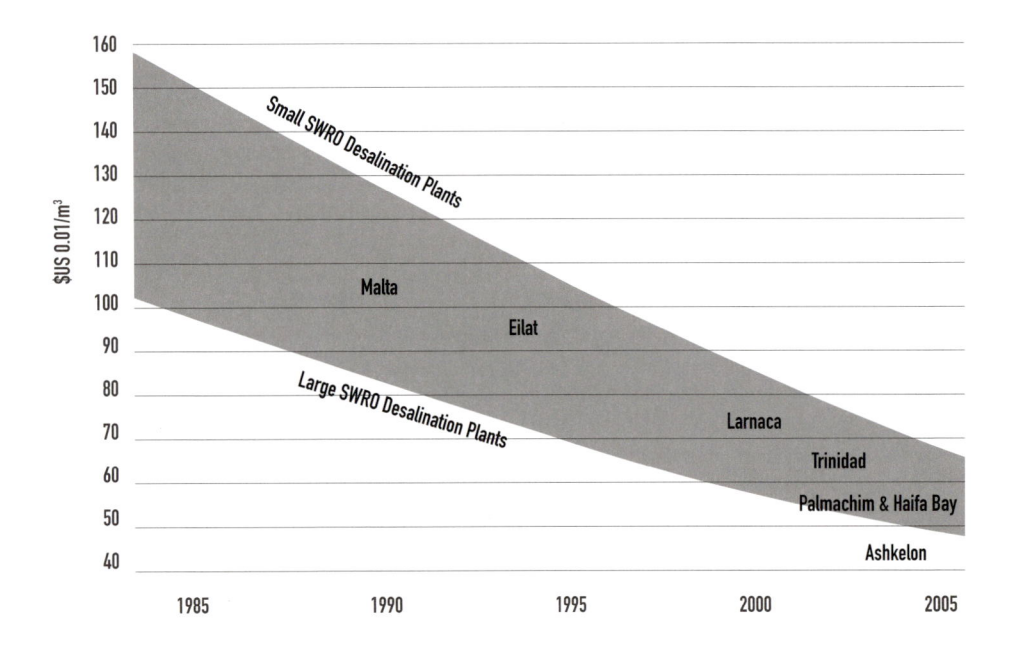

Figure 2a and 2b: Price of desalinated water 1985–2005

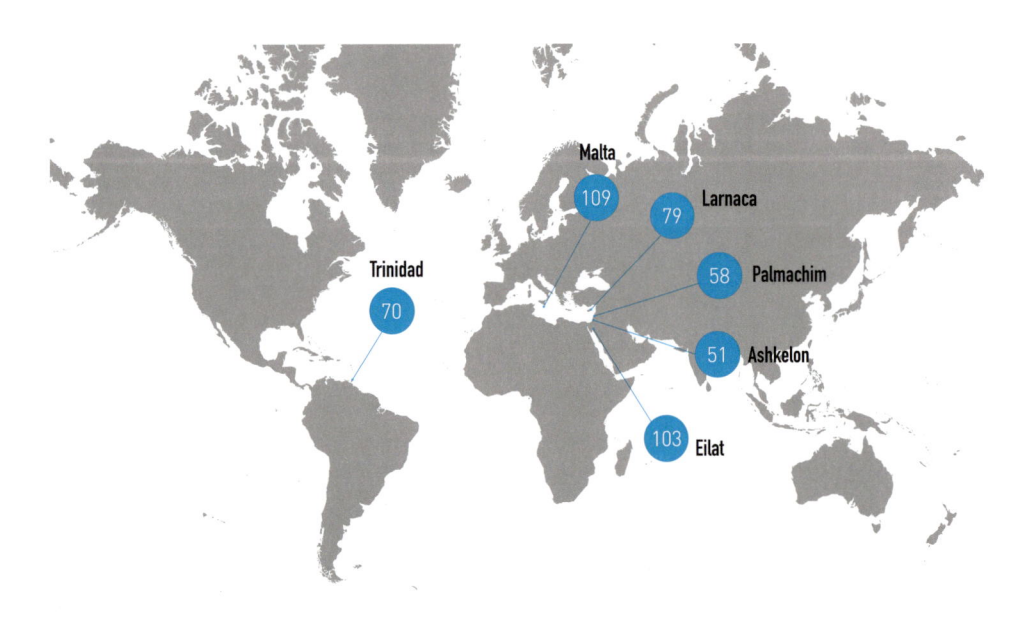

There is, of course, nothing new about removing salt from seawater to make it potable. Some 3,400 years ago, sailors were utilizing evaporation and condensation to produce fresh water in response to marine conditions. By 1907, the first industrial desalination facilities were built, with facilities later established by the military during World War II to provide drinking water to Allied soldiers. The economics of diffusion, however, constituted a serious barrier to its widespread use among civilians.

The past 20 years have seen reverse osmosis gradually emerge as the most cost-effective approach available for desalinating seawater, leaving behind competing technologies such as multiple-stage flash distillation or multiple-effect distillation. The process is relatively simple, involving a high-pressure diffusion of fluids which reverses the natural osmosis process. A thin, semi-permeable membrane separates the seawater into two streams: a pure H_2O stream and a concentrate stream. In other words, rather than moving salts from higher to lower concentration areas, the process uses tremendous pressure to move them in the opposite direction (Buros, 2000).

FIGURE 3: Seawater desalination capacity in the Mediterranean Sea (including all plants that are presumed online or in construction); see also caption of Figure 1

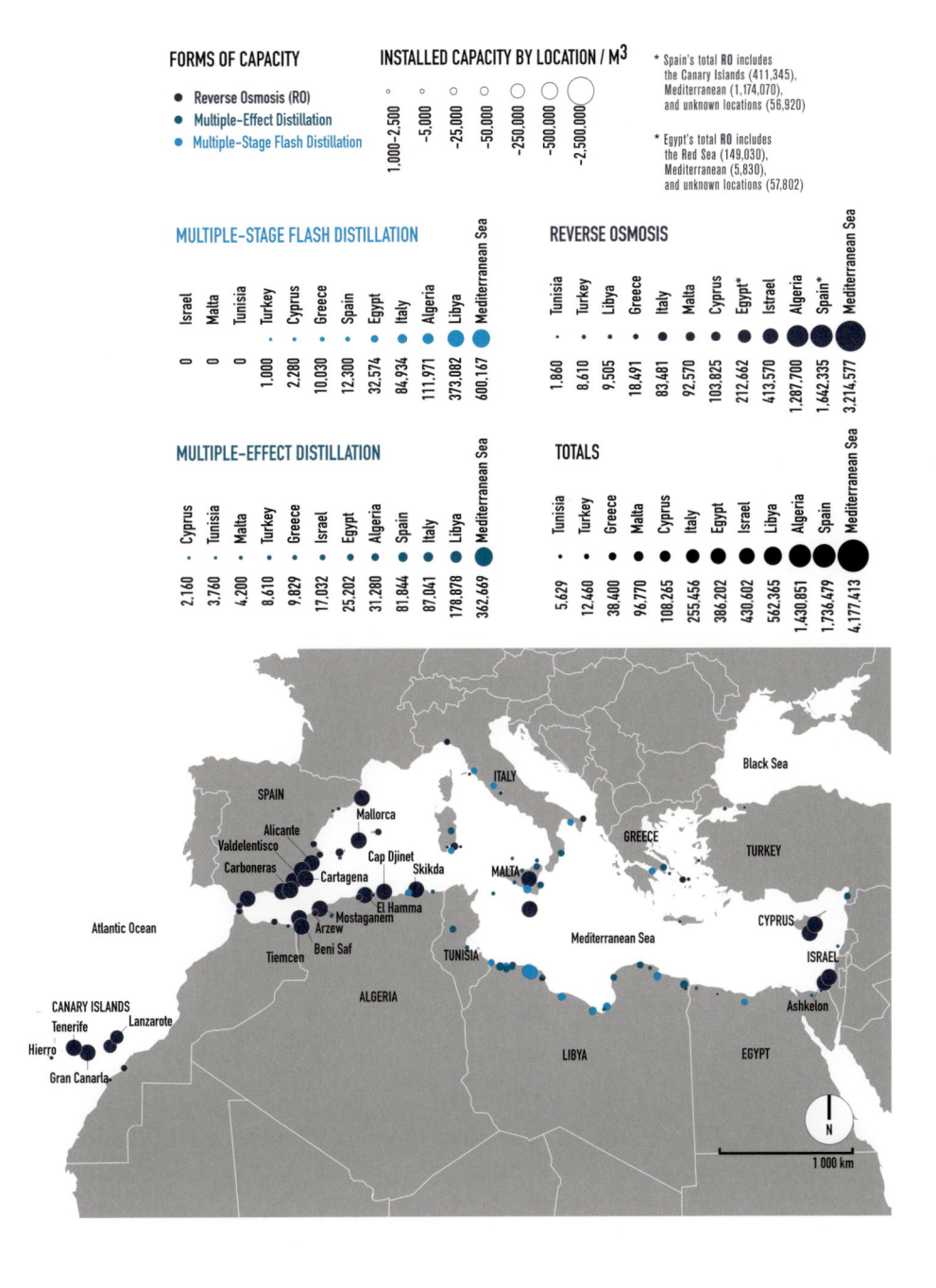

FORMS OF CAPACITY
- Reverse Osmosis (RO)
- Multiple-Effect Distillation
- Multiple-Stage Flash Distillation

INSTALLED CAPACITY BY LOCATION / M³
1.000–2.500 / 5.000 / 25.000 / 50.000 / 250.000 / 500.000 / 2.500.000

* Spain's total RO includes the Canary Islands (411,345), Mediterranean (1,174,070), and unknown locations (56,920)

* Egypt's total RO includes the Red Sea (149,030), Mediterranean (5,830), and unknown locations (57,802)

MULTIPLE-STAGE FLASH DISTILLATION

Israel	Malta	Tunisia	Turkey	Cyprus	Greece	Spain	Egypt	Italy	Algeria	Libya	Mediterranean Sea
0	0	0	1.000	2.280	10.030	12.300	32.574	84.934	111.971	373.082	600.167

REVERSE OSMOSIS

Tunisia	Turkey	Libya	Greece	Italy	Malta	Cyprus	Egypt*	Israel	Algeria	Spain*	Mediterranean Sea
1.860	8.610	9.505	18.491	83.481	92.570	103.825	212.662	413.570	1.287.700	1.642.335	3.214.577

MULTIPLE-EFFECT DISTILLATION

Cyprus	Tunisia	Malta	Turkey	Greece	Israel	Egypt	Algeria	Spain	Italy	Libya	Mediterranean Sea
2.160	3.760	4.200	8.610	9.829	17.032	25.202	31.280	81.844	87.041	178.878	362.669

TOTALS

Tunisia	Turkey	Greece	Malta	Cyprus	Italy	Egypt	Israel	Libya	Algeria	Spain	Mediterranean Sea
5.629	12.460	38.400	96.770	108.265	255.456	386.202	430.602	562.365	1.430.851	1.736.479	4.177.413

49

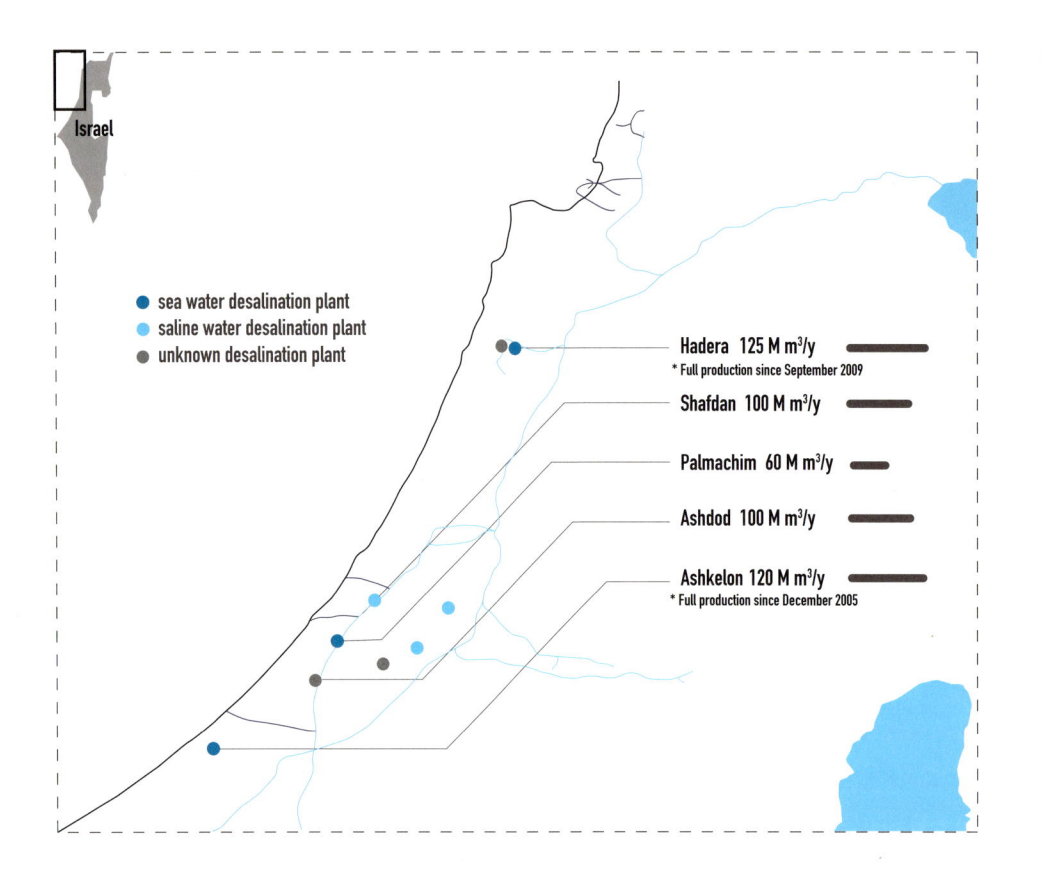

FIGURE 4a: Israel's desalination infrastructure

- sea water desalination plant
- saline water desalination plant
- unknown desalination plant

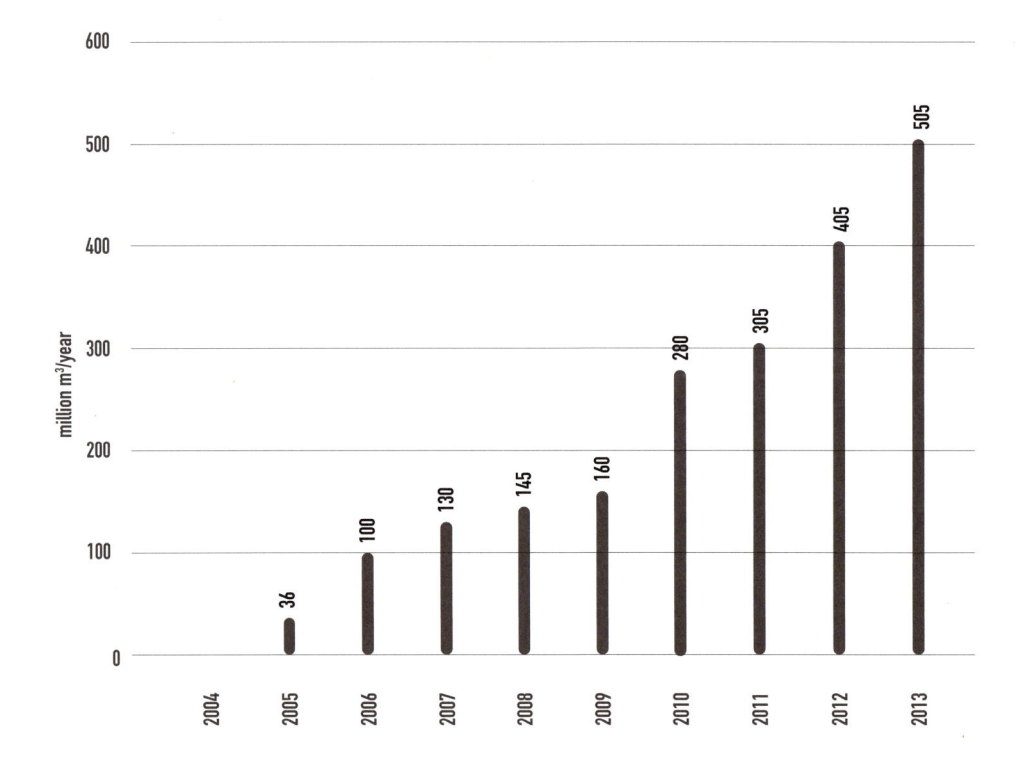

Hadera 125 M m³/y
* Full production since September 2009

Shafdan 100 M m³/y

Palmachim 60 M m³/y

Ashdod 100 M m³/y

Ashkelon 120 M m³/y
* Full production since December 2005

FIGURE 4b: The projected development of desalination plants in Israel 2004–2013

Year	million m³/year
2004	—
2005	36
2006	100
2007	130
2008	145
2009	160
2010	280
2011	305
2012	405
2013	505

The precipitous drop in the price of reverse osmosis production over the past few decades, as seen in Figure 2a and 2b, can be attributed to improvements in membrane and energy efficiency as well as to the economies of scale associated with large facilities. For instance, Israeli desal plants are probably the most efficient in the world, producing one cubic meter of water with 3.5 kWh of electricity. For many countries, this has led to a fundamental change in the economic calculus of drinking water policy.

While desalinated seawater still accounts for less than 2% of total planetary water consumption, the phenomenal growth rate of desalination, at 15% per year (European Commission, 2006), suggests that it may eventually make the world's perennial water shortages a thing of the past. The Mediterranean Sea (Figure 3) offers a dramatic example of the present expansion of desalination for drinking water and, in some cases, even for agricultural water supply (Yermiyahu, 2008).

Desalination is not without environmental ramifications—from anti-scalant discharges into the marine environment to the prodigious energy required to push the water through the desalination membranes (Lattemann and Höpner, 2008). But from the cornucopian, Promethean perspective, these are surmountable obstacles—production costs that are more than justified by the hydrological benefits.

As countries make this transition in their water supply portfolios, it is wise to consider their desal experiences and make an early assessment about the environmental implications of the process and the internal discourse that accompanies the transition into a brave new desalinated world. Accordingly, we now turn to lessons learned in Israel, Australia, and Spain.

Israel

Israel first turned to desalination to solve potable water delivery problems at the start of the 1950s, in the nascent port city of Eilat, located on the country's secluded southern tip on the Gulf of Aqaba. A variety of technologies were attempted as part of a trial-and-error process (Haupert, 1964; Lavie and Glueckstern, 1974; Manor and Weinberg, 1975). This eventually led to the establishment of the country's first reverse osmosis (RO) facility in 1973, on a site adjacent to a salty marsh, or sabha, after which the plant is named. About half of the production relies on brackish water, which could be produced at roughly half of the cost ($0.90/m^3) of desalinating Red Sea water (Tal, Ben-Gal, Lawhon, and Rassass, 2005). Since that time, desalination had remained a last resort, driven by the exigency of the lack of any alternative water sources for isolated desert communities.

Two factors combined to change these dynamics and make desalination a centerpiece in Israel's new water management strategy:

1. Three consecutive drought years, beginning in 1998, highlighted the vulnerability of Israel's agricultural sector to the ineluctable fluctuations in annual precipitation; and

2. Desalinated seawater became available at the bargain price of $0.52/m^3 (or $0.50/kl).

After years of stalling by treasury officials who sought to reduce agricultural water allocations, the Israeli cabinet approved a proposal put forward by the country's Water Commission and, on April 4, 2002, ruled to construct four sea desalination plants that were to produce at least 250 million m^3 of desalinized water (Dreizin, 2004). In fact, by 2011, this amount had actually reached 300 million m^3 in three plants, with additional facilities under construction that would double this capacity (Figure 4a, Figure 4b).

Not only were the scope of the plant and the membrane technology novel for Israel; so was the financing scheme. The new Israeli desalination ventures were privately financed Build-Operate-Transfer (BOT) ventures. For instance, the Israeli-French consortium VID Desalination Company opened the first of these Mediterranean plants in the southern city of Ashkelon in 2005, investing $250 million in a facility in return for the contractual rights to run it for 25 years (Kronenberg, 2004).

The presence of a reliable, inexpensive, high-quality water supply largely put an end to any serious discussions about previous proposals for Israeli acquisition of Turkish water via tankers, Medusa bags, or "Peace Pipes" (Gleick, 2002). Not only did desalination strengthen national hydrological independence, it was half the price of the alternative schemes.

Figure 5: Hadera Desalination Plant, Israel

The three major facilities established thus far, Ashkelon, Palmachim, and Hadera (Figure 5), are all based on slight variations of a common engineering approach. Open, submerged intake systems consisting of three plastic pipelines stretch as much as a kilometer into the sea, tapping the seawater at a depth of 7m. The parallel intakes reduce turbulence to a minimum, while the high-density plastic allows for relatively easy maintenance and inhibits bio-growth (Lokiec and Kronenberg, 2003). The seawater goes through a two-stage filtration process, and a pre-treatment unit adds chemicals to prevent water from fouling membrane stacks. Because Israel recycles over 75% of its sewage, boron in the water is a major concern, as it damages plant growth in high concentrations. Seawater typically has high natural boron concentrations. The desalination process was designed to include a boron removal phase, which brings concentrations down to negligible levels of 0.4mg/L.

One of the surprises in the Israeli desalination story is its impact on agriculture. The original Ashkelon plant (Figure 6) went online before the network of piping that would allow delivery into the national grid was available. Thus, for the initial period of production, after water was provided to the nearby southern cities and communities, a surfeit of hundreds of millions of liters remained. The surplus was delivered to the extensive agricultural operations in Israel's Negev southlands at no extra charge. This was seen as a magnanimous gesture. It was expected that the local fruit and vegetable farmers would regard this almost-pure H_2O—with a fifth of the salt content of the waters from Israel's national water carrier, which they had been utilizing for decades—as veritable "champagne." The lower Na^+/Cl^- levels, it was believed, should not only translate into better yields but also save water when leaching the reduced, residual salts from the soil (Shalhevet, 1993).

In fact, the farmers were not happy at all with the results. The previous water supply had contained sufficient nutrients (i.e., magnesium, sulfate, and calcium) that crops thrived without supplementary fertilizers for these elements. The desalinized water left crops such as tomatoes, basil, and flowers with nutrient deficiencies, requiring the hasty addition of chemical fertilizers and other minerals (Yermiyahu, et al., 2006).

After seven years of operation, the Ashkelon facility's initial environmental report card appears to correspond with what was projected. Because desal facilities have been sited contiguous to existing coastal infrastructures (e.g., electricity plants), almost none of Israel's limited beaches have been sacrificed thus far. There were concerns about the brine that the desalination process produces, which is discharged into the sea at a distance of one kilometer. Its temperature is higher than the seawater and it contains high concentrations of salt along with other chemicals and metals. Monitoring the flow of the fairly inert polyphosphate anti-scalants in the sea suggests that not only has marine water quality not suffered, but the high iron content in the discharged residuals has actually created a miniature fishery environment.

But it is energy that remains the major ecological concern. While the Ashkelon plant is powered by a self-generating energy supply system, the other facilities rely on electricity from the Israeli power grid—a coal-dominated system. According to one estimate, the facility's 60 MW/hour electricity demands can generate greenhouse gases at a level commensurate with a city of 45,000 people (Tenne, 2011). Ben-Gurion University's Yaakov Garb postulates about the implications for energy independence:

> Ironically, in creating a stable source of pure water, not subject to the climatic variations of our region, Israel has buffered itself to one source of vulnerability, but exposed itself to several others. With desalination, Israel is increasingly dependent on water quality in the Mediterranean, the terms of decade-long contracts, and, above all, to energy price variability. To the extent that a larger portion of the cost of desalinated water is a variable cost dependent on rising energy costs, the relative advantage of desalination with respect to other forms of water source augmentation with lower variable costs, for the short run, can be expected to decline. Desalination allows Israel to avoid hydrological constraints now, through a technological solution for meeting the inelastic demands for potable water; but it may introduce future energy constraints, as the world enters an era where limitations in energy supply and carbon emissions reach the forefront of the policy agenda (Garb, 2010, p. 245).

From a political perspective, Israel's transition towards desalination was relatively painless. There have been vague concerns expressed about the implications of privatizing water resources, but no meaningful protestations from Israel's typically aggressive environmental NGO sector about the shift to higher-energy water supplies or the associated financing modalities. As in the energy sector, occasional voices have wondered whether concentrating such high percentages of water supply in a single facility is wise, given the pervasive political instability. For instance, the Ashkelon plant is well within the range of the mortars and missiles that are intermittently directed from Gaza towards Israel. One could argue that diversification through a sprawling network of dozens of smaller desal plants could be a reasonable risk strategy. But the economic implications would be dramatic. These issues, however, have not been discussed in any serious public forum, either professional or journalistic. On the whole, opposition to Israel's bold desalination strategy has been marginal. There are several explanations for this conciliatory posture:

- The historic predilection of Israeli environmentalists towards technological optimism. (Tal, 2008).
- The recognition that desalination will be necessary in order to meet Palestinian water claims, and to diffuse much of the "hydro-hysteria" that has characterized peace negotiations in the region.
- The recognition that all river restoration strategies require a dramatic increase in the volume of Israel's depleted streams, whose flow is typically limited to municipal effluents and intermittent storm runoff. Desalination offers the possibility of restoring aquatic ecosystems and transforming the polluted trickles into recreational refuges.
- The fact that regulation by Israel's Water Authority has been highly effective, resulting in high-quality water at low prices—with none of the loss of services often seen internationally in water privatization.
- Israel is still categorized as a non–Annex I country under the UN Framework Convention for Climate Change, so while there is considerable lip service to global responsibilities, there is no immediate pressure to reduce greenhouse emissions.

The upshot of the above is a powerful consensus that desalination has already revolutionized Israel's water management strategy, producing myriad attendant geopolitical, economic, and environmental benefits. Until energy issues are addressed, by enhancing efficiency or tapping renewable sources, it is impossible to accord desalination the status of a "magic bullet." But it is surely a mighty step in the direction of hydrological sustainability.

Australia

As the driest of the world's continents, Australia has always faced water supply challenges. The worst drought in the country's recorded history, between 2003 and 2007, catapulted desalination onto the agendas of every major Australian population center. Until then, desalination was restricted to small remote urban communities like the Kangaroo and Rottnest Islands (URS Australia, 2002). The sense that climate change had exacerbated an already challenging hydrological predicament expedited one of the most dramatic and swiftest water infrastructure transitions in recorded history. A five-year process ending in 2012 will find 30% of the five major Australian cities' drinking water coming from desalination plants. The total cost of the enterprise is expected to reach $13 billion (Onishi, 2010).

Australia is the first country to power desalination with renewable energy. This makes the costs of Australian desalination the highest in the world (Figure 7). One estimate from the Water Services Association projects that the price of desalinated water will reach $2/m^3 when a full cost accounting is made. Defenders of the project claim that it is simply "the cost of adapting to climate change" (Onishi, 2010). Others, however, are critical of the transition, calling it economically wasteful and environmentally destructive.

The Australian initiative enjoys far less public support than does Israel's. Environmental and consumer advocates argue that a more prudent strategy would involve stringent water conservation programs. Drip irrigation, for instance, is surprisingly rare in many parts of rural Australia, notwithstanding its dramatic water-saving properties. The desalination debate also raised questions about the sustainability of the so-called "Big Australia" initiative, which would increase the nation's population from 22–36 million people. The dynamics of the Australian experience are perhaps best reflected in the story of Sydney's new desalination plant in Kurnel.

Precipitation in the catchment surrounding Australia's largest city is highly erratic, with unpredictable cycles of drought years that suddenly give way to floods. Creating massive water storage, as was done for other cities like Brisbane and Melbourne, was deemed the best response to this inherent uncertainty. Some 80% of the city's water needs are met by the reservoir system created by the Warragamba Dam in the Blue Mountains. During the 1990s, the city also sought to address the precipitation uncertainty issue and reduce its vulnerability by means of an emergency drought response program that was designed to ensure demand reduction. A comprehensive policy to reduce water demand was enacted that included mandatory water restrictions, investment in infrastructure to repair the city's leaking pipes, and water recycling and education campaigns. The approach was remarkably successful: By 2004, per capita water use in Sydney had fallen from 506L per person to 342, with aggregate water consumption returning to 1974 levels—despite the additional one million people receiving water (Lawhon Isler, 2010).

But the intensity of the most recent drought began to make local politicians nervous. In 2004, a Metropolitan Water Plan (MWP) replaced the Drought Response Management Plan. It allocated four million dollars to plan a desalination facility in order to "ensure that, if the drought continues beyond another two years, a desalination plant for Sydney could be constructed relatively quickly and efficiently" (New South Wales [NSW], 2004). A year later, with the drought showing no signs of relenting, state decision makers felt pressured to respond preemptively, and boldly, to the anticipated shortages. In the summer of 2005, the state declared its intention to build a two-billion-dollar desalination plant in Botany Bay, on Sydney's southern coast, in the event that the drought did not break within two years.

The election of a new state government in New South Wales, however, reflected a change in the political equation. Incoming Premier Morris Iemma announced his readiness to ensure a steady water supply for the Sydney region. The local public was less enthusiastic. A public opinion survey at the time suggested that some 60% of the local citizenry opposed the construction of a desalination plant, given the fact that the reservoir was still 41% full—enough water for two years (Lawhon Isler, 2010).

In what was to have been a textbook example of adaptive management, the government established a "trigger point": should water reserves drop to the point where the reservoir was only 30% full, the building of the desalination plant would commence immediately, with an anticipated construction time of 26 months (NSW, 2004). But with an election imminent, the

FIGURE 7: Cost of new Australian desalination infrastructure

- $1,200,000,000 GOLD COAST
- $2,400,000,000 SYDNEY
- $3,500,000,000 MELBOURNE
- $1,830,000,000 ADELAIDE
- $955,000,000 PERTH

allure of the political benefits of showing decisive leadership apparently proved too much for the premier to resist. Tenders were prepared for construction in February, 2007, even as the reservoir was still filled to 33.9% capacity. With an irony that could easily have been penned by a Hollywood scriptwriter, within a month the rains returned with a vengeance, filling the reservoir to 57% over four months. But construction of the desalination plant was already in motion and was built at the Kurnel site all the same (Lawhon Isler, 2010).

The upshot of the Sydney story is that local citizens faced an increase in their water rates averaging $110/year for five years. Again, greenhouse gas mitigation was a considerable part of the expense. Australia was among the last OECD countries to join the UN's Kyoto Protocol on greenhouse gas emissions, but once on board, it took its responsibilities seriously. Accordingly, it was decided to offset the anticipated increase in electricity demand by building wind farms.

Energy requirements and associated greenhouse gas emissions are the environmental concerns most often expressed about desalination. The Australian case is therefore particularly interesting for environmentalists to assess. On the one hand, the country has shown that desalination need not exacerbate carbon emissions. On the other, critics in Australia argue that the renewable energy capacity created to offset the desal plant could just as easily have been used to replace coal-generated electricity plants. Local energy experts Knights, MacGill, and Passey offer more muted criticism:

Because of electricity's unique physical characteristics, electricity supply must exactly match electricity demand at all times and at all points within a network. Furthermore, it is not possible to direct electricity flows from a particular generator to a particular load—the network effectively combines all electricity from all generators. The concept of reducing or eliminating the emissions from a grid-connected desalination plant is therefore necessarily somewhat abstract. For example, a desalination plant might be claimed to be greenhouse neutral if additional renewable generation is supplied to the network equivalent to the electricity consumption of the desalination plant over time. This renewable generation would have to be additional to what would have happened otherwise due, for example, to other policy drivers; again a somewhat abstract concept (Knights, MacGill, and Passey, 2009, p. 3).

In her recent review of the Sydney experience, Phoenix Lawhon Isler is more forceful in her argument that the overall Australian environmental balance sheet is negative:

"Desalination distracts from the need to build adaptive capacity and resilience into urban water systems through an integrated, whole-of-water-cycle approach. It also reflects a misguided pursuit of elimination of climate risk as a goal attainable through technical means rather than an ongoing process of adaptation of both technical and social systems to build resilience. Desalination reinforces the institutional tendency to rely on supply-side solutions, which in turn encourages wasteful consumption habits, and reduces incentives to adapt water-use behaviors ...Desalination plants may be doing more harm than good for Australian cities by locking in unsustainable patterns of water management and narrow climate adaptation trajectories" (Lawhon Isler, 2010, p. 36).

The plant in Kurnel is now up and running, with the potential to provide Sydney with 15% of its total water needs. For a brief period, it held the title of Australia's largest desalination facility. But it was surpassed in 2012, when the Wonthaggi desal plant went online to provide drinking water for Melbourne.

Spain

For decades, regulation of Spain's many rivers through a system of dams constituted the centerpiece of the country's national water management strategy. Spain is the fifth most dam-intensive country in the world; some 1,300 dams compound 53,500 million m^3 of water in reservoirs for utilization by agriculture (Martinez-Cortina, 2010). This constitutes 38% of the aggregate runoff potential. Without the dams, only 9% of runoff would be captured. The country is also blessed with almost 200,000km^2 of detritic, karstic, and volcanic aquifers. Most of the karstic aquifers are of high quality, although there are signs of steady salinization and nitrification of wells. However, Spanish water managers have believed for some time that these resources are insufficient. Accordingly, Spain is the most veteran and largest user of desalination in the Western world today, producing 7% of worldwide capacity. Spanish desalination pilot efforts started some 40 years ago in the water-scarce Canary Islands. In 2000, a major facility was installed there, processing 10,000m^3 per day (Nicoll, 2001).

During the 2000s, hydrological conditions on the mainland worsened, and by 2008 chronic drought conditions left water storage at a mere 46% of normal capacity. Precipitation was 40% below annual averages. Emergency measures were imposed, including fines of $3,850 for filling large swimming pools and $38 for watering gardens (Keely, 2008). In retrospect, the water crisis should not have come as a surprise. Spain has the highest per capita national water consumption rate in Europe. Combined with a Mediterranean climate in the large population centers and intensive irrigation in semi-arid zones, this made shortages inevitable (Global Water Intelligence, 2004). But whether mismanagement or unpredictable global warming was to blame, the crisis would not wait, and desalination became a national management priority overnight (Keely, 2008).

The present government assessed its options and concluded that previous plans to transport copious quantities of water in extensive carriers to desiccated Catalonia (where reservoirs had dropped to 20% capacity levels) were ill-advised. Rather, desalination was deemed a more cost-effective and more reliable long-term strategy. The Socialist government proposed an ambitious and controversial plan to build a new generation of desalination plants (Figure 8). Already, the desalination industry was humming in Spain. Some 950 desalination plants were making over 2 million m^3 of water a day, enough to supply 10 million people. But the new wave will be even greater. A new plant near Barcelona is expected to open in 2013, and when the $320-million Torrevieja desalination project near Madrid finally opens, it will be the second-largest desal facility in the world (Nicol, 2009).

Many were unhappy with the decision to abandon water transport as a national strategy in favor of desalination. While not quite a "water war," the issue became a source of considerable tension between the Catalonian and central Spanish governments. Among the environmental critics was the World Wildlife Fund, which went on record castigating present policy as "frenetic," expensive, and energy-intensive. At the heart of WWF's concern was the damage expected to occur to the Spanish coastline as a result of the planned facilities. The associated greenhouse gas emissions were also part of the local critique. The Spanish Association for the Technological Treatment of Water reported that a full million tons of carbon dioxide would be emitted annually by each major desal plant (Keely, 2008).

FIGURE 8: Desalination production in Spain

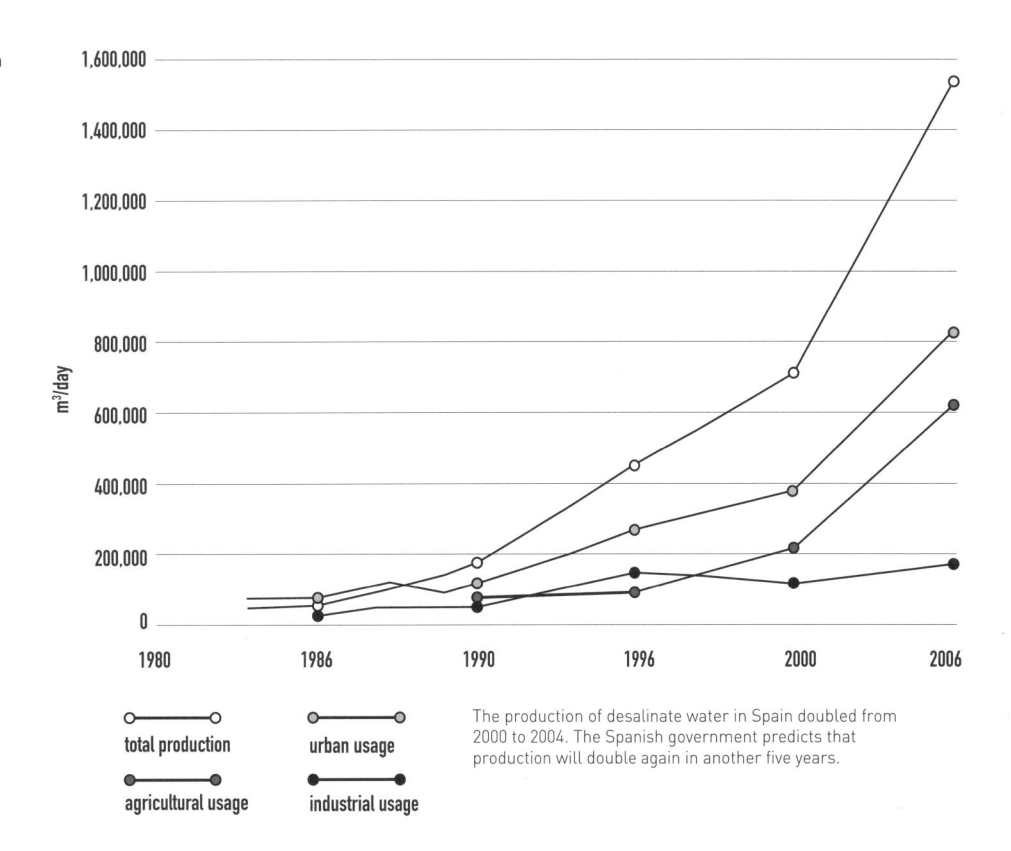

- total production
- urban usage
- agricultural usage
- industrial usage

The production of desalinate water in Spain doubled from 2000 to 2004. The Spanish government predicts that production will double again in another five years.

As in Israel, the environmental impact of desalination in Spain is probably mixed, and there are those who claim that overall, its benefits actually trump its downsides. Alternative sources of water involve diversion of rivers, which would lead to decimation of aquatic habitats. The potential introduction of invasive species, such as zebra mussels, presents another ecological risk from long-distance river-water delivery. At the political level, the debate became partisan when Mariano Rajoy, then-leader of the opposition, attacked desalination, stating that he would prefer to transport water rather than support CO_2-emitting desal plants that would consequently contribute to climate change.

Regardless of which side is correct, there is considerable room for additional water conservation, which should be pursued before supply-side solutions are funded. The price of water in Spain is among the lowest in Europe. Cities like Barcelona suffer from leaky infrastructure, leading to losses of millions of cubic meters a year. Also, it is not clear that groundwater resources have been fully utilized. At present, Spain utilizes some 34.7% of available surface water and groundwater resources.

Although there are signs of steady improvement in the efficiency of Spain's water utilization, annual demand for water increases at a rate of 1.6%, largely due to economic development and improved standards of living (Maestu and Gomez, 2010). And perverse incentives certainly do not promote efficiency. Some two-thirds of water is consumed by Spanish agricultural operations, which enjoy extremely favorable pricing—in some cases as low as 1/200th of actual operation costs (Manero, 2008). Such dynamics have led NGOs such as the Worldwide Fund for Nature, which are usually suspicious of water privatization and markets, to call for "water banks" where water could be bought and sold.

Conclusions

The desalination experiences of these three countries share certain elements: After decades of very modest application, seawater desalination recently came of age, due to a combination of extended droughts and anticipated shortages and the reduced costs of producing fresh water.

During the past few years, production has jumped by an order of magnitude, creating a surfeit of what was frequently considered the scarcest of resources. This development has not been universally popular, and in Spain and Australia has emerged as a politically divisive issue due to economic and environmental concerns. In the annals of water infrastructure controversies, it is conceivable that desalination facilities will soon become the dams of the 21st century.

Although desalination was originally envisioned as a way to meet demands for urban drinking water, there have been signs for some time that agriculture will become an increasingly substantial consumer. According to a UN Food and Agriculture Organization study, some 22% of the water produced by Spanish desalination plants is delivered to farmers (Beltran, 2006). A third of farmers surveyed in Israel five years ago anticipated that new crops would allow them to profit from additional desal allocation. Since that time, both the quantity of desalinated water and public awareness about its availability have grown geometrically, so enthusiasm for the process in the agricultural sector today is probably be even greater (Rassas, 2007). Some 53% of Australians envisioned desalinated water as supplying future irrigation of vegetables—almost twice the percentage that anticipated its use as household drinking and bathing water (Dolnicar and Schafer, 2006).

It is important to note, however, that for the foreseeable future, agricultural utilization of desalinated water, even at newly reduced rates, will only be economically feasible for the highest-value cash crops (e.g., flowers, specialty fruits, etc.). These are typically grown in developed countries. Developing countries with access to coastal or brackish waters, in which agriculture is largely subsistence level, will probably find that desal facilities are only cost effective for providing drinking water. The World Health Organization (WHO) recommends 100L per person per day as a minimal level of access for human well-being. Accordingly, a back-of-the-envelope calculation would suggest that at $0.50/m^3 of water, the full individual supply of absolutely clean water can be provided for $0.50 per day—a rate that many poor communities may be able to afford. Surely, people who are already buying bottled water or receiving water from tankers would enjoy exceptional savings from a desalinated water supply. In short, international development agencies should include desal plants in their menu of aid alternatives.

Beyond the human health and agricultural dividends, typically there are meaningful environmental advantages that desalination brings to dryland communities—as well as to their non-human counterparts in parched aquatic ecosystems. Rivers can be restored; ecosystems sustained; salinity in aquifers reduced. But the environmental scorecard is surely not perfect. Desalinated water does not provide a "free lunch." At present, it is not clear that the ecological downsides of desalination are always fully considered, especially if reduction of greenhouse gas emissions remains an environmental priority. Based on the Australian experience, the case for the economic feasibility of desalination is not as compelling if these full environmental costs of production are internalized. Public support will tend to have an inverse relationship to the price of water.

For many years, green orthodoxy has preached the Malthusian gospel of sacrifice, self-discipline, and limitations. It is no surprise, therefore, that environmentalists are uncomfortable with a technology which calls many of their basic assumptions into question. Environmental advocates are paid to worry and to be suspicious of good news. But for countries like Israel, where water allocation constitutes a volatile diplomatic issue, advancement in desal technology is very good news. Indeed, one can argue that the national commitment to desalination is actually an expensive gamble on a peaceful future. With each of Israel's recent wars, the range of its neighbors' missiles has expanded, and it is likely that these facilities will be targeted in future conflicts. In all three countries, desalination's energy intensity offers the most convenient basis on which to object to the ebullient hydrological optimism of the cornucopians. But membrane technology is constantly improving, and desalination processes will undoubtedly grow increasingly efficient over time, with an attendant reduction in carbon footprints.

The magnitude of seawater desalination's proliferation has not yet been recognized and acknowledged by international environmental agencies. It may be that beyond the greenhouse gas issue, the environmental impacts of a desal plant are largely local, and international intervention is superfluous. But this is not yet certain. Surely the cumulative impact of thousands of desalination facilities and their anti-scalant discharges on the marine environment warrant some systematic thought. This should be studied by the United Nations Environmental Programme (UNEP) and be the topic of research that would monitor and model its effects. One could argue that until such "macro" thinking is better developed, demands for an international regulatory response are premature. But the precautionary principle posits otherwise.

In the interim, the greenhouse gas issue remains germane and should be addressed during the planning phase, as it has been in Australia. Among the clearer implications of present trends is that the water and energy sectors in countries that opt for desalination will be increasingly linked. To the extent that electricity is clean and renewable, the ambivalence of environmentalists towards this expanding technology can be ameliorated. Current water scarcity may one day be remembered as an ephemeral stage in the history of the world's water management. In the interim, water managers should continue to advance water conservation strategies. Even if farmers do not receive desalinated water directly, high levels of freshwater consumption by the agricultural sector contributes to a substantial desal investment for the municipal sector, with the associated increased carbon footprint and loss of coastal lands. Surely, selecting non-water-intensive crops, mandating drip irrigation, and expediting expanded effluent recycling should complement the present desalination bonanza.

As countries consider what an optimal desalination policy might be, there are several questions that could be the basis for drafting water management decision rules:

- What are the levels of present and projected water shortages in the country?
- What alternative measures exist for reducing water demand?
- Is local agriculture operating at maximal efficiency?
- What is the "shadow price" of desalinated water? Are there alternative water sources (e.g., high-quality tertiary treated waste water) that can be produced for a cheaper price?
- As seawater desalination is far more expensive than brackish water, might there be saline groundwater resources that make more sense to tap as a first step?
- What measures can reduce the carbon impact and other environmental results of the process? Can they be integrated into the desalination facility's operating license?
- Is the necessary public funding available for a meaningful desalination program? If privatized investment is available as an option, would it ensure that water is supplied to all sectors of the local population?

Desalinated water is here to stay, and will comprise an increasingly large percentage of the world's drinking water supply. It is already clear that seawater desalination can bring water-scarce countries many blessings, but it is surely not a panacea. It does not make water conservation programs any less relevant than in the past. Our common challenge is to ensure that the environmental disadvantages associated with desalination are identified and addressed, and that all human beings who suffer from water shortages can benefit from this new hydrological reality.

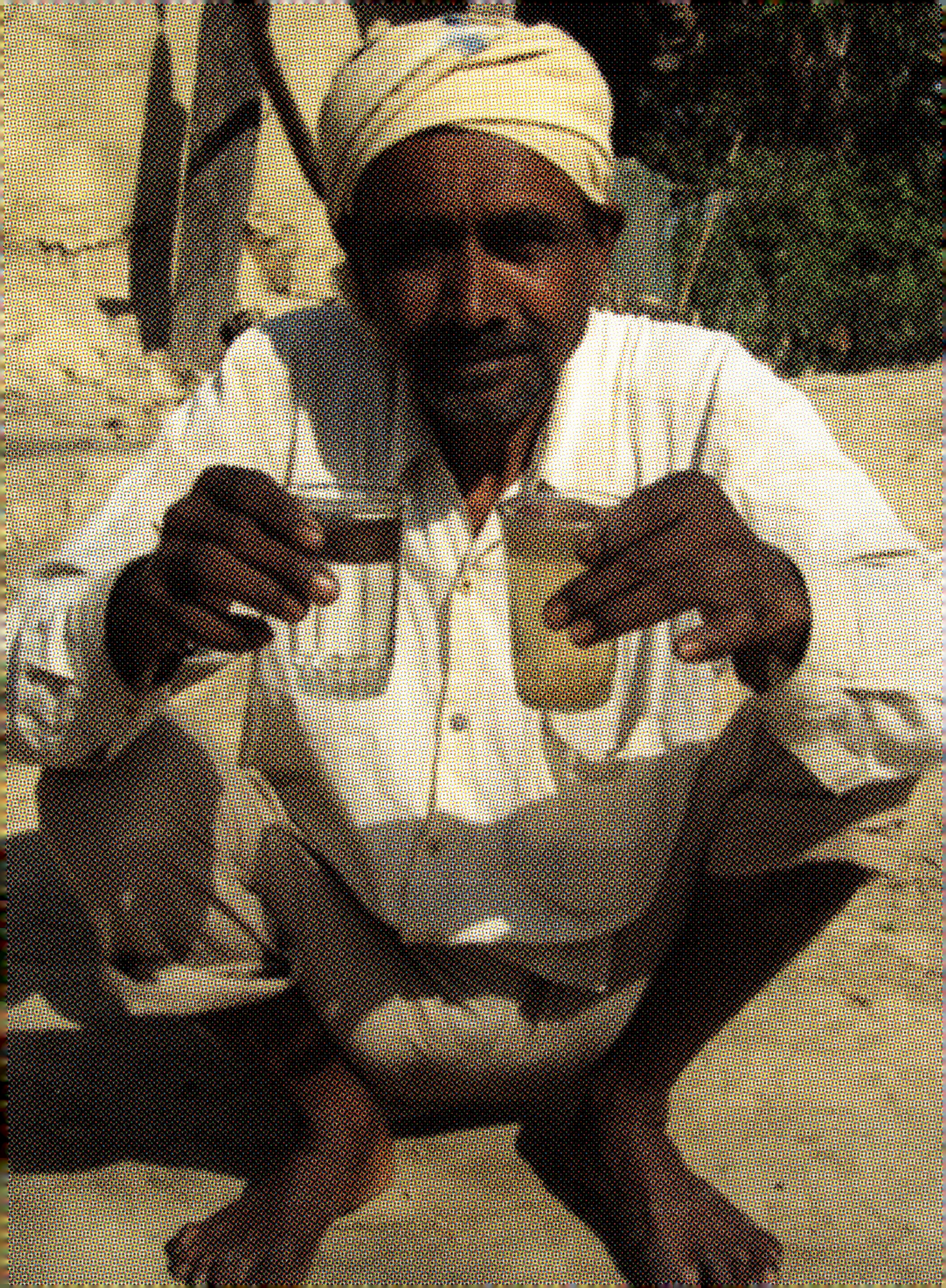

A New Model for Water Technology Dissemination: Reaching 20 Million People by 2020 with Better Water and Sanitation

Camille Dow Baker and Tommy Ka Kit Ngai

There is a tremendous need for better water and sanitation (W&S) services for the global poor. Although great progress has been made in the past decades, it is estimated that 780 million people in the world still lack access to improved water, and 2.5 billion lack sanitation (World Health Organization and United Nations Children's Fund [WHO/UNICEF], 2012). Across the globe, about 2.2 million deaths every year, mostly of children under the age of five, and over 7% of all burden of disease in low-income countries are directly caused by diarrheal diseases, which could be prevented by improving water, sanitation, and associated hygiene practices (WHO, 2008; Bartram and Cairncross, 2010).

In addition to their direct impact on child mortality and malnutrition, improvements in W&S contribute significantly to other human development concerns. For example, a reduction in illness and emotional hardship results in fewer medical expenses and an increased capacity to pursue income-generating activities, lifting families out of poverty (Hutton, Haller, and Bartram, 2007). Reducing the household labor burden on women and children—especially those in Africa, who often spend over 30 minutes per trip to collect water—allows them to engage in productive activities such as employment and schooling (WHO/UNICEF, 2010). The United Nations Millennium Project Task Force on Water and Sanitation (2005) claimed that investing in water and sanitation infrastructure and management is fundamental to the achievement of all other human development objectives.

Government agencies and non-governmental organizations (NGOs), which have the mandate to provide their constituents with W&S services, could play a key role in eradicating the health and economic threats caused by lack of adequate W&S services. However, they often lack the technical, institutional, and managerial capacity to do so effectively on a continual basis (IWA, 2010). Furthermore, research institutions around the world are generating clever insights at unprecedented levels; yet this knowledge often remains locked in scientific databases and research libraries, inaccessible and technically incomprehensible to the organizations in charge of implementing water and sanitation projects in the developing world. As a result, a large gap between knowledge and practice exists today, which seriously hinders the effectiveness of the implementation of both W&S policies, and design and infrastructure projects.

Narrowing the gap between knowledge regarding W&S technologies and strategies and their in situ implementation are vital to ensure long-lasting, sustainable solutions for the provision of basic services. To narrow this gap, we recommend promoting and building local ownership (responsibility for the problem and the solution) and leadership (ability to implement solutions), thereby strengthening the capacity of local institutions and populations to meet their own W&S needs.

Since the UN's International Drinking Water and Sanitation Decade of 1981–90, a plethora of scholars have stressed the crucial role played by a bottom-up approach to water management, enabled through education, training, and capacity building in local communities (McGarry, 1980; White, 1981; Kurup, 1991; Narayan, 1995; Carter, Tyrrel, and Howsam, 1999). The 1981–1990 period was designated by the United Nations as the First Water Decade to bring attention and support for clean water and sanitation worldwide. This ambitious UN program focused on safe water and sanitation for every person by 1990. Since the decade ended in 1990, hopes for improvement are centered on the World Water Assessment Program, a joint effort of the

FIGURE 3: Water before and after being filtered by the Kanchan Filter in Nepal

UN system and its member states, which includes a biennial assessment of the state of global freshwater resources. The launch of the second International Water Decade during 2005–15 will also provide much-needed impetus for the assessment program.)

The Centre for Affordable Water and Sanitation Technology (CAWST) is a Canadian-based non-profit engineering and training consultancy which was established in 2001. The unique and innovative institutional model of CAWST serves as a study in how to engage this bottom-up approach, and the strategies, achievements, and challenges that it entails.

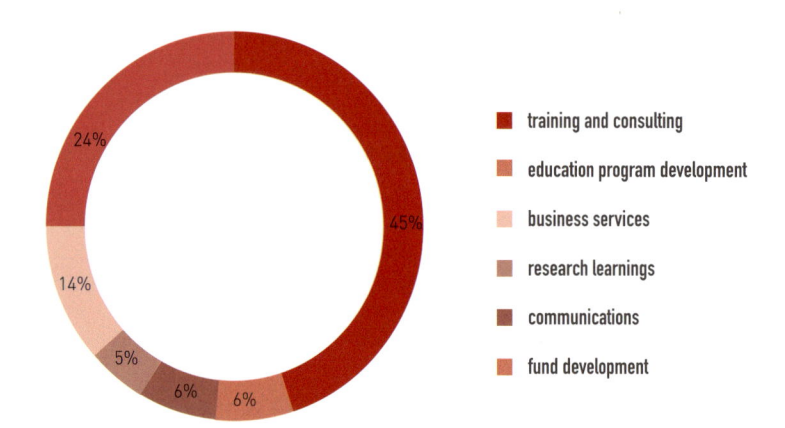

FIGURE 1: CAWST organizational budget by department

- training and consulting — 45%
- education program development — 24%
- business services — 14%
- research learnings — 5%
- communications — 6%
- fund development — 6%

A New Model for Water Technology Dissemination

Based in Calgary, Canada, CAWST compiles state-of-the-art knowledge on science, technology, public health, and international development, then distills and summarizes relevant material into easy-to-use, open-content educational materials that are freely downloadable from their website. Its team of international technical advisors assembles these materials for their work assignments around the world, and delivers training workshops to build the human capacity of local government officials, NGO workers, and community-based groups. The technical and managerial knowledge provided by the CAWST team, together with ongoing consulting support and follow-up field visits, catalyze self-reliant grassroots actions. Locals are empowered to build and maintain low-cost technologies appropriate to their own context.

CAWST is structured into six distinct functional departments, which receive varying budget shares (Figure 1). They focus their skills on different areas but share CAWST's overall goal and principles:

1. **Research Learning** reviews W&S–related research and policy documents from both academics and practitioners.
2. **Education Program Development** generates and maintains the educational materials used to implement CAWST's services and technical solutions.
3. **Training and Consulting** is responsible for technical and managerial training, as well as consulting with local groups in order to assist with the implementation of W&S technical solutions.
4. **Communications** disseminates CAWST's messages, materials, and knowledge locally and globally.
5. **Fund Development** leads CAWST's development of financial resources, with responsibility shared across the organization.
6. **Business Services** manages CAWST's policies, engages in financial stewardship, and provides systems support to the rest of the organization.

CAWST's unique approach to knowledge transfer is evident in the framework of its education programs. Unlike many educational institutions, its training programs are directed at non-professionals, and focused on actual and extensive implementation. Its services are subsidized and far-reaching, particularly aimed at those who have the greatest need. CAWST provides three-to-five-day training workshops, targeted at specific stakeholder groups that are involved in the implementation of community W&S programs.

CAWST trains organizations of all sizes, including larger, established NGOs and government agencies, as well as smaller community organizations and social entrepreneurs. Its workshops include a range of stakeholders, from project planners, to manufacturers, community health promoters, and regulators. The training focuses on the concrete implementation of W&S projects and programs, rather than policy development. With its robust and effective education and facilitation techniques, CAWST's training is designed to engage and motivate participants to take action. Educational materials are designed for trainers and include lesson plans, training curricula, posters, games, instructions, and suggestions. They are freely downloadable from the CAWST website.

FIGURE 2: Training social entrepreneurs on filter construction in Nepal

Following the initial training, about 10–20% of participating organizations initiate small pilots or demonstration projects, involving 100 households or fewer, that are intended to test demand at the community level. The pilot provides the organization with the experience and confidence to implement the full-scale program. An organization can recalibrate the technical and strategic details, based on lessons learned, and can maintain or attract support from donor and government agencies. CAWST provides support by email, phone and return visits to the pilot site to provide additional education and training support, help evaluate the projects, plan the next phase, and find program funding.

Over time, clients improve the quality of their projects and broaden their reach, both locally and across the region. At times, the replication of the project in other areas is undertaken by different organizations with the support of the original client and with specific training from CAWST. For example, in the case of a household-scale sand-filter project, CAWST offers training sessions on a diversity of topics: building a sand filter, implementing sand filter programs, training community health workers within the filter programs, providing household water treatment for people with HIV/AIDS, and teaching effective facilitation skills for trainers (Figure 2). Ultimately, CAWST's target is for the clients to quickly become independent by building their own capacity in all these areas.

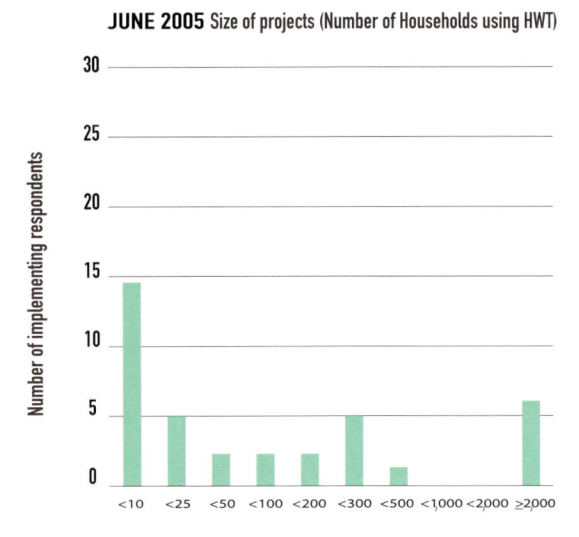

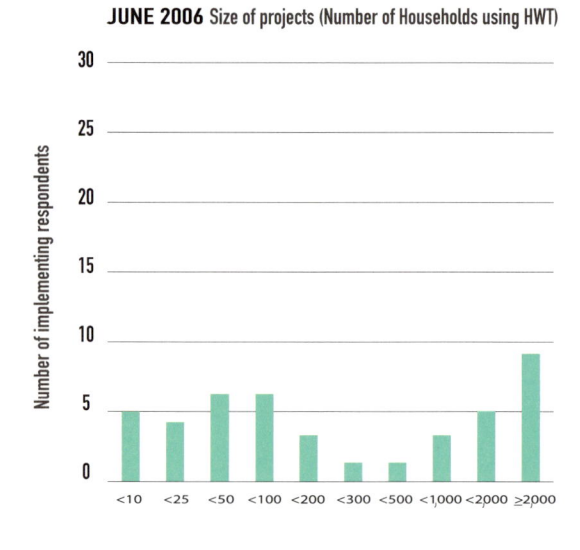

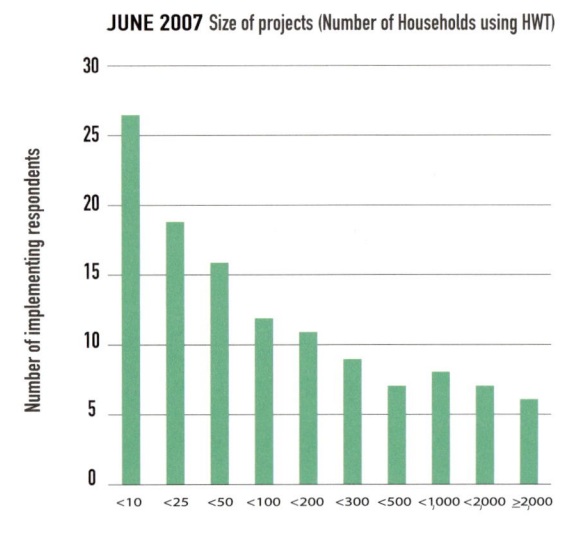

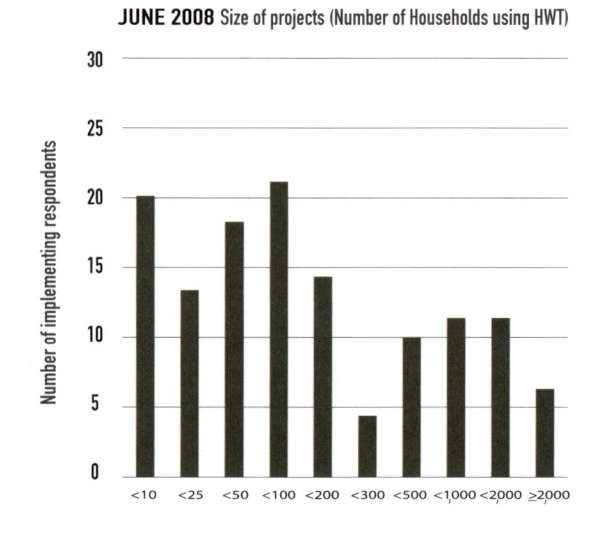

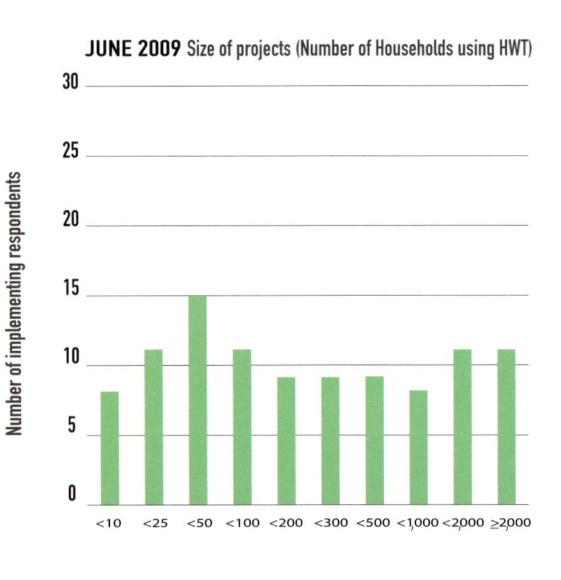

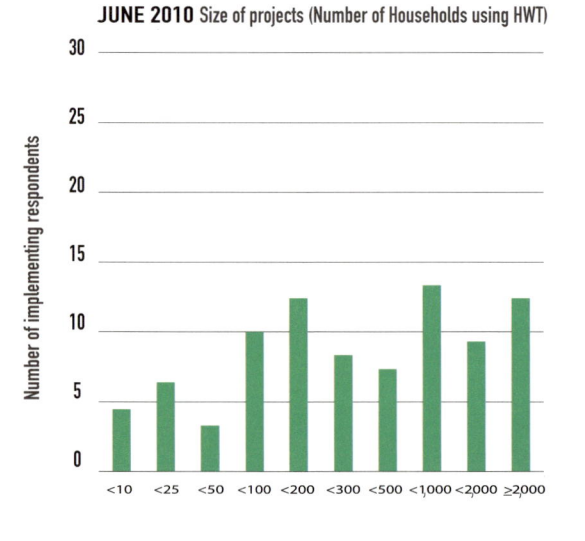

FIGURE 4: CAWST projects—evolution from 2005–2010

CAWST identifies local NGOs that currently provide training to community organizations at some level, or government agencies whose mandate is to build human resource capability in water and sanitation at the local levels, and shares its training know-how with them. Through these local organizations, CAWST establishes Water Expertise and Training Centres (WET Centres). As of 2012, CAWST was working with eight organizations in eight different countries, each at various stages of setting up WET Centres.

FIGURE 6: Installation of the Kanchan Filter at a household in Gorkha, Nepal, 2012 (top)

FIGURE 7: Filter testing in Cambodia, 2008 (bottom)

PEOPLE IMPACTED

FIGURE 5: Evolution of people impacted by CAWST from June 2009 to June 2020

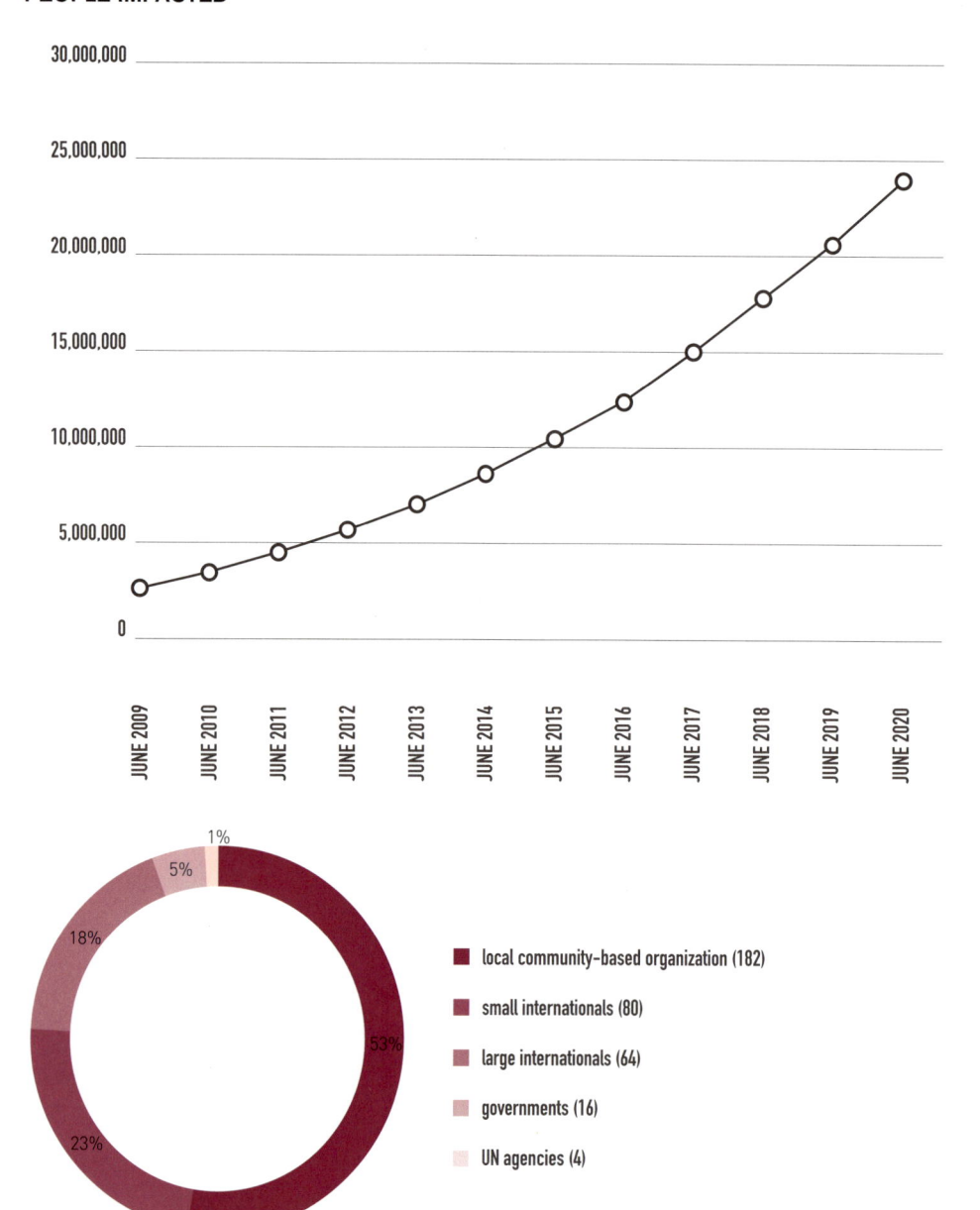

FIGURE 8: CAWST clients

- local community-based organization (182) — 53%
- small internationals (80) — 23%
- large internationals (64) — 18%
- governments (16) — 5%
- UN agencies (4) — 1%

Six Million People, 63 Countries: Results as of 2012

Focusing on technology dissemination at the local level has proved to be an effective solution. CAWST has demonstrated the efficacy of replicating numerous small projects, as opposed to attempting to deploy regional or national-scale mega-projects. Since its formation in 2001, CAWST has delivered 398 direct training workshops and 262 consulting support visits in 43 countries, including Afghanistan, Sudan, and Haiti. CAWST projects growth per household size between 2005–10 is illustrated in Figure 4.

1.5 million people have been trained by other organizations using CAWST education and training materials. Of CAWST's client organizations, 392 have implemented projects and reported to CAWST. Collectively, they have reached a total of 6 million people in 63 countries with access to safe drinking water and sanitation. If a linear growth is assumed, CAWST could affect around 24 million people in 2020 (Figure 5).

In the context of the developing world, the long-term sustainability of CAWST's strategy is rooted principally in the notion that communities can take ownership of their own W&S issues through education. This is crucial to fast and widespread implementation of new technologies and practices. CAWST relies on the local community's leadership structure and social relations for the dissemination and acceptance of innovations. Their specific content, and the pace at which they are introduced, are set by the community's leaders and customized according to site-specific needs and cultural conventions. The provision of W&S therefore starts with the individual implementation of water treatment devices in each household (Figure 6). This self-reliance empowers individuals to make the link between water, health, and sanitation from the outset.

Partnership Example:
Environment and Public Health Organization (ENPHO), Nepal

In 2000, in order to address arsenic contamination in Nepal, the Nepali NGO ENPHO and the Massachusetts Institute of Technology (MIT) collaborated on the development of a household-level arsenic removal filter called the Kanchan Arsenic Filter. The Kanchan Arsenic Filter is a modification of an intermittently operated slow sand filter, also known as the biosand filter, which CAWST has promoted since its inception in 2001 (Figure 7). Since 2003, CAWST and ENPHO have provided training to hundreds of social entrepreneurs in Nepal, which has consequently helped 300,000 people gain access to better water and sanitation.

CAWST's contributions have helped ENPHO in the following ways:
- strengthen its own institutional and technical capability;
- help establish local entrepreneurs, to supply Kanchan Arsenic Filters and biosand filters;
- improve access to technological options for organizations implementing W&S programs;
- train individuals, at levels ranging from grassroots to professional;
- make information accessible to all;
- provide ongoing technical consulting to implementers and promoters of W&S programs.

ENPHO now works in partnership with CAWST to develop ENPHO's capabilities as a WET Centre that can deliver W&S training and consulting services to other NGOs and government agencies in the region.

Challenges

Some of the biggest challenges facing CAWST include staying committed to the planned course of action; selling others on household water treatment and storage (HWTS) as the starting point for the sustainable delivery of W&S services; and finding the appropriate committed WET Centre partners to replicate services globally.

Keeping committed to the planned course of action is often difficult. CAWST can only motivate and support its diverse clientele (Figure 8); it has no control over its actions. At times, the pace of development is slower than projected, and CAWST has to resist the impulse to intervene, instead maintaining a disciplined respect for its mission to equip communities with the knowledge and confidence to self-manage. This has an impact on funding as well, as agencies determine their support based on actual results, not capacity building.

Household Water Treatment as the Starting Point

Many service providers are concerned that individuals cannot treat water in the home effectively and consistently over a period of time. This is because HWTS often does not improve water quality to the zero–*E. coli* level, which has been set as a minimum drinking water quality standard in many countries. Although HWTS does not always meet this standard, it has been extensively demonstrated that it can improve water quality and significantly decrease diarrheal disease in a consistent manner and under a diversity of conditions. Unfortunately, incremental improvement in water quality is dismissed in favour of "perfect" water quality. This is an issue in cases where "perfect" water quality is neither affordable nor technically possible. Furthermore, due to their distributed and autonomous nature, governments do not have the know-how to effectively regulate and monitor HWTS. As a consequence, the potential for HWTS to improve water quality is significantly reduced.

Finding Committed Partners for Service Replication

Finding the right WET Centre partners, organizations that are able and willing to replicate CAWST's services globally, is challenging. Often, partners fail to recognize the need to appoint a dedicated leader and staff to the WET Centre, and instead have their current staff take on the burden of training in addition to their regular workload. Partners are also sometimes hesitant to implement the three critical functions of a WET Centre: actively searching for and marketing WET Centre services to potential implementing organizations, providing continuous consulting support after the training, and measuring results in terms of number of people with better W&S.

CAWST's WET Centre program has successfully demonstrated that the CAWST organizational model is replicable globally. Each WET Centre provides the same core services as CAWST: training, consulting support, and education. However, each WET Centre differs in its capabilities and local needs. For example, CAWST's Afghanistan partner DACAAR, is a long-standing organization in the country providing services to government at all levels and local and international NGOs of all sizes; whereas CAWST's Zambian partner, SHIP, was founded more recently and has primarily trained local organizations and district/municipal level government responding to a need in Zambia and regionally across Africa.

Conclusions

Based on our forecast model, and assuming that current trends in investments, macroeconomics, and policy environments continue in the future, CAWST expects to impact 20 million people with better W&S by 2020. Given the increasing client interest in the WET Centre program, the current and expected improvements to the business model and increases in efficiency, and the potential for other organizations to implement the business model, the impact of the project could be much higher.

The Centre for Affordable Water and Sanitation Technology has developed and implemented an innovative institutional model for W&S technology dissemination to the poor in developing countries. It is a model that has proven to be effective, sustainable, replicable, and capable of impacting the billions of people who need better access to W&S services.

Changing the current deteriorating trajectory of water quality and water availability globally will require action and water education at the household level. Household decision-making is crucial because behaviour change is central to achieving health gains in sanitation. Service providers need to focus on this level. Furthermore, investment in physical infrastructure must be accompanied by development of the "soft" infrastructure of policies, legal systems, and human capacity. Yet, much bilateral aid for sanitation and drinking water fails to achieve a balance between soft and hard infrastructure. It is this gap that CAWST fills.

KANCHAN ARSENIC FILTER

Global Water & Sanitation (WatSan), Nepal's Environment and Public Health Organization (ENPHO) and Rural Water Supply and Sanitation Support Programme (RWSSSP)

Site: Biratnagar, Terai Region, Nepal
Longitude & Latitude: 26°28'N 87°16'E
Annual Precipitation: 2,500mm

Year: 2000–2004
Status: Completed
Water Volume/Day: 24–36L
Dimensions: 0.94m x 0.35m x 0.35m

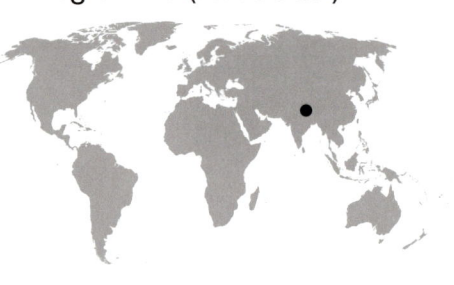

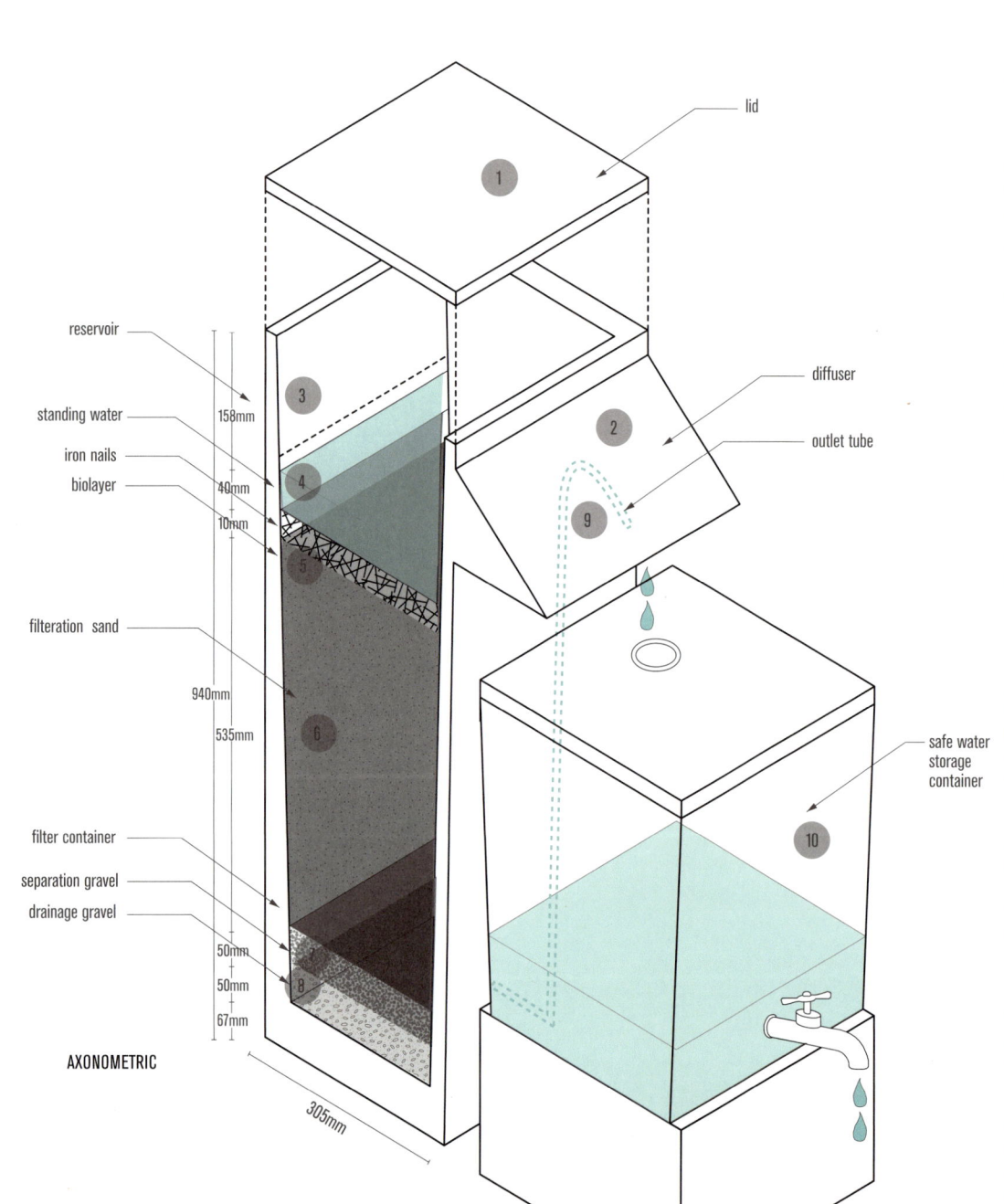

AXONOMETRIC

1 LID
A tightly placed lid prevents contamination and pests

2 DIFFUSER
The diffuser is filled with 5–6kg of non-galvanized iron nails and covered by a layer of bricks to prevent displacement

3 RESERVOIR
The reservoir sits on top of the filter and holds 12L

4 STANDING WATER
A 5cm layer of water settles on top of the sand biolayer layer to maintain constant wetness and effective biological function. The water layer can provide the necessary oxygen for the biolayer

5 BIOLAYER
The biolayer consists of a 1–2cm layer of sand which develops the biological mechanism (i.e. bacteria) needed for the treatment of pathogens

6 FILTRATION SAND
A 54.5cm layer of sand removes 85–95% of arsenic, 90–99% of iron, and 87–98% of bacteria while reducing turbidity by 80–95%. The sand used is sifted and cleaned prior to usage

7 SEPERATION GRAVEL
The separation gravel layer consists of small-sized mineral aggregate which prevents sand particles from clogging the outlet tube

8 DRAINAGE GRAVEL
The drainage gravel layer consists of large-sized mineral aggregate and also prevents sand from clogging the outlet tube

9 OUTLET TUBE
The outlet tube is made of plastic or copper and outflows water that is safe to drink

10 SAFE STORAGE
The safe water storage container holds the treated water

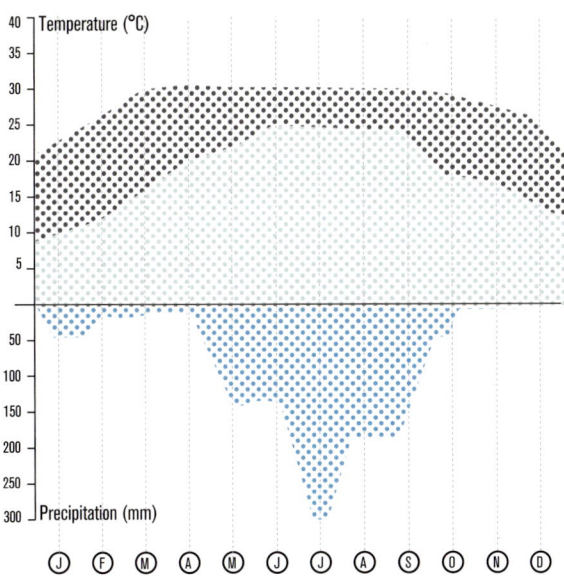

The Kanchan Arsenic Filter (KAF) is a household device that removes arsenic from drinking water through a layer of rusty nails in the filter's diffuser basin, in addition to providing microbiological water treatment. An adaptation of the biosand filter, the KAF was developed by the Massachusetts Institute of Technology (MIT) Global Water & Sanitation (WatSan) Projects in collaboration with Nepal's Environment and Public Health Organization (ENPHO) and Rural Water Supply and Sanitation Support Programme (RWSSSP) to address the widespread arsenic and fecal bacteria pollution in the rural Terai region of Nepal (MIT, 2008; Ngai, et al., 2006). Long-term exposure to arsenic through drinking water and food has resulted in adverse health effects including dermal and vascular diseases, birth defects, low IQ, and cancer of the lungs, kidneys, and skin (Hussain, Haque, Islam, and Hossen, 2001).

The KAF was conceived as an affordable and feasible solution for the improvement of safe drinking water to be widely implemented through capacity building and training activities (see Baker and Ngai, p. 61-68). The treatment of up to 99% of arsenic-laden groundwater is a well-understood science (Robins, Nishimura, and Singh, 2001; Hussain, et al., 2001). MIT's WatSan offers a review of approaches and techniques for the removal of arsenic (MIT, 2008), but the implementation of low-cost treatment systems on a wide scale has proved an ongoing challenge. KAF responds to this challenge by being affordable—$12–40 per unit of concrete, or $75 per unit of plastic (Center for Affordable Water and Sanitation Technology [CAWST], 2012)—and easily installed and maintained, using locally-sourced materials and requiring no electricity or chemicals to operate.

The device is composed of a concrete or plastic container, 94cm tall by 30cm wide, which includes from top to bottom a lid, reservoir, diffuser, bio-filter, and outlet tube. The reservoir is designed to hold up to 12L of water. The diffuser is filled with 5-6 kg of non-galvanized iron nails and covered by a layer of bricks to prevent displacement. The bio-filter is composed of a 54.5cm layer of sand, a separation gravel layer to stop the sand from blocking the outlet tube, and a drainage gravel layer (Ngai, et al., 2007). A recommended filter loading rate of 600 liters/hour/m^2 and flow rate of 0.4 L/min will produce 24–36L of daily water supply (CAWST, 2012). The estimated lifespan of the device is 10 years; lids and diffusers may need more frequent replacement and nails should be replaced every 2–3 years.

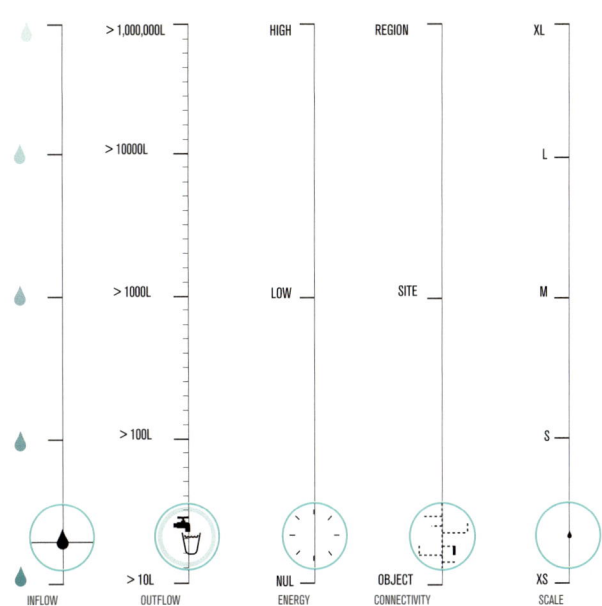

The Kanchan Arsenic Filter removes 85–95% of arsenic, 90–99% of iron, and 87–98% of bacteria while reducing turbidity by 80–95% (CAWST, 2012). Arsenic removal is achieved by incorporating a layer of rusty nails in the diffuser basin of the filter, since arsenic binds to ferric hydroxide by adsorption. The oxide surface of the nails bonds with arsenate ions to form an insoluble ferric arsenate compound, which could be easily blocked by a sand filter. It takes up to two weeks to establish rust on the nails, depending on inlet water quality and usage (CAWST, 2012; Frazer, 2005; Robins, et al., 2001).

Other pathogens are removed by the KAF thanks to a complex biological film that grows naturally on the surface of sand. The underlying sand also acts as a substrate or support medium for the purification treatment, as demonstrated in slow sand filters. The biological film is a gelatinous layer called the hypogeal layer or Schmutzdecke and is located at the top few millimeters of the fine sand layer. The biological film consists of bacteria, fungi, protozoa, rotifera, and a range of aquatic insect larvae. As water passes through the film, particles of foreign matter are trapped in the mucilaginous matrix and dissolved organic material is adsorbed and metabolized by the bacteria, fungi, and protozoa. It takes up to 30 days to establish the biolayer (CAWST, 2012; Huisman and Wood, 1974).

Despite its numerous advantages, the KAF has several limitations. The device cannot be relocated once installed, since cracking or breakage may occur due to its weight. Changing water sources, particularly to rainwater, may compromise the removal of arsenic. The filter must be used almost every day to maintain the biological layer; the recommended pause period is 6–12 hours with a minimum of 1 hour and maximum of 48 hours. In addition, sufficient treatment efficacy has not been consistently demonstrated for certain influents: high phosphate and pH levels lead to decreases in the efficiency of the arsenic removal process (Mahin and Ngai, 2008). The KAF cannot remove pesticides or organic fertilizer chemicals, salt, hardness, or scale (dissolved compounds). Finally, the filter poses some potential health risk associated with the elevated nitrate levels produced in the effluent within the filter, possibly due to nitrification and high levels of ammonia in the groundwater (Chiew, et al., 2009).

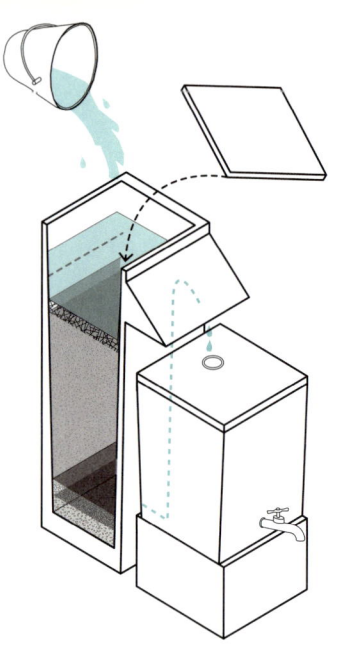

PROCESS DIAGRAM

1. Contaminated water is poured into the reservoir, located at the top of the BioSand Filter (BSF) device the top lid serves to keep the water from further contamination and pests - the filter is filled 1–4 times daily

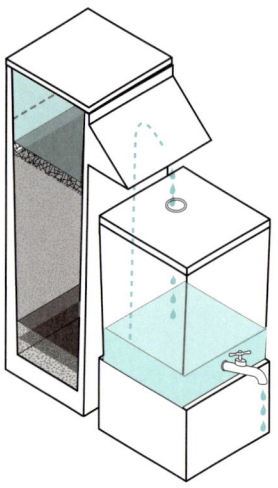

2. The reservoir should be filled to its maximum capacity (12L) to ensure consistent flow

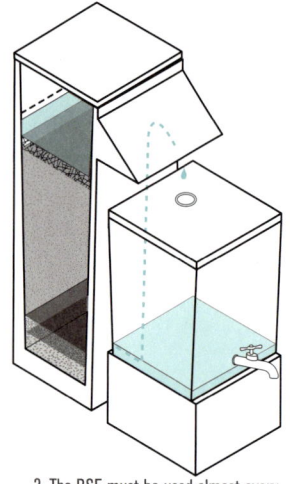

3. The BSF must be used almost every day to maintain the biological layer; the recommended pause period is 6–12 hours with a minimum of 1 hour and maximum of 48 hours

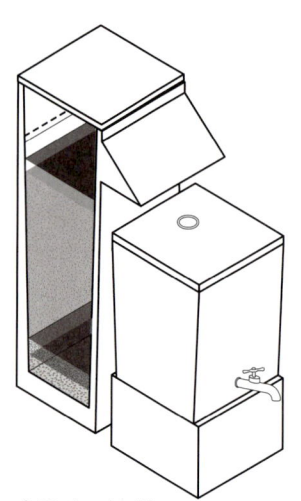

4. Filtration takes 1 hour

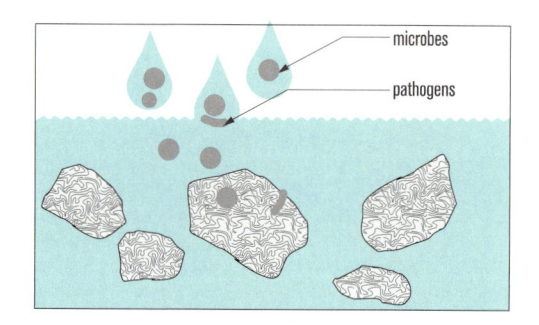

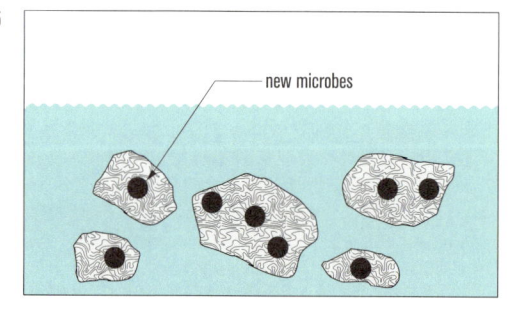

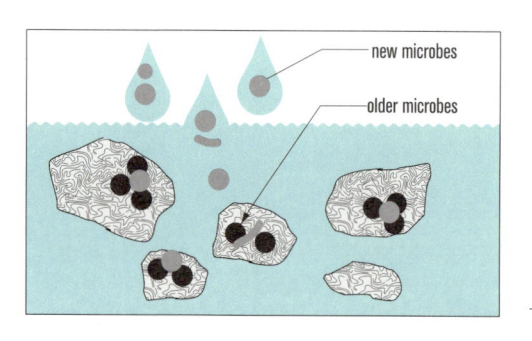

Day 1 — microbes, pathogens

Day 15 — new microbes

Day 30 — new microbes, older microbes

Pathogens are removed by the BSF via a complex biological film that grows naturally on the surface of sand

The biological film is a gelatinous layer called the hypogeal layer or Schmutzdecke, which is located within the top few millimeters of the fine sand layer

The biological film consists of bacteria, fungi, protozoa, rotifera and a range of aquatic insect larvae

As water passes through the film, particles of foreign matter are trapped in the mucilaginous matrix and dissolved organic material is adsorbed and tabolized by the bacteria, fungi and protozoa

It takes up to 30 days to establish a biolayer

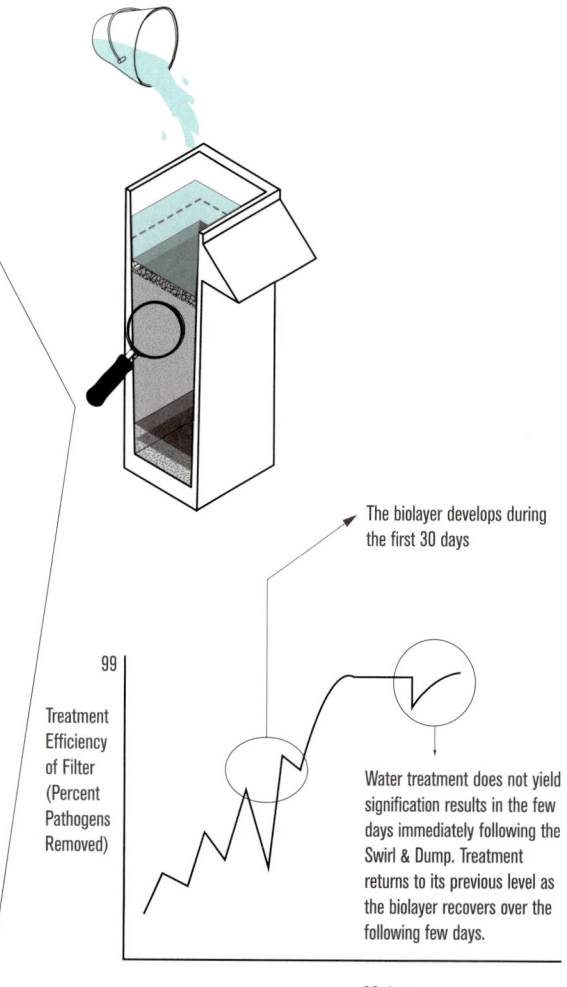

The biolayer develops during the first 30 days

Treatment Efficiency of Filter (Percent Pathogens Removed)

99

Water treatment does not yield signification results in the few days immediately following the Swirl & Dump. Treatment returns to its previous level as the biolayer recovers over the following few days.

30 days

THE MULTI-BARRIER APPROACH TO SAFE DRINKING WATER

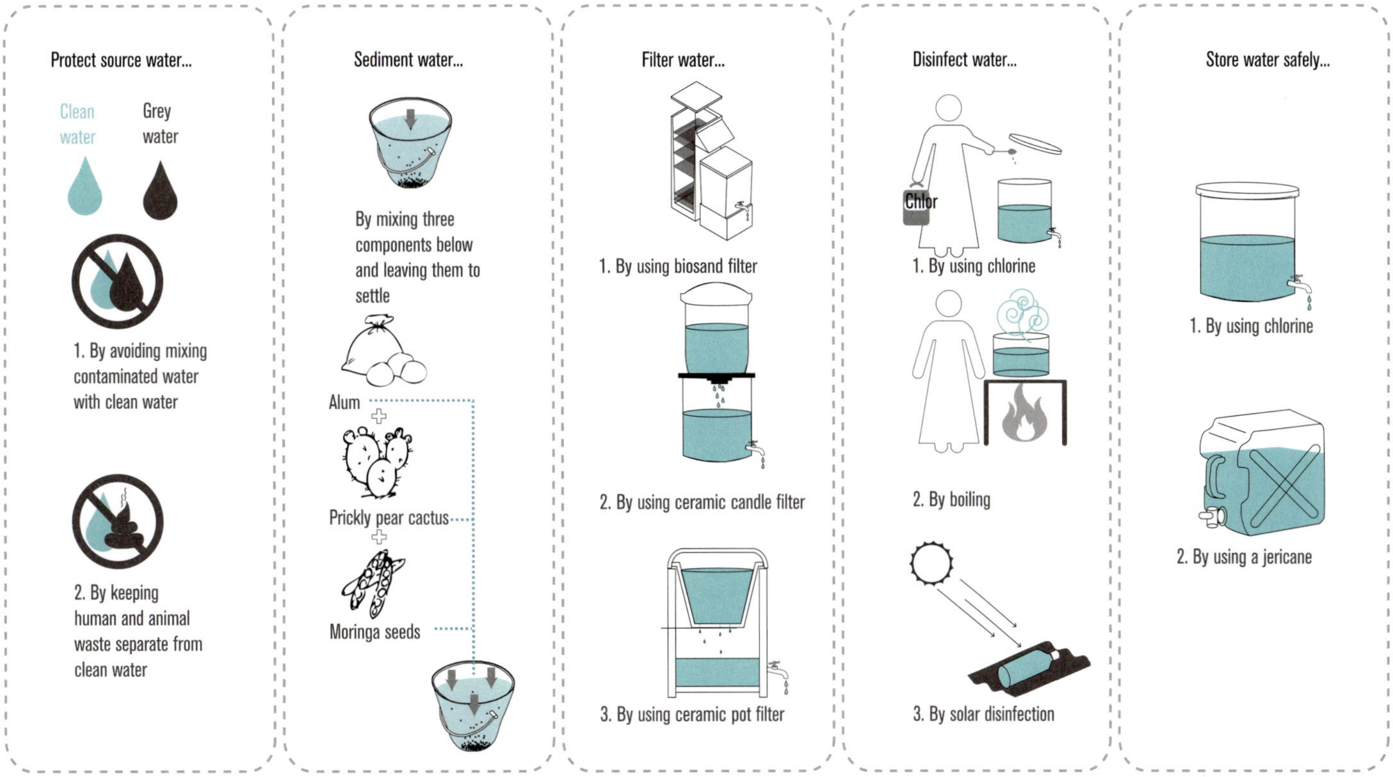

Protect source water...

Clean water / Grey water

1. By avoiding mixing contaminated water with clean water

2. By keeping human and animal waste separate from clean water

Sediment water...

By mixing three components below and leaving them to settle

Alum +
Prickly pear cactus +
Moringa seeds

Filter water...

1. By using biosand filter

2. By using ceramic candle filter

3. By using ceramic pot filter

Disinfect water...

1. By using chlorine

2. By boiling

3. By solar disinfection

Store water safely...

1. By using chlorine

2. By using a jericane

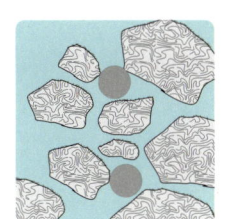

PATHOGENS FILTRATION MECHANISM

Mechanical Trapping

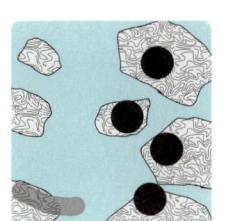

Adsorption

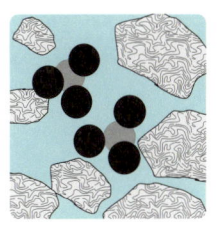

Predation

Expiration

BIOSAND FILTER CONSTRUCTION

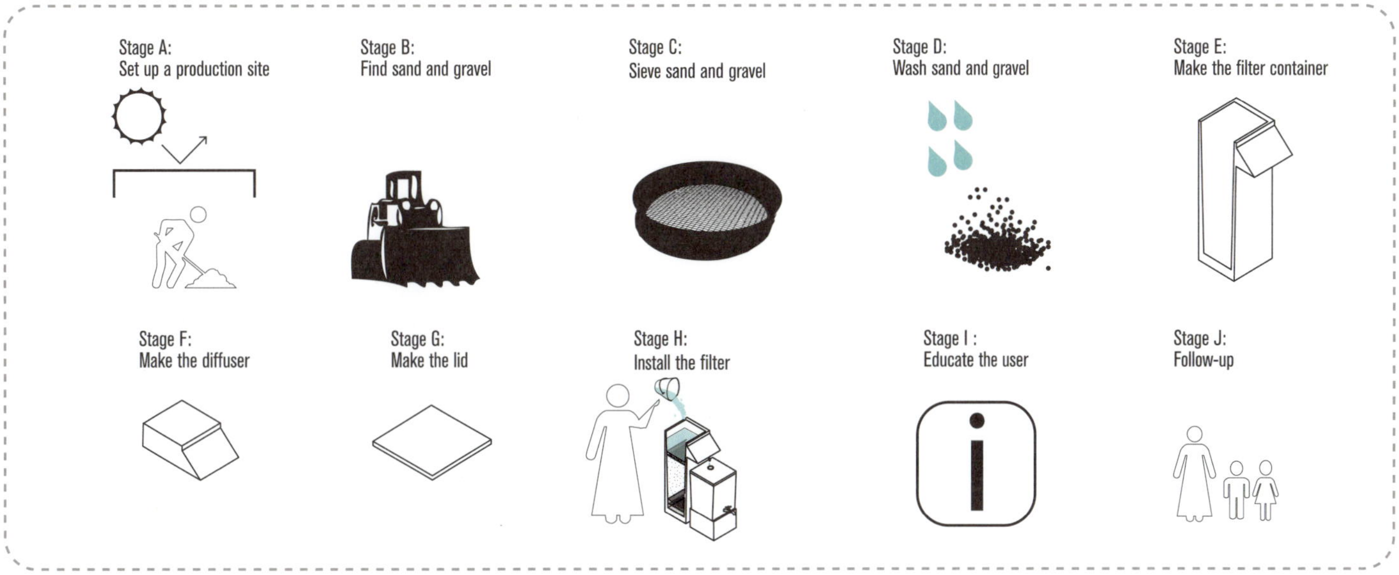

Stage A: Set up a production site

Stage B: Find sand and gravel

Stage C: Sieve sand and gravel

Stage D: Wash sand and gravel

Stage E: Make the filter container

Stage F: Make the diffuser

Stage G: Make the lid

Stage H: Install the filter

Stage I: Educate the user

Stage J: Follow-up

LIQUID WRAP
Proxy Architects

Site: Za'atari Refugee Camp, Jordan
Longitude & Latitude: 32°17'N 36°15'50"E
Annual Precipitation: 150mm

Year: 2008
Status: Prototype
Water Volume/Day: 20L
Dimensions: 11.85m x 0.6m

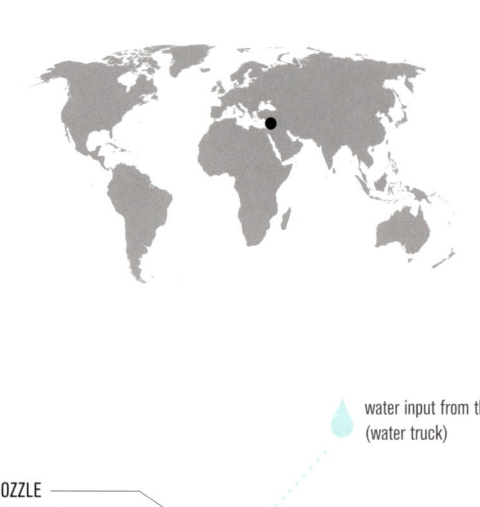

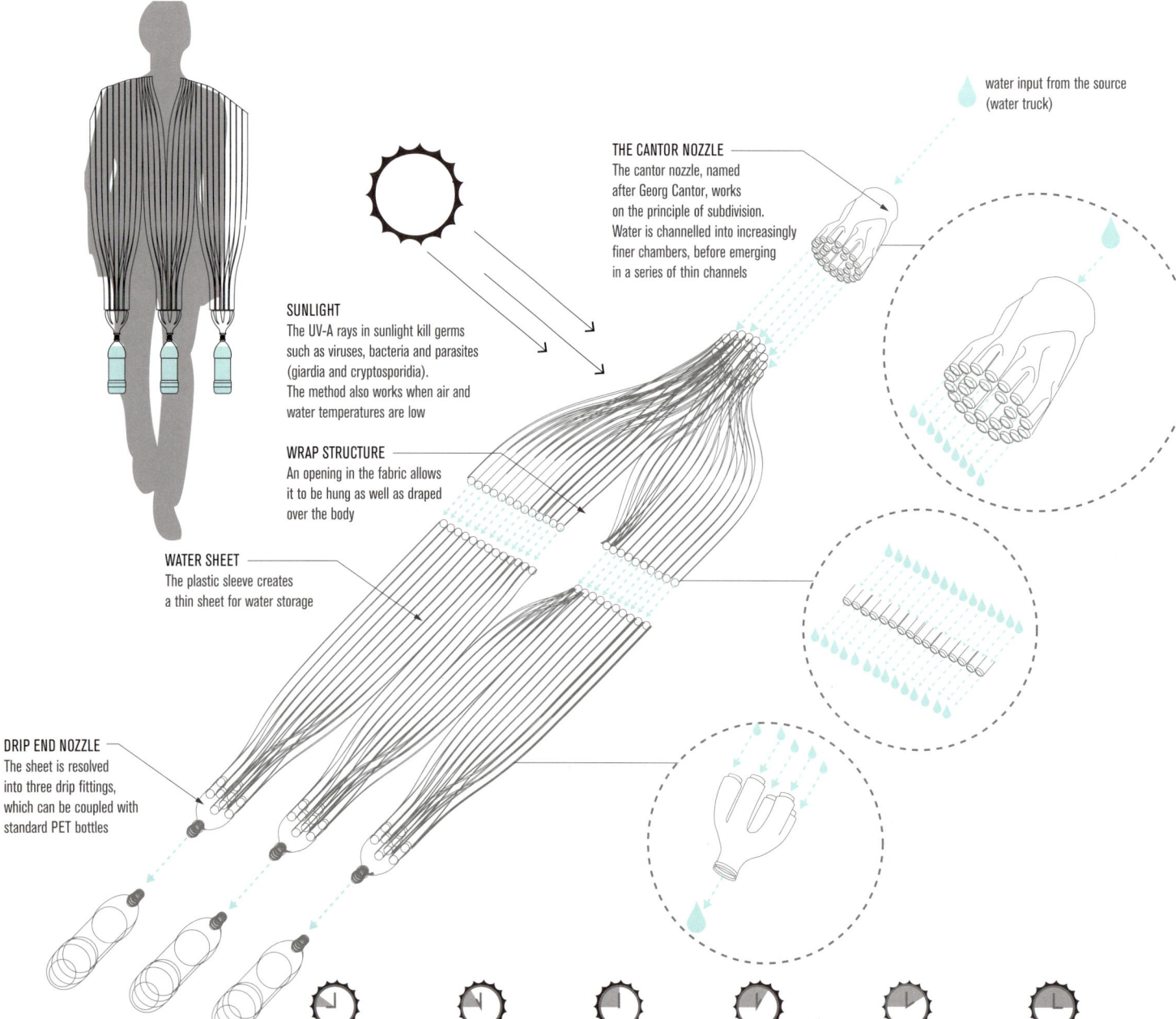

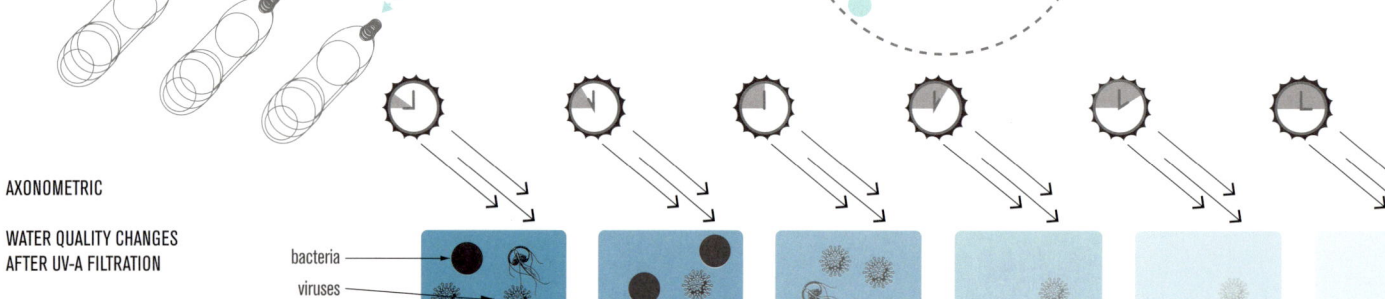

THE CANTOR NOZZLE
The cantor nozzle, named after Georg Cantor, works on the principle of subdivision. Water is channelled into increasingly finer chambers, before emerging in a series of thin channels

water input from the source (water truck)

SUNLIGHT
The UV-A rays in sunlight kill germs such as viruses, bacteria and parasites (giardia and cryptosporidia). The method also works when air and water temperatures are low

WRAP STRUCTURE
An opening in the fabric allows it to be hung as well as draped over the body

WATER SHEET
The plastic sleeve creates a thin sheet for water storage

DRIP END NOZZLE
The sheet is resolved into three drip fittings, which can be coupled with standard PET bottles

AXONOMETRIC

WATER QUALITY CHANGES AFTER UV-A FILTRATION

bacteria
viruses
parasites (giardia and cyptosporidia)

74

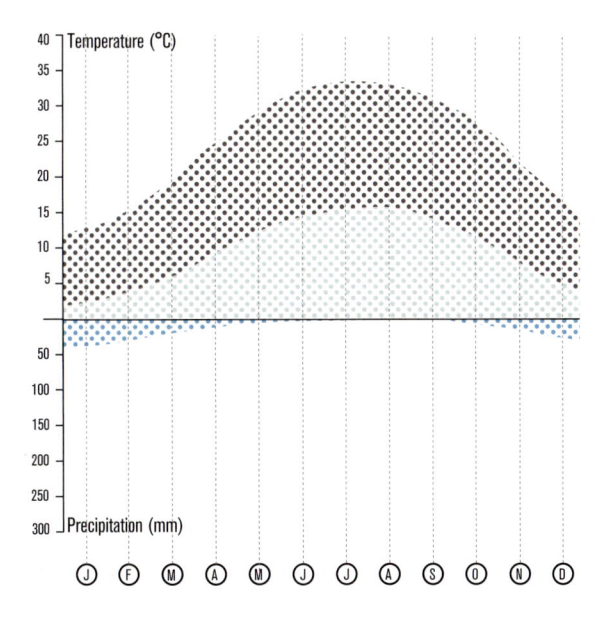

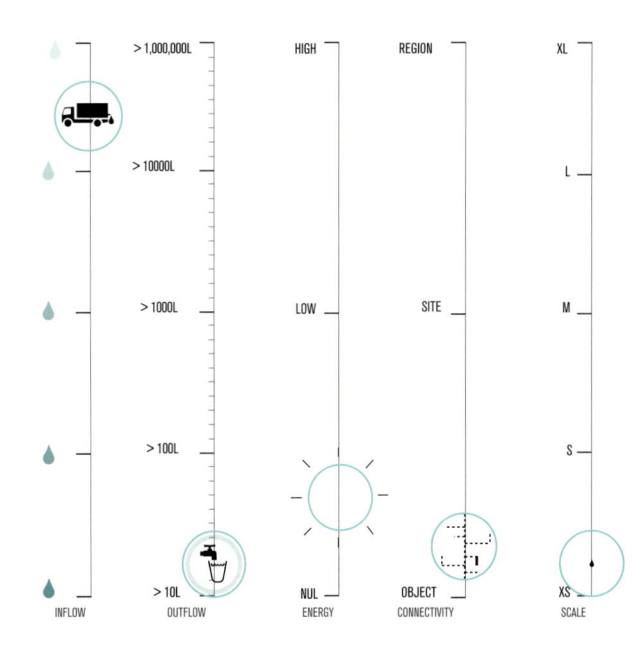

Liquid Wrap is a small-scale device designed for the conveyance, storage, and solar disinfection of contaminated water obtained from informal sources such as rivers, runoff catchments, and private truck vendors. Liquid Wrap is a 20L plastic pouch composed of one fractal input nozzle that branches into increasingly finer chambers, before emerging into thin channels. These channels then bundle into four fractal output nozzles. The extremities of the output and input nozzles are equipped with a drip fitting that can be connected to a standard PET bottle.

Liquid Wrap's design is inspired by the Cantor set, developed by German mathematician Georg Cantor in 1883. The Cantor set is produced by starting with a unit interval and taking out the center open interval, leaving two closed intervals (Bovill, 1996). This operation can be repeated an infinite number of times, generating clustered layouts (Peitgen, Jürgens, and Saupe, 1992). The integration of the cantor concept into the design of Liquid Wrap resulted in subdividing chambers, narrowing, and decreasing depth crescendo, thereby maximizing the surface area of water exposed to the sun's rays. By increasing exposure to solar radiation, water disinfection efficiency is enhanced (Kehoe, et al., 2001; Mani, Kanjur, Bright Singh, and Reed, 2006). Liquid Wrap's chambers are built by heat-sealing two plastic sheets together, while the plastic fractal nozzles are mass-produced using molds shaped through rapid prototyping. The design is ergonomic: the user can easily carry it while keeping both hands free. Also, Liquid Wrap can be hung, preferably near highly reflective or black surfaces to maximize solar exposure.

Solar water disinfection (SODIS) is an ancient process that can be traced to nearly 2,000 years ago (Baker, 1949). Even though the bactericidal effect of sunlight was thoroughly investigated by Downes and Blunt in 1877, it was not until the 1980s that Aftim Acra and collaborators at the University of Beirut published their seminal research on disinfecting contaminated water via sunlight for use in oral rehydration solutions (Acra, Karahogopian, Raffoul, and Dajani, 1980; Acra, et al., 1989). Acra and his colleagues' work spurred the Integrated Rural Energy Systems Association (INRESA) to launch a network project in 1985. The Brace Research Institute in Montreal organized a workshop in 1988 to review the results of INRESA's field research (Lawand, et al., 1988). Since then, the full potential of SODIS to inactivate a wide range of waterborne pathogens has been investigated by several scholars (e.g., Conroy et al., 1996).

Two different water treatment processes using solar energy were found to improve microbiological water quality (Conroy et al., 1998). The first, UV radiation, was used for its bactericidal effect. The second, using infrared radiation to raise water temperature, is known as pasteurization. Like the SODIS system using PET bottles, developed conjointly by the Swiss Federal Institute of Environmental Science and Technology (EAWAG) and the Department of Water Sanitation in Developing Countries (SANDEC), Liquid Wrap combines both processes.

The first process involves ultraviolet radiation that reaches the surface of the earth, called UV-A. UV-A radiation has a lethal effect on pathogens present in water: it directly interacts with the DNA, nucleic acids, and enzymes of the living cells, changing their molecular structure and causing death (Wegelin, et al., 1994). Ultraviolet radiation also reacts with oxygen dissolved in the water and produces highly reactive forms of oxygen (oxygen free radicals and hydrogen peroxides). These reactive molecules also interfere with cell structures, killing the pathogens (Reed, Mani, and Meyer, 2000).

The second process involves the long-wave radiation called infrared, which heats water as it is absorbed. Sufficient heat eliminates 99.9% of microorganisms in water (Feachem, Bradley, Garelick, and Mara, 1983; Joyce, McGuigan, Elmore-Meegan, and Conroy, 1996). At a water temperature of about 30° C, about five hours at a threshold solar radiation intensity of at least 500 W/m² is required for the Liquid Wrap system to be efficient (Conroy, et al., 2012).

Liquid Wrap's SODIS system has many benefits: improvement of the microbiological quality of drinking water; inactivation of pathogens causing diarrhea, thanks to solar UV-A radiation and temperature; outdoor and household use under the direct responsibility of the individual user; simplicity in application due to reliance on sunlight, a renewable energy source; the lack of need for fuel or chemicals for disinfection; reduction in the need for traditional energy sources such as firewood or gas fuel, limiting deforestation; and reduction in workload for women and children, who usually fetch and boil water (SANDEC, 2002).

A number of parameters affect the efficacy of the Liquid Wrap SODIS process: solar irradiance availability and quality of the water to be treated, as well as the nature of the contamination, as some pathogens are more resistant to SODIS than others (Byrne, et al., 2011). Additional concerns with wide implementation of the Liquid Wrap system include the difficulty of replicating the manufacturing process, and the cost of the system.

Liquid Wrap's success is contingent on populations "buying in," which necessitates change in behaviors and household practices. The commitment and the changes that are needed could be instigated by educational programs, community meetings, and support groups (Bhutta, 2009).

city water system   neighbors line

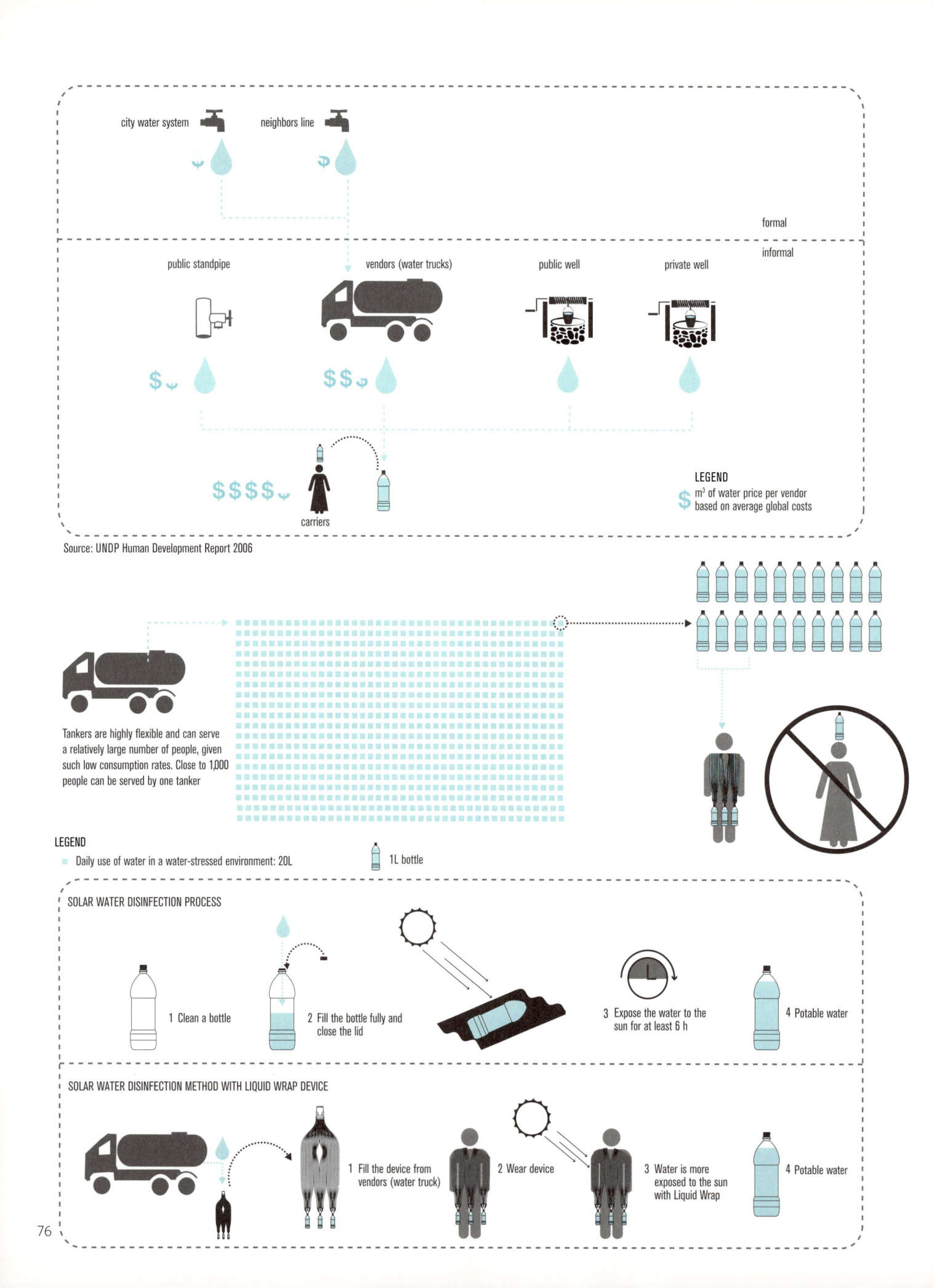

formal
informal

public standpipe   vendors (water trucks)   public well   private well

$ $$

$$$$
carriers

LEGEND
$ m³ of water price per vendor based on average global costs

Source: UNDP Human Development Report 2006

Tankers are highly flexible and can serve a relatively large number of people, given such low consumption rates. Close to 1,000 people can be served by one tanker

LEGEND
■ Daily use of water in a water-stressed environment: 20L
▯ 1L bottle

SOLAR WATER DISINFECTION PROCESS

1 Clean a bottle
2 Fill the bottle fully and close the lid
3 Expose the water to the sun for at least 6 h
4 Potable water

SOLAR WATER DISINFECTION METHOD WITH LIQUID WRAP DEVICE

1 Fill the device from vendors (water truck)
2 Wear device
3 Water is more exposed to the sun with Liquid Wrap
4 Potable water

76

PLAN
0.15m
0.25m

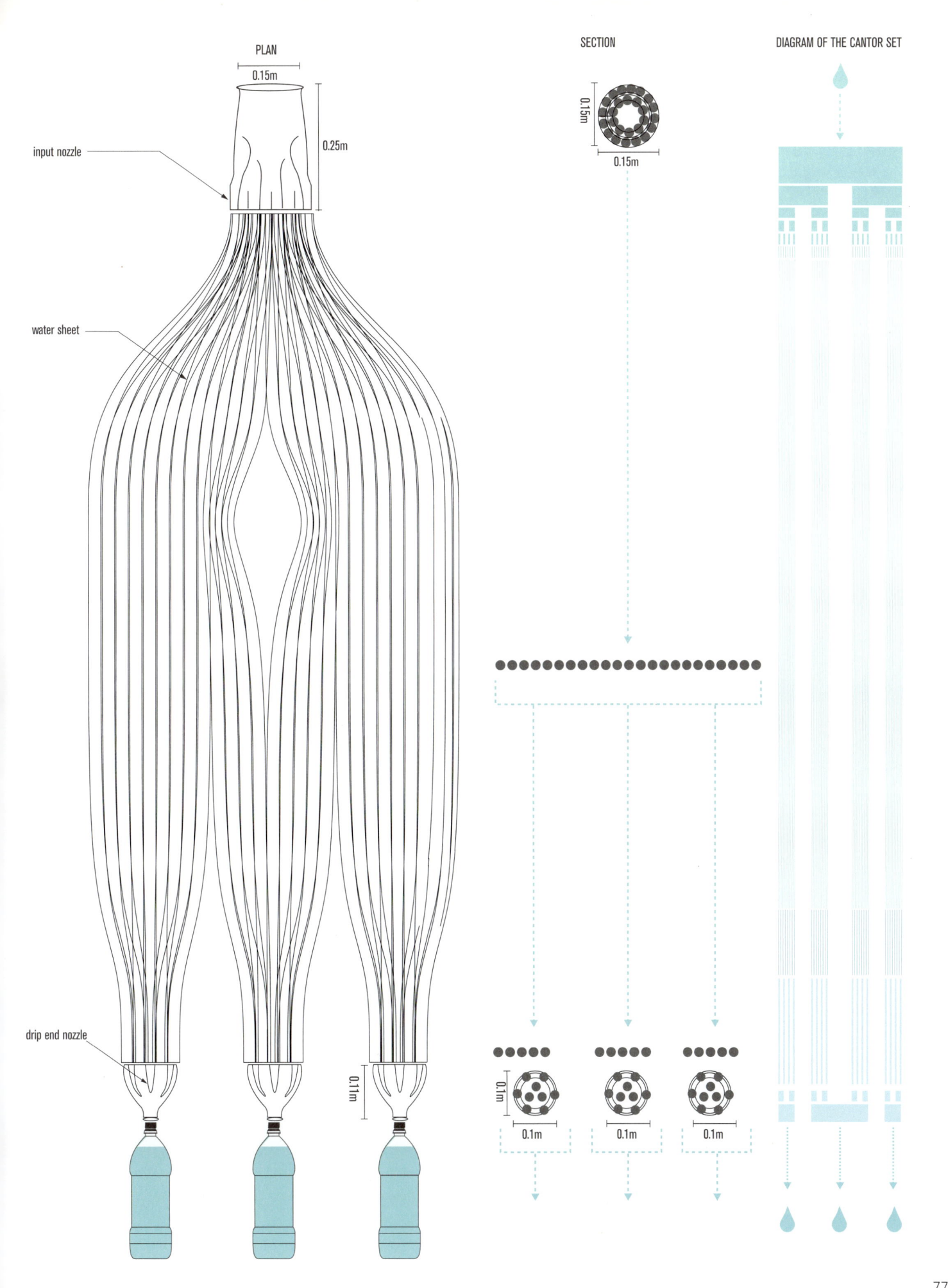

input nozzle

water sheet

drip end nozzle

0.11m

SECTION
0.15m
0.15m

0.1m
0.1m 0.1m 0.1m

DIAGRAM OF THE CANTOR SET

77

VENA WATER CONDENSER
ORE Design + Technology

Site: Sana'a, Yemen
Longitude & Latitude: 15°45'N 44°20'E
Annual Precipitation: 200mm

Year: 2009
Status: Schematic design
Water Volume/Day: 10–15L
Dimensions: 60cm x 460cm

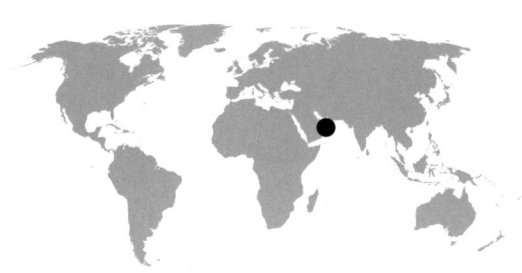

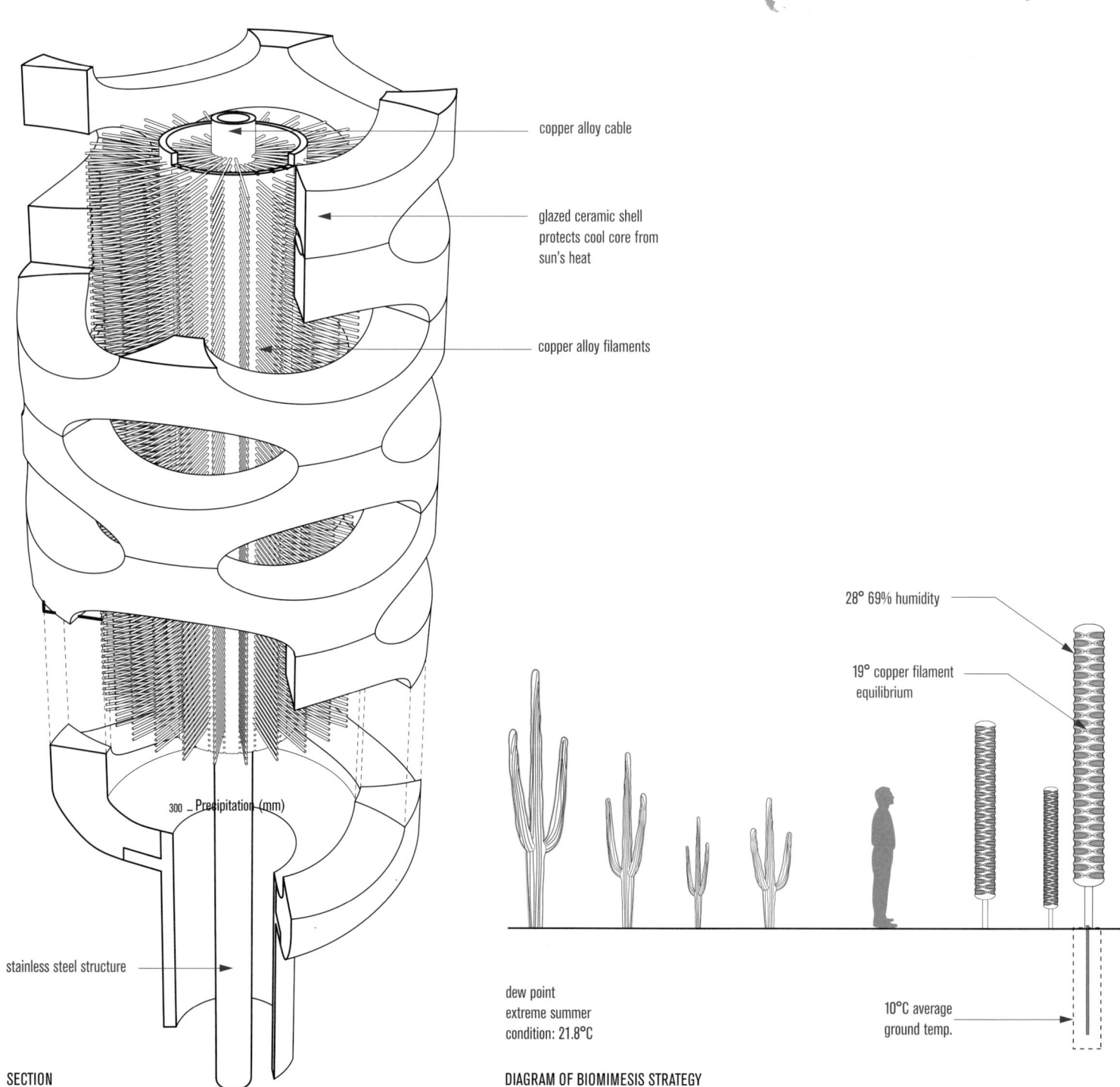

- copper alloy cable
- glazed ceramic shell protects cool core from sun's heat
- copper alloy filaments
- 300 _ Precipitation (mm)
- stainless steel structure

SECTION

- 28° 69% humidity
- 19° copper filament equilibrium

dew point extreme summer condition: 21.8°C

10°C average ground temp.

DIAGRAM OF BIOMIMESIS STRATEGY

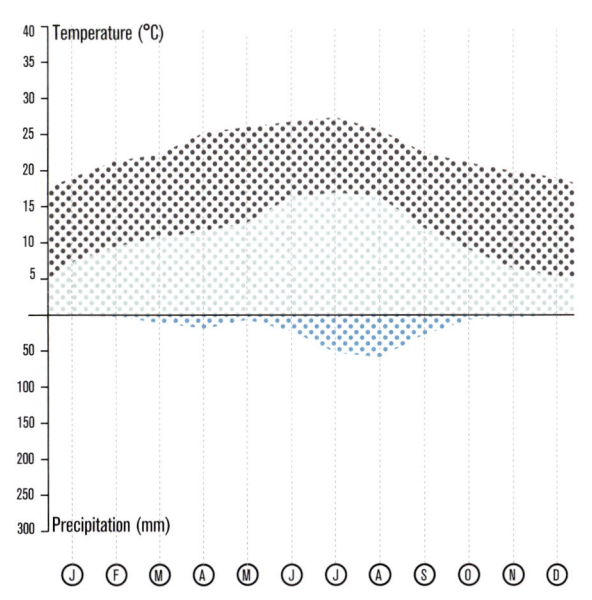

The VENA water condenser, designed by Ore Design + Technology, is a prototype for a vapor condensation device which is particularly suitable for arid climates, areas that are disconnected from water infrastructure, or areas where water sources are polluted. The design is based on heat transfer. Daytime ambient temperature is typically 5–15° C hotter than belowground temperature; spanning this differential can trigger dew point. Ore's main objective was to generate a small-scale, modular assembly of relatively low-cost, simple components, requiring no electrical input or coolants for operation. The device is intended to harvest and deliver water on-site, reducing sole dependency on centralized water conveyance. The VENA collector is conceived as an easily deployable single- or multi-unit installation, responsive to water demand and availability of space (Ore Design + Technology, 2009).

The water condenser extracts water from air by transferring cool belowground temperatures to an elevated network of copper alloy filaments, around which latent airborne water condenses and is collected. The core of this vertical assembly is an alloy cable, the key thermal conductor, which reaches up 2m from the top surface of a 20m-deep underground cistern. Extending from the conductive copper cable are angled copper alloy filaments which remain 5–15° C cooler than daytime ambient temperature. The copper cable is encased in a perforated stainless steel tube out of which the copper filaments come into contact with the ambient temperature. When air comes in contact with the cooler copper filaments, dew point is triggered; vapor condenses and continually flows down the copper cable into the cistern.

The efficiency of the system is highly dependent on local conditions. For example, Sana'a, Yemen, is 2,250m above sea level and receives about 250–300mm of rainfall per year. In these conditions, at 30° C with 60% humidity, a cubic meter of air contains 18g of vapor, out of which an estimated 35% (6.3g) could condense and drain into the cistern (Ore, 2011).

A series of interlocking ceramic discs, 60cm in diameter and 15cm in height, are stacked to form a protective shell around the copper core. The white, high-gloss ceramic discs reflect solar radiation and protect the core from heat gain. When stacked, the sectional profile of the discs forms a series of open apertures, designed to channel prevailing hot winds through the metal core.

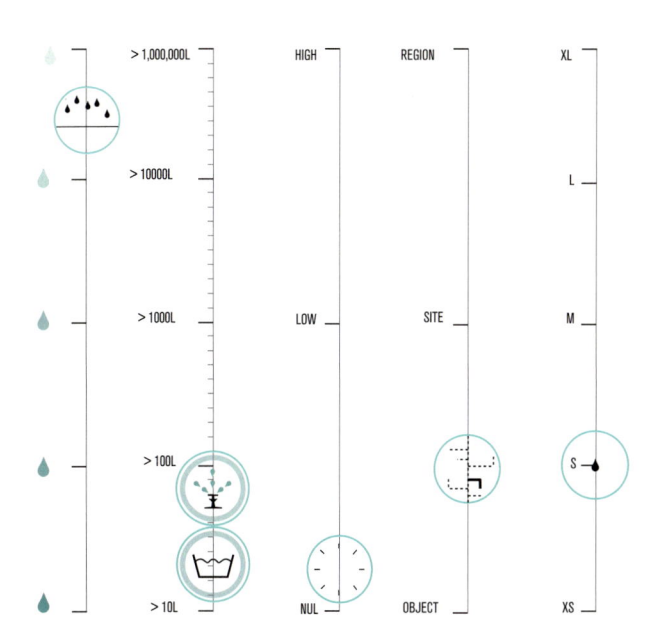

Despite VENA's many assets, it has some limitations. For instance, it is inoperable during cooler months due to lower temperature differentials. Also, since water collection from the atmosphere is dependent on the location, time of year, and relative humidity (Kogan and Trahtman, 2003), VENA cannot provide a sustained water volume and should thus be complemented with other water sources. Gandhidasan and Abualhamayel (2005) offer a wide literature review of various experiments and geographically specific metrics associated with dew collection. Their own study of dew formation on radiatively cooled pigmented polyethylene foils in Dhahran, Saudi Arabia, showed that as wind speed increases, dew collection rates increase in humid climate, whereas they decrease in relatively dry climate. Furthermore, a clear sky with humid atmosphere is required for maximum dew collection.

A study in Israel's Negev Desert demonstrated that average dew and fog amount increase with topographical elevation. Despite the greater distance from the sea, the study showed an increase of 0.015 and 0.03mm in daily dew and fog amounts, respectively, per 100m increase in elevation, resulting in a two- to three-fold increase in average daily dew and fog amounts from mean sea level to 1,000m above. A larger proportion of days with heavy dew or fog as altitude increases was also noted (Kidron, 1999).

Collection of water from the atmosphere is advantageous due to the fact that atmospheric water is of high quality (Kogan and Trahtman, 2003). However the chemistry of the water may vary from location to location and the treatment of harvested water must be taken into account prior to consumption (Lekouch, et al., 2011). For example, dew water collected in Chile was found to have very high ionic concentrations and was noted to be very corrosive, while elevated concentrations of sulfates and nitrates were found in water collected in Japan (Lekouch, et al., 2011). Dew water quality can be affected by factors such as pollution, salt from marine origin, the enhanced deposition of aerosols from the dry, arid soil, and small bacterial contents.

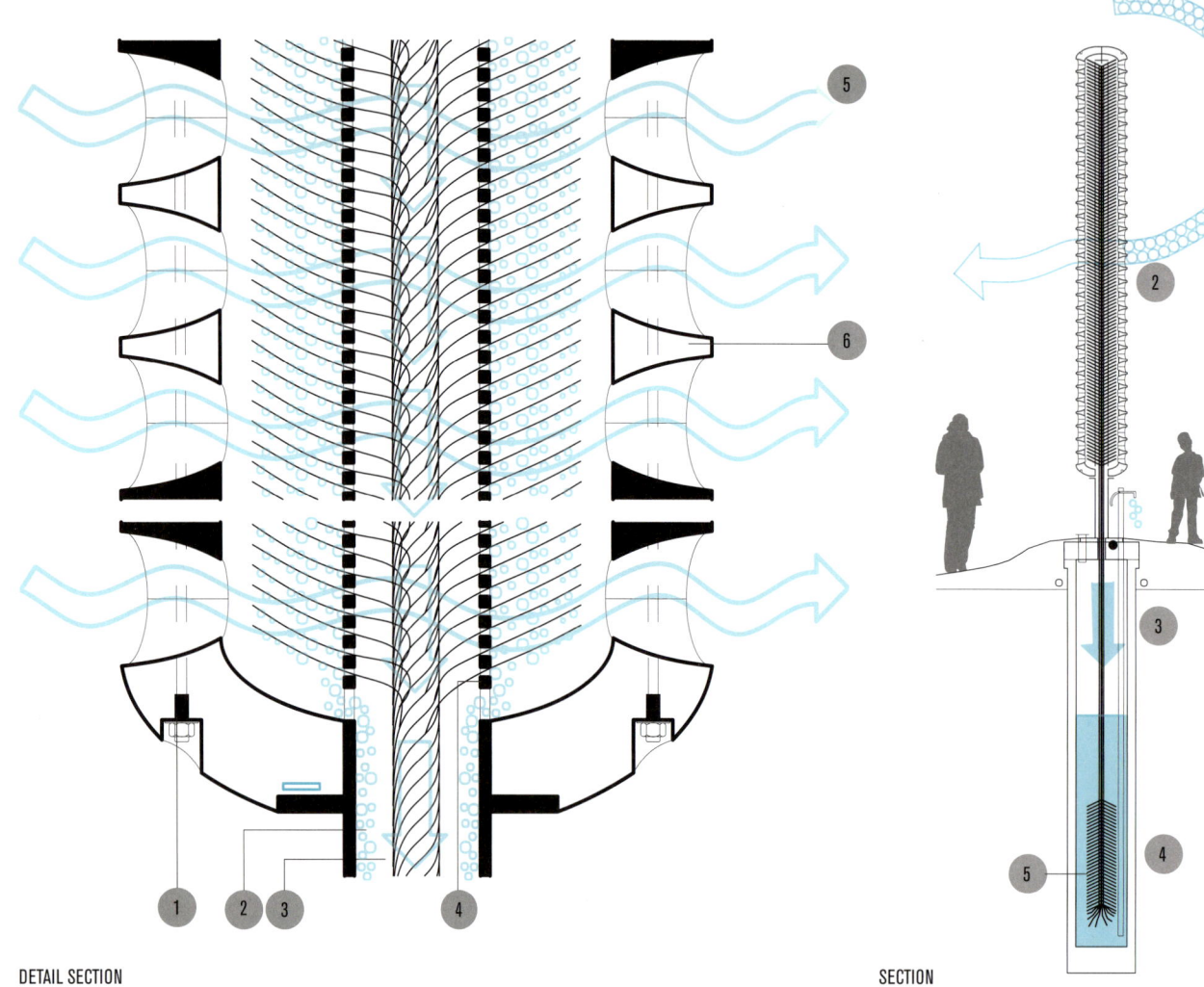

DETAIL SECTION
1 tension cable secures ceramic rings
2 condensed water drips down through tube into reservoir
3 heat is exchanged with cool well below ground
4 stainless steel structural tube is perforated within
4 shell to expose cooled earth copper filaments to
4 water laden air
5 hot air passes through cold copper coils
6 ceramic fins

SECTION
1 hot air passes through copper coils
2 hot air cools due to temperature differential
3 condensed water extracted from cooled air drips down
4 underground water reservoir
5 hot air passes through cold copper coils
6 copper coils cooled due to low belowground temperature

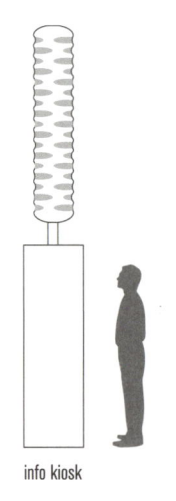

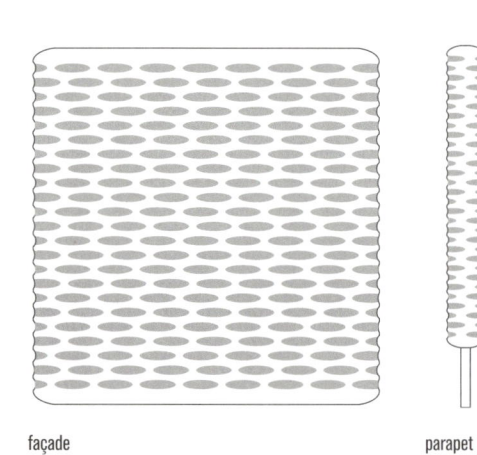

seating   info kiosk   façade   parapet

VENA AS URBAN FURNITURE   **VENA AS ARCHITECTURE**

80

MODULAR SCALABILITY BASED ON BELOWGROUND HEAT CAPACITY

AA: shallow reservoir/cool temperature
AB: shallow reservoir/cold temperature
BA: deep reservoir/cool temperature
BB: deep reservoir/cold temperature

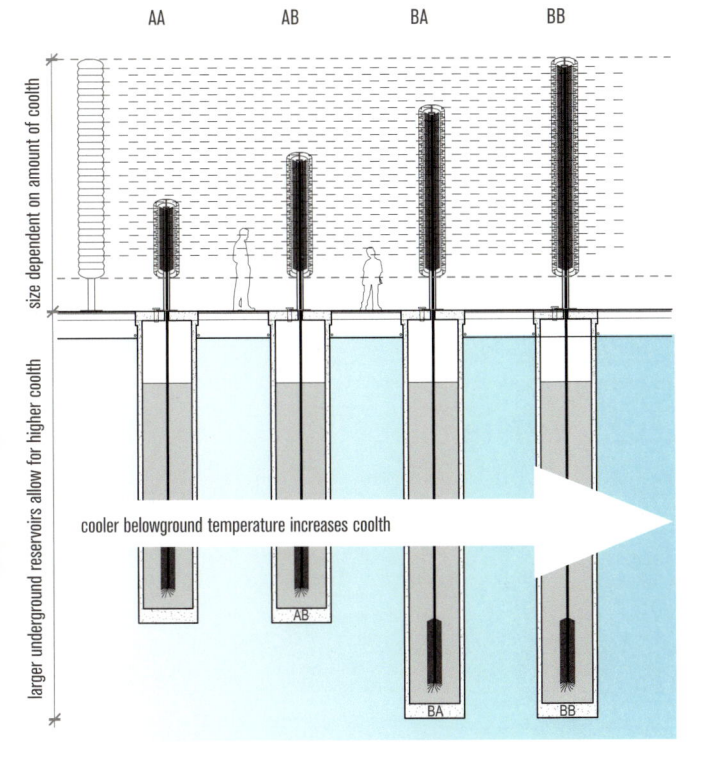

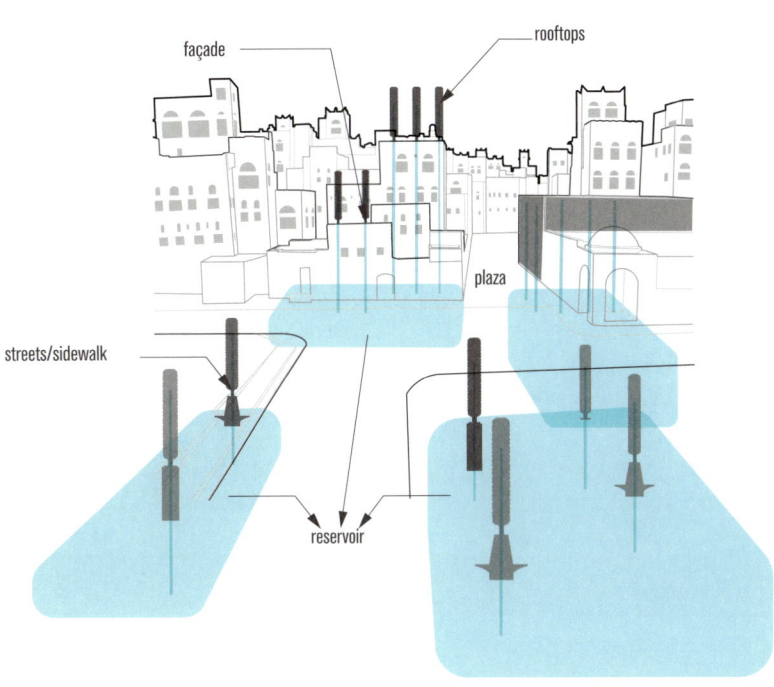

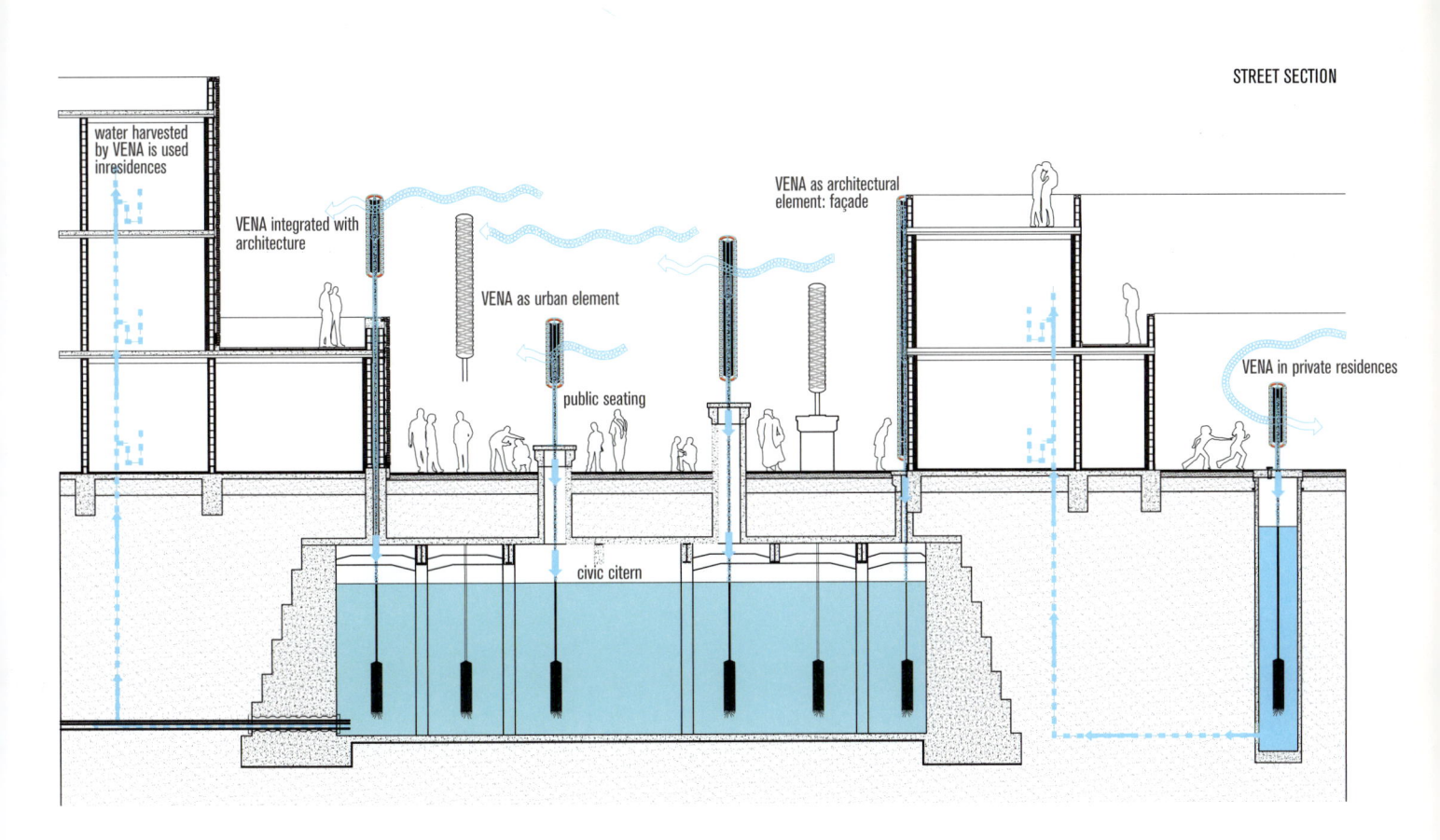

size dependent on amount of coolth
larger underground reservoirs allow for higher coolth
cooler belowground temperature increases coolth

URBAN INTEGRATION DIAGRAM

façade, rooftops, plaza, streets/sidewalk, reservoir

STREET SECTION

- water harvested by VENA is used in residences
- VENA integrated with architecture
- VENA as urban element
- public seating
- VENA as architectural element: façade
- VENA in private residences
- civic citern

81

ISLA URBANA
NGO Isla Urbana

Site: Mexico City, Mexico
Longitude & Latitude: 19°16'N 99°12'E
Annual Precipitation: 1000mm

Year: 2009
Status: Ongoing
Water Volume/Day: 163–173L
Dimensions: 10,000L/70m² rooftop surface

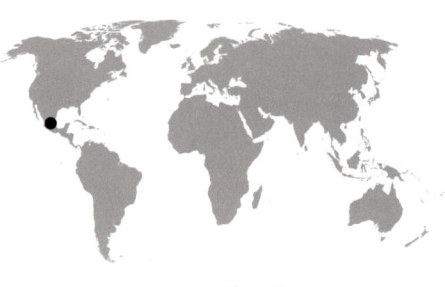

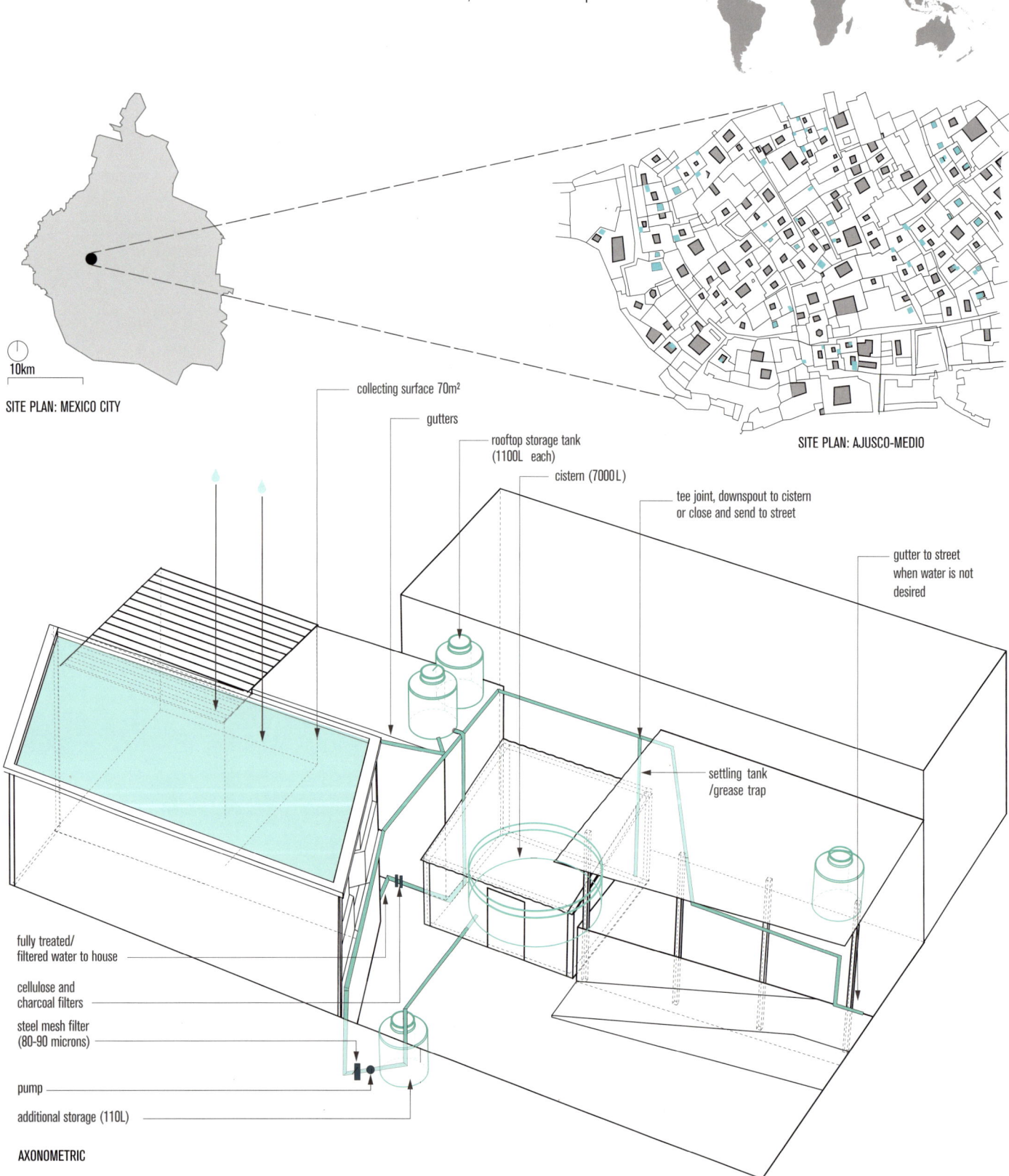

SITE PLAN: MEXICO CITY

SITE PLAN: AJUSCO-MEDIO

collecting surface 70m²
gutters
rooftop storage tank (1100L each)
cistern (7000L)
tee joint, downspout to cistern or close and send to street
gutter to street when water is not desired
settling tank /grease trap

fully treated/ filtered water to house
cellulose and charcoal filters
steel mesh filter (80-90 microns)
pump
additional storage (110L)

AXONOMETRIC

82

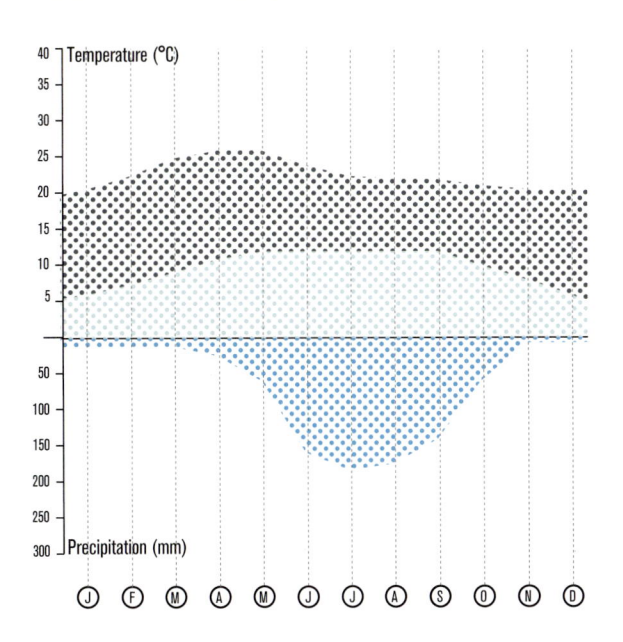

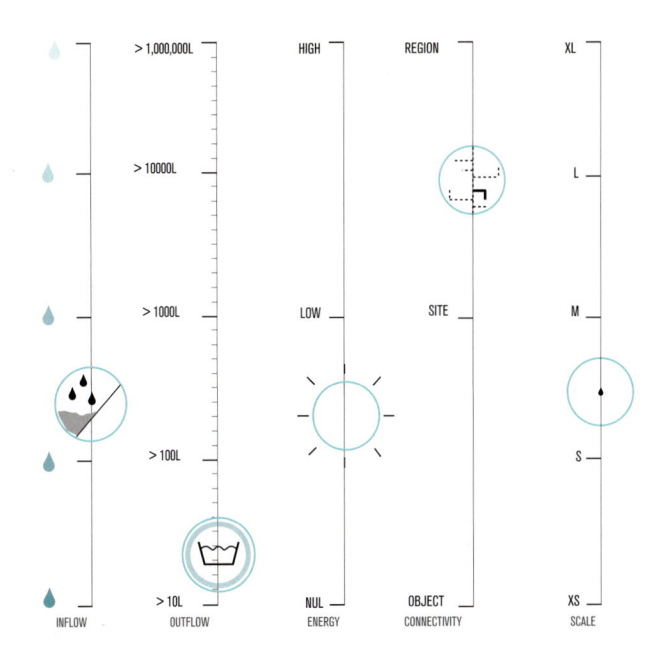

Launched in 2009, the Isla Urbana Project consists of a low-cost, low-tech, and low-maintenance system for rainwater harvesting (RWH) that can be installed and implemented for individual households within a day. The system was developed by the NGO Isla Urbana in response to the staggering number of people that suffer from inadequate water supply in Mexico City—8 million, or 36% of households. It is intended to provide about 50% of a household's annual water need (Isla Urbana [IU], 2013). The system uses commonly available materials, such as plastic pipes and fittings, rain barrels, and mesh filters, and can be assembled to retrofit any housing structure. Aside from employing economical materials, Isla Urbana importantly engages in capacity building, which includes training local plumbers in system installation and direct beneficiaries in post-installation maintenance and use. Isla Urbana's multidisciplinary team of industrial designers, engineers, urban planners, and sociologists work closely with local community group, local businesses, non-profits, NGOs, and the Mexico City government to facilitate the widespread adoption of rainwater harvesting as a viable solution to the prevalent water crisis.

Currently, Mexico City receives 70% of its water supply from the Valley of Mexico aquifer, which is greatly overexploited. This groundwater extraction contributes to the City's ongoing subsidence (~1m per 10 years) which results in broken and leaky pipes and groundwater contamination (Tortajada and Castelán, 2003). An additional 20% of the city's water supply is pumped from as far as 127km away, from a 1-km-high mountain (Grillo, 2009). The energy used to pump such vast quantities of water is the equivalent of the total energy used by as many as 8 million people in Mexico City. IU estimates that if implemented city-wide, its RWH system could provide 30% of Mexico City's water supply. Rainwater harvesting can also reduce severe flooding, which occurs during the rainy season and requires significant energy daily to pump stormwater out of the city. Hence, the colossal hydrological and structural issues that Mexico City faces could be alleviated to a certain degree in the immediate term, using affordable and simple means. At the time of publication, more than 1,100 systems had been installed, providing over 54 million liters of water to nearly 13,000 people in primarily marginalized informal urban and rural areas.

IU's RWH system includes rooftop plastic cisterns or rain barrels and conventional PVC plumbing pipes which convey the water to a sedimentation trap and mesh filter before entering a storage tank. The water is disinfected with chlorine and colloidal silver and is eventually gravity-fed through a PVC pipe to the house. Based on annual rainfall in Mexico City, IU estimates that a single 70m^2 roof, equipped with four storage tanks, can capture 60,000L/year (Isla Urbana [IU], 2013).

Four main factors affect the efficiency of the RWH. These are the nature of the catchment surface (roof) and filter, as well as tank size and water consumption. Roof orientation, design, and materials account for losses that are measured using a runoff coefficient, typically measured at 0.8–0.9 for a sloping tiled roof (Fewkes, 1999). Pitched roofs oriented towards the dominant wind, covered with an impervious surface such as bitumen, have lower runoff loss than horizontal roofs with gravel, for example. A second factor involves the coarse filter, which removes larger debris, such as leaves, moss, and grit, before runoff enters the tank. The filter usually accounts for volumetric losses at a coefficient of 0.9 (Leggett, et al., 2001). Finally, water tank size and water consumption are interdependent factors. The design volume of the tank is dependent on household water consumption rather than on the contributing area of the roof (Vaes and Berlamont, 1999).

As well as directly installing RWH systems, IU trains plumbers to not only implement RWH within their communities but also to maintain leaking or deficient water infrastructure. This investment in developing local RWH knowledge contributes to the long-term sustainability of the project and to wide dissemination of the system. (For additional information on capacity-building strategies, see Baker & Ngai, p. 61-68).

The main challenge of IU and other RWH systems is to confront the persistent skepticism vis-à-vis technologies for water harvesting (Domènech and Saurí, 2011). This skepticism is partially founded, because even though rainwater harvested from residential roofs can meet WHO standards with regard to measured inorganic compounds, fecal coliform levels have been found to exceed the safe limits for drinking water (Abdulla and Al-Shareef, 2009). Hence, to obtain potable water from RWH systems, affordable water purification systems, such as the Kanchan Arsenic Filter (p. 70-73), should be added.

Since the initial capital required to install RWH is significant, long payback periods constitute a problem for low income households, unless this cost is mitigated, as is the case for the Isla Urbana Project, by startup capital grants and material and installation assistance.

Valley of Mexico

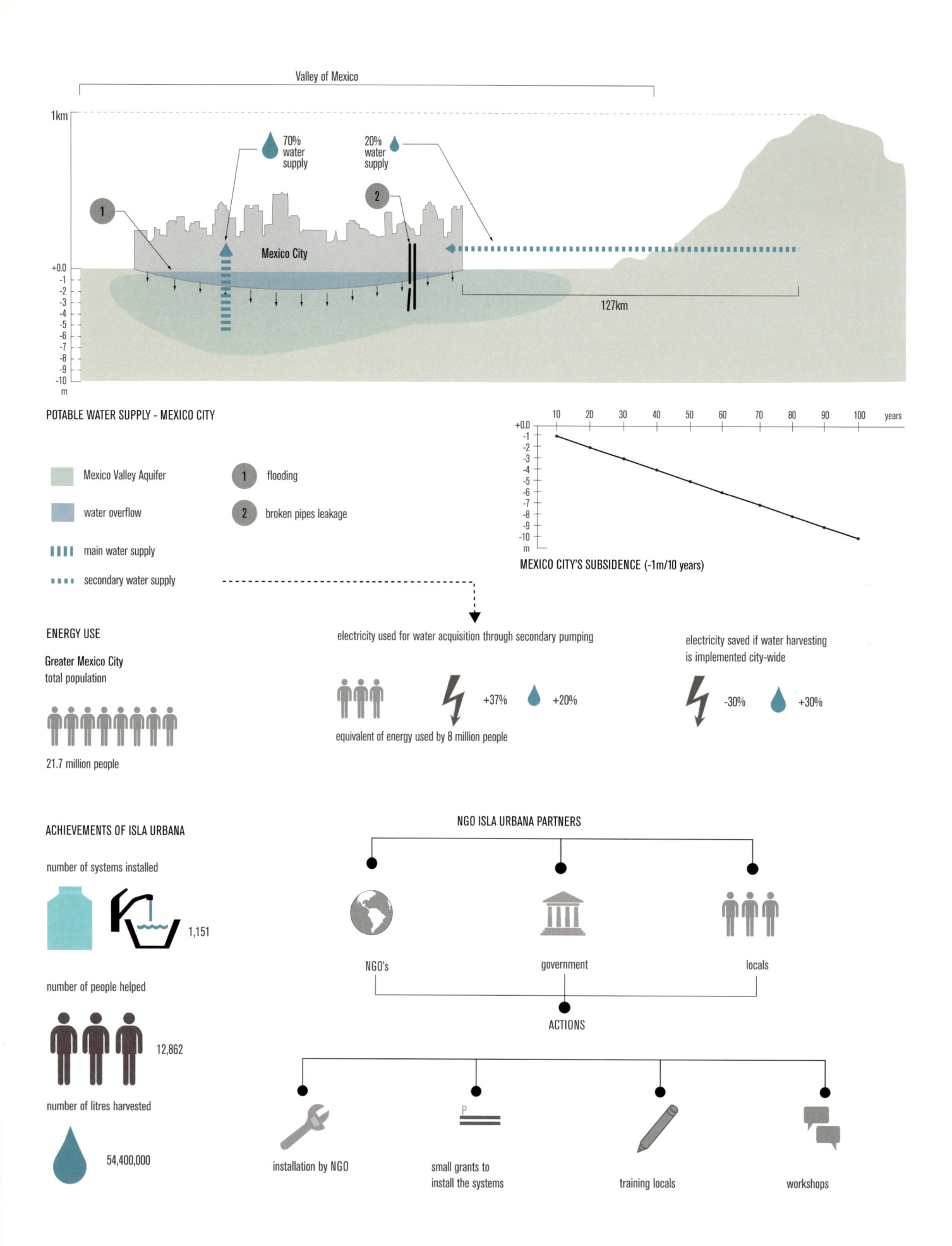

POTABLE WATER SUPPLY - MEXICO CITY

- Mexico Valley Aquifer
- water overflow
- main water supply
- secondary water supply

1. flooding
2. broken pipes leakage

70% water supply
20% water supply
127km

MEXICO CITY'S SUBSIDENCE (-1m/10 years)

ENERGY USE

Greater Mexico City total population

21.7 million people

electricity used for water acquisition through secondary pumping
+37% +20%
equivalent of energy used by 8 million people

electricity saved if water harvesting is implemented city-wide
-30% +30%

ACHIEVEMENTS OF ISLA URBANA

number of systems installed
1,151

number of people helped
12,862

number of litres harvested
54,400,000

NGO ISLA URBANA PARTNERS

- NGO's
- government
- locals

ACTIONS

- installation by NGO
- small grants to install the systems
- training locals
- workshops

STAGE 1　　　　　　　　STAGE 2　　　　　　　　STAGE 3　　　　　　　　STAGE 4

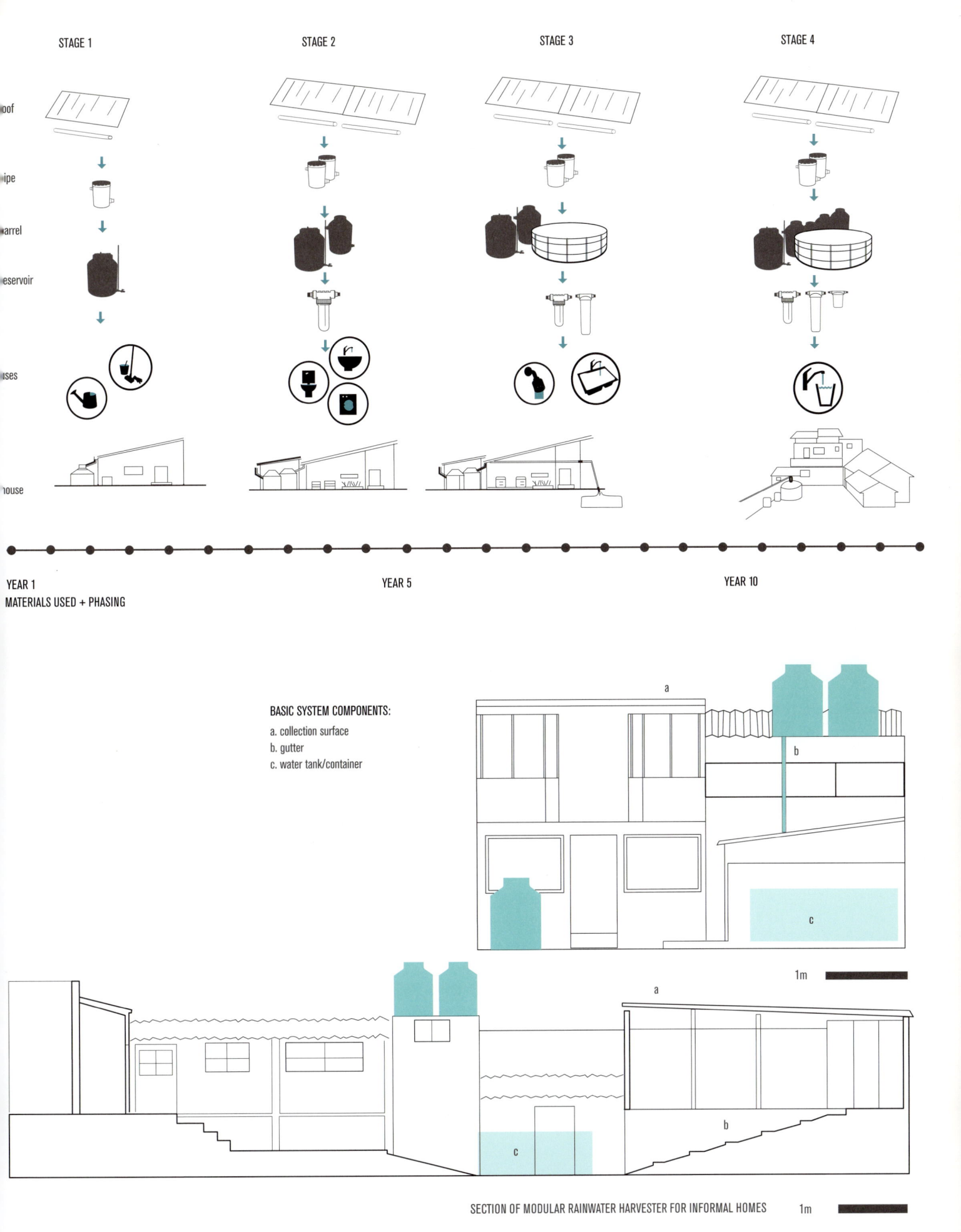

roof

pipe

barrel

reservoir

uses

house

YEAR 1　　　　　　　　　　　　　　YEAR 5　　　　　　　　　　　　　　YEAR 10
MATERIALS USED + PHASING

BASIC SYSTEM COMPONENTS:
a. collection surface
b. gutter
c. water tank/container

1m

SECTION OF MODULAR RAINWATER HARVESTER FOR INFORMAL HOMES　　1m

85

DOWN TO EARTH
Ruth Kedar

Site: Negev Desert, Israel
Longitude & Latitude: 30°15'N 35°0'E
Annual Precipitation: 100mm

Year: 2007
Status: Schematic Design
Water Volume/Day: 39L
Dimensions: Prototype catchment area is 521,384m²

LEGEND
- Jewish town
- Bedouin town
- planned reservoir
- existing reservoir
- municipal boundary

SITE PLAN

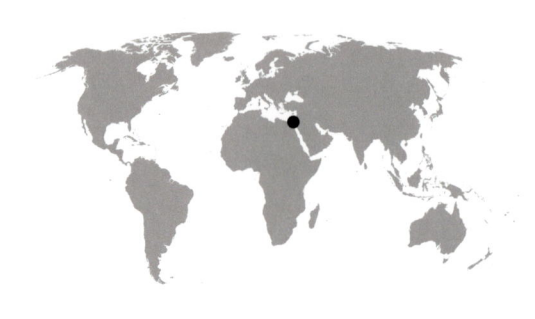

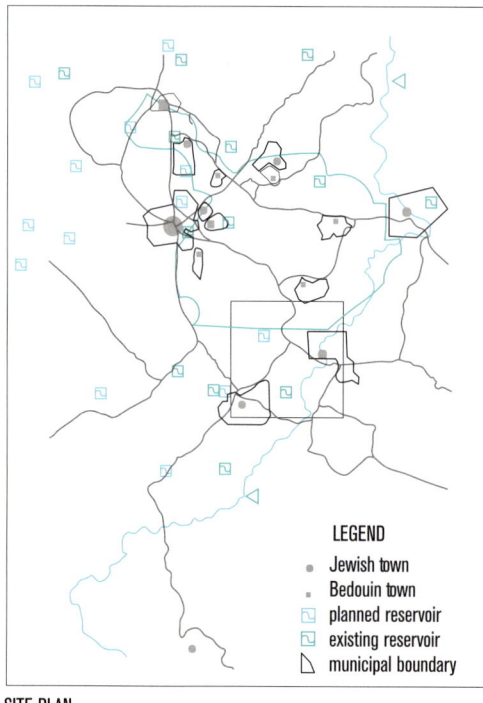

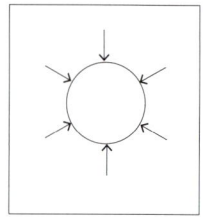

UNRECOGNIZED VILLAGES AS PERIPHERY OF EXISTING URBAN SETTLEMENTS
The unrecognized villages are often located in the periphery of existing urban settlements, taking advantage of the services and amenities of the towns while preserving a non-urban character

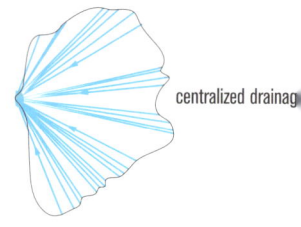

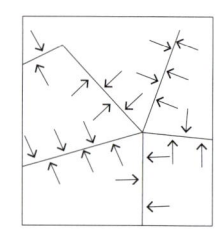

UNRECOGNIZED VILLAGES OCCUPYING THE "NEUTRAL" INFRASTRUCTURE
- Infrastructure is often perceived as neutral territory
- The unrecognized villages are often located by the roads, and inhabitants use them in order to reach urban centers and services

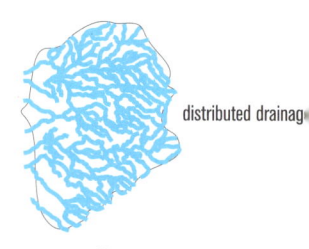

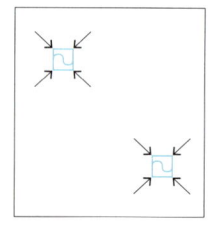

NEW SETTLEMENTS AS "PARASITES" ON NEW WATER
- Around 100 new reservoirs are planned to be built by the JNF, many of which are located in the Negev
- By locating the new inhabitable platforms near or in place of the planned reservoirs, it is possible to develop a water infrastructure which branches from the centralized water system, and is therefore not dependent on political policies

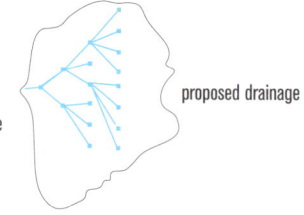

EXISTING AND PROPOSED WATER SYSTEM

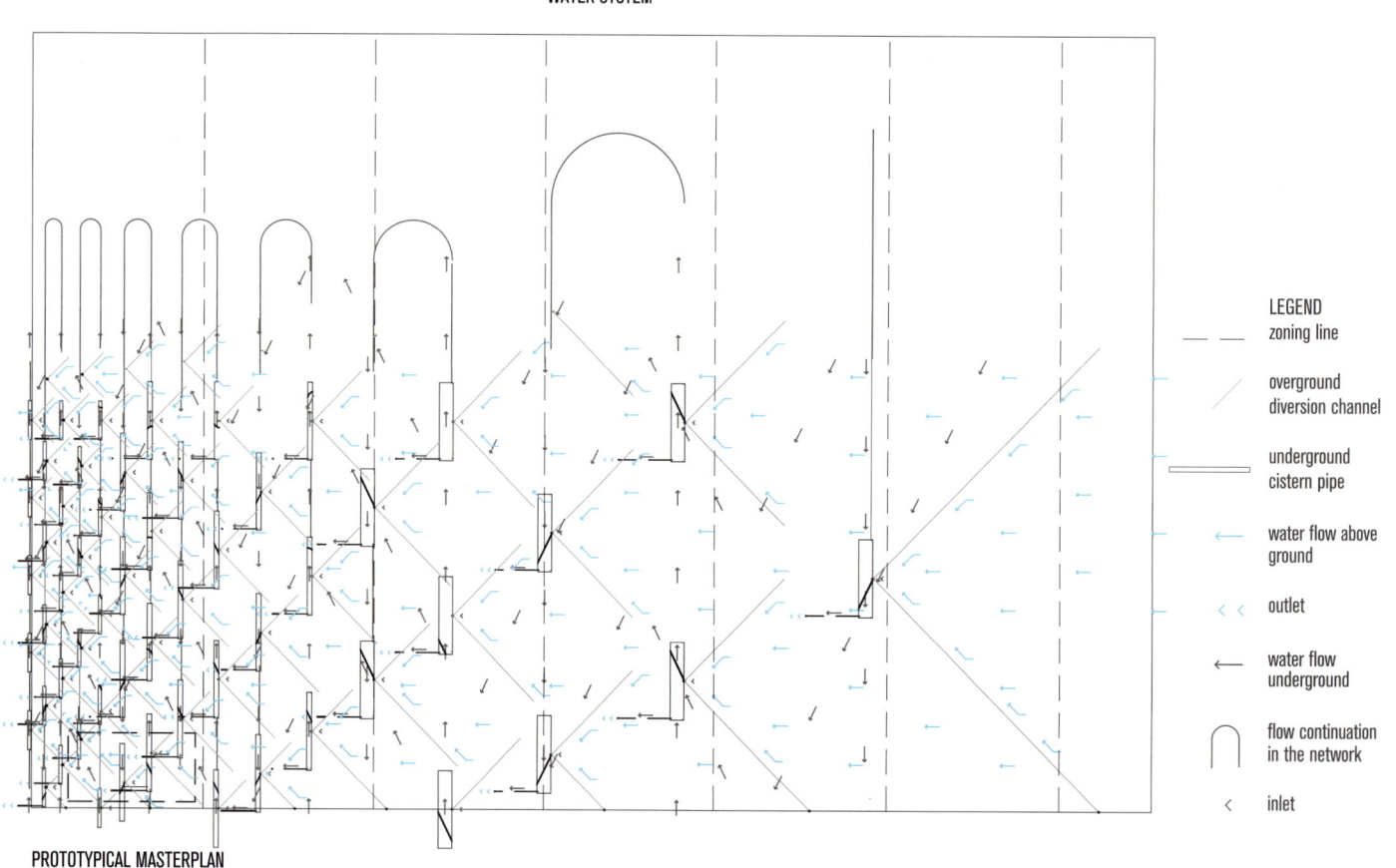

centralized drainage

distributed drainage

proposed drainage

LEGEND
- zoning line
- overground diversion channel
- underground cistern pipe
- water flow above ground
- outlet
- water flow underground
- flow continuation in the network
- inlet

PROTOTYPICAL MASTERPLAN

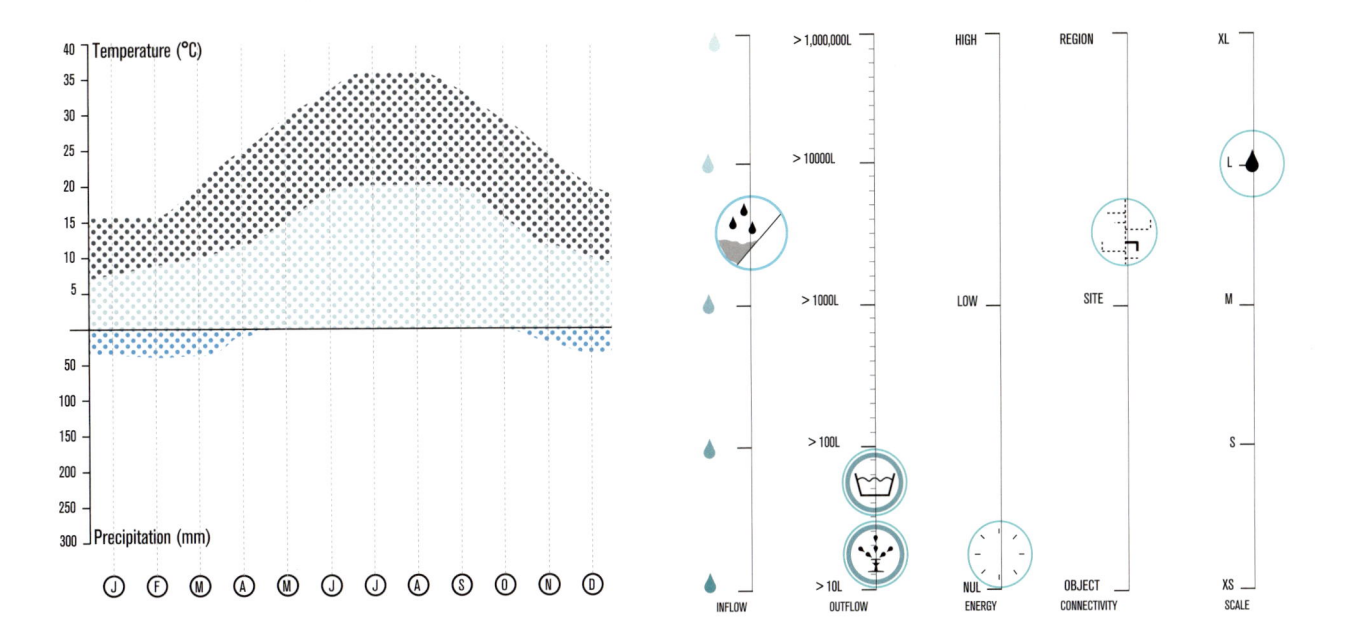

The Down to Earth project by Ruth Kedar proposes a stormwater or rainwater runoff collection system for semi-nomadic communities, some of which do not have full access to public water infrastructure, in the Negev Desert's mountain region. In some of these areas, the depth of local aquifers and their brackish water prevent construction of conventional wells from being a viable solution. In response, the Down to Earth project proposes an underground cistern, integrated into the foundation of each individual house, to capture stormwater runoff during the rainy season in order to increase water reserves. By adapting ancient technology for contemporary use, the project aims to increase water availability in areas where it is an increasingly rare resource.

The cistern consists of modular precast concrete components that can be assembled using basic construction techniques. Its design represents a contemporary adaptation of historical and regional desert technologies, including the quanat, a horizontal tunnel that taps underground water in an alluvial fan without pumps or equipment and brings it to the surface so that the water can be used. These tunnels typically have a 1-2% slope ratio and run for up to 30km (Lightfoot, 1997; Prinz, 2002). The project also borrows from ancient Nabatean systems of runoff irrigation, which employed shallow channels, minor topographic grading, rock-lined soil, and stone weirs to redirect and retain water in low-lying agricultural fields (Evaneri, Shanan, and Tadmor, 1968).

Runoff is first collected by aboveground channels and then diverted to an underground cistern sized according to slope ratio, catchment area, and quantity of water needs. The cisterns are also equipped with a flow valve to account for overflow. This would allow each individual unit to connect to other subterranean reservoirs down the slope in the same community. In this respect, the networked water reserve can expand to accommodate a growing population by constructing and connecting additional subterranean structures. Runoff catchment is also thought to be a means to mitigate soil erosion during flash floods, which are common occurrences in desert conditions.

Rubin (1988) describes that as early as the 4th century, cisterns were common in desert areas throughout the region, particularly as part of house foundations in towns. The cisterns proved to be a more efficient solution than dams, which were often abandoned because of evaporation and siltation problems. Consecutive years of drought are common in these areas, and precipitation occurs in short, heavy storms, causing floods and only allowing for very low infiltration rates. Rubin's study confirmed that ancient inhabitants used various methods of collecting water to compensate for the low rainfall and high annual variability.

It is important to note that while perennial springs do exist in the Negev, they are often located in deep wadis, unsuitable for settlement or transport of the water via aqueducts. In addition, the flow rate of these springs is too low and infrequent to be a permanent water source. Therefore, the most common technologies found in the Negev are cisterns. The cisterns found in towns are built as part of the foundation of each house with hydraulic plaster (Rubin, 1988). Large public cisterns are also found throughout the region, with capacities ranging up to 40,000m^3 (Cowan, 2008).

Down to Earth does not specify the target use of the harvested water. While in ancient times runoff harvesting was used for all household uses including drinking and bathing, much of the literature on the subject indicates that the primary use of runoff catchment is irrigation. Prinz (2002) promotes the revival of traditional runoff collection for irrigation uses in arid and semi-arid areas and offers a matrix of water harvesting and storage techniques. Likewise, Boers and Ben-Asher (1982) cite a range of literature about rainwater harvesting for irrigation uses and outline technical instructions with respect to micro-catchment sizes, ratio of contributing area to collecting area, and layout.

Zhu and colleagues (2004) also suggest runoff reuse for irrigation, as opposed to drinking. Their study found that rainwater can be collected from different catchment surfaces, such as mortar roofs, cement-paved courtyards, and compacted land or road surfaces, and stored effectively in cisterns. However, for water collected from the land and road surfaces which showed elevated levels of inorganic, organic, and bacteriological contaminants, water purification is necessary. Rice (2004) found that the provision of drinking water to wildlife via subsurface water harvesting in Idaho's semi-arid and remote rangelands was highly effective. Underground cisterns, whether individually employed or networked across multiple households and buildings, are more viable in low density areas where runoff water is of high quality, for household and animal husbandry or wildlife use, or relatively clean, for irrigation purposes.

In areas where the process of desertification continues to reduce the available arable land and where water is a rare resource, runoff-rainwater irrigation should become a valuable option. These areas can be found in Syria, Jordan, Yemen, Southern Arabia, Sinai, Northern Sahara/Tunisia, Afghanistan, Pakistan, Southern Spain, Kenya, Mali, Nigeria, Australia, and parts of North and South America (Lüttge, 2010). Although the applicability of these techniques depends on geomorphological conditions and soil types, many regions meet these criteria, and in fact already practice such techniques to some extent.

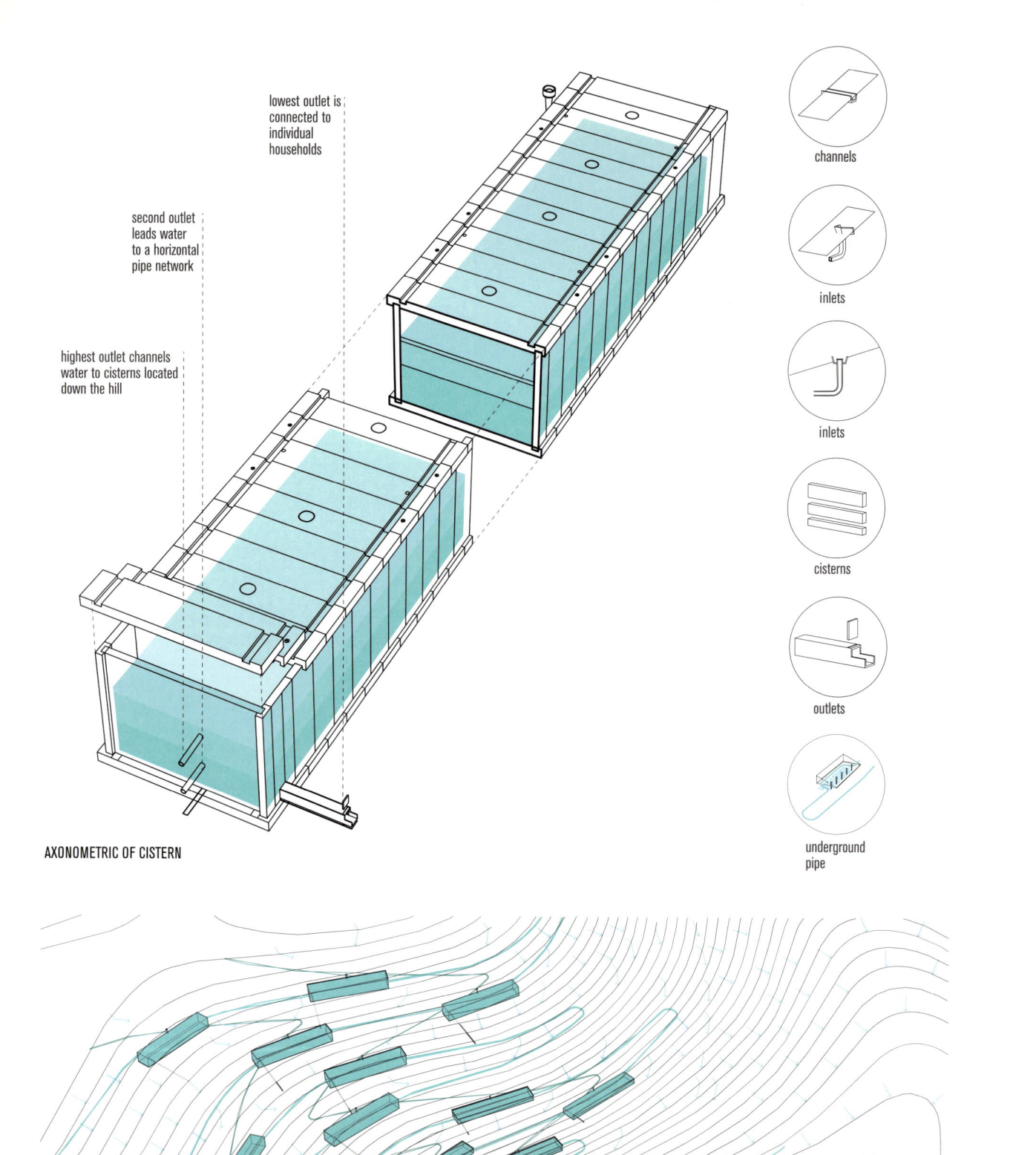

lowest outlet is connected to individual households

second outlet leads water to a horizontal pipe network

highest outlet channels water to cisterns located down the hill

channels

inlets

inlets

cisterns

outlets

underground pipe

AXONOMETRIC OF CISTERN

LEGEND
inlet
outlet
storage
pipe
over ground water flow

PLAN OF UNDERGROUND PIPES

88

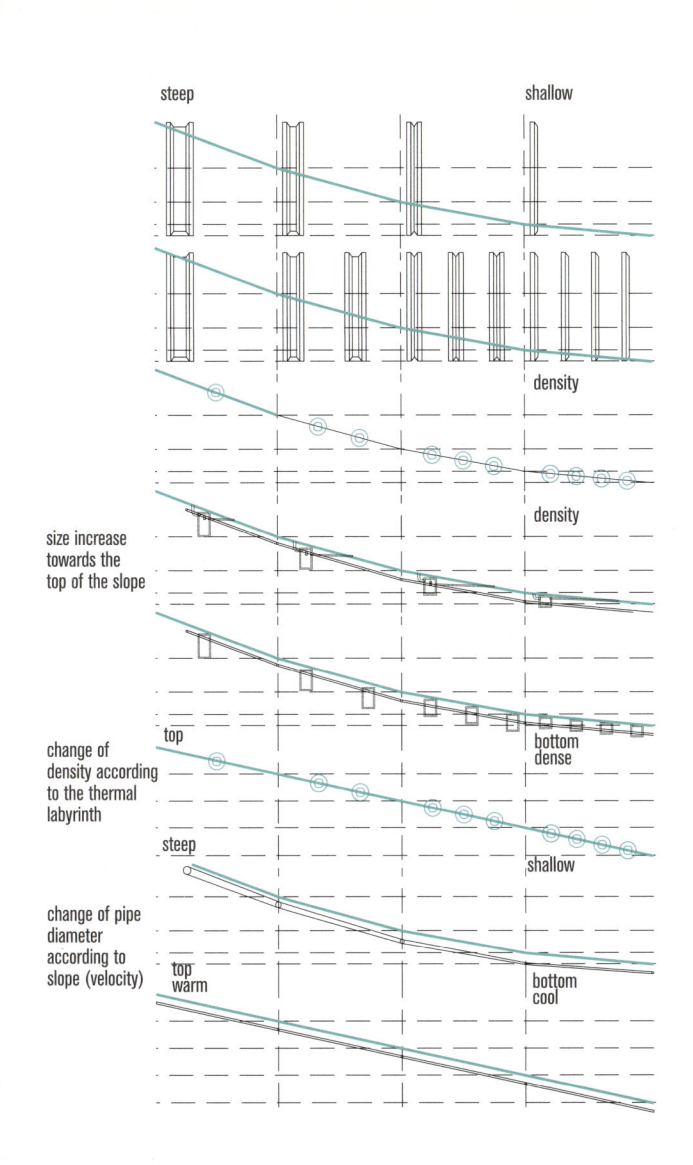

steep **shallow**

density

size increase towards the top of the slope

density

change of density according to the thermal labyrinth

top — bottom dense

change of pipe diameter according to slope (velocity)

steep — shallow

top warm — bottom cool

CISTERN-TO-SLOPE RATIO DIAGRAMS

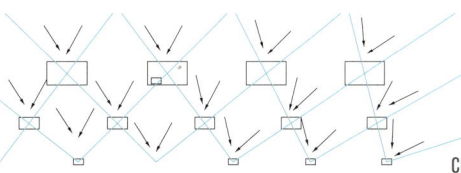

CATCHMENT AREA SIZES

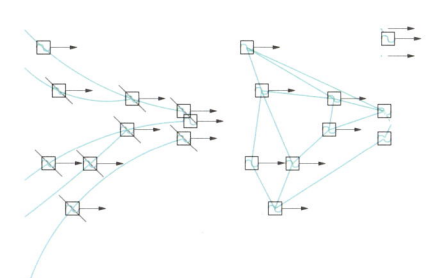

MAINTENANCE - INDIVIDUAL

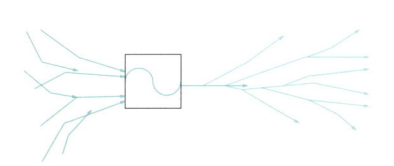

MAINTENANCE - COMMUNITY

CHANNEL
1. Channel water to underground network as fast as possible to reduce loss by evaporation (divert water towards inlets)
2. Reduce velocity to reduce erosion and make water flow but not sediment into the underground system

INLETS
1. Allow water into underground system but reduce sediment excess located at bottom of each catchment area

CISTERNS
1. Store water at time of plenty
2. Delay the 'flood' effect - gain control of water use
3. Keep water at higher areas of the site to be able to use gravity
4. Correlation between catchment area and cistern size

OUTLETS
1. Requires control to open and close
2. Location will dictate later occupation of the site
3. Suggest uses of irrigation or inhabitation in nearby area
4. Density of outlets is defined by location on the underground thermal network

UNDERGROUND PIPES
1. Connecting underground storage and creating a storage network which is based on water level and gravity
2. Creating underground thermal labyrinth system
3. The thermal network is suggesting zoning according to change of temperature

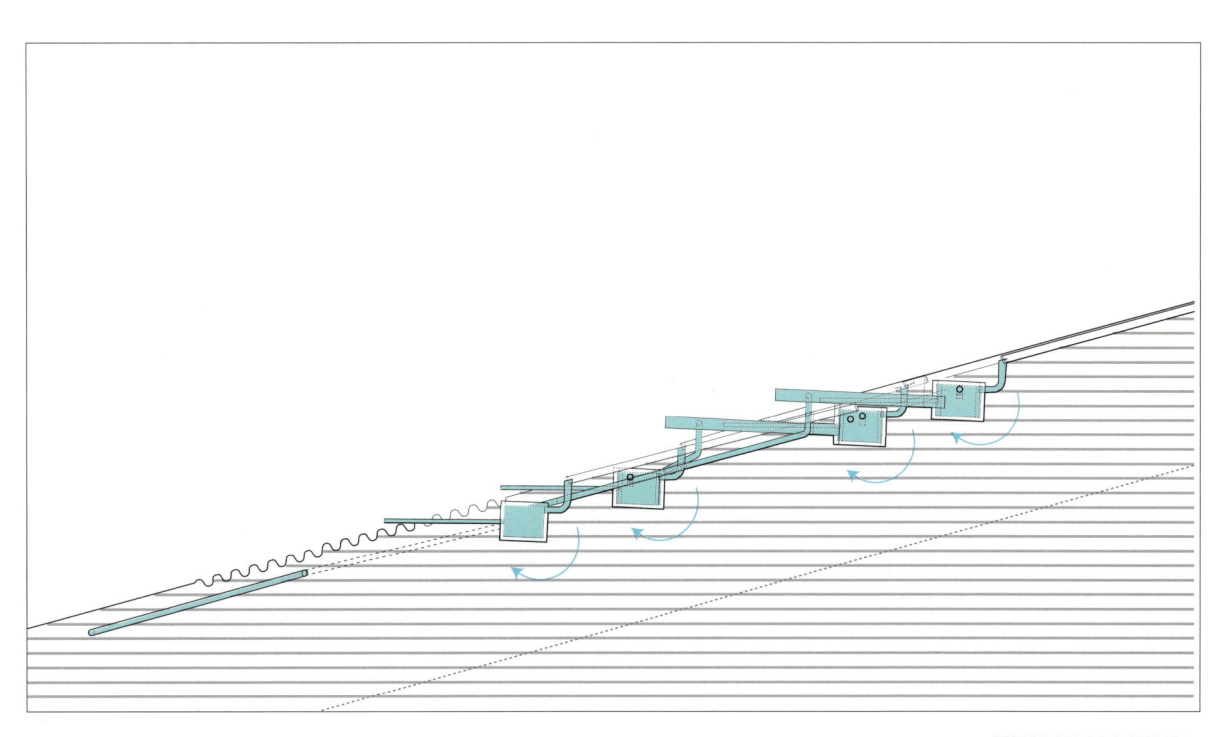

SECTION OF WATER STORAGE

2
WATER
FOR
AGRICULTURAL
PRODUCTION

Introduction: Water Equals Food

Water equals food. Conversely, water scarcity equals famine, which is inextricably linked to poverty and underdevelopment. Although agriculture accounts for 70% of all water withdrawn by the agricultural, municipal, and industrial (including energy) sectors worldwide (World Water Assessment Programme, 2012), there are 842 million hungry people in the world and 98% of them are in developing countries (World Food Programme, 2014). Three-quarters of all hungry people live in rural areas, mainly in the villages of Asia and Africa. Around half of the world's hungry people are from smallholder farming communities, surviving off marginal lands prone to natural disasters like drought or flood. Another 20% belong to landless families dependent on farming and about 10% live in communities whose livelihoods depend on herding, fishing, or forest resources. The remaining 20% live in shantytowns on the periphery of the biggest cities in developing countries. The numbers of poor and hungry city dwellers are rising rapidly along with the world's total urban population (World Food Programme, 2014).

Food demand is predicted to increase 60% by 2050, and at the same time, economic growth and individual wealth are shifting diets from predominantly starches to meat and dairy, which require more water. Furthermore, the distance food travels from field to fork along an extensive supply chain results in wasted food at each step along the way, which also equals wasted water (World Food Programme, 2014).

Another aspect to the relation between water and food is that agricultural practices are often associated with environmental degradation including, among many other negative impacts, the rapid depletion of aquifers and the degradation of aquatic ecologies as a result of over-extraction, damming, diversion, and contamination. Today, 250 million hectares of land are cultivated, which amounts to about five times more area than at the beginning of the 20th century. This exponential expansion is a key factor in the vast deforestation and decline of biodiversity worldwide, which results in recurrent flooding, erosion, and loss of viable agricultural land, not to mention loss of human communities.

Globally, we are not "out of water." In fact, there is enough water for present and future needs for food cultivation. Clearly, water availability and high agricultural productivity is not only a question of geographical distribution and climate patterns, but also a question of management and technology. The Sudano Sahel region, for instance, has ample surface and underground water resources, yet 80% of the population derives its income from rain-fed agriculture. A combination of drought, poor soils, and inappropriate crop selection results in low agriculture productivity and endemic poverty. As authors Dov Pasterank and Lennart Woltering demonstrate, a transition to irrigated agricultural practices, which utilize the existing water resources, is the necessary solution to alleviate famine and poverty. In contrast, irrigated arid and non-arid regions alike still depend on non-renewable fresh water resources as the primary water source. Here, a technological shift to desalinated water and/or treated wastewater would ensure a consistent water supply.

The Design Perspective

Given the recent interest in urban agriculture among the architectural design fields, the questions we wish to raise here pertain to how design can contribute to rethinking food production in relation to land use and water management, particularly in context of the above-mentioned issues, such as the redevelopment of rural areas and shantytowns, the environmental mitigation of aquatic ecosystems, and the integration of urban food production as a means to increase urban food security and water conservation.

This chapter invites a diversity of perspectives from the fields of agronomy, hydrology, and water engineering, as well as architecture, landscape architecture, and urban design, to open up a discourse around the following questions:

- How is water configured in urban agriculture today?
- What are some of the most progressive water management strategies for agriculture in arid regions?
- How can these approaches serve as design principles for urban design?
- Finally, what are the potentials for arriving at a unified water management strategy that would synergistically serve agriculture, urban design, and aquatic ecosystems?

Urban Agriculture

The topic of urban food production is at the forefront of contemporary architectural discourse. Several publications and conferences (Side Note 1) that investigate the relationship between food and cities have surfaced in recent years partly as a response to sustainability, namely issues of environmental mitigation and adaptation, human health, and social equity. Although urban agriculture is not a new concept or practice, the subject has evolved as an extension of design objectives such as smart growth that supports mixed land use developments as a means to achieve livable cities, the repurposing of urban dross and vacant lots, and the design of productive and performative landscapes such as constructed ecologies and green infrastructure. Urban food production ultimately addresses a life style question concerning the individual's stake in making decisions about where food comes from and how it affects one's health.

The subject of food production in urban contexts touches upon a vast array of technical and logistical details ranging from horticulture and greenhouses, to policy and business strategies, to community engagement. Within the discipline of urban design, the subject links to a lineage of 20th century Modernist visions for urban planning and ambitions for social engineering (Waldheim, 2010), as well as more contemporary Everyday Urbanism (Chase, Crawford, and Kaliski, 2008) which includes backyard kitchen gardens, community gardens, and farmer's markets. The focus is primarily on the transformation of built form and program. The efforts, thus far, have been in generating visions for a new life style and getting various stakeholders to buy into the general idea. Few publications have focused on analyzing the pro forma of urban agriculture and associated implications on infrastructure (e.g., increased water demand, potential for a dual water system), environmental impact (e.g., effect of fertilizer runoff on water bodies), and economic feasibility (e.g., labor, distribution) (see, for example, Viljoen, Bohn, and Howe, 2005).

Fadi Masoud critiques the superficial imagery that the New Urbanist model paints of "(an) agrarian landscape as a backdrop to settlement" for neglecting to consider and reconfigure water infrastructure. Masoud calls for an integrated water cycle management where water supply, stormwater, wastewater, and aquatic ecosystems are managed as interconnected systems that span multiple organizational, neighborhood, and regional boundaries, and where the flows and cycles of resources are embedded in architectural and urban code. Such a charge is important insofar as it shifts the focus from haphazard urban agriculture as it primarily manifests in the form of community-run gardens, and opens up a bigger question to decision makers about transitioning to closed loop urban water-sanitation systems and systemizing a new productive landscape typology within the built environment.

That said, the essays by Masoud and Chaouni highlight the important role that an integrated approach to landscape, urban, and architectural design can play in hydrologic analysis and projective modeling of water management in relation to food production. Designers have the capacity to envision new and unconventional scenarios and produce multi-functional solutions by synthesizing and materializing diverse sets of scientific data. The authors, however, encourage designers to collaborate with the natural and social science disciplines in order to quantify the performance metrics of their proposals. They also highlight the relevance of often forgotten, or abandoned vernacular building practices that not only have high performance attributes, but also have an ongoing cultural significance.

Closed Loop Systems

As Eilon Adar describes, a major shift in approaching water in context of agricultural production is to consider water a commodity, not a resource. Although contradictory to the notion that water is a human right with regards to drinking water supply, in context of the economics of food production, water as commodity means that its utilization is extremely efficient. Since every drop counts, farmers use a range of water qualities including brackish water and treated municipal or agricultural effluent, as well as efficient and smart (e.g. sensor activated) irrigation control methods. In effect, water's monetary value incentivizes invention and inventiveness, and a zero-waste policy.

---

1. Design publications: *On Farming (2010), Carrot City: Creating Places for Urban Agriculture (2011), Urban Agriculture: Growing Healthy, Sustainable Places (2011), Designing Urban Agriculture: A Complete Guide to the Planning, Design, Construction, Maintenance and Management of Edible Landscapes (2013)*.

Design conferences: 6th International AESOP Sustainable Food Planning Conference, Leeuwarden, The Netherlands, 2014; Global Urban Agriculture Summit, Bonn, Germany, 2014; Urban Agriculture Summit, Toronto, Canada, 2012; Food and the City, Dumbarton Oaks Research Library and Collection, Washington, DC, 2012.

A few nations have systematically replaced potable water with alternative water sources, including treated wastewater and desalinated water. Water conservation is further optimized through an industrial ecology approach, whereby water cascades through a network of end users to produce a closed loop system in which waste becomes input for new processes (by-product synergy, "waste-to-feed" exchanges), as well as smart irrigation techniques and appropriate crop selection.

Effluent reclamation and reuse on a national scale in Israel, for example, is highly effective in bridging the gap between demand and availability. Moreover, it is infinitely more reliable than annual rainfall thanks to the year-round supply of municipal sewage. The extensive treatment method, which includes stabilization reservoirs or constructed wetlands, is massive in size at the city-region scale but offers seasonal and multi-year storage which bridges seasonal and annual gaps of drought with the potential for constant irrigation and peak irrigation in the summer.

At a business-to-business scale, networks of end users synergistically exchange surplus low-quality water and residue. In effect, multiple end users utilize the same unit of water for their crops and operations. For instance, surplus water collected from peppers and tomatoes is redirected to a grape variety that can tolerate a higher level of salinity and benefit from the residual fertilizers. Brackish water is used in aquaculture and then reused for irrigation of a salt-tolerant olive tree. Surplus nitrate from ornamental fish cultivation is used for aquatic flowers, while the effluent from fish farms is used in date palm plantations. The final residue, sludge, is digested into methane and redistributed to the fish farms. In addition to achieving zero waste, each end user has the ability to custom-formulate the appropriate water quality flowing through their operation.

Technological Adaptation

According to Dov Pasternak and Lennart Woltering, the Sudano Sahelian region is not "out of water" but lacking in the appropriate irrigation technology. The region has significant quantity of underground and surface water, but less than 1% of its cultivated land is irrigated even though 80% of the population is dependent on subsistence agriculture. The International Crops Research Institute for the Semi-Arid Tropics (ICRISAT) specifically targets millions of smallholder producers who currently use labor-intensive and wasteful manual irrigation methods that result in low agricultural productivity. Its African Market Garden (AMG) system is a kit comprised of a low-pressure drip irrigation that is complemented with suitable varieties of high-value vegetable and fruit crops. It allows small producers to have access to drip irrigation, usually limited to large commercial farms, thereby improving their productivity. This case demonstrates that the informal (private) small-scale irrigation sector, which operates in a more market-driven fashion, is more profitable than more expensive formal sector irrigation initiatives.

According to the World Food Programme, women are the world's primary food producers, yet cultural traditions and social structures often mean women are much more affected by hunger and poverty than men (World Food Programme, 2014). The AMG provides a return on labor that is 3 to 3.5 times greater than that of a traditional system, and 15 to 18 times greater than the average daily income in Niger. Aside from numerous benefits such as increased production, yield, and income, the kit reduces water chores usually assigned to women. It also reduces the labor required for irrigation by about 80%; this reduces the operation cost to the producer by about 40%, and allows women to fully participate in irrigated horticulture. AMG can triple yields in long-duration vegetable crops. Women could cultivate 10 times more land while spending half as much time in the garden as they had spent with the traditional system. As a result of this extra time, they had almost four times the earnings from non-agricultural activities as before. Water technologies often have impacts on the socio-economic structure of societies where they are used.

Tool Kit: Food Production Issues for Project Design Briefs

In order to achieve the ambition to synergistically integrate food production with cities and aquatic ecosystems, designers must be provided with a tool kit, a set of criteria that can figure in design briefs. Some of these criteria are outlined below:

Conceptual Framework
- Water is a commodity and has a market value; water utilization is therefore highly efficient.
- There is no water shortage but a shortage of water quality and/or technology to efficiently collect and distribute water.
- Innovative technology and cycling of water can bridge the gap between availability and demand.
- Water cascades through a chain or network of end users to produce a closed loop system; the same unit of water is used multiple times.
- Automating operations (e.g., water collection, irrigation) can create significant savings in labor and increase overall earnings from non-agricultural activities for smallholder producers.
- Vernacular water budgeting and crop cultivation (e.g., quanats, seguias) can offer both technical and spatial models for contemporary design schemes.
- Analytical and projective modeling of water availability for both ecological systems and agricultural production could benefit from investigating the existing and potential implications of urban, landscape, and architectural form, technology, materiality, and environmental performance on water (e.g., water harvesting and reuse, pervious vs. impervious surfaces, preservation of canopy, urban density).
- Diversify the scale, type, and distribution of water solutions. Develop multi-functional solutions.

Water Collection, Treatment, and Delivery
- Distribute a variety of water qualities (potable, effluent, treated effluent, brackish) via different colored pipe networks.
- Each end user customizes water quality according to crop requirements.
- Conserve water, fertilizer, and soil through drip irrigation to deliver both water and fertilizer, confine root zone and reduction of percolation, and implement smart irrigation control (e.g., calculation of transpiration rates through the use of sensors).
- Adapt technology through testing from large-scale to small-scale operations (e.g., low-pressure drip irrigation is suitable for small plots).
- Use of alternative energy sources like solar radiation, gravitation, or artesian pressure to further cut down the costs of water supply.
- Construct attenuation reservoirs to collect runoff water, settle sediment, recharge aquifer, and store for irrigation during peak demand.
- Construct stabilization ponds and reservoirs for extensive treatment and storage of municipal effluent to provide constant supply and bridge seasonal and annual gaps in precipitation.

Planting and Other Agricultural Activities
- Match crops with irrigation method.
- Select water-thrifty crops and crops that can tolerate low-quality water.
- Graft commercial crop species with salt-tolerant plant shoots.
- Identify unconventional agricultural activities (e.g., algae production) and potential use of by-products (e.g., sludge converted into methane for energy).
- Refer to traditional oasian agriculture for planting schemes whereby a tall canopy provides shade and evapotranspiration; mid-height fruit trees are planted below; and the groundcover consists of legumes, grains, and a range of vegetables.

Spatial Organization
- The spatial extent of wastewater reclamation can be local, regional, or inter-regional.
- Consider the potential overlap and synergy between hydrological structures and water-sanitation infrastructure (e.g., hydrological corridors can integrate wastewater treatment via bioremediation and public recreation space, while providing ecological habitat).
- Topography, geology, and microclimate variation form the basis for the organization of cities and land uses.
- Housing and streetscape design play a role in on site water recycling.
- Cluster and communal systems allow producers to benefit from the collective use of water, energy resources, land, purchasing, and marketing.

REFERENCES

Chase, J., Crawford, C., and Kaliski, J., eds. (2008). *Everyday Urbanism*. New York: Monacelli Press.

Gorgolewski, M., Komisar, J., and Nasr, J. (2011). *Carrot City: Creating Places for Urban Agriculture*. New York: Monacelli Press.

Hodgson, K., Campbell, M.C., Bailkey, M. (2011). *Urban Agriculture: Growing Healthy, Sustainable Places*. Chicago: American Planning Association.

Philips, A. (2013). *Designing Urban Agriculture: A Complete Guide to the Planning, Design, Construction, Maintenance and Management of Edible Landscapes*. New Jersey: John Wiley & Sons.

Viljoen, A., Bohn, K., and Howe, J., eds. (2005). *Continuous Productive Urban Landscapes: Designing Urban Agriculture for Sustainable Cities*. Oxford: Elsevier Architectural Press.

Waldheim, C. (2010). "Notes towards a history of agrarian urbanism," in M. White and M. Przybylski (eds.), *On Farming*. Barcelona: Actar.

White, M., Przybylski, M., eds. (2010). *On Farming*. Barcelona: Actar.

World Food Programme. (2014). "Who are the hungry?" *World Food Programme*. http://www.wfp.org/hunger/who-are

World Water Assessment Programme. (2012). *UN World Water Development Report: Managing Water under Uncertainty and Risk*. UNESCO. unesdoc.unesco.org/images/0021/002156/215644e.pdf

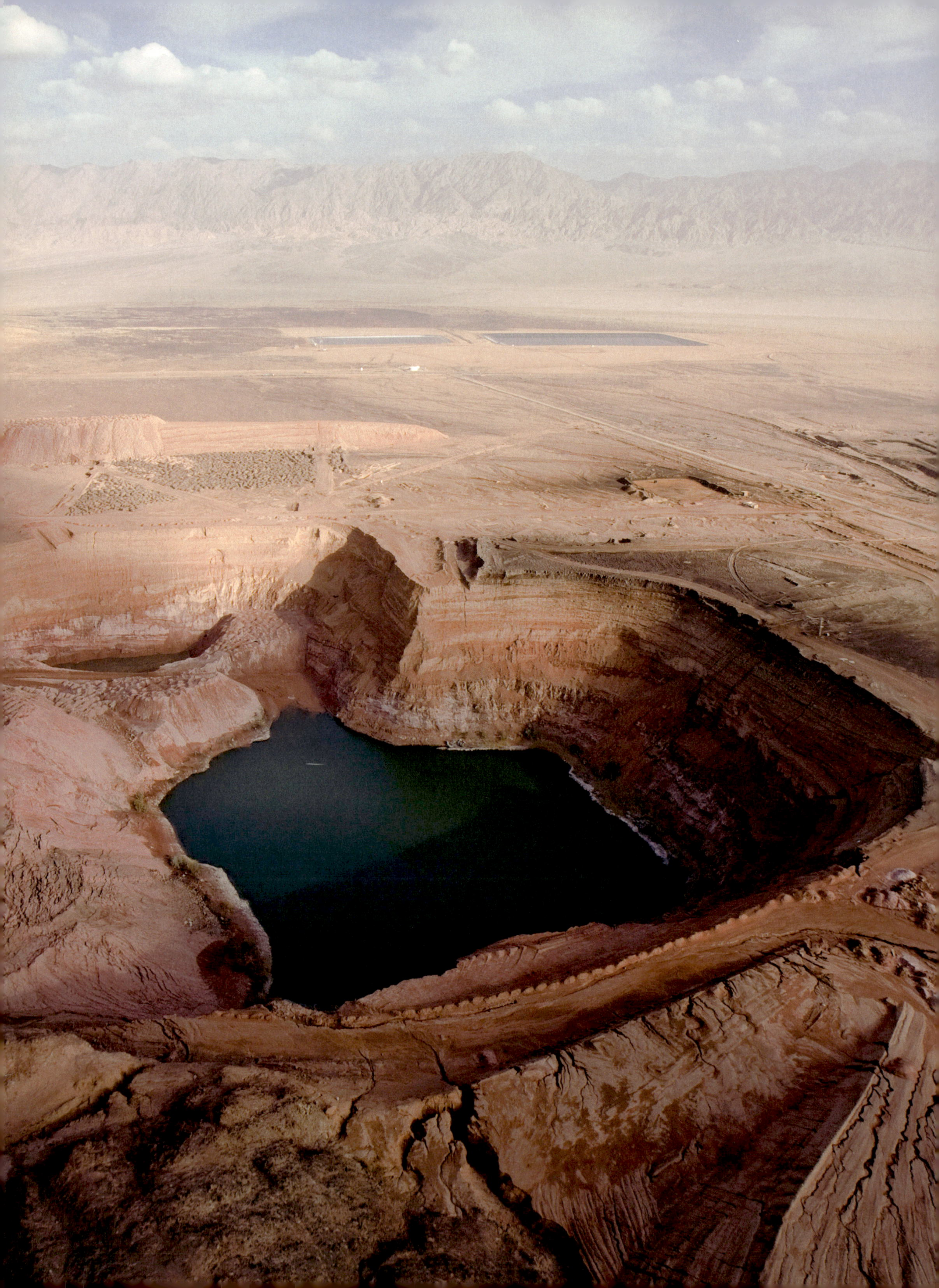

Bridging the Gap between Available Water and Water Demand: Water Technologies for Agricultural Production in Israel

Eilon M. Adar

The following is an edited transcript of Eilon Adar's lecture delivered at the "Out of Water" conference, April 2, 2011.

Israel is located in an extremely arid region. Yet, despite its ongoing population growth, it does not suffer from desertification; the average water availability in the Middle East reaches a mere 1,400 m^3 per person per year—less than 20% of the global average, according to the World Bank and the UN. Agricultural production thrives in Israel, despite the fact that water availability amounts to only 225 m^3/person/year, a total of 1,800 million m^3/year for less than 8 million people. This figure includes all available water sources: water from the Sea of Galilee, groundwater, reclaimed sewage water, and desalinated groundwater and seawater.

Water in the Middle East is indeed a scarce commodity, and we should emphasize the word commodity rather than resource; Israel was the first country to nationalize its water, and remains one of only a few countries to do so. This gives water a monetary value. Private well owners are not allowed to pump as much as they want; rather, they are allotted a yearly quota, and they pay for the water they pump from their own private wells. The consumption of water is far beyond the rate of replenishment, exceeding the safe yield. Therefore, in the same way that many countries mine for oil, Israel used to mine fresh water from the aquifers and from the Sea of Galilee. Only recently did desalination mega-plants begin providing the amount of water that enabled Israel to bridge demand and supply.

Looked at closely, the entire Northern Negev desert is no longer in fact a desert; it is cultivated semi-arid and arid land. How did this come about? The answer lies in cutting-edge innovation and technologies that bridge the gap between available water and water demand, some of which have been developed at Ben Gurion University of the Negev (BGU). Israel serves as a good example for the rest of the global desert belt. Despite its relatively small area, it contains a diversity of desert types, all of which have been cultivated. The salient question here concerns the approach to water availability and water scarcity. I will argue that we should not despair due to a lack of water.

Water Use Efficiency

Israel has created a unified water distribution system—infrastructure that allows water to be transported from north to south and from west to east. Agricultural end users and 95% of the population are connected to this main distribution system. The fresh water network, Blue Water, is intended not only to transfer water from one place to another, but also to provide each end user with the specific mélange of water qualities that is appropriate to their demands.

The Red Lines transport a treated effluent to regions where it may safely be used for irrigation; the Green Lines supply salty to brackish water for the agriculture sector in selected basins, mainly in the Negev and the Arava basins. The national water carrier allows the combination and connection of groundwater from different aquifers (Coastal, Mountain, and Galilee) into a unified pipeline, which diverts water from 212m below the surface of the Sea

Figure 6a: Timna Mine water reservoir is used to collect runoff for aquifer recharge and irrigation

Figure 1: PVC mesh–covered greenhouses

of Galilee to areas up to 890m above sea level in the Negev highlands. This system's ability to connect groundwater and surface water accounts for Israel's extensive countrywide irrigation.

The most important principle of water management is that water supply must be secured for future generations. Israel implements two approaches to prevent resources from being exhausted. The first has to do with identifying end users who can accommodate low-quality water. For example, the groundwater of the Nubian Aquifer is brackish to saline; however, some agricultural users can utilize this water as is, or with minimal treatment. It is important to note that the region does not suffer from a shortage of water, but rather a shortage of water quality.

The second approach focuses on bridging the gap between availability and demand. The population of Israel and Palestine west of the Jordan River is projected to double in the next 18–22 years, which will mean a need for more food and, hence, more water. Arable land in the region has already reached capacity, and therefore the focus has shifted to the desert. In 1959, the Negev desert was completely uncultivated and relatively barren. By the late 1970s, it had been proven that open-field agriculture was feasible in the desert, but from a water-saving point of view it remained unaffordable due to daily evaporation rates of 8mm (winter) to 12mm (summer).

Irrigation Control

PVC mesh–covered greenhouses form the primary system for cultivation in the desert (Figure 1). Drip irrigation and, more recently, subsurface, pulse-responsive drip irrigation are used to eliminate moisture evaporation from soil and conserve water usage. Although drip irrigation is by now used worldwide, there are several particular adaptations in the methodology of cultivation and water application. The topsoil is lined to avoid soil moisture evaporation. In addition, an impermeable lining is introduced beneath the crops to prevent deep percolation of irrigation surplus. The lining is introduced to eliminate soil moisture evaporation—not only to conserve water, but also to conserve the precious soil itself. Otherwise, only pure H_2O would evaporate from the soil, leaving a residue of minerals and salts which are extremely difficult to remove, making the soil unusable (Figure 2).

In order to improve the growing micro-climate, simple plastic airbags are used during peak daytime heat to cool the greenhouses, and at night to circulate warm air and create optimal growing conditions. The crop's root zone is actually confined within a plastic sleeve which captures every drop of water. The subsurface drip irrigation system allows the farmer to introduce fertilizer, again without losing a drop. The other advantage is that the surplus water

Figure 2: An impermeable lining beneath the crops prevents deep percolation of irrigation surplus and soil moisture evaporation

collected is rich with residual fertilizer, a relatively expensive commodity, and is further used downstream for other types of crops that can tolerate higher salinity.

An important aspect of irrigation control is the calculation of transpiration rates. This is the achieved through integration of solar radiation sensors, soil and air temperature sensors, and irrigation activated by soil-moisture sensors. Many years ago, commercials on the radio rallied farmers to wake up in the middle of the night and irrigate their fields to reduce water losses by evaporation. It was later understood that it makes no sense to recharge the root zone at night and wait for plants to uptake the water during daytime, as soil moisture is lost due to deep percolation below the root zone by gravity.

In most cases today, plants are irrigated only when they are ready to photosynthesize and transpire. This means that the plants are irrigated, not the soil. This responsive irrigation system, which includes subsurface drippers with almost no drainage and no deep percolation, results in an unparalleled 85–92% irrigation efficiency without damaging the soil. Each farmer can therefore configure his or her own isolated growing environment and formulate the appropriate and profitable mélange of water qualities (brackish, fresh, occasionally effluent), according to his or her specific goals and budget.

A Chain of End Users

Along with improved growing technologies, another important strategy to increase water use efficiency is to set up a chain of water users—in other words, to identify multiple end users who are able to utilize the same unit of water for their crops and operations. For instance, surplus water collected from peppers and tomatoes is redirected to a grape variety that can tolerate a somewhat higher level of salinity and benefit from the residual fertilizers (Figure 3).

Ultimately, these strategies mitigate the negative anthropogenic impact of intensive agricultural activity. The root zone is isolated in a small volume of soil in an individual plastic sleeve, maintaining a healthy soil environment. At the end of the growing season, this small quantity of soil can be easily extracted and sterilized to ensure that pests, fungus, and disease are not proliferated from one growing season to another. The use of pesticides and herbicides is also diluted, due to restricted deep-water percolation and consequent reduction of fertilizer loss.

To make use of this abundant resource of brackish water in the Nubian Aquifer, commercial crop species have been grafted with a variety of salt-tolerant plant shoots (Figure 4). Crops are irrigated with brackish water only in places where the soil can be collected after two or three

Figure 3: Surplus water collected from peppers and tomatoes is redirected to a salt-tolerant grape variety (top)

Figure 5: Algae production uses brackish water and is then sold to salmon farms in Europe (middle)

Figure 7: Ben Gurion University (formerly the Negev Research Institute) Professor Sidney Loeb and his technician in the Reverse Osmosis pilot desalination plant in Kibbutz Yotvata, southern Arava Valley, 1968 (bottom)

Figure 4: Commercial crop species are grafted with a variety of salt-tolerant plant shoots

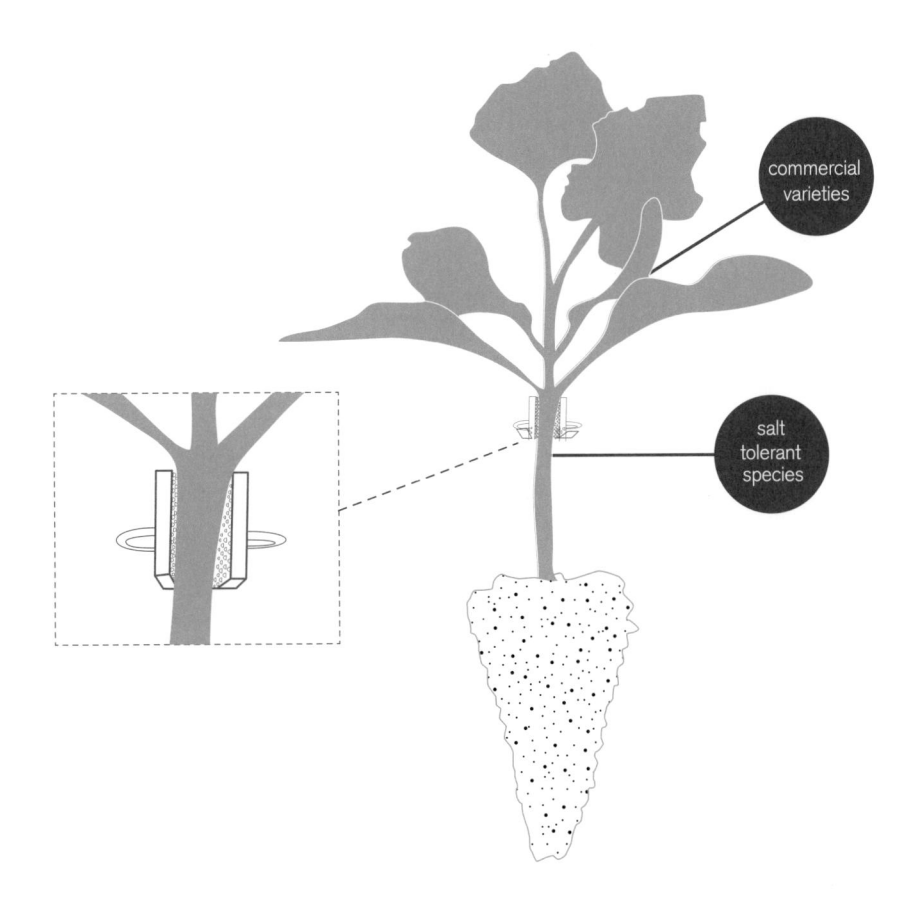

seasons and washed or incinerated. Thanks to this technique, the Negev Desert is now the home of 16 budding wineries featuring several grape varieties, and the producer of a diverse variety of tomatoes and miniature watermelons that are exported to the European market.

Another group of end users are those engaged in unconventional agricultural activities, such as algae production (Figure 5). The type of algae being farmed is the natural food of salmon (via ingestion of shrimp and krill), and gives the fish's flesh its pink color. The algae are only pink when the temperature of the water is above 22° C. Therefore, salmon harvested in Norway is naturally grey; since the pink color is expected by consumers, most salmon is artificially colored with a pigment manufactured by a Swiss company at a cost of $2,400/kg. Though naturally found in salt water, the algae thrive in brackish water if provided with the necessary nutrients. The algae turn pink with sun exposure and are immediately harvested, dried, and sold to the same Swiss company at $5,200/kg. The company then sells the product as "organic" pigment for "organically cultivated salmon," which has a high market value.

The warm desert climate also permits the raising of high-demand equatorial warm-water fish species such as tilapia and Australian barramundi. These are raised in very small pools, since the water used is pumped from the aquifer at 1,000–1,300m below the surface and is therefore costly. To avoid the buildup of parasites and the need for antibiotics, the water is disposed of after a number of cycles. Though highly saline, this water is redirected to irrigate a special type of olive tree that can tolerate brackish water. Today, the Negev desert boasts numerous plantations, with a ratio of 0.4ha of fish farm to every 25–30 olive trees, equipped with subsurface drip irrigation and plastic covers to limit evaporation and accumulation of salt. Until recently, Israel was an importer of olive oil; today, it exports olive oil even to olive-rich countries such as Spain and Italy.

Another closed-loop system is used by the ornamental fish and aquatic flower industries. Fish waste is converted to nitrate via algae, which are fed back into the fish farms to give the fish their flamboyant colors. The surplus nitrate is used in water lily cultivation. Finally, the effluent from these farms is redirected to date palm plantations. In this way, three distinct industries use the same unit of water. Sludge, the final residue, is anaerobically digested into methane which is then redistributed back to the fish farms.

Groundwater Recharge and Desalination

One promising method of replenishing water resources is through artificial recharge. Groundwater in the desert is replenished naturally by stream infiltration during floods. However, in many instances this surface runoff contains 30–35% sediment and does not percolate. To mitigate this, constructed attenuation dumps allow the sediments to settle and clean water to replenish the aquifer after three to four days. In some cases, farming communities use the retained water for irrigation, but these reservoirs are always covered; open water reservoirs are inappropriate for arid climates due to the high evaporation rates (Figure 6a and 6b).

Ultimately, all these increases in water use efficiency will be insufficient to meet Israel's future water demands, in light of population growth projections and diminishing non-renewable resources. It is still necessary to create "new" water through desalination. Reverse osmosis was developed in 1966 at what was then the Negev Institute and is now BGU (Figure 7). Today, 300 million m^3 of seawater and nearly 40 million m^3 of brackish water is desalinated yearly. This water is fed into the national water distribution system, allowing the National Water Authority to provide enough adequate-quality water to every end user.

In reverse osmosis, water is pushed through a membrane to separate the pre-permeate from the brine. The main challenge is to protect the membrane from biofouling; the accumulation of seawater biomass on the membrane eventually destroys it. Therefore, only 17% of the total cost of desalination is for energy. The rest goes into operation and pretreatment. Researchers at BGU have developed peptides that can be applied to the membrane to kill the bacteria without the need for antibiotics.

Another technology developed at BGU is electrodialysis, which utilizes an ion separation membrane to desalinate industrial effluents and allow factories to release the effluents into the municipal waste system. The residual salt is dried and harvested for reuse. It is a common misconception that the elevated level of salinity in the sea is due to the desalination process. The primary cause is not generally the brine effluent, but rather the loss of freshwater drainage from rivers to the sea, due to various anthropogenic factors (e.g., dams, extraction for irrigation, etc.) and climate patterns (e.g., drought).

Undoubtedly, the critical factors that will have to be managed to ensure the long-term viability of large-scale desalination will be energy use and CO_2 emissions. Various new solutions are becoming available, including improved solar energy technologies and a Dutch vacuum thermal membrane, which requires less than half the usual energy supply. Wind energy is another option that is currently under development at BGU—not for energy production, but to provide the water pressure needed in the reverse osmosis process.

Water must be regarded as a commodity with a market value. Setting up a chain of water end users is paramount to water use efficiency, but cannot be accomplished without the cooperation of highly educated farmers. Ultimately, if its population grows as projected, the Middle East will have no option but to intensify desalination to meet increasing food and water demands.

Figure 6b: Enhanced groundwater recharge and storage increases local water availability at Hatzeva, along the Arava Wash (opposite)

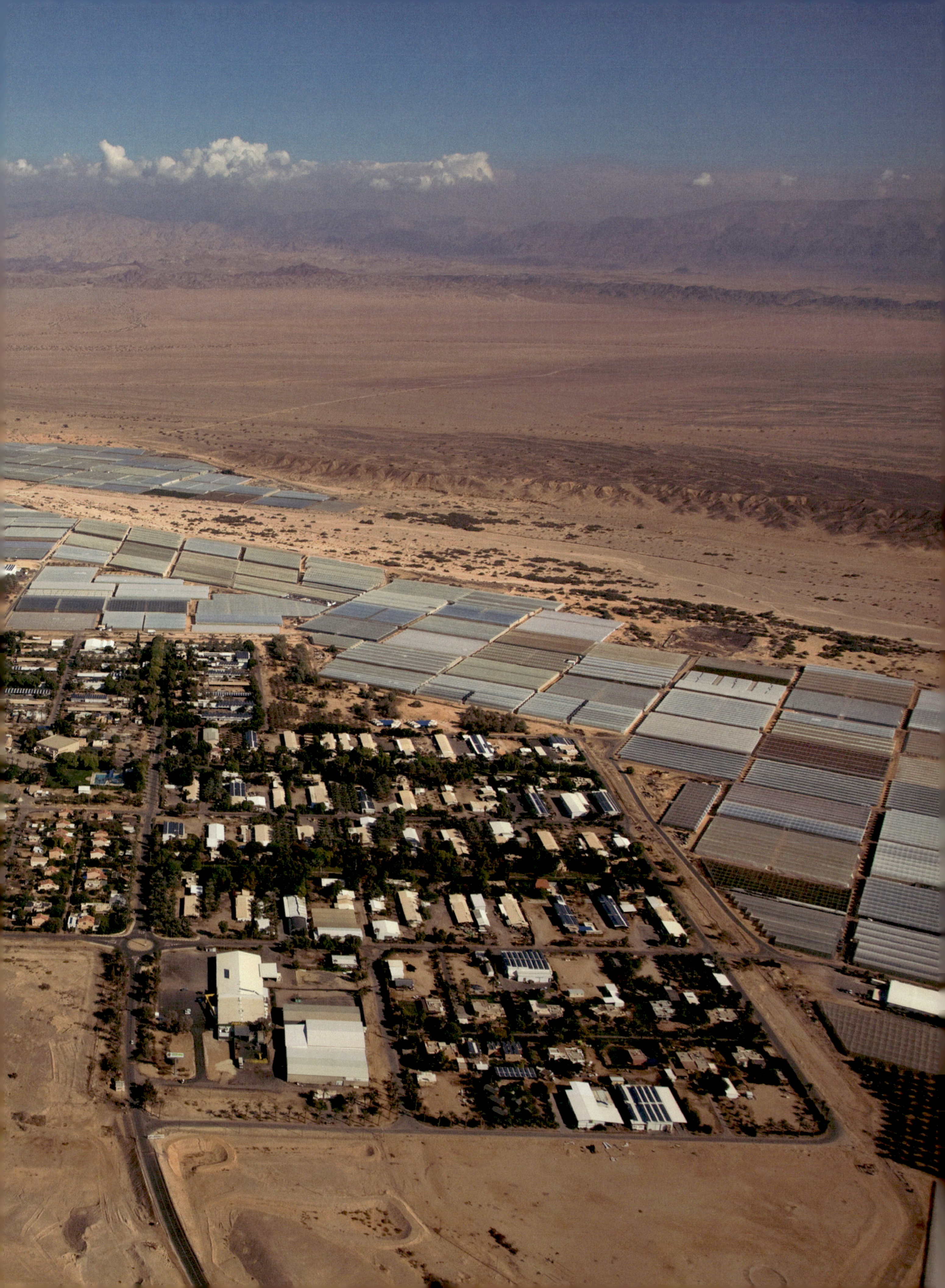

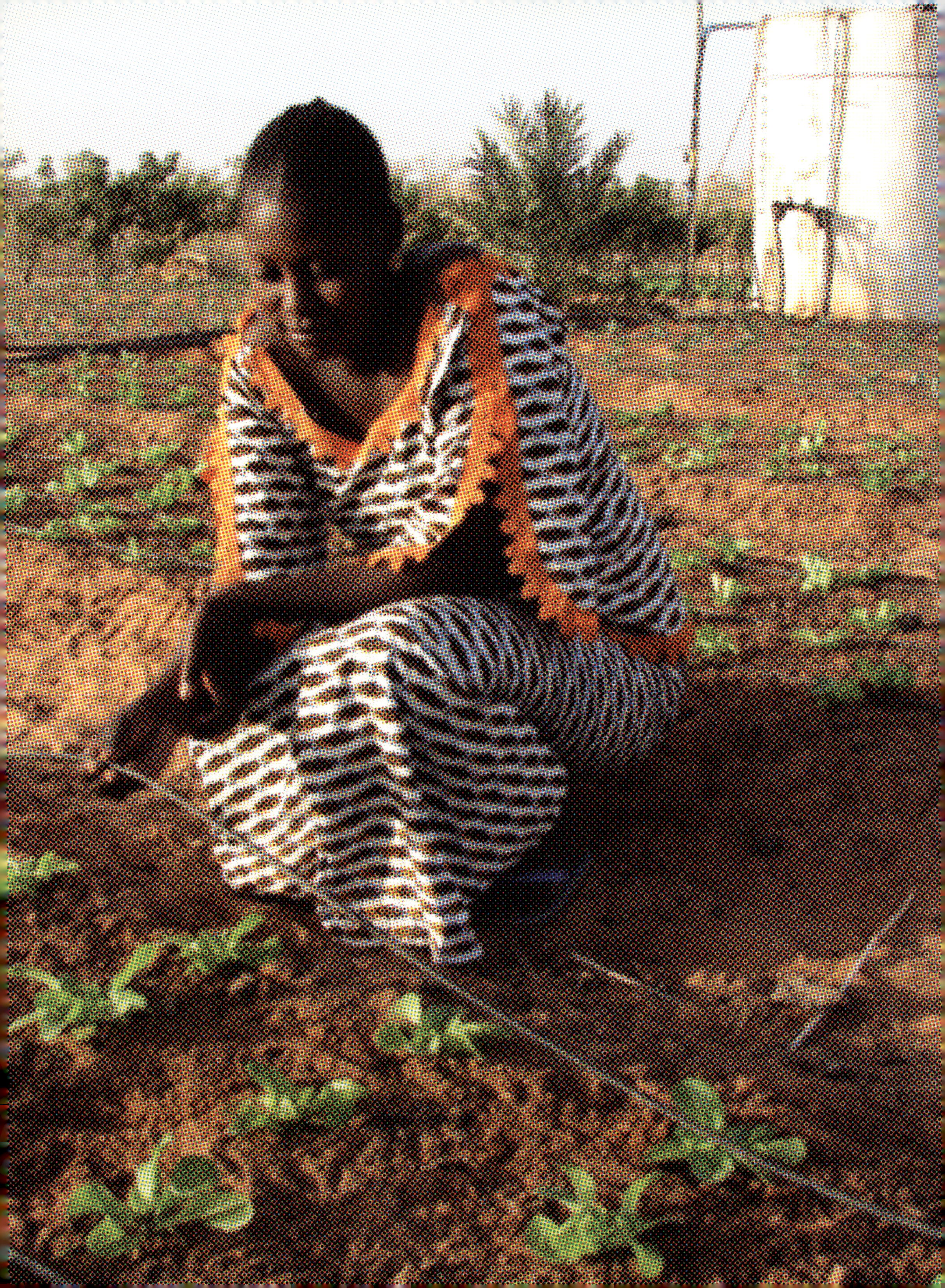

The African Market Garden: Introduction of Drip Irrigation to the Sudano Sahel Region

Dov Pasternak and Lennart Woltering

Irrigated horticultural production is a major source of income and employment for millions of smallholder producers in the Sudano Sahel. The International Crops Research Institute for the Semi-Arid Tropics (ICRISAT) developed a holistic horticultural production system in Niger for small producers, based on low-pressure drip irrigation combined with a crops management package, and called it the African Market Garden (AMG). This system allows horticulture producers in the Sahel to benefit from drip irrigation, a technology often associated with large commercial farms in the developed world.

We will describe the development pathways of the four different AMG models—Thrifty, Commercial, Cluster, and Communal—and assess their returns to investment. The AMG reduces the labor required for irrigation by about 80%; this reduces the operation cost to the producer by about 40%, and allows women to fully participate in irrigated horticulture (Figure 1). At the same time, the AMG can triple yields in long-duration vegetable crops. The Cluster and Communal systems were developed to allow producers to benefit from the collective use of water, energy resources, land, purchasing, and marketing. These models have been tested using alternative energy sources like solar radiation, gravitation, or artesian pressure, to further cut down the costs of water supply.

The Sudano Sahel is a region located south of the Sahara, between the 300 and 800mm isohyets. About 80% of its population derives its income from rain-fed agriculture and pastoralism, but the area's combination of droughts and poor soils results in very low agriculture productivity and endemic poverty. A shift from rain-fed to irrigated agriculture is probably the best solution for development in this region, as it was in other regions of the world (Postel, 2011).

The Sudano Sahel is rich in both surface and underground water. The combined annual discharge of the Senegal, Niger, and Chari Rivers is estimated at 80 billion m^3/year, more than the discharge of the Nile River. The quantity of water stored in shallow aquifers is also significant. For example, it is estimated that the amount of renewable water in the many shallow aquifers of Niger is about 3 billion m^3/year (World Bank, 2004). Artificial and natural lakes also store billions of cubic meters of water (Direction Génerale de l'Hydraulique [DGIRH], 2001). Moreover, the Sudano Sahel and the Sahara are underlined by a series of aquifers extending over more than 4 million km^2 (Burdon, 1985). Currently, the Sudano Sahel is definitely not "out of water." However, less than 1% of its cultivated land is irrigated (Food and Agriculture Organization of the UN [FAO], 2005). Past attempts to promote irrigation in the Sudano Sahel by the formal sector were expensive and, in many cases, unsuccessful (World Bank, 2008). Investments have shifted in the last decades towards the informal (private) small-scale irrigation sector, which operates in a more market-driven fashion and has proved to be more profitable.

The African Market Garden

Low-Pressure Drip Irrigation for Smallholder Horticulture Producers

Millions of smallholder producers in sub-Saharan Africa practice and live on small-scale production of irrigated vegetables (Weinberger and Lumpkin, 2005). They use manual irrigation or small gasoline-powered pumps to lift water from wells or surface water. The water is then distributed over the field using traditional irrigation and production methods. These are labor

FIGURE 1: The AMG reduces the labor required for irrigation and allows women to fully participate in irrigated horticulture

intensive and wasteful of water and energy, resulting in low productivity. Drip irrigation is the most efficient irrigation technology, as it delivers water and fertilizer directly to the root zone of the crops through a network of pipes and emitters. This saves water, energy, and labor, and allows maintenance of healthy soil moisture for the crops. Since the 1990s, low-pressure drip irrigation systems have become available for small areas where an operating pressure of 1m (0.1 bars) is required, instead of the 20m (2 bars) needed for conventional drip irrigation systems.

The African Market Garden first developed by Pasternak and Bustan (2003) is a holistic system incorporating a low-pressure drip irrigation system and a crop management package. The AMG was tested over a period of nine years in eight Sahelian countries. The evolution of the AMG incorporated the testing and improvement of the drip system, the selection and breeding of vegetable varieties for the Sudano Sahel, the formulation of a horticulture management system, and the development of new AMG models that take advantage of economies of scale and alternative energy sources.

Testing and Improving the Drip System

Uniform distribution of water and placement of soluble fertilizers along the drip line are some of the principal advantages of the drip system over other systems. When all plants in a given field receive the exact amounts of water and fertilizer that they need for growth, yields are maximized, as are water and fertilizer efficiency. In developing this system, three main types of drip emitters were tested: low-cost micro-tubes, inserted in a thin polyethylene line; drip-tape made out of very thin-walled laterals (0.3mm), inserted with low-cost emitters; and high-quality in-line emitters, inserted in relatively thick-walled (0.9mm) laterals.

The micro-tube system showed poor uniformity of water distribution: at a distance of 5m from the water source the discharge was 4.5L/h, but it went down to about 2.5L/h at 30m (Figure 2). The drip-tape and in-line emitters showed low and uniform discharge along the 30m lateral length. Pasternak and Bustan (2003) found that high discharge rates result in vertical leaching of solutes in the soil. The micro-tube system, with discharges ranging from 2.5–4.5L/h, would therefore cause a much higher vertical leaching of fertilizers than the other two systems.

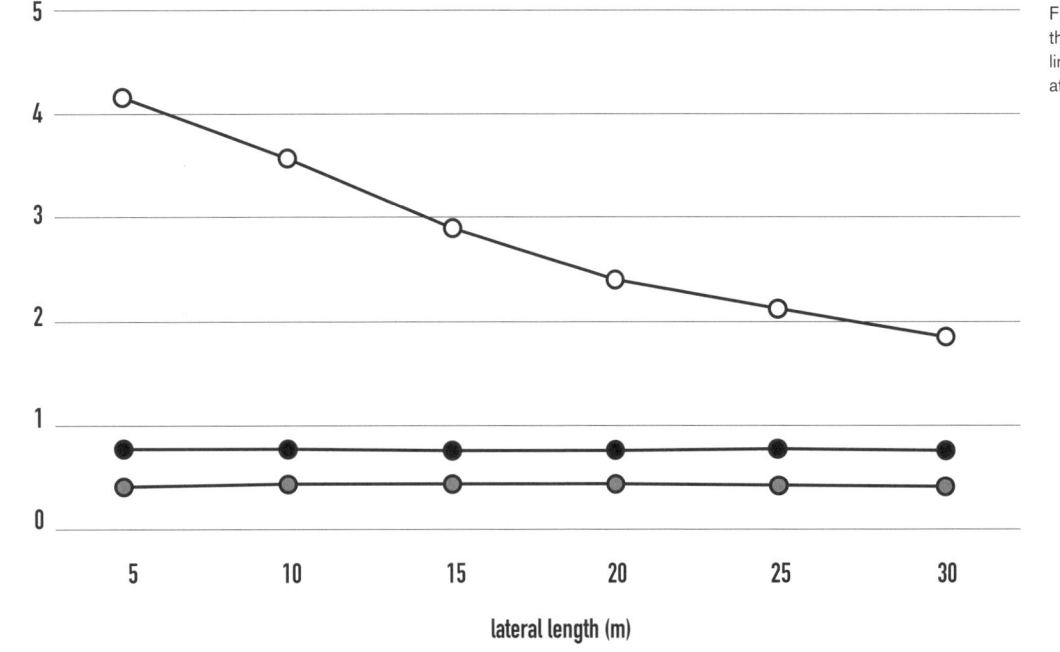

FIGURE 2: Emitter discharge of three main types of drip irrigation lines, as a function of lateral length at a water head of one meter

Figure 3: The drip system is connected to a reservoir that provides daily water required by the crops

An important advantage of the micro-tube system for developing countries is its low emitter discharge rate (around 0.4L/h), as the lower levels of vertical leaching are important when soluble phosphorus (P) and potassium (K) are not readily available for fertigation. The tested drip-tape gave good and uniform water distribution, and its cost is relatively low, but it has an estimated lifespan of only two years. Therefore, the thick-walled in-line drip is recommended, because of the rigidity of these laterals and their longer lifespan, an estimated seven years. In developing countries, the longevity and rigidity of the drip emitters and laterals and their resistance to clogging are very important considerations, as poor farmers often do not replace damaged equipment.

Designing the AMG System in the Local Context

Technologies that are appropriate for large commercial farms have to be re-engineered to suit smallholders' unique characteristics (Keller, 1990). Technological features that are important to smallholders include low investment and operation cost, rapid return on investment, and simple operation and maintenance. However, ICRISAT learned that affordability and simplicity should not come at the cost of longevity and quality of equipment (Woltering, Pasternak, and Ndjeunga, 2011). The AMG is designed in such a way that it can be easily operated and maintained. The drip system is connected to a reservoir of standard size, which the farmer must fill and empty once a day to provide exactly the daily water requirement for the crops (Figure 3).

Producers can mix fertilizer with the water simply by pouring it in the reservoir. The reservoir also provides enough pressure to allow uniform water distribution over the field. Whereas with traditional methods the size of the area one could irrigate depended on one's muscle power, the AMG allows women to cultivate large areas with ease, as one only needs to open a tap to irrigate areas of 500, 1,000, or 5,000m^2. Table 1 shows that after the introduction of the AMG, women could cultivate 10 times more land while spending half as much time in the garden as they had spent with the traditional system. As a result of this extra time, they had almost four times the earnings from non-agricultural activities as before.

	HAND LIFTING & WATERING CAN	SOLAR PUMP & DRIP
area cultivated	12m²	120m²
time spent in garden	5 hours/day	2.5 hours/day
non-agricultural earnings	US$45 (±$24)	US$169 (±$65)

TABLE 1: Impact of changing from traditional irrigation to AMG for three groups of women in northern Benin

	HAND LIFTING UNIT				TREADLE PUMP UNIT				MOTOR PUMP UNIT				SOLAR PUMP UNIT			
	qty	cost $	total $	amount $/y	qty	cost $	total $	amount $/y	qty	cost $	total $	amount $/y	qty	cost $	total $	amount $/y
equipment	12	10	120	60	3	70	210	53	1	400	400	80	1	6000	6000	600
well	12	30	360	90	3	100	300	30	1	200	200	20	1	200	200	20
water distr. network	0			0	3	75	225	23	1	400	400	40	1	400	400	40
maintenance				12				45				120				30
fuel				0				0				1.920				0
labour@$2/person day	2.222	2		4.444	556	2		1.111				50				13
labour@$1/person day	2.222	1		2.222	556	1		556				25				6
total labour @$2/day				4.606				1.261				2.255				709
total labour @$1/day				2.384				706				2.205				696

TABLE 2: Annual cost for different water abstraction technologies to irrigate a 1ha field, at labour cost of US$1 and $2 per person day

Water Delivery for Small-Scale Irrigation

The most common method of subtracting water for irrigation in countries like Niger is by hauling water from a well using a simple half-gourd with a long cord attached (Norman and Walter, 1994). This method is very labor intensive and can only be used at shallow depth. Based on their successful introduction in Asia, various NGOs promoted treadle and hand pumps operated with human energy. Some farmers use small gasoline-powered pump sets that can pump from a maximum depth of seven meters. Fuel is not always available in rural areas, and farmer cooperatives often have difficulties collecting funds for fuel or maintenance when sharing a pump. Solar pumps, on the other hand, are independent of fuel availability and have hardly any operating costs. As well, solar water pumping and crop water demand are driven by the same force—namely solar radiation, available throughout the year. The price of solar pumps has decreased significantly over the last few years, turning solar pumps into an attractive water-lifting alternative for small-scale irrigated horticulture.

We calculated the cost of water delivery to a one-hectare field in Niger using the four above-mentioned options. Water delivery cost is dependent on the depth of the well (or borehole), the number of wells or boreholes that must be dug to supply water to the field, the amortization of the various pumps and auxiliary equipment, and the cost of labor or fuel needed to irrigate the field. Table 2 shows that the annual operation cost of the solar pump is the lowest of all options, followed by the treadle pump and the motor pump. The hand-lifting technology carries the highest cost.

Crop Management Package

The crop management package incorporates the production of healthy plants in the nursery, proper planting beds preparation, and application of standard quantities of inputs such as manure (4kg/m^2), fertilizer (NPK at 100g/m^2), irrigation (at 100% evaporation from a USWB Class A evaporation pan), and fertigation (nitrogen from urea at 50ppm in irrigation water). In a controlled experiment (Woltering, Ibrahim, Pasternak, and Ndjeunga, 2011) it was found that just the application of manure, basic fertilizers, and urea without any changes to the traditional watering technology tripled the fruit yield of eggplants.

In addition to adapting drip technology to the needs of smallholder farmers, ICRISAT in Niger is also running a long-term project, begun in 2002, that aims to select adapted vegetable varieties for the region. Most vegetable varieties used in the Sudano Sahel are imported from Europe and many are not adapted to the climate and soils of this region. For the project, between 20 and 100 varieties of each species were tested, and best varieties were selected and multiplied (Gowda, et al., 2010). In many instances, local land races and varieties such as the Xina tomato or the Konni okra were superior to imported varieties. Emphasis was given to varieties that produce well in the rainy or in the hot dry season, to allow year-round production of vegetables. In all cases, there was a need to purify the varieties to achieve quality, uniformity, and high yields. All selected and improved varieties were open pollinated. This means that the vegetable farmers can produce the seeds by themselves after receiving training, thus solving a perennial and severe problem of seed supply.

The Development Pathway of the African Market Garden

The development pathway of the AMG as described in Figure 4 can be divided into four phases.

1. **Phase 1 (1998–2001):** Development and testing of the AMG at Ben Gurion University in Israel (Pasternak and Bustan, 2003).

2. **Phase 2 (2001–2005):** First testing of the single 80m^2 (Thrifty) and 500m^2 (Commercial) AMG units, development of the management package, and beginning the selection of adapted vegetable varieties. Socioeconomic studies (Mahamadou, 2005; Intermediate Technology Consultants, 2003) demonstrated that small 80m^2 units have no economic advantage over traditional irrigation methods. The maximum benefit from the AMG can be achieved when many 500m^2 units are clustered in a single field, creating an economy of scale.

3. **Phase 3 (2005–2008):** Development of the Cluster and the Communal systems. The Cluster system is composed of many single 500m^2 units; they receive water from a single source, but each is operated individually by the producer. In the Communal system, one central water source supplies water to a large drip system (usually 5,000m^2) that is managed by a producers' association. The field is divided into units, from 120–500m^2 in size, which are given to individual women (Figure 5). Representatives of the association are responsible for the purchasing of inputs, marketing, irrigation, fertigation, and crop spraying. Growers need to prepare the land, plant the crops, weed, and harvest. This system is particularly suitable for women, as they can cultivate large areas and save a lot of time, which they spend on other income-generating activities or caring for their families (Figure 6). In this third phase, the use of low-energy water sources (low hydraulic gradients between water dams and the field, artesian water, and solar pumps) was tested and quantified. The use of these water sources significantly cuts down the energy needed for water pumping and delivery.

4. **Phase 4 (2008–current):** System refinement, and beginning of mass dissemination of the AMG in West Africa. It is estimated that 3,000 AMG units are currently operating in the region. By the end of 2012, about 5,000 new systems will have been added, mainly in Niger and Senegal.

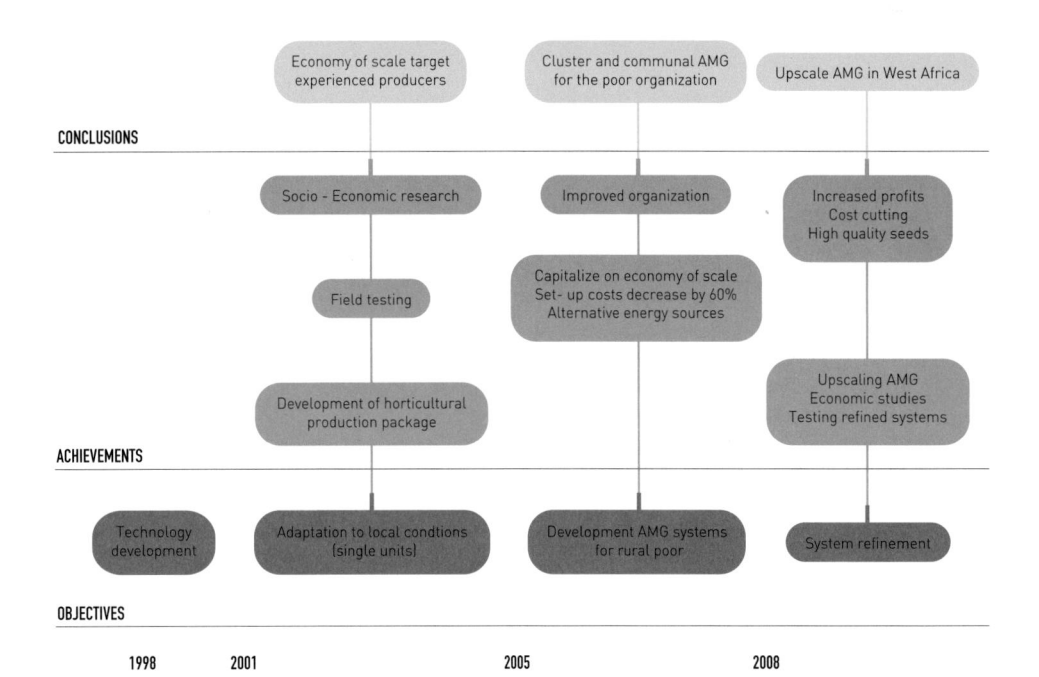

FIGURE 4: The development pathway of the AMG technology in West Africa 1998–2011

TABLE 3: Setup costs, gross revenue, payback period, and return to land and labor for a 500m² production unit in a traditional system, versus a Commercial, Cluster, and Communal AMG system (Woltering, et al., 2011)

	TRADITIONAL AFRICAN MARKET SYSTEM	COMMERCIAL SYSTEM	CLUSTER SYSTEM	COMMUNAL AMG SYSTEM
	500m²	500m²	10 x 500m²	5000m² for 10 prod.
drip system	US$0	371	3,710	3,000
reservoir	100	400	560	2,000
pump and connections [2]	420	420	970	420
well or borehole [3]	160	160	160	160
fence [4]	104	104	1,392	1,296
farming tools	140	110	564	564
training [5]	0	50	500	500
investment cost	924	1,615	7,856	7,940
production cost	764	585	5,526	5,526
gross revenues	1,500	2,000	20,000	20,000
payback period (years)	1.3	1.2	0.5	0.6
return to land ($/m²)	1.1	2.3	2.6	2.6
return to labour ($/person/day)	2.7	16.8	19.4	19.6
benefit-cost ratio	1.57	2.34	2.99	3.02

1 thrifty and cluster: 200L oil drum; other systems: concrete reservoir
2 thrifty: hand lifting; other systems: 3 hp motor pump
3 thrifty: hand-dug well <4m; other systems: 110mm hand-drilled borehole to 12m depth
4 for individual gardens, cheap $1/m fence is used, with a lifetime of 3 years; for gardens of 0.5ha, $4/m fence, with a lifespan of 10 years, is used
5 training for thrifty and commercial AMG at $50 against $500 for producer groups

FIGURE 5: The field is divided into units, from 120–500m² in size. The AMG is ideal for women, as they can cultivate large areas and save a lot of time, which they spend on other income-generating activities or caring for their families

Economic Analysis

The economics of a traditional 500m² vegetable garden were compared with those of a Commercial, a Cluster, and a Communal AMG system.

The AMG provides a return on labor that is 3–3.5 times greater than that of a traditional system, and 15–18 times greater than the average daily income in Niger. One of the major deterrents for investment in low-pressure drip irrigation is the high setup cost of this system compared with a traditional system. However, drip irrigation benefits a lot from economies of scale. As can be seen in Table 2, the setup cost of a 500m² garden unit in the Cluster system is the same as that of a 500m² traditional garden, but the payback period of the Cluster system is less than half that of the traditional system.

Conclusions

ICRISAT's systematic development of the African Market Garden serves as an instructive example of addressing water supply problems by introducing innovative technologies and systems. The productivity of the AMG can be optimized only when the drip system is matched with suitable varieties and an appropriate and holistic crop management package. The use of drip irrigation alone, without the implementation of the management package and without using the right crop varieties, would have very little effect on crop productivity. The AMG is a production system for high-value crops, such as vegetables and fruit. A further task will be developing profitable technologies for the production of field crops that have lower value than vegetables, with the objective of fully converting the Sudano Sahel from rain-fed to irrigated agriculture.

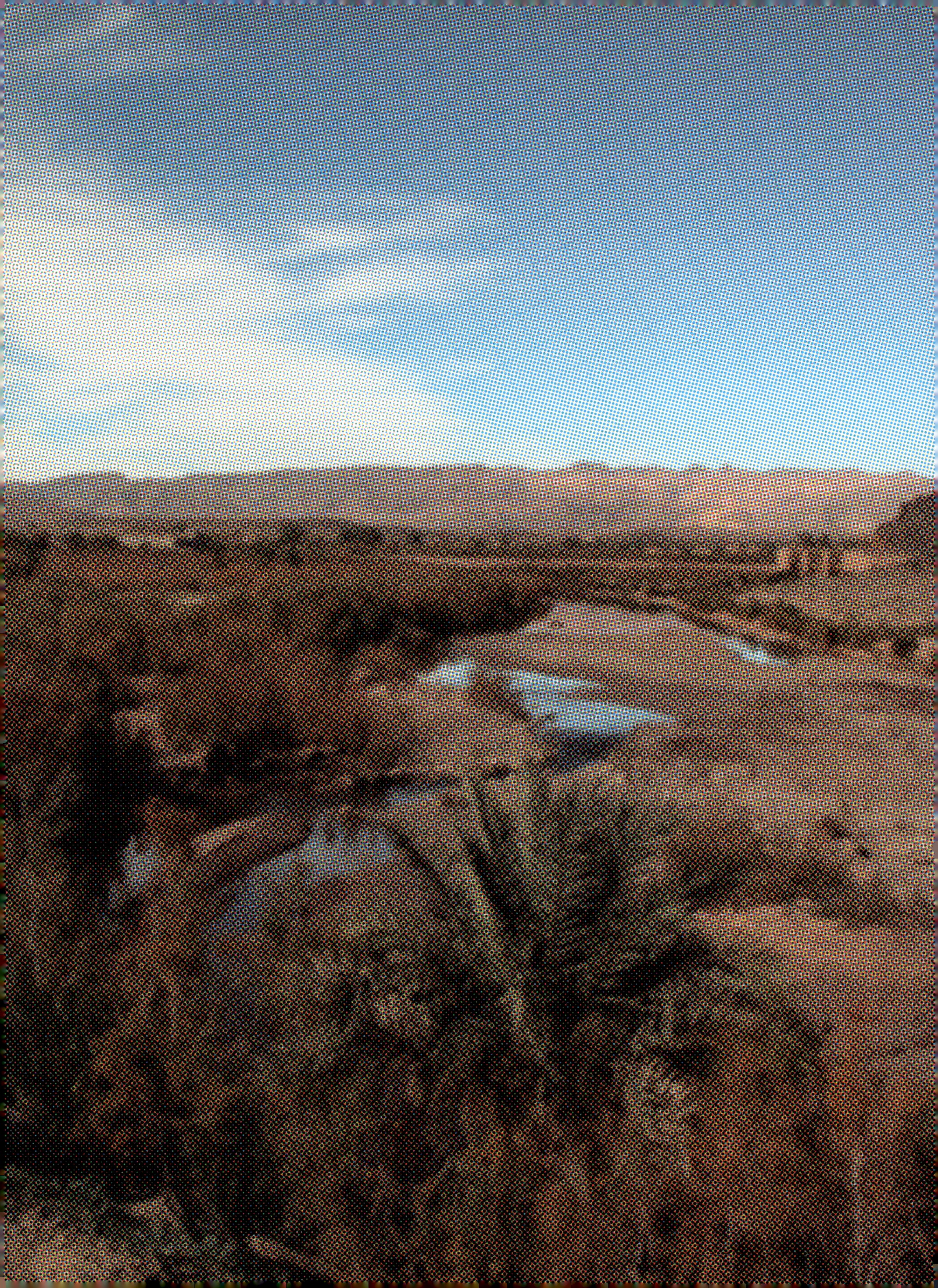

The Role of Design in Hydrological Modeling of River Basins: The Drâa Oasis Valley

Aziza Chaouni

River basins are complex environmental and social systems; such complexity demands that researchers employ equally complex tools. Hydrological modeling is a projective, probabilistic process that is useful for experimenting with the dynamics that govern complex environmental and social systems such as river basins. By using this method to evaluate outcomes at the local and regional scale, multifaceted solutions can be identified and put into action. Current hydrological modeling research focuses on investigating the potential impacts of climate and land-cover changes on water quantity, quality, and management, for the purposes of scenario development for river basins (Chang, et al., 2001). In fact, both climate and land-cover change are major drivers of global change which are expected to persist throughout the 21st century (Olson, et al., 2008; Intergovernmental Panel on Climate Change [IPCC], 2007). The complex and dynamic nature of river basins necessitates multidisciplinary analysis and projective modeling, whose algorithms often include data from the fields of political science, economics, sociology, and geography, as well as hydrology, geology, ecology, climatology, and agronomy.

Often, the design fields are excluded from the analytical and strategic planning and modeling process. Consequently, the outcomes of such projective models neglect to consider the impact of urban and architectural form, technology, materiality, and environmental performance. It is therefore important to recognize the role that landscape, urban, and architectural design can play in envisioning new and unconventional scenarios and means by which these data sets may produce optimized and multi-functional results. For instance, urban development significantly affects both surface water and groundwater conditions through its impact on water runoff, infiltration, evapotranspiration, and water quality (Vörösmarty, et al., 2000; Alcamo, et al., 2007; Wang, 2006; Dunne and Leopold, 1978). Landscape architects who work at the urban and regional scale typically consider hydrological models as an integrative part of urban and infrastructural development, as evidenced in the work of Carl Steinitz of the Harvard Graduate School of Design in his San Pedro River project (Steinitz, et al., 2000, 2003) and Christophe Girot of ETH Zurich in his Ciliwung River Watershed study (Future Cities Laboratory, 2012).

Linking the realm of fundamental scientific research in applied terrestrial and hydrological ecology with that of empirical and heuristic methods of landscape architecture and urban design, Steinitz's and Girot's approaches echo a larger trend within the design disciplines. The past decade has indeed seen an unprecedented expansion of the agency of architects, landscape architects, and urban designers within the ecological and infrastructural dimensions of the built environment (Mostafavi, 2010). This trend has facilitated not only multidisciplinary endeavors, but also the conceptualization of strategies for resilient cities—that is, cities which could adapt to change, whether that change is environmental, climatic, economic, or socio-political (Lister, 2009; Ahern, 2012).

In this context, the current investigation concerns the potential contribution of the design disciplines to integrated hydrological modeling. It will do so by focusing on an arid oasis valley river basin typology whose modeling has not yet been extended to include design criteria. In the face of scarce water supply, limited land resources, and dwindling economies, oasis river basins require new modeling approaches that take into account both climate change and anthropogenic impacts, in order to support sustainable development that preserves the ecological and cultural heritage.

Figure 1 : Drâa River Oasis at the Oasis of Agdz

The case study I will use is that of the Drâa Valley, which is one of the driest basins in the world (Revenga, et al., 1998) and which has been the subject of a holistic model developed at the University of Bonn (Schulz and Judex, 2008). This approach incorporates hydrologic and economic modules in one integrative model, where water demand and water supply are solved simultaneously. IMPETUS is a collaborative research project involving a unique mix of scientists from the social sciences, natural sciences, agriculture, and medicine which aims to study these disciplines' interrelation with hydrological modeling. Since the IMPETUS project does not consider the potential impact of existing and new urban, landscape, and architectural models on hydrological modeling, it offers an ideal ground on which to test the hypothesis.

FIGURE 2: Inside the oasis of M'hamid, Drâa Valley

The Drâa Valley: Changes and Challenges

Fed by the Drâa River, which takes sources in the Atlas Mountains, the arid Drâa Valley is composed of six palm groves or oases located in southern Morocco (Figure 1). The uniqueness of this pre-Saharan valley lies in its stunning cultural and ecological landscapes, comprised of more than 1,000 rammed-earth houses called *kasbahs*, assembled in villages called *ksour*, which are surrounded by lush, oasian agricultural fields (Mouline and Hensens, 2005). The *ksar* (singular of *ksour*) and its oasis form a dual ensemble of rural domestic and work spaces, intrinsically connected and supportive of each other. The *ksar*, built on non-fertile high ground, is an assembly of two to five dozen high-walled courtyard houses, with a central square and mosque as public space. Its dense and compact structure, with rammed-earth walls 0.5m thick and four stories high and shaded pedestrian streets 2m wide, creates a microclimate that is up to 10°C cooler than the exterior temperature.

The Drâa Valley oases are also man-made, artificial landscapes built on the fertile riverbanks. They are typically composed of three vertical layers of different plants: vegetables, fruit trees, and date palms (Figure 2). The canopy combination creates a microclimate propitious to plant growth and to minimizing soil evaporation and plant evapotranspiration. The oasian landscapes, predominantly composed of cereals such as wheat and date palms, have been constructed and sustained not only by the sophisticated irrigation and agricultural techniques that have evolved in response to aridity and water scarcity, but also by a rigorous communal management of water resources.

According to the Morocco 1996 Agricultural Census, micro-properties are the norm in the Drâa Valley; holdings range in size from 0.5–5ha. Due to the combined effects of inheritance divisions and demographic pressure, more than 80% of the region's farmers own less than one hectare. Palm trees often fall under a separate property title; several tenants can share ownership of a single date palm tree, by inheritance or purchase (Ait Hamza, et al., 2007).

With half the surface area of the Drâa Valley oases having already vanished over the course of the 20th century (Association de Développement de la Vallée du Drâa [ADRERA], 2012), the socio-environmental balance is today being further compromised by several factors: the spread of diseases such as the Bayoud, a virus that attacks palm trees; successive droughts; and, most importantly, the over-pumping of scarce water resources.

The vulnerability of the Valley's water resources is attributed to population growth and the emergence and expansion of urban centers, along with the development of modern means for groundwater withdrawal (e.g., motor pumps), the introduction of a dam upstream, and the absence of an integrated basin-wide management policy, all of which have been ongoing issues since the late 1970s. The compounded effects have resulted in the over-pumping of groundwater resources and a loss of the natural groundwater recharge. Consequently, piezometric levels have decreased, underground water supplies have been depleted, traditional irrigation systems and oasis landscapes have deteriorated, and soil salinity has increased. Both water scarcity and soil salinity may worsen in the future due to climate change.

Despite these hurdles and transformations, the Drâa Valley remains the "date basket" of Morocco; agriculture, and date palm cultivation in particular, still constitutes the Valley's main economic activity. However, it is becoming an unreliable endeavor and is slowly being abandoned. The abandonment of agricultural land is ominous in many regards: it is often followed by the advancement of sand dunes into the oasis, the exodus of inhabitants from the *ksar* to new urban centers which have sprung up along the Valley's main paved road, N101, and the ultimate loss of the cultural landscape heritage associated with the *ksar*-oasis system.

Given the dependence of the *ksour* and oases on water availability and agricultural cultivation, what water management model would be the most appropriate here? What approach would support the economic betterment of the inhabitants, while preserving the agricultural landscape and architectural heritage? Bypassing, on one hand, the pastiche preservationist approach that advocates for the nostalgic return to a vanished oasian past (Shoay, 1999), and on the other, the Moroccan state's focus on potable water access only, a new water model should integrate not only new economic activities, but also the re-design of built environments and agricultural landscape models as hybrid systems which combine both innovative technologies and traditional methods.

The IMPETUS model, called MIDAV (*Modèle intégré de la vallée du Drâa*), integrates climate, water, and economic data, but stops short of envisioning drastic changes in the built environment or in crop types and agricultural practices. Hence, it can serve as a foundation for discussing a new approach to hydrological modeling. Before introducing this subject, a brief description of the Valley's hydrology, built environment, and economy will contextualize IMPETUS's site of study.

Surface and Ground Water Resources

The Drâa River is the longest river in Morocco at 1,100km. It flows from the Atlas Mountains southwards to Tagounite and, from there, westwards to the Atlantic Ocean. The Upper Drâa is part of the province of Ouarzazate and ends with the Mansour Eddahbi dam and reservoir, constructed in 1972 in order to ensure regular access to water for irrigation, hydroelectric energy, and flood reduction (Office Régional de Mise en Valeur Agricole de Ouarzazate [ORMVAO], 1995). The area under discussion—the middle part of the watershed, called the Middle Drâa—is 200km long and belongs to the province of Zagora. The Middle Drâa starts at the intersection of the River Dades and the River Ouarzazate, runs along six oases, and then drains into the saltwater Lake Iriki in the far south (Ouhajou, 1996). The six oases—from north to south, Mezguita, Tinzouline, Ternata, Fezouata, Ktaoua and M'Hamid—cover a total surface area of 18,500 hectares. Each oasis has its own small reservoir, starting from Agdz and ending in the Bounou reservoir near M'Hamid (Figure 3). The area beyond the last oasis of the Middle Drâa is predominantly a dry riverbed, which has not reached the Atlantic Ocean for decades.

The Middle Drâa Valley watershed receives most of its water resources from the high Atlas Mountains' ice melts and precipitations. Seventy-five percent of this water is lost by evaporation (Schulz and Judex, 2008), from the tributary rivers of the M'goun, Dades, and Ouarzazate, and from three underground water tables (Figure 4). The annual average precipitation in the Middle Drâa ranges from 50–80mm, while month to month precipitation variability is very large. For instance, mean monthly precipitation in Agdz is 6.5mm, but the standard deviation is 3.8. Moving from north to south, average monthly precipitation decreases (Figure 5). There are two rainfall peaks per year: one in October–December and one in February–March. The latter is essential to the viability of agricultural sowing (ORMVAO, 2000).

Within the watershed, air temperature and evaporation are higher along the aridity gradient of the Saharan promontory. In the southernmost oasis, M'Hamid, evaporation reaches 2,500mm/year; temperatures are high, especially between June and September, when they range from 43°–50° C. The vegetation of the Drâa watershed changes according to this climatic gradient, from Mediterranean savannah in the north to desert biomes in the south. Similarly, there is a large variation in precipitation within the watershed, depending on topography: Ouarzazate, at the north of the Middle Drâa Valley, receives 117mm of rain a year, whereas Lake Iriki, at the east of M'hamid, located at 450m above sea level, receives only 50mm annually, scattered between October and February. The Mansour Eddahbi reservoir receives an average of 350mm/year, whereas Bounou, near M'hamid, receives only 30–40mm/year.

It is important to note that precipitation throughout the Middle Drâa watershed has irregular patterns, which may range from aggressive, heavy rainfalls to frequent periods of drought averaging four to five years, followed by flash floods. Consequently, the releases from the dam are dependent on the filling level and manifest a high inter-year variability (Figure 6). The aim of a yearly outlet of 250mm was reached in only 43% of cases before 2007. Usually, with levels below 250mm, the six oases south of the dam cannot benefit from the dam's water releases at all, and rely mainly on water from the groundwater table accessed using motorized pumps. Groundwater aquifers thus play an important role to supplement and stabilize the availability of surface water in the Middle Drâa Valley. Aquifer recharge depends mainly on the infiltration of irrigation water in the oasian farmlands, as well as the infiltration of water from the riverbed (Hiedecke, 2009).

FIGURE 3: Drâa Valley watershed

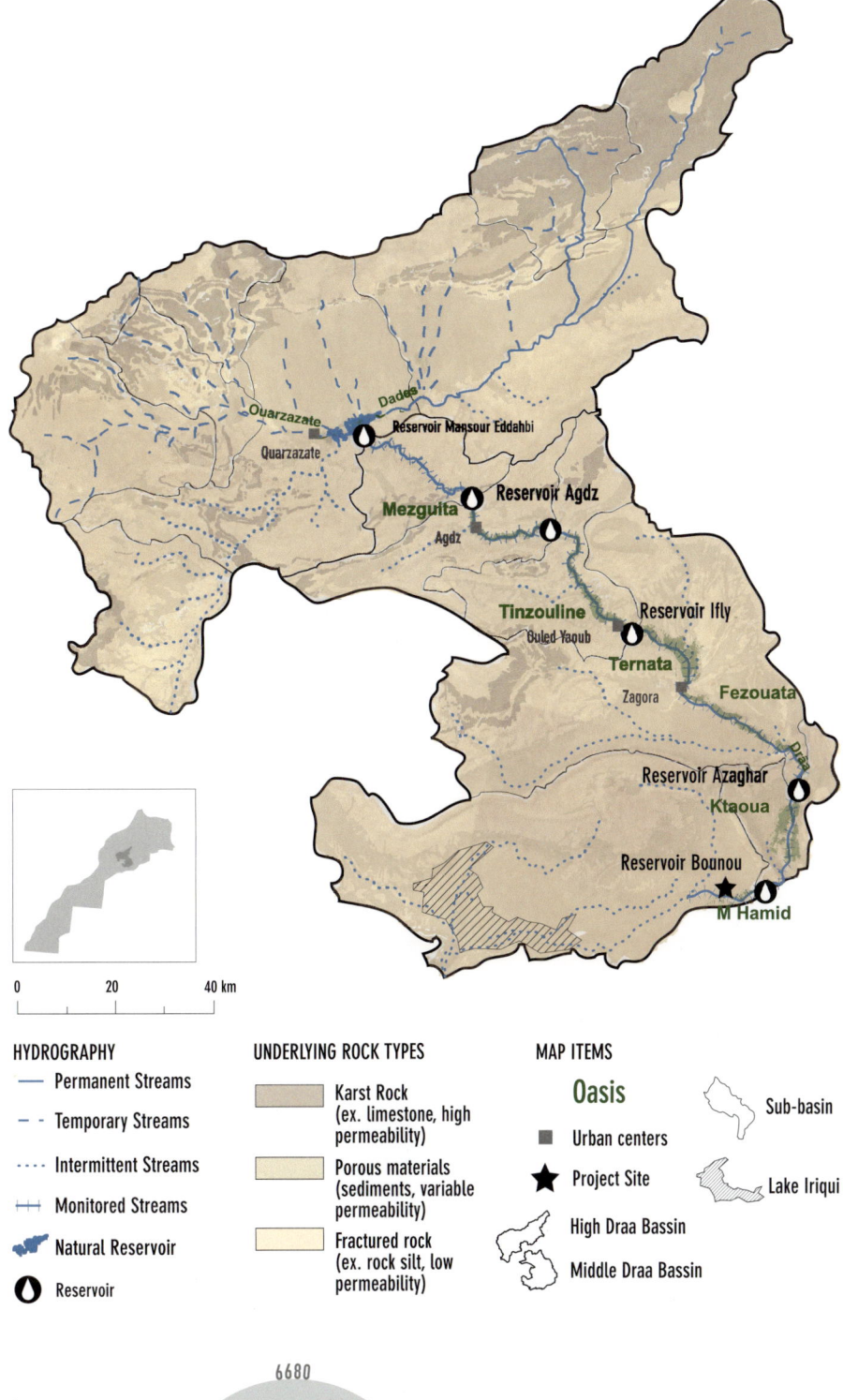

HYDROGRAPHY
— Permanent Streams
- - Temporary Streams
⋯ Intermittent Streams
⊢⊢⊢ Monitored Streams
▬ Natural Reservoir
⬤ Reservoir

UNDERLYING ROCK TYPES
Karst Rock (ex. limestone, high permeability)
Porous materials (sediments, variable permeability)
Fractured rock (ex. rock silt, low permeability)

MAP ITEMS
Oasis
■ Urban centers
★ Project Site
Sub-basin
Lake Iriqui
High Draa Bassin
Middle Draa Bassin

FIGURE 4: Contribution of rivers to the Drâa River Valley water regime

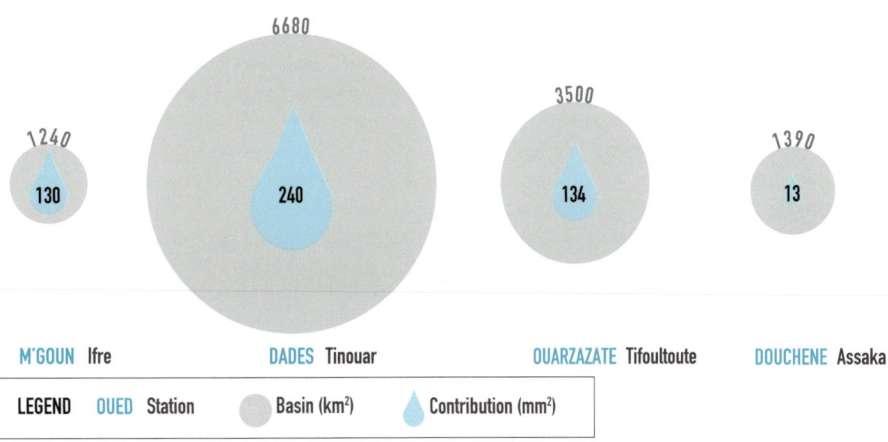

M'GOUN Ifre	DADES Tinouar	OUARZAZATE Tifoultoute	DOUCHENE Assaka
1240 / 130	6680 / 240	3500 / 134	1390 / 13

LEGEND OUED Station Basin (km²) Contribution (mm²)

FIGURE 5: Precipitation patterns in the Drâa Valley

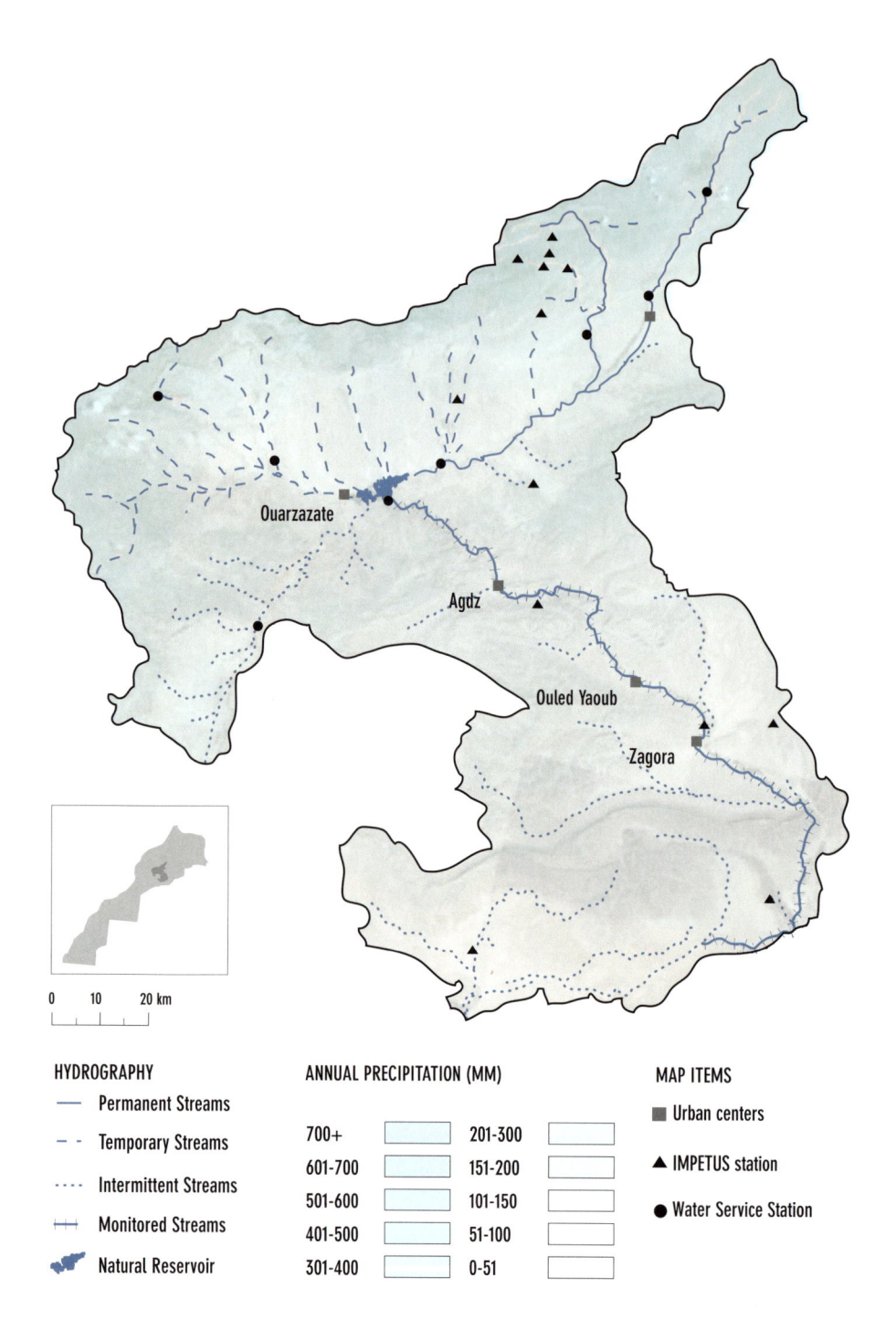

HYDROGRAPHY
— Permanent Streams
- - Temporary Streams
···· Intermittent Streams
⊢⊢⊢ Monitored Streams
 Natural Reservoir

ANNUAL PRECIPITATION (MM)
700+
601-700
501-600
401-500
301-400
201-300
151-200
101-150
51-100
0-51

MAP ITEMS
■ Urban centers
▲ IMPETUS station
● Water Service Station

Groundwater resources in the Middle Drâa Valley vary among its six oases. Aquifer size and total reserves of groundwater fluctuate from one oasis to the next (Klose, et al., 2008) (Figure 7). The largest groundwater reserve can be found in Fezouata, with a volume of 127 million m³. Mezguita and M'Hamid have the lowest groundwater reserves, with less than 30 million m³ combined. During the infamous 1974 and 1984–88 droughts, low precipitations and surface water lowered the aquifers' levels by several meters. High soil salinity and contamination of the groundwater by chemical fertilizers have led to a severe water stress situation. The once lush and active oases of the Middle Drâa are today partly abandoned and lacking irrigation water, forming fragile and perilously damaged systems.

FIGURE 6: Water balance of the Mansour Eddahbi from 1972–73 until 2002–03

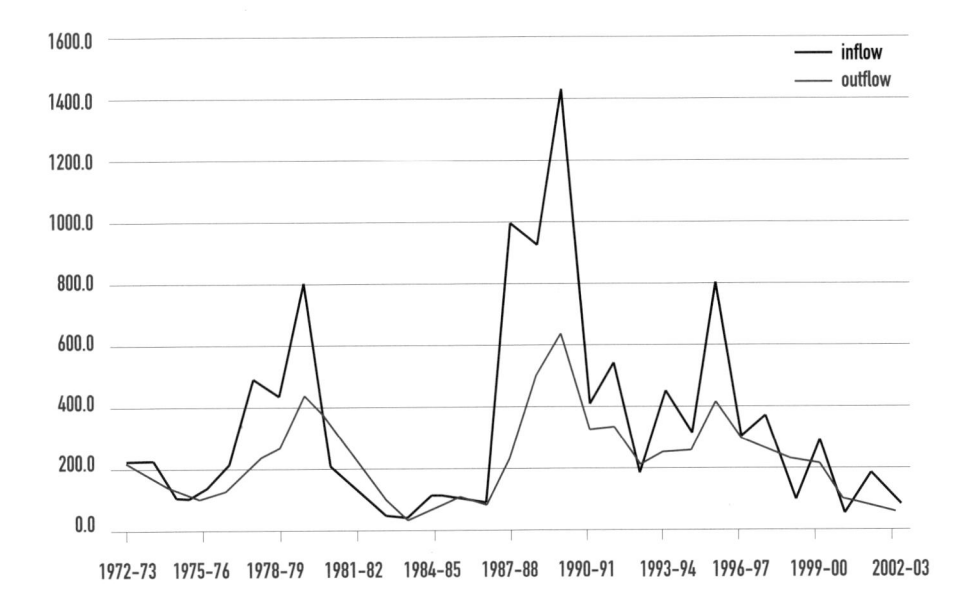

Water Use

Water use in the Drâa Valley falls into three main categories—domestic, tourism-related, and agricultural—with agriculture being the largest consumer of water (Office National de l'Eau Potable [ONEP], 2008). Few published reports are available regarding water usage in tourism; an unpublished 2006 survey, based on interviews with hotel owners, concludes that the tourism sector uses 100,000m³/year. Of all the water used by hotels, 15% is groundwater, and each tourist uses, on average, 1.2m³ of water per day (Heidecke, 2009).

Within the municipalities of the Middle Drâa, which include Zagora, Agdz, Tagounite, and M'Hamid, drinking water demand was estimated in 2003 at 1.2 million m³ in urban centers and 2.3 million m³ in rural areas (Schulz and Judex, 2008). One million m³ was the estimated use for cattle husbandry (Office National de l'Eau Potable [ONEP], 1995).

Interestingly, drinking water demand in rural areas is not included in the data provided by the official water authority, ONEP, although 70% of that population has had access to a municipal pipeline system since 2002 (Direction de la Recherche et de la Planification de l'Eau [DRPE], 1998). Despite this omission, agricultural irrigation use remains by far the most significant water demand in the Valley. It is important to note that this demand is not often fulfilled, as water supply is highly variable due to severe and prolonged droughts, such as the ones that occurred in the mid-1980s and early 2000s.

In fact, farmers in the Middle Drâa obtain water either from periodic water releases from the dam, called *lâché*, or by pumping shallow groundwater. While 85% of the water used during non-drought years is surface water from the Drâa River, during drought years their reliance on groundwater resources significantly increases. In 1977, there were about 2,000 motor pumps in the six oases; by 1985, that number had doubled (Faouzi, 1986), then up to 7,000 in 2005 (Centre de Mise en Valeur [CMV], 2005). In other basins in Morocco, water pricing has been implemented as a tool to prevent unsustainable depletion. In the Drâa Valley, however, groundwater usage is not yet supervised or disincentivized.

Oasian Irrigation Systems and Water Management

The traditional irrigation systems in the pre-Saharan oasis valleys of Morocco rely not only on water conveyance and distribution techniques, but also on communal water resource management. Most farmers in the Drâa Valley used to convey water to their agricultural plots from the river (*oued*), either through clay canals (*seguias*) or from underground water table troughs (*khetarras*). Traditional seguias are not as efficient as non-porous canals, but the water that is lost replenishes the water table.

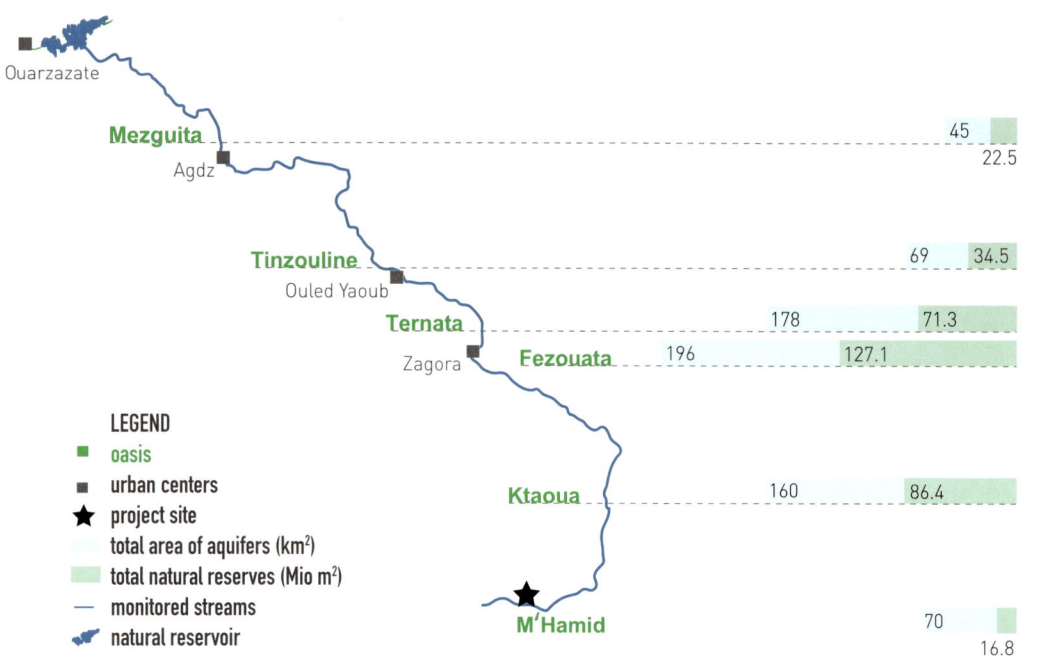

FIGURE 7: Area of aquifers and total natural reserves in the Drâa oases

FIGURE 8: Section of a khetarra

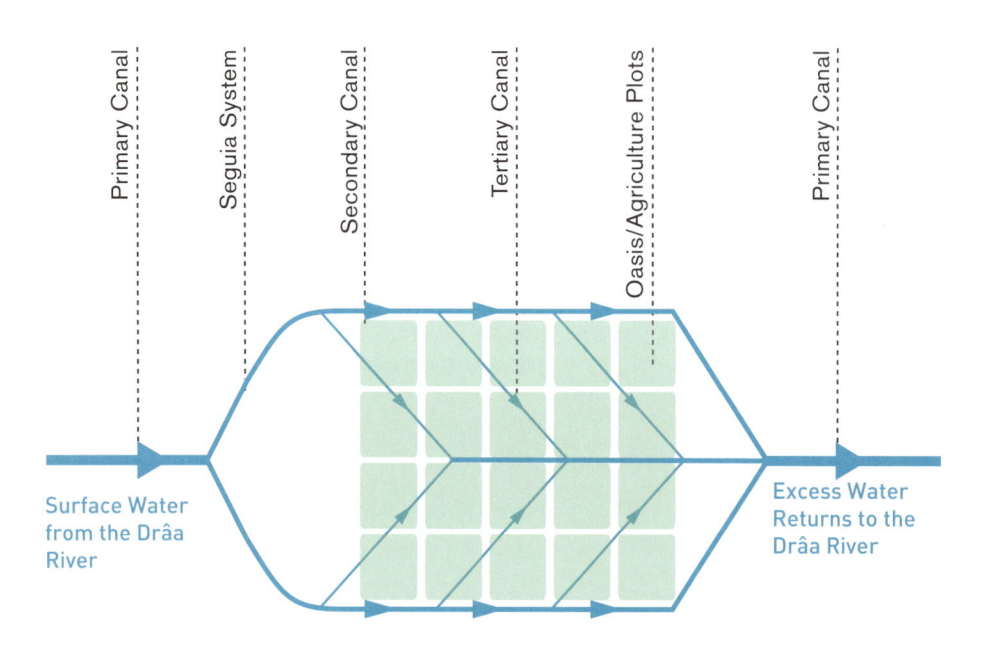

FIGURE 9: Fish bone pattern of irrigation canals ("seguias")

Similar to the Iranian *qanats, khetarras* are underground canal systems that use gravity to collect and channel water towards the oasis (Figure 8). Their average water flow is 10L/s (Simon, 2011). In contrast, the withdrawal of water by motor pumps can lead to aquifer depletion, since this technology has the capacity to extract large amounts of water from deep aquifers (Lightfoot, 1996). *Khetarras* in the Drâa Valley are still used today by some farmers; however, many have become obsolete due to the ongoing and expert maintenance they require. Today, most of these canals can be found in a state of ruin, or filled with sand.

Once water reaches the oasis, it is distributed across the oasis through a network of *seguias* organized in a fishbone pattern (Figure 9). The main *seguia*, which brings water from the river to the oasis, is subdivided into secondary channels called *mesrefs*. An irrigation schedule, *noubas*, determines the sequence of use by each farmer. This sequence depends on three factors: the farmer's location vis-à-vis topography, the rule of the *rebta wa-jartha* ("one division after another," or from upstream to downstream; La Roche, 1946), and a complex set of agreements between tribes. These agreements recognize two types of *seguias*: *melk seguias* allow partial private ownership of the water received, while *allam seguias* are collective. In both systems, an elected member of the community, the *amazzal*, manages water distribution, ensures fair distribution of water, and manages conflicts. These two water management systems still exist today, yet the tight community bonds and cohesion that they rely on have been eroded by exodus to cities.

Following the construction of the Mansour Eddahbi dam in 1972, surface water allocation in the Drâa Valley has been managed by local water associations and the regional office of agriculture, ORMVAO. Water allocation is predominantly carried out through *lâchés*, directed southward to the six oases via channels and ditches.

Architectural Heritage and Urban Transformation

The upper and middle zones of the watershed are home to 780,000 inhabitants who live in *ksour*. These are scattered along the riverbanks of the oases and maintain a relatively low density of 29 inhabitants per km². The Valley was designated in 2000 as part of the UNESCO Man and Biosphere Program (MAB) for its unique agricultural and riparian ecosystems, and its rammed-earth *ksour*.

Launched in the early 1970s, "the MAB Program proposes an interdisciplinary research agenda and capacity building that target the ecological, social and economic dimensions of biodiversity loss and the reduction of this loss" (UNESCO, 2013). Areas that are part of this Network of Biosphere Reserves have to conduct programs for the preservation of biodiversity and share their outcomes. In the Drâa Valley, these have included programs to prevent the advancement of sand dunes into the oasis, including sand dune stabilization via biodegradable geotextiles and tamarisk tree planting; the substitution of gas for wood in pottery production; and environmental awareness campaigns. The Agriculture Services, Waters, and Forests Departments, Public Works Services, and the Civil Society lead these actions. Despite these efforts, the stability of the *ksour* and oases is tenuous.

Today, however, this self-sufficient micro-urbanism, which is defined by an agro-social economy, is facing crisis on two fronts. First, the economic viability of small-scale oasian agriculture is diminishing each year. In fact, in the past two decades, oasian farmers have been increasingly relying on remittances from relatives. Many agricultural plots have been abandoned, which has allowed the advancement of sand dunes into the oases. Secondly, the once-vibrant walled *ksour* have been deserted, forming a series of ruins along the Drâa Valley (Figure 10). As early as the 1950s, *ksour* inhabitants began relocating to generic concrete houses near the winding reconnaissance road, which was built along the Drâa River and offered water-sanitation infrastructure and a supply of electricity, previously unavailable in the *ksour* (Mouline, 1991; Hensens, 1991). The new settlements took a linear form, with stores and amenities organized along the road and housing informally scattered nearby.

The houses in these new settlements are problematic on many levels. Their construction materials—brick and concrete—and their lack of insulation are not suited to the Valley's arid climate, which is characterized by warm days and cool evenings. Rammed earth has a low thermal resistance, countered by its large thermal mass. Thermal mass allows a material to absorb heat during the day and then release this absorbed heat over the cool evening. The thermal mass of rammed earth mitigates internal temperature fluctuations when applied to a building envelope, unlike brick and concrete. Overall, this increases internal thermal comfort and energy efficiency.

FIGURE 10: Ruins along the Drâa Valley

Unlike the tight layout of the *ksar's* buildings and streets, which is conducive to generating a microclimate, the scattered placement of houses in the new urban centers increases the heat gain of buildings and produces unshaded, unpleasant circulation systems. In addition, the water scarcity measures commonly used in the *ksour*, such as communal rainwater reservoirs, composting toilets, and grey water reuse for irrigation, are not present in the new urban centers.

Today, according to our 2009 survey, M'Hamid and Tagounite are the poorest oases of the Valley and remain inhabited at a 50% occupancy rate, while the rest of the rammed-earth building stock is either abandoned or used as pens for animals. Unfortunately, the local population of the Valley views rammed-earth construction as archaic, despite its success in recent tourism developments, where *kasbahs* have been rehabilitated and converted to hotels (Chaouni, 2012).

The IMPETUS Drâa Valley Project, the MIDAV Model, and Alternatives

Developed by researchers at the University of Bonn, the Drâa Valley IMPETUS project proposes a model for the Drâa River basin based on a conjunctive hydro-economy, to be studied over a period of three years. One of its key goals is to propose possible conjunctive water management solutions and water pricing policies for the Drâa Valley, with agriculture as the main activity. Conjunctive water management refers to the coordinated operation of a groundwater basin and a surface water system to increase total supplies and enhance total water supply reliability. In fact, ground and surface water sources are seen as two components of single system that should be managed accordingly (Gemma and Tsur, 2007).

The complex relationships between crop yields and water quality and quantity (Roseta-Palma, 2006), and between various water supply and user types (Heidecke, 2009), necessitate a model which integrates hydrological as well as socioeconomic data. Such conjunctive models (e.g. Ringler, 2002; Cai, et al., 2006) emerged within the field of hydrology as an alternative to simple models, which derive the value of water analytically, bypassing empirical data on the site's socio-cultural and economic characteristics (Tsur and Graham-Tomassi, 1991; Provencher and Burt, 1994).

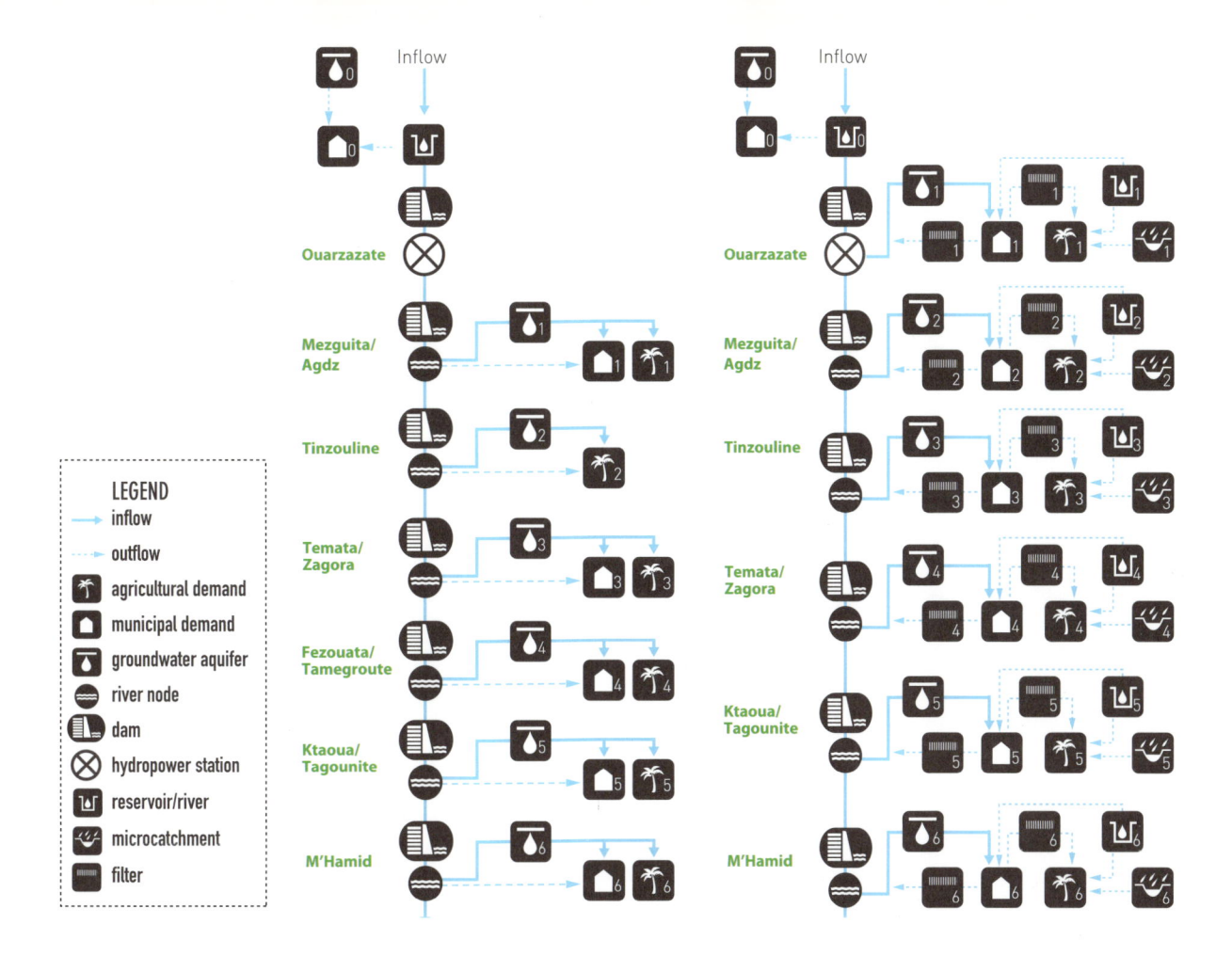

FIGURE 11a: Water network for the Drâa Basin in the MIDAV model (left)

FIGURE 11b: MIDAV model and proposed water reuse strategies (right)

Due to increased demand for available water resources by multiple users and the increased economic difficulty in constructing large-scale projects such as dams, there is a need for basin-wide management strategies that are based on the conjunctive model, such as the MIDAV model developed by IMPETUS. This model proposes long-term water budgeting which balances water surplus during wet years with water deficit during drought years. During the wet years, surface water would be used for irrigation and aquifer recharge, thus replenishing and conserving groundwater for withdrawal during periods of deficit. The model also proposes water metering, proportional to source and availability, as a means to decrease groundwater depletion and ensure the viability of the oasis ecologically and economically (Figure 11a).

A limitation of the MIDAV model is its failure to anticipate any change in the dynamics between the new urban centers and *ksour*, urban sprawl, land use zoning, or agricultural practices. The model also does not consider alternative solutions to water management, such as artificial groundwater recharge, return flow from irrigation and sewage, and stream-aquifer interaction (Figure 11b and Figure 12). Different architectural typologies, landscape strategies, and urban design principles could be used in the MIDAV model to delineate alternative futures for the Drâa Valley, distinct from the status quo of the Valley's built and rural environments.

An increase in impervious surface area accompanied by urban development and vegetative loss is well-established to significantly alter the hydrological cycle, in particular by increasing the flow volume and velocity of stormwater runoff (Dunne and Leopold, 1978). Impervious surfaces displace water from its natural locations of retention and infiltration, which can cause a loss of local groundwater recharge and an increase in floods elsewhere. The lack of local infiltration decreases groundwater recharge, while the loss of vegetative cover results in a decrease of evapotranspiration and evaporative cooling, thus changing climate patterns. Moreover, the combination of stormwater runoff and loss of vegetation increases erosion of fertile topsoil, which consequently impacts agricultural practices. Hence, urbanization, and the means by which it takes form, has tremendous impact on the hydrological cycle (Figure 12).

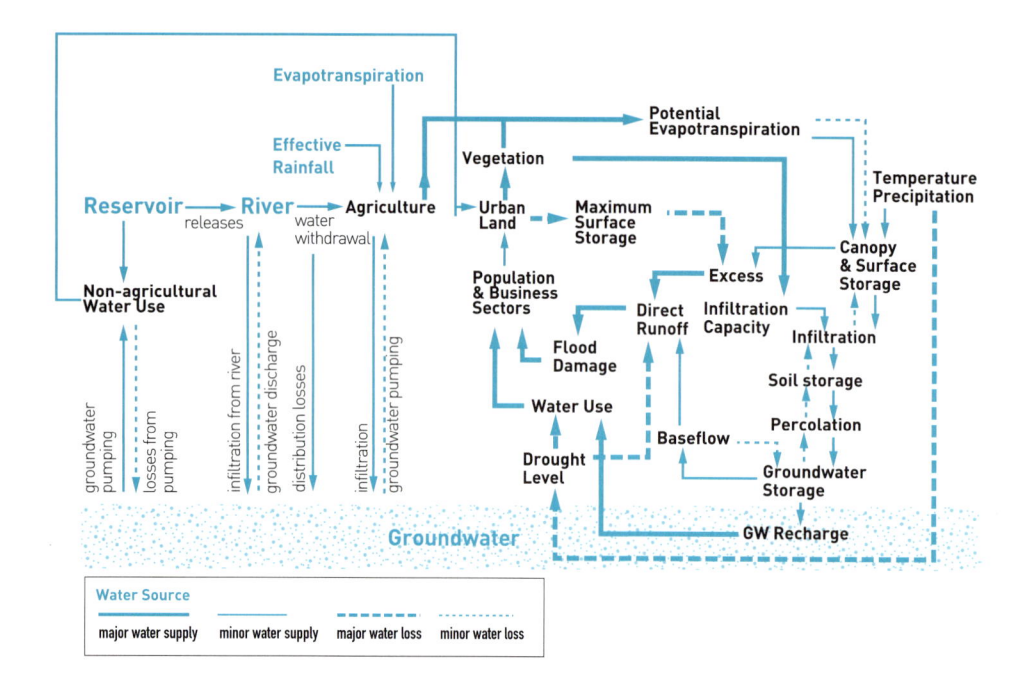

FIGURE 12: Feedback loop between hydrologic and urban/socioeconomic components: MIDAV model with proposed urban strategies

Alternative solutions for augmenting water availability may include retrofitting existing buildings or designing new ones to collect and store rainwater and dew. Urban wastewater can be collected and treated for reuse in agriculture, thus increasing water availability for irrigation, or for groundwater recharge. This may affect the pricing of water, allowing the agriculture-based economy to remain viable. New urban areas can be integrated with tree canopy to offset ambient temperatures; streets can be designed with water-retaining landscapes, such as bio-swales and rain gardens, that would capture and infiltrate water on-site; and pervious, unpaved, landscaped public spaces can be integrated into the public realm. Such architectural and urban guidelines and bylaws should have their water management capacity quantified, and be incorporated into the MIDAV model.

Similarly, rural domestic water use in the Valley could be viewed through a finer lens. Farmers' incomes are often used to upgrade housing or build new concrete homes. Guidelines for retrofitting *kasbahs* could change this trend, and encourage locals to maintain use of the *kasbahs* by introducing strategies that provide both the modern amenities sought by local populations (such as indoor toilets and showers) and water conservation features (such as new-generation composting toilets, water reservoirs, and subterranean wetlands to clean grey water). In addition, rammed-earth, off-the-grid housing typologies could be developed to minimize both heat gain and water use. The Desert House, by Moroccan design firm Aziza Chaouni Projects illustrates this new sustainable typology. Located in the Saharan region of Erfoud, the house incorporates affordable rammed earth constructed techniques (Figure 13a and 13b).

Tourism is another important factor which is currently overlooked by the MIDAV model. In fact, tourism will be the primary economic focus for Morocco over the next few decades. Plan Azur 2010 aimed to attract 10 million tourists annually, which was achieved; Plan 2020 (Chaouni, 2012) aims for 20 million tourists annually, along with a sustainable tourism agenda. One of the aspects of Plan 2020 calls for an emphasis on rural areas, including the Drâa Valley. Already a popular tourist destination, the Drâa Valley will certainly attract more visitors in the near future thanks to its UNESCO Biosphere status. Unplanned growth in tourism may promote further abandonment of agriculture in favor of more lucrative tourism jobs. It may also promote the development of unsustainable and inappropriate forms of tourism, such as large hotels built with concrete and air conditioning systems, swimming pools, golf courses, water-intensive gardens, and so on.

FIGURE 13a: Desert House by Aziza Chaouni Projects, Erfoud, Ziz Valley, Morocco

AXONOMETRIC

TENT FABRIC (WOOL)

- pvc tubular structure
- wool fabric (light color)
- wind tower
- rain water collector

TICK EARTH WALL CONSTRUCTION

- southern wall (50cm)

a well
b drinking water reservoir
c rain water reservoir
d natural refrigerator

PHASING DIAGRAMS

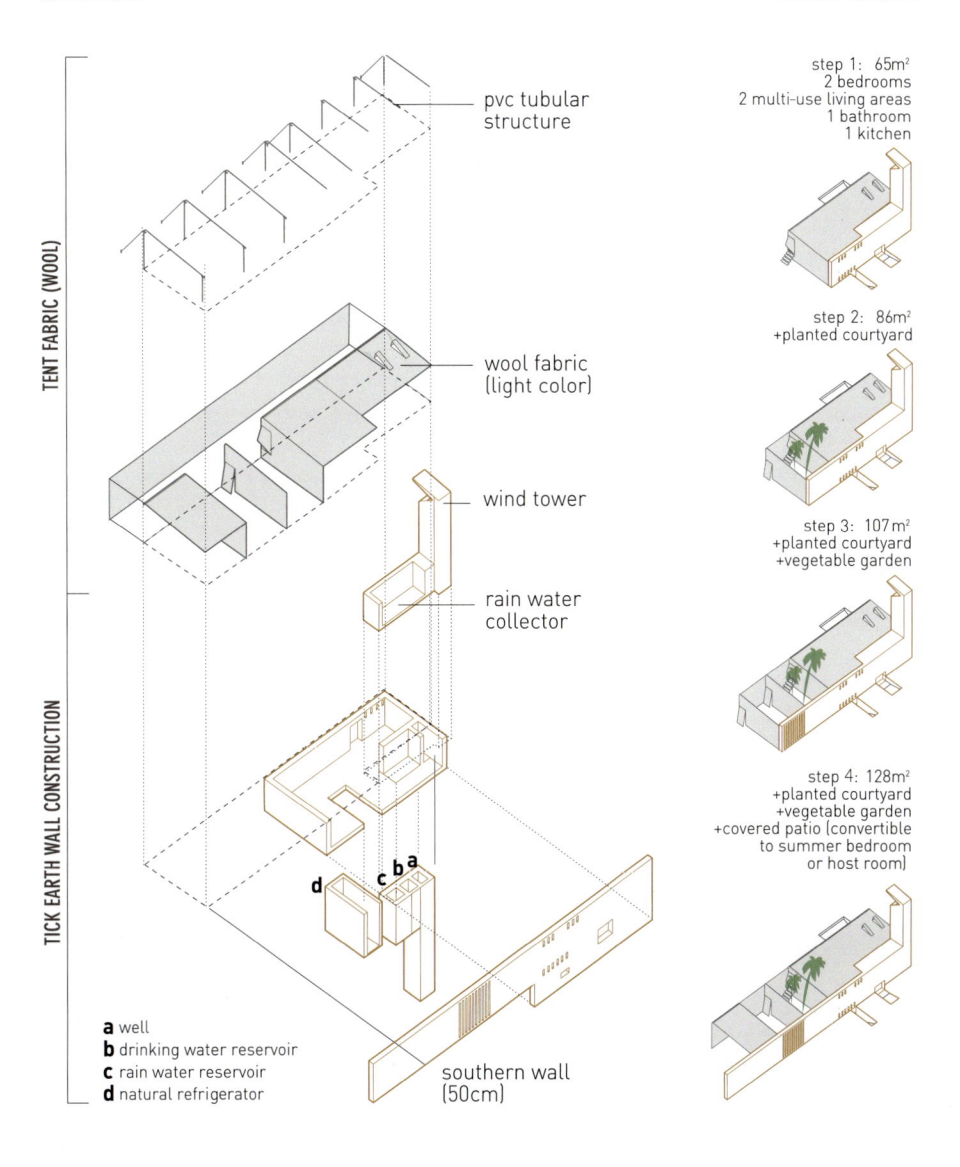

step 1: 65m²
2 bedrooms
2 multi-use living areas
1 bathroom
1 kitchen

step 2: 86m²
+planted courtyard

step 3: 107m²
+planted courtyard
+vegetable garden

step 4: 128m²
+planted courtyard
+vegetable garden
+covered patio (convertible to summer bedroom or host room)

SUSTAINABLE DEVICES FOR EVERYDAY ACTIVITIES

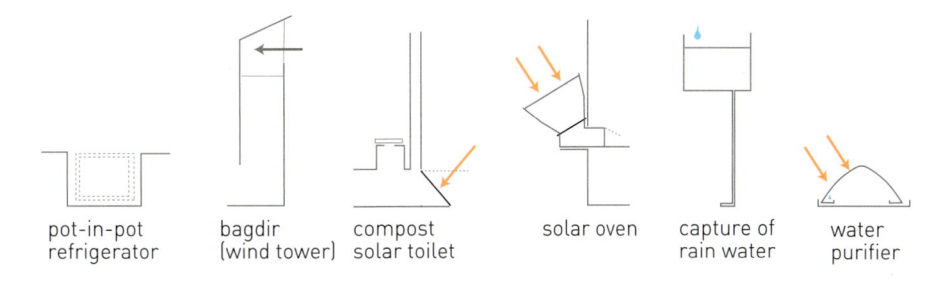

- pot-in-pot refrigerator
- bagdir (wind tower)
- compost solar toilet
- solar oven
- capture of rain water
- water purifier

Such hotels have already begun to appear, primarily along the main road in the new urban area, as described previously. In response, Morocco's Ministry of Tourism has been promoting ecotourism and sustainable building approaches, as developed in the agro-tourism masterplan of SMIT (Société Marocaine d'Ingénieurie Touristique) and DET (Designing Ecological Tourism). The masterplan calls for a focus on the Valley's unique agricultural landscape, which is defined by the relationships between the oasis and ksar, its associated ecology, architecture, and cultural practices. It proposes an infill strategy, whereby uncultivated agricultural sites within the oasis would be rehabilitated for tourism activities. The masterplan identifies priority areas for land cultivation, the selection of endemic crops, sustainable agricultural practices, construction of "eco-lodges" (for example, see Taragalte Ecolodge, pp.178–179) in place of large hotels, and guidelines for the appropriate siting of built structures, trails, and tours. The ambition of the masterplan is to improve the socioeconomic conditions of farmers through landscape management of oasis ecology and hydrology.

While today the Drâa Valley is primarily characterized by subsistence agriculture with the exception of date exports, the masterplan proposes that crops be introduced and sold locally to the tourism industry (hotels currently import food products from other regions in Morocco). Such crops may include not only food products, but also high-value cosmetic and health products such as henna and Argan oil—in the oasis of Tinzouline, henna currently represents a mere 3.9% of the total crops produced (Roth, 2008). The masterplan would entail the introduction of the henna plant (*Lawsonia inermis*) and Argan tree (*Argania spinosa*) to this region, both of which are particularly suitable for arid conditions. For instance, the Argan tree is uniquely suited to this arid climate due to its 250m long taproots (Préau, 2004).

The ecotourism model addresses the hydro-ecological, socioeconomic, and design dimensions as a single integrated design problem. This speculative plan, however, would greatly benefit by drawing from the MIDAV model for the testing of its proposed strategies, associated metrics, and phasing with respect to environmental and socioeconomic criteria. For instance, in the MIDAV model, the recommended set price for ground and surface water is $0.03/L. If this pricing regulation was put in place conjointly with the ecotourism masterplan, extra ecotourism income could help farmers gain access to more water and thereby cultivate more land. What remains to be studied under the ecotourism masterplan scenario is how much of the Drâa Valley's fertile lands could be cultivated without compromising the water balance of the Valley while accommodating climate change, urban expansion, and population growth.

Conclusion

The agro-tourism masterplan, rural and urban design, architectural and landscape retrofit, new typologies, and the MIDAV water regulation strategies are mutually beneficial: the successful implementation of one profits the others. Speculative scenarios that include land use patterns and urban-architectural innovations, climate data, and soil and water quality criteria could significantly affect the modeling of hydrological basins. Likewise, the Drâa Valley ecotourism masterplan could benefit immensely by testing its scale, metrics, and phasing propositions using the MIDAV model.

Implementation of the design strategies and MIDAV financial regulation requires intervention by provincial actors. In the case of the Drâa Valley, the Agence du Bassin Hydraulique de Souss Massa, a government agency which regulates the Drâa River basin among other basins in southwestern Morocco, would benefit from collaborating with the Urban Agency of Ouarzazate and the Ministry of Tourism in order to develop a masterplan for both rural and urban areas of the Valley. Such a multidisciplinary collaboration could certainly produce the nuanced hydrological models needed to tackle the Drâa Valley's new economic and climatic challenges, utilizing modern as well as ancient technologies.

Acknowledgements

The author would like to thank the Moroccan Ministry of Tourism, the Aga Khan Program at the Harvard Graduate School of Design, and Halim Sbai from the NGO Zaila.

FIGURE 13b: Desert House by Aziza Chaouni Projects, Erfoud, Ziz Valley, Morocco

PLANS

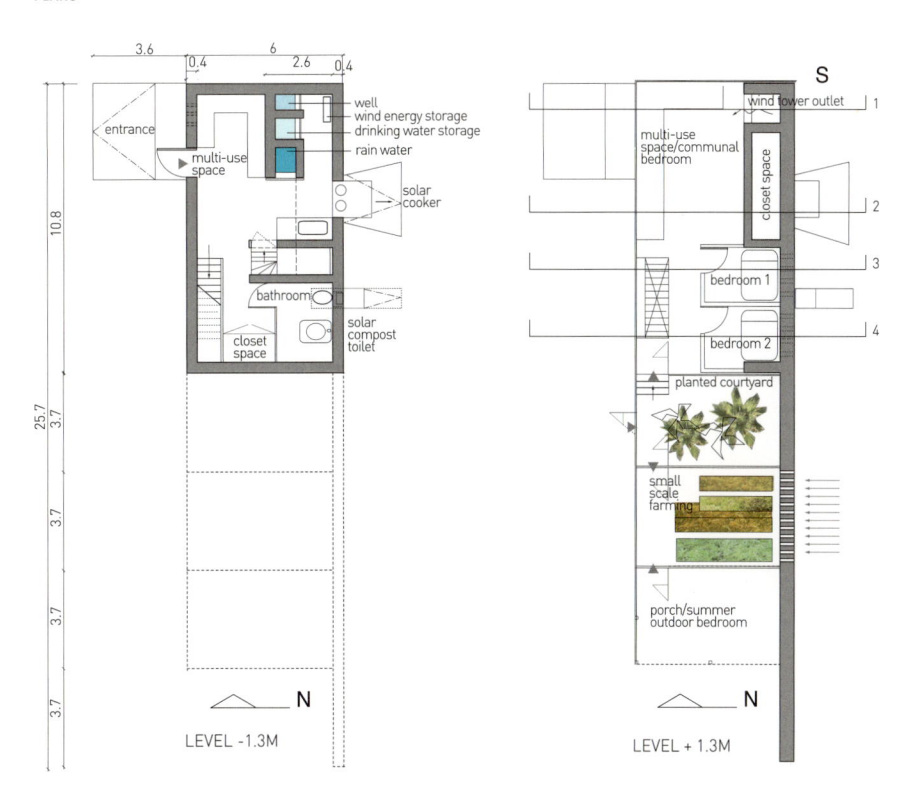

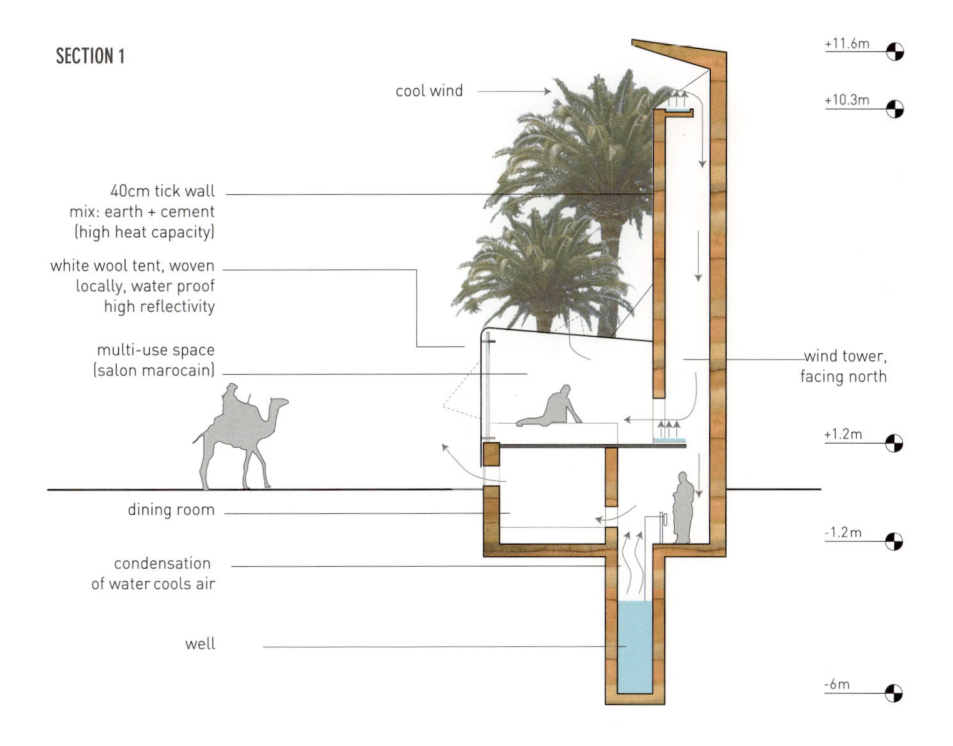

LEVEL -1.3M
- entrance
- multi-use space
- well
- wind energy storage
- drinking water storage
- rain water
- solar cooker
- bathroom
- solar compost toilet
- closet space

LEVEL +1.3M
- wind tower outlet
- multi-use space/communal bedroom
- closet space
- bedroom 1
- bedroom 2
- planted courtyard
- small scale farming
- porch/summer outdoor bedroom

SECTION 1

- cool wind
- 40cm tick wall mix: earth + cement (high heat capacity)
- white wool tent, woven locally, water proof high reflectivity
- multi-use space (salon marocain)
- wind tower, facing north
- dining room
- condensation of water cools air
- well

+11.6m
+10.3m
+1.2m
-1.2m
-6m

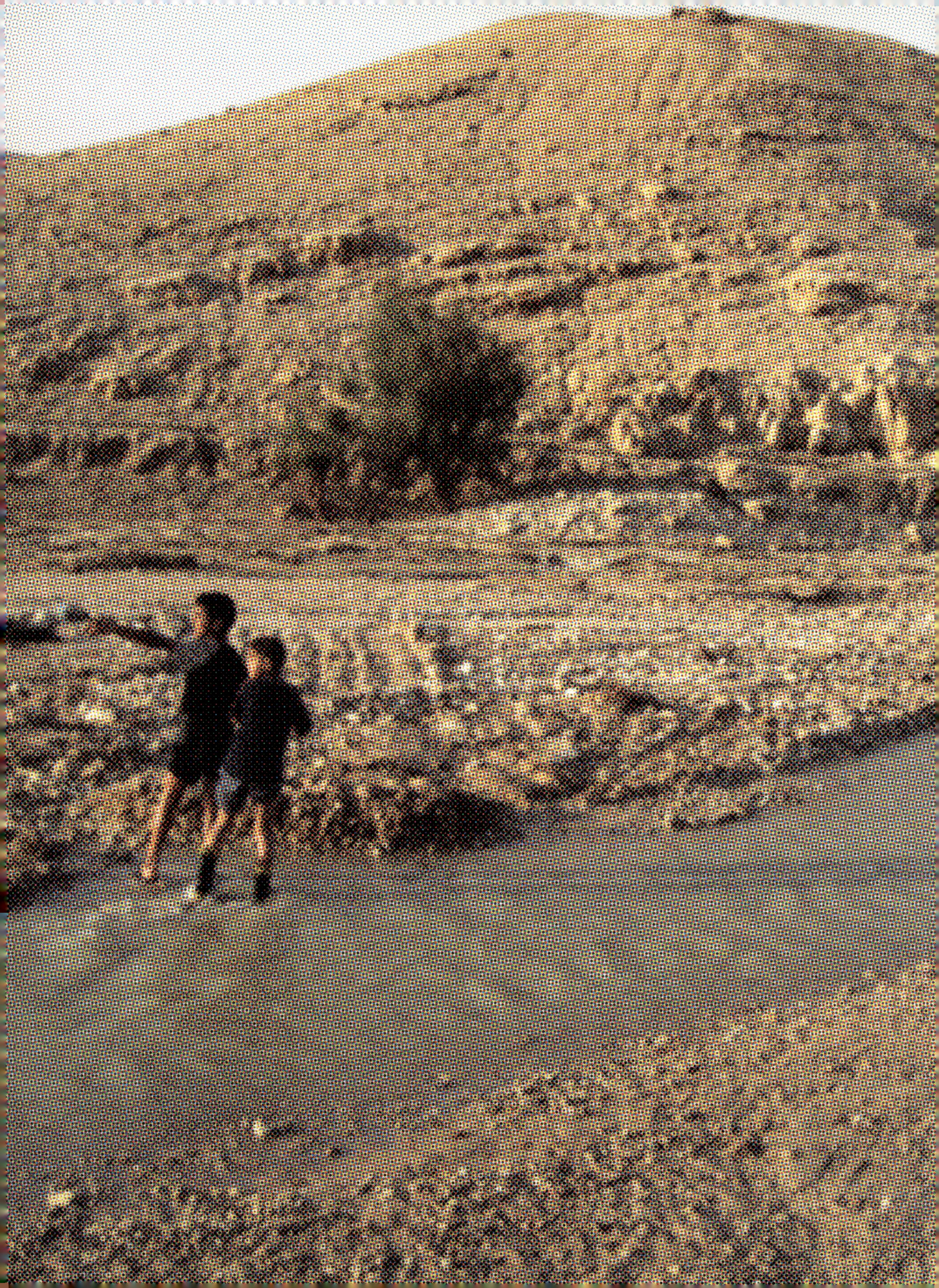

A Model for Integrated Agrarian Urbanism: Water Management in the Jordan River Basin

Fadi Masoud

The concepts of the urban and the agrarian have often been polarized in a way which has consequences for issues of water resources. This polarity has existed for centuries across various geographies, cultures, and disciplines. In contrast, contemporary design and planning discourse has sought to redefine what constitutes the physical limit of the city, given that its resources and infrastructure, including water, food, energy, waste management, and mobility, extend far beyond city limits (Brenner, 2001; Corner, 1999; Soja, 2000; Guillart, 2008; Bélanger, 2010). Existing legislative tools and administrative boundaries often disrupt socioeconomic and ecological flows that would otherwise conjoin regional geographies in a globalized condition (Brenner, 2008).

This essay advances a speculative proposal for agrarian urbanism, whereby agricultural production would be integrated into the urban context through the realignment of hydrology and water-sanitation infrastructure at the watershed and sub-watershed scales. Key to this proposal is the idea that landscape and the agrarian condition are formative elements of city structure, with profound influences on the shape and eventual distribution of resources at the regional scale. The proposal focuses on the Jordan River valley—one of the world's most contested and symbolic border river regions—and suggests a transition from an ineffective, ancient agrarian condition, which is subject to displacement by conventional urban or suburban models, to that of an efficient and environmentally sustainable growth model.

The Agrarian Urbanism Model

The proposed renewal of an urban-agrarian system is not a nostalgic call for a return to pastoral life, but rather a recognition of the fact that resilient systems can emerge from the coupling and diversification of land uses (Lister, 2007), and moreover from the integration of natural resource management. While much has been written about the implications of urban farming for agricultural production and public policy (e.g., Parham, 2011; Smit and Nasr, 1992; Pothukuchi and Kaufman, 2000), little has been written about the potentially profound implications for the shape and structure of the city itself.

Urban agriculture incorporates agriculture into the existing city structure by growing food in residual or abandoned open spaces (Mougeot, 2000). This may include livestock in backyards and parks, and along roadsides and utility right-of-ways; orchards, vineyards, and street and private lot trees that produce fruit; and vegetable crops grown on rooftops, backyards, vacant lots, institutional lots, and utility right-of-ways (DeKay, 1997). Agrarian urbanism, on the other hand, holds agrarian production as the principal organizing urban element in relation to open space and landscape functions (Parham, 2011; Duany, 2011; Pothukuchi and Kaufman, 2000).

Employing agrarian urbanism also means that cities are intrinsically transformed from places of consumption into important resource generators that are shaped by their agrarian flows and structures. The integration of urban elements (e.g., streets, buildings, parks, and infrastructure) with landscape processes would develop self-sufficiency and resilience with respect to food security, and at the same time make use of urban fresh water and wastewater resources (Arroyo, 2000; Pearson, 2007).

FIGURE 1: The southern region of the Jordan River is classified as arid African sub-Saharan

According to Duany (2011), agrarian urbanism is a model in which communities' settlement patterns support an agrarian society, whereby members are involved in the cultivation, economy, and consumption of their own food. The agrarian urban model seeks to erase the cultural divide between urban and rural, and further transform affluent suburban life and habits into productive preoccupation with food cultivation. This model, however, is strictly concerned with the cultural implications of the idealized lifestyle that it imagines; it falls short of addressing the most fundamental practical aspects of agriculture, which include the provision and management of water, waste, and energy, and their environmental, technological, economic, and political implications. In other words, it presents the agrarian landscape as a backdrop to settlement. It envisions a community where agriculture is a hobby, rather than one where the capture, treatment, and reuse of water for agricultural use is integrated into individuals' daily lives, thus lowering the community's environmental footprint.

Waldheim (2010) points to three agrarian urbanism precedents in which the spatial, ecological, and infrastructural import of agricultural production becomes the formative element of the peri-urban. Frank Lloyd Wright's Broadacre City (1932), Ludwig Hilberseimer's New Regional Pattern (1949), and Andrea Branzi's Agronica (1994) assume that the city-region would continue to be decentralized and that landscape would become the primary medium of urban form. These projects encompass large regional networks of infrastructure that synthesize natural environments with planned agricultural and urban landscapes. Perhaps in contrast to Duany's proposition, these models seemingly concern themselves with issues of social justice and environmental health; yet, these too neglect to provide any urban or architectural code that resolves hydrologic and hydraulic infrastructure across these agro-urban terrains.

In recent years, a paradigmatic change has begun to emerge globally in the way waste and wastewater are regarded, and how they are integrated into the built environment (Kurian and McCarney, 2010). This is most evident in arid regions, where water availability is limited, and in low-income regions, where the cost of chemical fertilizers is prohibitive (Mougeot, 2000; van Hirtum, et al., 2002). Wastewater treatment structures are often sited on steep slopes, terraces, agriculture fields, or integrated agro-water catchment basins, and can be designed to be multi-functional, with uses such as slope stabilization and aquifer recharge (Arroyo, 2000; Pearson, 2007).

The proposal for the Jordan Valley discussed here reconceives the region, imagining dissolution of the urban form into a productive agrarian landscape based on a decentralized wastewater infrastructure. Urban elements such as buildings would become agricultural terraces, streets would become water conduits, and valleys would become infrastructure for water catchment and treatment. The conventional distinctions between urban, suburban, and rural become irrelevant as the synthesis between urban and agricultural water uses is foregrounded as a primary driver of urban form.

The Jordan Valley Context

The Jordan Valley runs along the African Rift; it rises from the Earth's lowest point on dry land, 450m below sea level, to over 1,000m above sea level in the Jordan Highlands. The overall width of the Valley ranges between 4–25km (Venot, 2003). An extreme climatic gradient characterizes the Valley's 100km stretch. The northern Highlands have a temperate Mediterranean climate (Figure 1), whereas the southern end—close to the Dead Sea—is classified as arid African sub-Saharan (Venot, 2003; Figure 2). This ancient, fertile region has witnessed the flourishing of some of the world's earliest civilizations. In the last 60 years, however, modern engineering schemes for freshwater diversion have reduced the Jordan River to a fraction of its original flow (Figure 3). This is a result of increasing extraction by the river's four riparian countries (Lebanon, Syria, Israel, and Jordan), and it leaves the Lower Jordan with less than 100 million m^3/year—more than 1 billion cubic meters less than its original flow (Laster and Livney, 2010).

The Jordan Valley is an ideal testing ground for urban-agrarian morphologies, as its fragmented geopolitical situation (Zeiton, 2011), misallocation of water resources (Shuval, 2007), reliance on wasteful single-function centralized water-sanitation systems (Tal, 2010), increasing population's water demands (Rumman, 2010), and extreme topographic, geologic, and geographic conditions (Venot, 2003) have all led to a state of perceived water scarcity.

Figure 2: The northern Highlands of the Jordan River have a temperate Mediterranean climate

It is fair to assume that continuing the current mode of agriculture and urban settlement along the Jordan River, without adapting to social and environmental changes, may contribute to ongoing geopolitical disputes.

Existing and Proposed Hydraulic Systems

As the Middle East's population increases, so too does the demand for water, expediting the need for multi-scalar watershed management. Current proposals focus primarily on large-scale engineering solutions and neglect to consider a broader set of solutions that may be more environmentally and politically appropriate (Laster and Livney, 2010; Rumman, 2010; Orthofer, 2007; Assaf, 2007; Lipchin, 2007). Given pervasive water shortages in the region, seawater desalination is often seen as the primary solutions for the region's water scarcity crisis (Schiffler, 2003; Government of Jordan, 2009; and see Tal, (p. 47-59). Major hydraulic infrastructure in the region includes water diversion carriers from the Jordan River and desalination plants. The latest and largest project proposed is the Red Sea–Dead Sea Canal, which is intended to provide up to 850 million m^3/year of desalinated water to Jordan, Israel, and Palestine through hydroelectric generation and reverse osmosis (Environmental Resources Management [ERM], 2012).

Exclusive reliance on centralized technical fixes such as channels, desalination plants, and deep aquifer pumps reflects insufficient diversification of solutions. This produces extreme vulnerability. In a fragile geopolitical region, relying completely on a single source of water that is carried in channels along seismic fault lines carries a high risk. The potential environmental and economic costs generated by such a process are yet another concern (Tal and Rabbo, 2010; Schwaback, 1999). Large-scale engineering projects can conceal fluctuations in climate, context, and quantity, leading the public to believe that water supplies are abundant (de Châtel, 2007). In response, current discourse on water management includes arguments for more adaptive, resilient, and flexible solutions, to accommodate for population growth and extreme climatic and political uncertainties (Pahl-Wostl, 2007).

Water Consumption Priorities

The most controversial aspect of water management in the Jordan River basin is not scarcity but rather uneven distribution and consumption, resulting from geopolitical power instabilities, dated infrastructure, and wasteful agricultural practices (Orthofer, 2007). Recent technological and infrastructural advancements have propelled inequitable water allocation, leading to

FIGURE 3: Jordan River water diversion schemes over the past 60 years

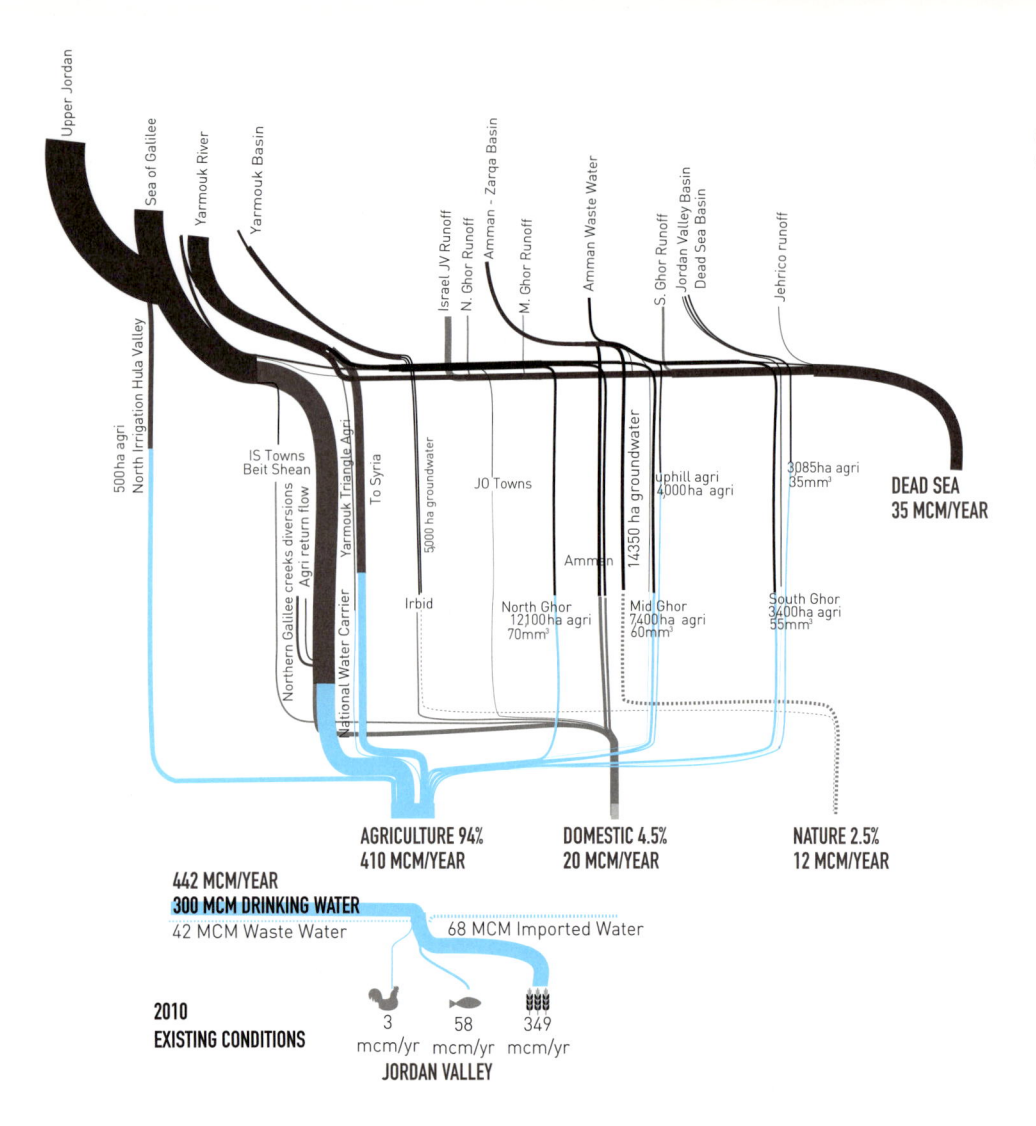

unsustainable modes of land development and rates of resource consumption. Currently, only 6% of fresh water in the Jordan Valley is allocated for domestic use. The other 94% is diverted for water-intensive subsidized agriculture (Shuval, 2007); a significant percentage of this is exported, but nevertheless, it represents a low economic yield. A defining ethos of cultural claim to the land often justifies this disproportionate allocation of fresh water towards agriculture, since it is perceived to be connected to the agrarian identity of the regional landscape (Lipchin, 2003; de Châtel, 2007; Tal and Rabbo, 2010; Tagar, 2007).

The Jordan Valley's 94% of fresh water dedicated to agriculture is among the highest percentages in the world (the world average sits at 62%). Egypt, which has a single source of water, dedicates 80% of its fresh water to agriculture; the Mediterranean average is 63%, while the UK's is only 3% (Shuval, 2007). The amount of water exported from Israel alone in agricultural products amounted to 257 million m^3/year, yet agriculture's contribution to the gross domestic product (GDP) is only 2.77%, and the sector employs less than 2% of the population (Tagar, 2007; Lipchin, 2007).

The Minimum Water Requirement (MWR) needed to maintain a reasonable level of social and economic life and to meet vital human needs in the Middle East is about 125m^3/person/year. Based on estimates from the World Bank, the 2005 availability of water resources per person in the watershed is 200m^3/person/year for Jordan; 240m^3/person/year for Israel; and 70m^3/person/year for Palestine. To dispel the myth of scarce availability of water in the Jordan Valley, one need look no further than the amount available almost exclusively to agriculture in the Valley: 1,800m^3/person/year. This figure is much higher when uncaptured seasonal rainwater, untreated wastewater, agricultural runoff, and evapotranspiration are accounted (Shuval, 2007).

Agricultural intensification and land-use shifts in many Mediterranean hinterlands have sometimes involved the replacement of local varieties by unsuitable cultivars of grain crops and fruit trees that are not adapted to the environment (Al-Bakri, et al., 2008; Lasanta, Begueria, and Garcia-Ruiz, 2006). This may be a major threat to local water sources (Khresat, Rawajfih, and Mohammad, 1998). The water availability and use figures above make a compelling case for a switch in the hydrological priorities for the Jordan Valley, where a high portion of the water now allocated to agriculture would be allocated instead to the Valley's 250,000 inhabitants, and urban wastewater would be recycled for use in agriculture.

There are several benefits in using treated wastewater for agriculture. First, it conserves scarce and costly fresh water for potable use (Pearson, 2007). Second, the cost of secondary-level treatment for domestic wastewater in the Jordan Valley, at an average of $0.65/m^3 (Water Authority of Jordan, 2010), is cheaper than developing new drinking water supplies in the region (World Bank, 2000). Third, treated wastewater can be used to recharge aquifers. If the benefits of environmental and public health protection were correctly factored into economic analyses, wastewater collection, treatment, and reuse would be among the highest priorities for scarce public and development funds (World Bank, 2000).

Urban agriculture is also a growing trend in the region. For instance, 16% of the households in Amman include urban food gardens, with annual revenue estimated at $4 million, or 2.5% of the value of agriculture in Jordan as a whole (Government of Jordan, 2002). With less fresh water available for agriculture in the region, one way to address the threat to food security would be to treat and reuse domestic wastewater. Another report, by the International Development Research Centre (IDRC), found that 16% of the households in Amman practice decentralized wastewater treatment and irrigation, primarily for the production of household fruits, vegetables, and herbs. The IRDC's projects in the Middle East have demonstrated that it is possible to develop decentralized wastewater-treatment systems that meet the standards for restricted irrigation in urban agriculture (World Bank, 2000).

The IDRC's Cities Feeding People program is currently developing a network of decentralized, low-cost natural waste-treatment systems for use in the Jordan Valley. Pilot projects include trickling filters for grey water reuse in the low-density hilly settlements surrounding East Jerusalem; aquatic wetlands using water lettuce or duckweed for poultry feed near Jericho; and the implementation of new cultivation techniques (e.g., transplanting shrubs in contour furrows, and restoring well-adapted native plants and landraces) in relation to water harvesting and reuse techniques (Rerkasem, et al., 2002; Gerritsen and Wiersum, 2005). These projects aim to protect the environment and improve food security by pilot-testing the use of decentralized wastewater treatment using hydrological flows in small communities in the Jordan Valley.

Non-Contextual Urban Paradigms

While many developments in the Jordan Valley on the Jordanian and Palestinian sides are unplanned and informal, official proposals for the region's development are more disquieting. National-scale master planning projects for the region are associated primarily with large-scale infrastructure proposals, incompatible with the initiatives outlined above. These proposed projects have limited the design vocabulary for urban development in the region.

A Strategic Master Plan for the Dead Sea completed in 2012 by Sasaki Associates for the Jordan Development Zones Commission lays out a "sustainable tourism-based economy at the Dead Sea" (Sasaki Associates, 2012). The commercially driven masterplan accepts existing and proposed tourist resorts and gated communities, which have been designed with complete disregard to the ecological and hydrological constraints of the Valley. While the masterplan designates some ecological areas for conservation and includes a wastewater treatment plant, it does not propose a new approach to reverse the environmental degradation that threatens the very core of tourism—the landscape. Jordan, like many developing countries, demonstrates a misalignment between existing and proposed land use due to a lack of planning and geographic suitability analysis. Consequently, an increasing percentage of arable land in Jordan is being lost due to economic pressures to develop agricultural land (Millington, Al-Hussein, and Dutton, 1999; Al-Bakri, Taylor, and Brewer, 2001). Despite Sasaki's proposal of discrete sustainable or green building elements, their masterplan arguably does not offer an alternative to the current direction of development patterns.

Likewise, the "Red-Dead Canal" proposal envisions the Jordan Valley following in the footsteps of the oil-rich Arab Peninsula (Schiffler, 2003). The $4.5-billion Jordan Red Sea Project (JRSP) sees desalination infrastructure as the basis for economic urban development projects in some of the most arid regions of the country (ERM, 2012; World Bank, 2012). The development program will involve the planning, financing, design, and construction of multiple residential developments, skyscrapers, shopping malls, commercial areas, industrial centers, resort villages, and other JRSP-related business support functions (ERM, 2012).

So long as desalination is one of the most pervasive solutions for future growth in the Middle East, and environmental impacts are overshadowed by the thirst for urbanism driven by speculation in real estate, centralized infrastructure will continue to produce building projects that are regionally inappropriate. Air-conditioned glass-and-steel skyscrapers, resorts, informal concrete settlement blocks, and sprawling, American-style suburban gated community compounds will have no relation to the operative potentials of the landscape they occupy. Their form, placement, and materiality are detached from any hydrological, climatic, ecological, or geophysical system that may encompass them. As such, they are solely reliant on centralized, energy-intensive infrastructural technologies (Schiffler, 2003; Schwaback, 1999).

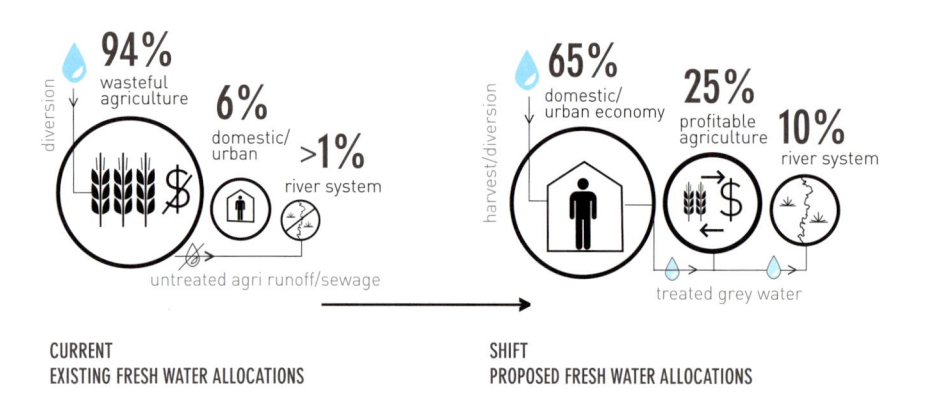

Figure 4: Shifting hydro-economics from wasteful agriculture to productive domestic uses

Mapping a Unified Watershed

The proposal showcased in this essay calls for the establishment of a regional cross-boundary watershed authority, in order to address the watershed relative to its hydrological and ecological attributes, as well as with respect to anticipated population growth. The proposal's analytical mapping of the watershed region as a unit, irrespective of national boundaries, is politically controversial, but is also highly informative. Its comprehensive inventory of the systems of extraction and diversion that are in place has consequently had an impact on human settlement, agriculture, and growth patterns. The mapping and analysis of the Valley according to its hydrology, rather than its fragmented legislative territories, confirms that current agricultural activities and urban settlements are contributing to water scarcity and environmental degradation (Assaf, 2007; Orthofer, 2007; Lipchin, 2007). The proposal assumes the continued political apportion between various countries in the Valley, but asserts that an intervention strategy is plausible in spite of it.

The proposal outlines the reallocation of fresh water supply for domestic and urban use, anticipation of ongoing population increases, and integration of runoff capture, wastewater treatment, and reuse to maintain agricultural activities and groundwater recharge (Figure 4). It also calls for a shift from highly water-consumptive crops—such as bananas, citrus, and cotton—to crops designated for domestic consumption and food security, and to highly profitable but water-thrifty crops including olives, figs, grapes, almonds, and jojoba (Figure 5). This change

Figure 5: New crop selections based on climatic conditions

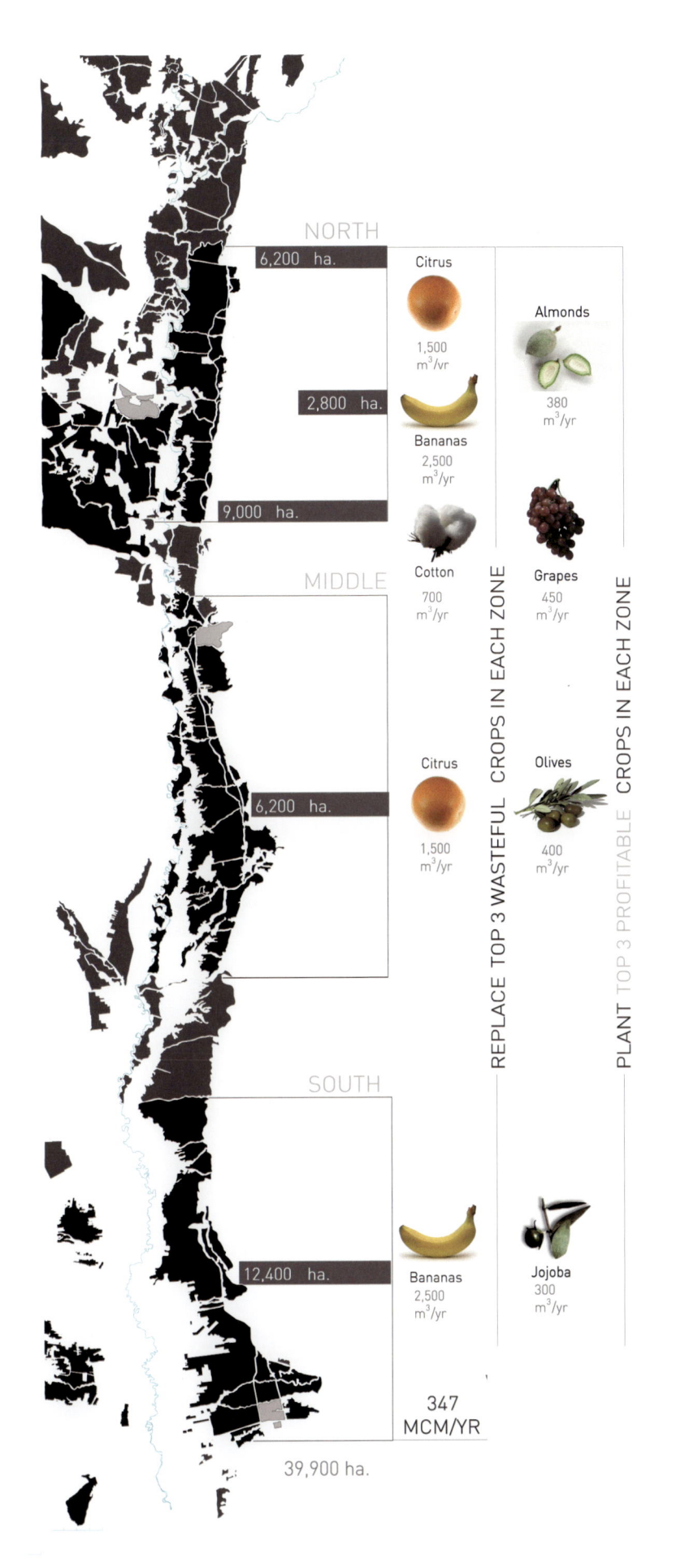

NORTH

6,200 ha. — Citrus — 1,500 m³/yr — Almonds — 380 m³/yr
2,800 ha. — Bananas — 2,500 m³/yr
9,000 ha. — Cotton — 700 m³/yr — Grapes — 450 m³/yr

MIDDLE

6,200 ha. — Citrus — 1,500 m³/yr — Olives — 400 m³/yr

REPLACE TOP 3 WASTEFUL CROPS IN EACH ZONE

PLANT TOP 3 PROFITABLE CROPS IN EACH ZONE

SOUTH

12,400 ha. — Bananas — 2,500 m³/yr — Jojoba — 300 m³/yr

347 MCM/YR

39,900 ha.

135

in crop selection would free up approximately 200 million m³/year of water—enough to supply fresh water for over 1.5 million people per year, and irrigate 10,000ha with treated wastewater (Shuval, 2007). The proposed hydro-economic shift may call into question the aforementioned large-scale engineering and urban schemes.

Two Valley Cross-Sections

The primary organizational mechanisms for the proposed integration of urban water-sanitation infrastructure and agricultural structures are based on two Valley cross-sections. The east-west latitudinal section takes the geologic condition of the Valley as the basis for the organization of land uses. It leverages the topographic edge for terracing buildings, streets, and infrastructure to create a productive landscape of wastewater treatment facilities, orchards, and farms. The north-south longitudinal section is based on the climatic gradient which characterizes the Valley's 100km stretch, which ranges from semi-arid in the north to sub-Saharan in the south.

The sectional (as opposed to planometric) approach clarifies the relation between surface and groundwater and their associated geology and vegetative cover, prioritizes the preservation of definitive view-sheds that are distinctive of the Valley's topography, and differentiates between design approaches appropriate to each microclimate. It enables a design process in which the dynamics of hydro-ecology and the dynamics of urban systems intersect technologically and spatially. Ultimately, these organizational mechanisms are intended to set guidelines for how agricultural production could be integrated into the urban context through realignment of hydrology and water-sanitation infrastructure at the watershed and sub-watershed scales.

Latitudinal Sections – Geologic Sectional Zoning

The east-west latitudinal section of the Jordan Valley functions as a form of sectional zoning and is broken into four distinct zones, based on its topographic and geologic features: the Zor, Katar, Ghor, and Jabal (Figure 6a, 6b and 6c).

The Zor is the floodplain zone of the Jordan River, originally covered by meadows subject to flooding and by forests of tamarisks and poplar trees. It is currently proposed to become a protected ecological zone to maintain vital habitat linkages and wildlife corridors. This area is essential for the recharge of aquifers closer to the river's flow (Venot, 2003).

The Katar is designated in this proposal as a geologic buffer zone. According to Venot (2003), the Katar is defined as an area made of outcropping calcareous marls. Due to its bad soil condition, it is an area of uncultivated land which marks the separation between the floodplain and the rest of the fertile valley floor. The unique spine of geological formations is a defining characteristic of the landscape and provides an opportunity to channel the proposed treated water back into the floodplain.

FIGURE 6a: Proposed Valley cross-section: The Zor and the Katar (top)
FIGURE 6b: Proposed Valley cross-section: The Ghor (middle)
FIGURE 6c: Proposed Valley cross-section: The Jabal (bottom)

FIGURE 7: Proposed agrarian urbanism plan

    The Ghor is designated in this proposal as the agricultural spine. Venot (2003) describes its lacustrine deposits, which are made up of mostly fertile, deep clay-loam soils. This portion of the valley was home to the earliest farming activities on Earth, some 12,000 years ago. Since this area accounts for 67% of Jordan's agricultural lands, it is proposed that the Ghor remain the agricultural spine of the country and support minimum urban development. From north to south, crop selection is determined according to the microclimate gradient. The goal is to maintain food production for local consumption, but reduce cultivation for international export. Treated wastewater from proposed urban areas is reused for irrigation in the Ghor.

    Lastly, the Jabal, or Highlands, are the proposed areas for urban expansion. Capitalizing on the slopes that form the valley, it is envisioned that buildings and agrarian fields be terraced topographically. This is for two main reasons: to maximize and protect as much of the fertile Ghor lands below as possible, and to capture runoff. The plan for this zone, as described below, includes new architectural and urban design codes pertaining to water management in relation to housing and agriculture.

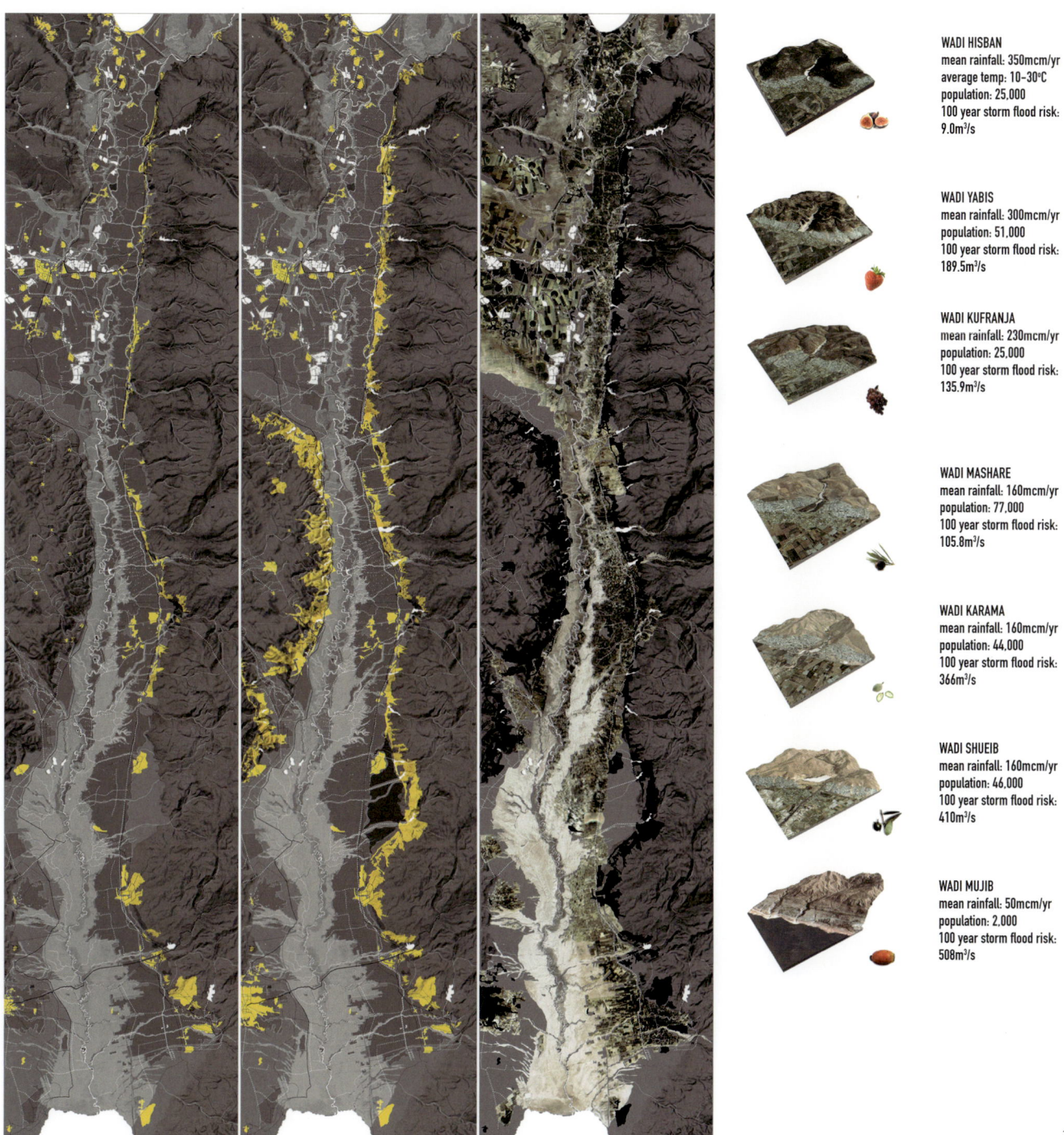

WADI HISBAN
mean rainfall: 350mcm/yr
average temp: 10–30°C
population: 25,000
100 year storm flood risk: 9.0m^3/s

WADI YABIS
mean rainfall: 300mcm/yr
population: 51,000
100 year storm flood risk: 189.5m^3/s

WADI KUFRANJA
mean rainfall: 230mcm/yr
population: 25,000
100 year storm flood risk: 135.9m^3/s

WADI MASHARE
mean rainfall: 160mcm/yr
population: 77,000
100 year storm flood risk: 105.8m^3/s

WADI KARAMA
mean rainfall: 160mcm/yr
population: 44,000
100 year storm flood risk: 366m^3/s

WADI SHUEIB
mean rainfall: 160mcm/yr
population: 46,000
100 year storm flood risk: 410m^3/s

WADI MUJIB
mean rainfall: 50mcm/yr
population: 2,000
100 year storm flood risk: 508m^3/s

FIGURE 8: The *wadis* serve as the hydrological armature for urban development (top)

FIGURE 9: A variety of water catchment and treatment techniques are incorporated into the *wadi* and water hub (bottom)

Longitudinal Section—Agrarian Urbanism Design Strategies

The 100-km section along the north-south axis corresponds to the Valley's extreme geophysical and climatic gradient. Along this axis, a series of proposed public water hubs will define the agrarian urbanity of the Valley.

The highland topography features a series of *wadis* (ephemeral streams) that naturally drain to the floodplain. In this proposal, these serve as the armature for an open-space network through the urban area, and as public water hubs (Figure 7). The entire length of the *wadi* functions as a water reservoir and park system, while its water hubs, situated at the lower elevations of the slope, are conceived to function as town centers. Growth limit is predetermined by local water-carrying capacity and by the preservation of ridgeline, agricultural spine, and floodplain (Figure 8).

Various water catchment technologies, including earth or concrete check dams, are incorporated along the *wadi's* span in order to re-establish vegetation and habitat. The vegetation would then provide erosion control and water retention. Existing freshwater channels that currently divert water from the Jordan River's headwaters to agriculture are redirected to each hub's reservoir at the terminus of each *wadi*. Urban wastewater is also redirected to a series of wastewater treatment facilities located within the *wadi*. Following preliminary treatment, water is released into sub-surface wetlands that follow the *wadi's* natural incline, prior to its distribution for agricultural use (Figure 9).

The water hubs are also designed to function as urban nodes around which civic, commercial, and educational institutions are located. The aggregation of these nodes along the Valley forms an urban corridor which is connected by transportation corridors and rail lines. Growth limit is again predetermined by the water-carrying capacity along the climatic gradient (Figure 10). The proposal also envisions retrofitting the hydro infrastructure of existing older towns. This means that simple technologies, such as rain catchers and stone- or pebble-distilled grey water treatment systems, are installed and connected to the wastewater grid in order to contribute to the hydrological armature.

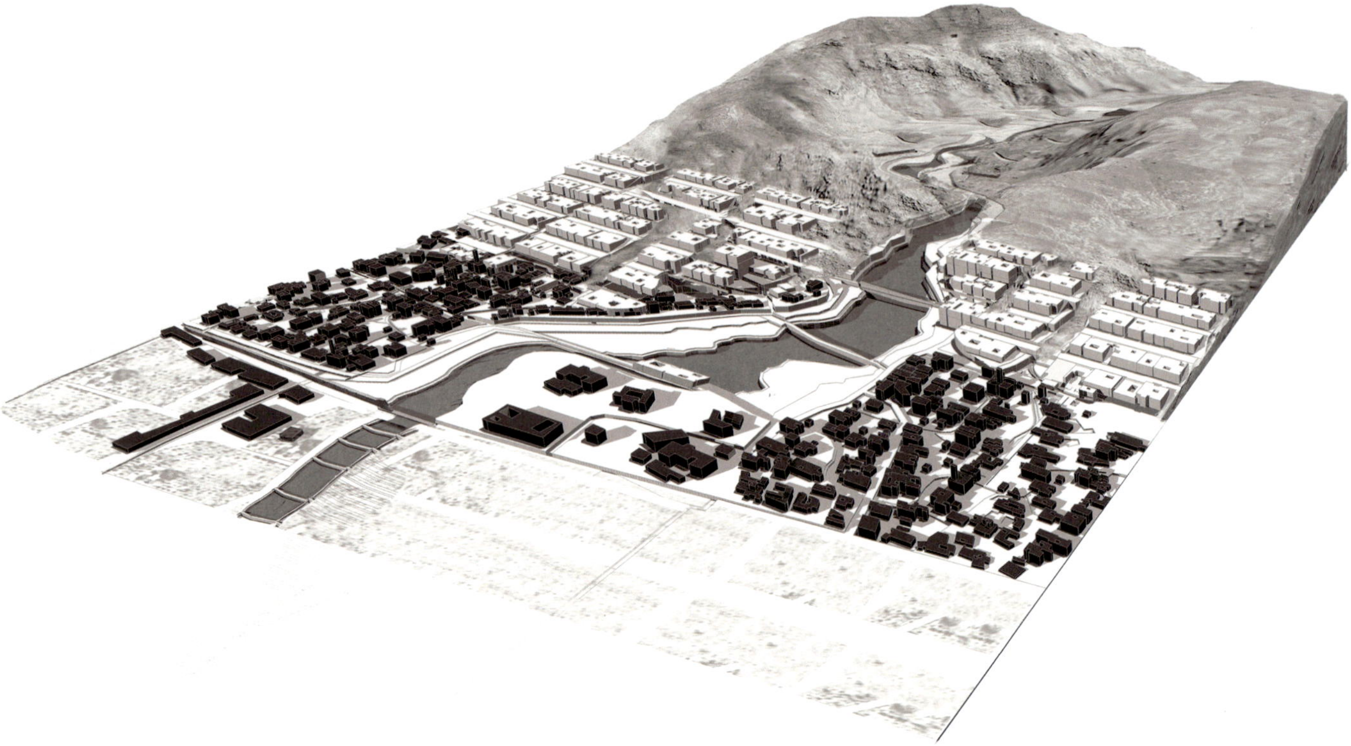

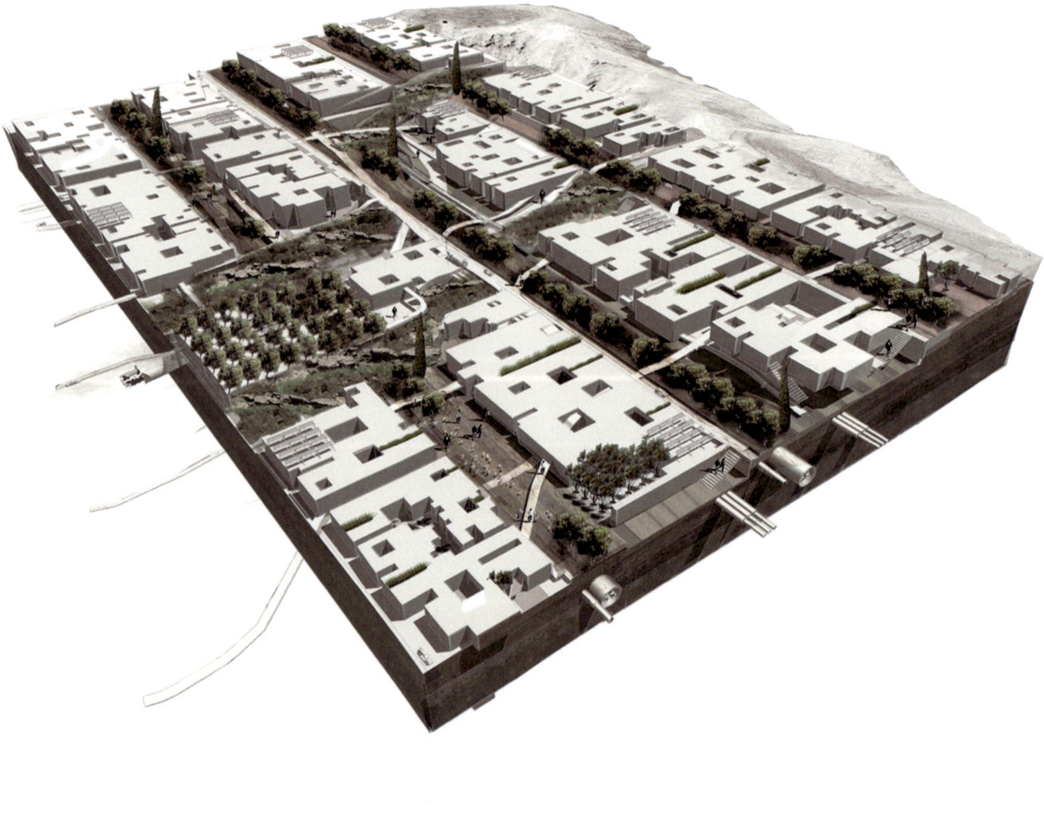

FIGURE 10: Water hubs serve as centers of civic life (opposite top)

FIGURE 11: Proposed hillside design guidelines integrate urban development with agriculture and water management (opposite bottom)

The new agrarian urbanism model produces a 100-km linear route from north to south, which includes the Valley's heritage landscapes and archaeological sites, as well as reconfigured agricultural production and integrated water management (Figure 10). The proposed urban design guidelines include a terracing system that alternates between cultivated orchard zones and built structures (Figure 11). Each architectural structure and street profile is equipped with water catchment mechanisms (e.g., cisterns, runnels, and pipes) which outflow into a treatment facility in the center of the water hub. The proposed synthesis between landscape, agriculture, and urban infrastructure is meant to address the need for increased housing while reducing the population's environmental footprint in many respects, improving hydro-ecology, and preserving the landscape heritage of the Jordan Valley.

Conclusions

Lister (2007) states that the ecological systems upon which we ultimately depend for clean air, water, and food are examples of resilient, flexible, and highly adaptive systems that operate on many levels, in multiple contexts and scales, and with a lot of redundancy. In parallel, Pahl-Wostl (2007) cautions us against relying solely on mono-functional, inflexible, large-scale technologies or infrastructure. Across the fields of design, policy, science, and engineering, scholars and practitioners have begun to acknowledge the need for multi-functional, decentralized, and diverse sets of solutions concerning water management. The prevalent notion is that environmental and ecological systems, which are conventionally perceived as peripheral to the city, should in fact be seen as a continuum of inputs and outputs within interdependent systems.

In the field of landscape architecture, in particular, practitioners are trained to consider both environmental and urban dynamics and conceive of their formal and functional synthesis. While a few proposals and guides have outlined the integration of agricultural production with the urban fabric, none have described or detailed the integration of hydrological and hydraulic management. Although the speculative proposal discussed here is conceptual and schematic, it calls for a continuation of such detailing which can begin to develop urban and architectural codes, and expand the vocabulary of governing bodies, commercial developers, and design professionals.

The Jordan Valley's *wadis*, hillside topography, and hydro-geological features serve as the basis for an urban agrarian system conceived as a watershed-wide transformation. However, each *wadi* zone and associated urban development is independent of the full implementation at the watershed or river basin scale. The transformation of the Valley can occur incrementally, under different authorities and in response to local circumstances. The proposed latitudinal cross-section design approach facilitates decentralized management of resources, whereby water harvesting, storage, recycling, and reuse in irrigation can partially occur independently of the larger network. Arguably, due to the inherent flexibility of the proposed system, the insurmountable challenges of uniting multi-sectorial and multi-national parties in this region would not preclude the realization of a single sub-basin unit.

Finally, the agrarian urbanism model addresses Pahl-Wostl's (2007) call to increase the adaptive capacity of water systems. Accordingly, the proposal suggests introducing a new socio-technical system, where social capital increases and its members are active in the management of the integrated system, and in the overall restoration and maintenance of a multi-functional landscape.

WASTEWATER TREATMENT AND RECLAMATION IN ISRAEL
Jewish National Fund (JNF) and Mekorot

Site: State of Israel
Longitude & Latitude: 31°30'N 34°45'E
Annual Precipitation: 30-900mm

Year: 1970s
Status: Ongoing
Water Volume/Day: 270 million m³
Dimensions: Varies

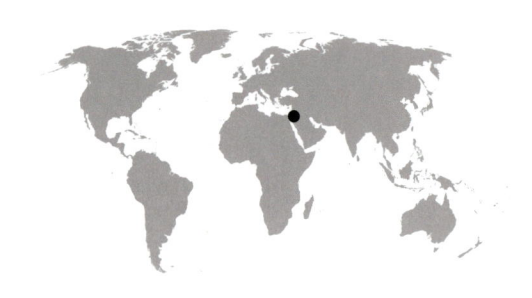

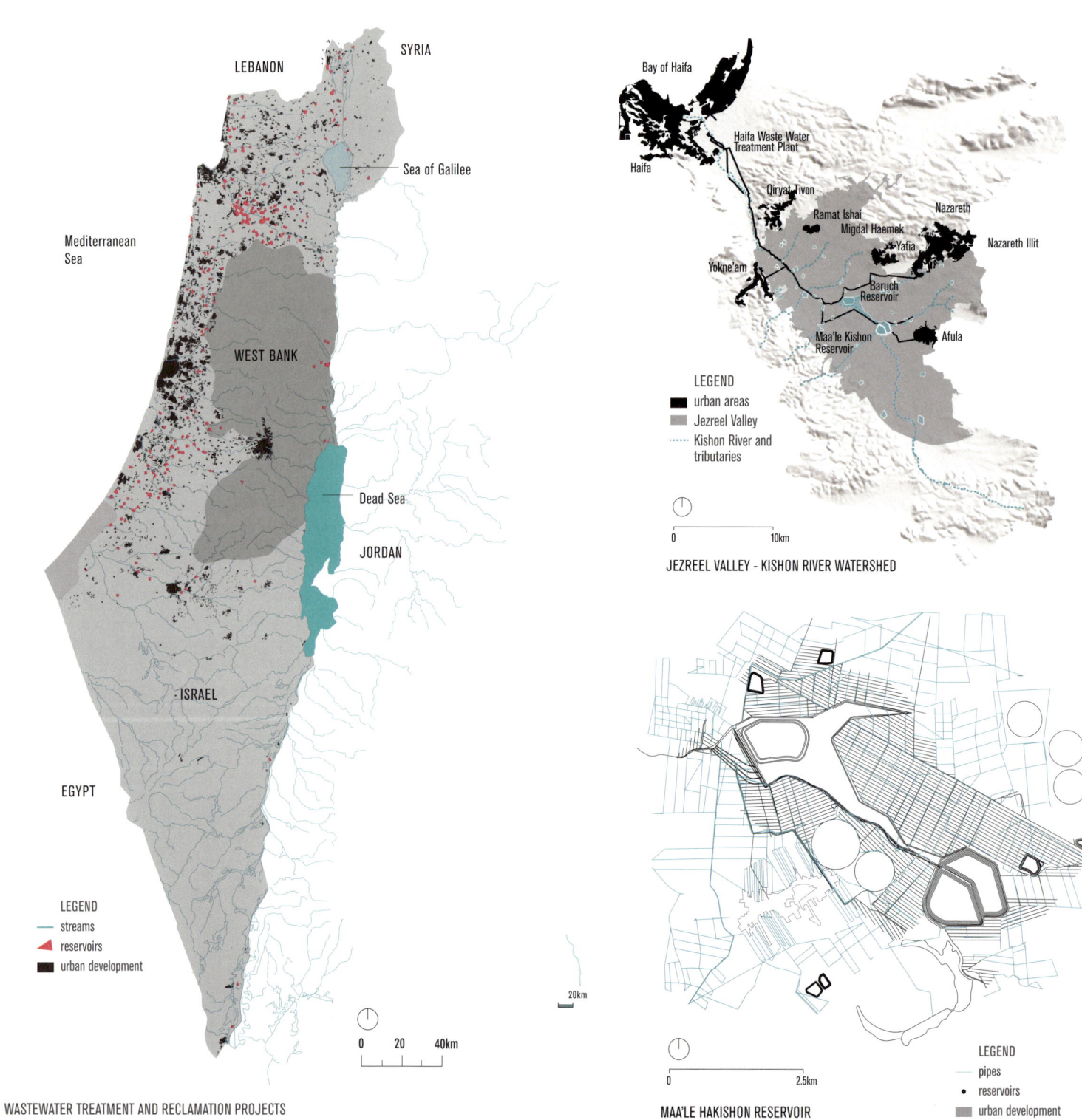

JEZREEL VALLEY - KISHON RIVER WATERSHED

LEGEND
- urban areas
- Jezreel Valley
- Kishon River and tributaries

WASTEWATER TREATMENT AND RECLAMATION PROJECTS

LEGEND
- streams
- reservoirs
- urban development

MAA'LE HAKISHON RESERVOIR

LEGEND
- pipes
- reservoirs
- urban development

142

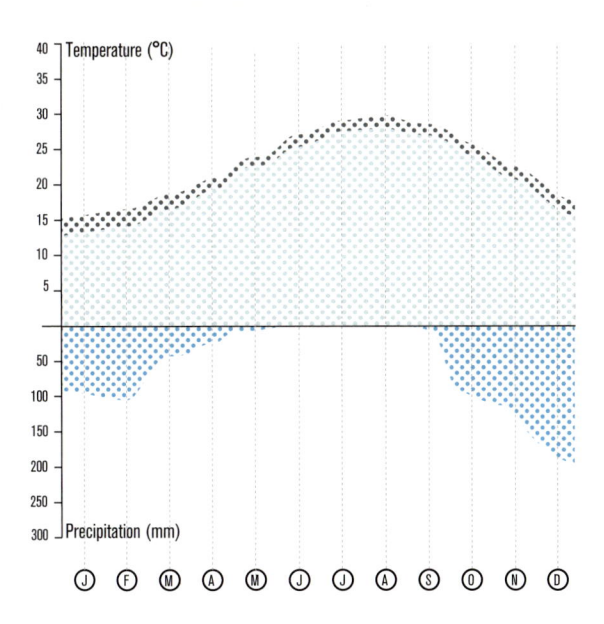

Israel's nationwide treatment and reuse strategy uses wastewater in place of conventional (potable) water for irrigation or other purposes that do not require water of drinkable quality, releasing some of the pressure on conventional water resources. Reclaimed wastewater (RW) reduces the water balance deficit in a region where all drinkable surface and groundwater resources are already used to their maximum capacity (Friedler, 2001). Approximately 92% of the wastewater in Israel is treated, and around 75% (350 million m³) of this is used for agricultural irrigation—the highest percentage of such utilization in the world, in stark contrast to countries such as Spain (12%), Australia (9%), Italy (8%), Greece (5%), Central Europe (1%), and the U.S. (1%; Mekorot, 2013).

Reclaimed wastewater is also used for artificial groundwater recharge, another component of the national water management plan. The artificial recharge programs have improved the quality of groundwater, and have succeeded in restoring higher groundwater levels to Israel's Coastal Aquifer, offsetting seawater intrusion which occurs due to the overpumping of groundwater (Mekorot, 2013). Juanico and Friedler (1999) found that RW may be the primary available source—perhaps the only available source—of water for the recovery of dried or polluted rivers in arid and semi-arid countries suffering water shortage. The capture of downstream river discharge and its reuse can be yet another method to intensify water reuse.

Restoration of Israel's rivers would not have a significant impact without water supply from RW (Gafni, 2010). Finally, RW diverts sewage from entering surface and subsurface water sources, including rivers, lakes, aquifers, and seas. Friedler (2001) states that even in regions with abundant water resources, environmental degradation due to wastewater pollution may be offset with long-term retention in reservoirs.

The initial treatment of wastewater takes place in wastewater treatment plants throughout the country and typically includes four stages: pre-treatment, followed by primary, secondary, and tertiary treatments. These processes include oxidation ponds, activated sludge, and mechanical bioreactors (MBR; Mekorot, 2013). Treated effluent (partly purified wastewater) is then distributed to over 200 open-air reservoirs for additional polishing by means of settling and oxygenation processes, microbial metabolism of organic matter, and pathogenic disinfection with ultraviolet exposure. Built by the quasi-governmental non-profit organization Jewish National Fund (JNF), the reservoirs hold a static volume of 150 million m³ and a dynamic (emptying and refilling) volume of approximately 270 million m³ annually (Gafni, 2010). The reservoirs are designed for both storage and treatment. In the case of the Jezreel Valley, the most productive agricultural valley in Israel, 20–28 million m³ of effluent per year enables the irrigation of 20,000 hectares (Friedler, 1999; Mekorot, 2007b; Tahal, 2013).

The goal of storage is to bridge the gap between the continuous supply of sewage and seasonal irrigation needs, which are higher in the summer. Agricultural water demand also varies from year to year, according to annual rainfall, distribution of rain events, and the intensity of each rain event, and therefore multi-year storage capacity in both open-air and aquifer reservoirs can optimize wastewater resources (Friedler, 2001).

Reclaimed wastewater is very reliable due to its relatively constant supply during the year and from year to year, with an increase over time. This allows for investments in intensive agriculture, which are not feasible with infrequent precipitation in semi-arid regions (Friedler, 2001). Yet, wastewater reuse in agricultural irrigation necessitates the compliance with three dissimilar quality requirements: agrotechnic—low salt concentration and storage capacity; environmental—low concentration of heavy metals and xenobiotic compounds, controlled levels of nutrients and salts, and no malodors; and sanitary—removal of viruses, bacteria, and parasites. For instance, nutrient load needs to be as low as possible to meet environmental quality, while relatively high levels of nutrients are desirable in achieving agrotechnic quality due to savings in the use of costly fertilizers (Friedler, 2001).

There are two main technological approaches for wastewater treatment. In the first, intensive sewage treatment systems such as activated sludge are optimized for biological oxygen demand (BOD) removal, but not for the removal of detergents, heavy metals, xenobiotics, and pathogens. Such facilities do not have any significant storage capacity to accommodate for the seasonal gap. Thus, intensive systems alone cannot achieve the requirements for agricultural irrigation and have to be followed by polishing treatment systems, which can be achieved in two ways:

The addition of advanced intensive treatment units, including disinfection units (chlorination, ozonation, UV, etc.), membrane filtration, activated carbon treatment, etc. Although these processes can be accomplished in a matter of hours, they require high investment and operational costs, high energy consumption, and the release of series of sludges which are difficult and costly to treat and dispose of.

The addition of extensive treatment units such as stabilization reservoirs or constructed wetlands. Although these processes require several weeks or months to process, they are relatively resilient to break down, and more effective with respect to the removal of pollutants such as organic matter, detergents, heavy metals, and fecal coliforms (Friedler, 2001).

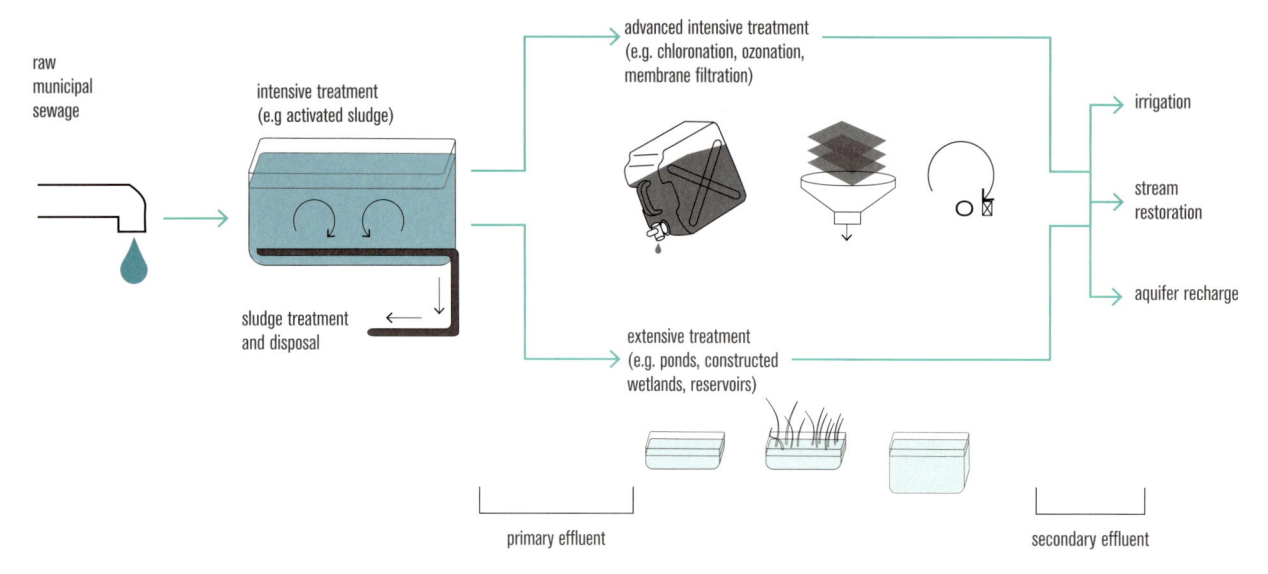

INTENSIVE AND EXTENSIVE WASTEWATER TREATMENT PROCESSES DIAGRAM

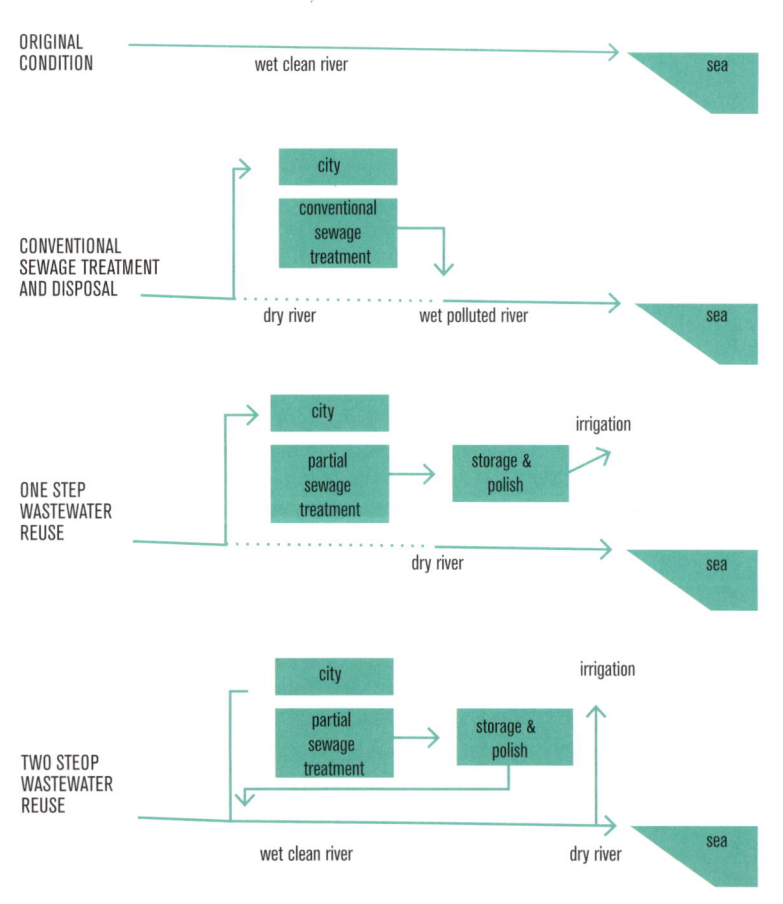

The second approach to wastewater treatment involves extensive sewage treatment systems, such as stabilization ponds and reservoirs, constructed wetlands, and so on. These are constrained by their requirement of very large land areas; however, with the high storage capacity needed to regulate seasonal and annual demand for sewage and irrigation, such solutions are nevertheless necessary (Friedler, 2001). Ultimately, the combination of both intensive and extensive treatment technologies would improve the quality of effluent for agricultural irrigation, especially in arid or semi-arid countries.

Using RW necessitates constructing dual distribution pipelines in order to eliminate the risk of accidental interconnection between drinking and irrigation water supplies—in Israel, wastewater pipes are purple, while potable water pipes are blue. While the challenges are real, the cost of RW is about 50% of the cost of desalinating seawater and is of great significance to severe shortages of potable fresh water (Mekorot, 2007a).

RIVER RESTORATION WITH TREATED EFFLUENT DIAGRAM

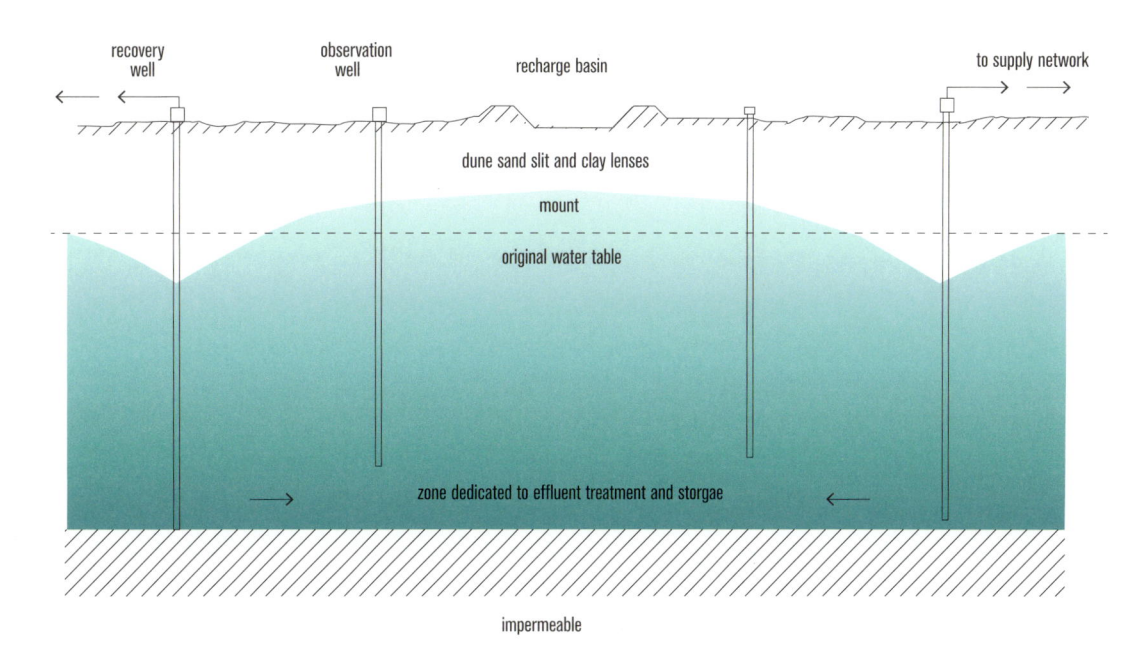

COASTAL AQUIFER ARTIFICIAL RECHARGE DIAGRAM

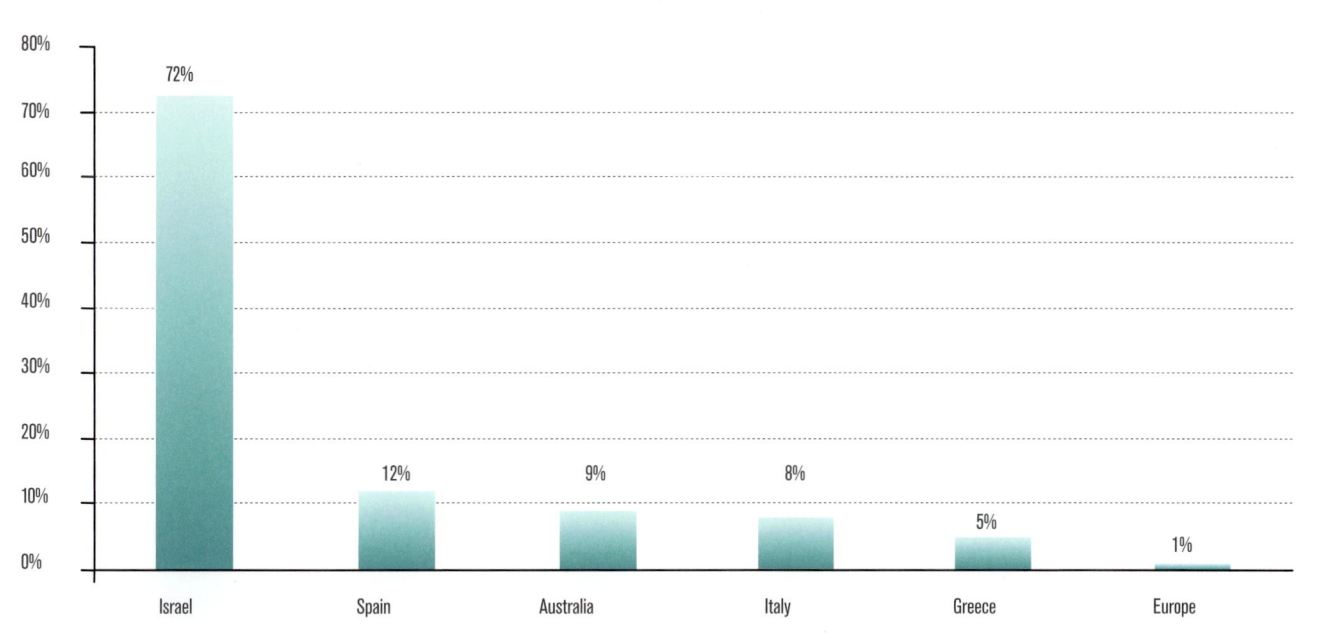

Labels: recovery well, observation well, recharge basin, to supply network, dune sand slit and clay lenses, mount, original water table, zone dedicated to effluent treatment and storgae, impermeable

EFFLUENT REUSE COMPARISON WORLDWIDE

Country	Percentage
Israel	72%
Spain	12%
Australia	9%
Italy	8%
Greece	5%
Europe	1%

3
WATER
FOR
ECOSYSTEM
SERVICES

Introduction: Urban Aquatic Ecosystems

The term "ecosystem services" refers to the benefits that humans gain from the functions of ecosystems, which are often assigned economic values. The Millennium Ecosystem Assessment has designated several categories of ecosystem services, which include provisioning (e.g., food, water), regulation (e.g., climate and water flow), support (e.g., nutrient cycling, pollination), and culture (e.g., aesthetic value, recreation, sense of place). With respect to water and cities, ecosystem services such as flood mitigation, erosion control, and the protection of property and human life, as well as water quality improvement and conservation, wastewater treatment, the creation of habitat, and provision of education, recreation, and aesthetic value, can all be derived from urban aquatic ecosystems.

At the same time, the extreme manipulation of urban aquatic ecosystems (e.g., damming, discharge of contaminated water to waterways), coupled with the increase of impervious surfaces and aging or inadequate water-sanitation infrastructure, results in degraded ecological functioning of waterways and increased risk to human life through flooding, water contamination, and so on (Larson, et al., 2013). Aridland aquatic ecosystems are all the more vulnerable to both natural and anthropogenic disturbances due to their limited and unpredictable water availability. The following three sections provide a framework for understanding the temporal and spatial scales of water availability in relation to existing and possible aridland habitation.

Hydrological Flux

One of the key attributes of desert streams and rivers is the high inter-annual variability in water flow availability (Larson, et al., 2013). Aridland aquatic systems are largely characterized by intermittent ephemeral water systems due to low precipitation and long periods of drought, as well as elevated temperatures and high evaporation rates. Equally severe is the infrequent yet voracious flooding that rapidly transforms the landscape from a dune scape or barren land to a surging river or a waterhole as large as a lake. Such conditions may also be further intensified with urban and regional development and infrastructure, as well as with changes to climate patterns.

The extreme hydrological flux between desiccation and flood, and consequent unpredictability in water availability, have influenced the way water in drylands is perceived. For example, Gini Lee's essay in this part recounts the long-standing view of Central Australia's arid landscape as a "hideous blank—a barren, alien, and useless place," which "comes alive" once record-breaking rains fill inland waters and lakes with more water than has been seen for years. The primary theme that emerges here is the recurring loss of cultural and institutional memory of such profound hydrological transformation. This loss often results in the gradual encroachment of habitation into waterways during prolonged periods of drought. The Wadi Hanifah case study illustrates this phenomenon. With an unprecedented growth and rapid urbanization of Riyadh, Saudi Arabia, parts of the ephemeral waterways (*wadis*) were quarried and mined for construction materials, while other parts have been filled in to accommodate new subdivisions, roads, and infrastructure. Many areas had become dumping grounds for as much as 1,000,000m^3 of solid waste.

The southern reaches of the Drâa River (described in Chapter 2) convey a similar lapse of memory. The river had been significantly desiccated over the last 40 years due to both anthropogenic factors, such as construction of a dam upstream, increase of population and water demand, and rise in tourism, as well as natural factors, such as climate change. During the rain event in 2009, which was of a magnitude that had not been seen in more than 15 years, the tourist lodges built within the flood plain during this prolonged period of drought were washed away, and one fatality was reported. Children under the age of 15 had never seen a full river flowing through their town. Old men strolled along the river hand in hand, reminiscing of the last time the river was full.

Lee argues that in order to fully comprehend aridland habitation and associated technical or technological approaches to hydrology, we must first examine the etymological origins of technology as a synthesis of *techne* (skill, craft) and *logia* (knowledge). In other words, local knowledge of natural and constructed systems, both past and present, must be viewed as a crucial part of technology. In her work, Lee traces the character and coexistence of human and hydrological systems and the remnant structures that frame the landscape—bridges, overpasses, dams, towns, and cultivated gardens. She argues that in order to understand the arid terrain, one must look for these cues to fully comprehend and anticipate the location, quantity, and quality of water. Whether they are ancient or modern, man-made or geomorphological structures, the observation of landscape cues, Lee argues, has been an integral part of indigenous knowledge as a way of reading, inhabiting, and working with the landscape. It is a cultural knowledge and set of skills embedded within a community that should inform land use and spatial planning.

Another key attribute of arid landscapes is their fragility, both ecological and cultural. As Lee points out, the limited presence of critical refugia waterholes in the Central Australian landscape jeopardizes the existence of relict species that depend on the ecological habitats the waterholes provide. And while the rise in tourism has shifted government attention and funding to better protect these barren lands, the accompanying increase in water demand in turn puts additional pressure on their fragile ecologies. Aziza Chaouni's account of the Drâa Valley (see Part 2) describes the gradual decline of the oasian ecology, which has a direct and significant impact on human habitation, economy, and culture. Chaouni's essay and the Taragalte Ecolodge case study describe a process of desertification, or land degradation (Side Note 1).

Most importantly, the loss of ecological quality contributes to the loss of an integrated cultural knowledge; conversely, the ongoing cultural transformation furthers the ecological degradation. As a result, the ministerial solutions to the ecological problems are divorced from the ways in which people now inhabit and engage with the landscape. They are merely technical and isolated solutions to ecological problems (e.g., dune stabilization) but lack a comprehensive approach to aridland habitation, both past and present, and vernacular practices to manage flooding. It is no surprise then to identify the didactic aspiration of the Taragalte Ecolodge, Hiriya Landfill Recycling Park, and Wadi Hanifah projects. The aim to restore the ecological health of these landscapes is embedded in their commercial and civic redefinition.

In the same capacity that urbanization can alter natural hydrology and exacerbate water scarcity, urban effluent maintains a constant flow into otherwise dry natural water systems. In other words, urban water systems greatly alter the natural hydrological flux, and herein lies the potential to hybridize and integrate urban water management and natural hydrology as a synergistic system.

The case of Wadi Hanifah provides a good example. Despite the increase in water supply, due to stormwater runoff and sewage dumping from the city of Riyadh, until very recently the quality of the water was so poor that it was considered an open-air sewer. The massive restoration project, led by Moriyama and Teshima and Buro Happold, radically recovered this condition as both runoff and sewage are treated via a variety of bioremediation techniques. Fadi Masoud's essay on the Jordan River (see Chapter 2) describes a similar condition where decades of water diversion, low precipitation, and urban effluent have left the river a polluted trickle, although the 2013 restoration project has begun to remediate and replenish the river with desalinated and treated wastewater (Abdelrahman and Jägerskog, 2013). In the same vein, the River Restoration Project, described in the Wastewater Treatment and Reclamation in Israel case study (see Part 2), greatly depends on reclaimed wastewater supply to maintain surface flows in streams and, conversely, it diverts wastewater away from surface and subsurface water resources.

Tools for Water Conserving Design

The design of aridland habitation has been traditionally structured around the variability between scarcity and surplus. The legacy of this design approach, as Wescoat tells us in his essay, is rooted in water budget analysis and water conserving design, and in methods of regulating the presence of water. The idea is that while having no water or too much water is often seen as a vulnerability, it can also be thought of as an opportunity to develop joint strategies for water management that mediate the two ends of the spectrum.

Water budget analysis is the evaluation of water demand for natural and constructed landscapes with respect to temporality—frequency, intensity, and duration of weather events—

1. Land degradation points to the interdependent relations between water, soil, and vegetation. For example, hydrological changes affect plant and soil ecology; the loss of vegetation leads to topsoil erosion and decrease in soil infiltration capacity; over-pumping of groundwater increases salinity in the soil, impacting the viability of plant growth, and so on.

2. Online tools, such as the California Irrigation Management Information System (CIMIS), provide hourly, daily, monthly, and annual water budgets for user-specified time periods, weather stations, and regions. An online tool called WebWIMP (Web-Based Water-Budget Interactive Modeling Program) calculates water budgets globally at a half-degree grid cell resolution, and can incorporate variations in soil depth, infiltration rates, and climate change scenarios. The U.S. Environmental Protection Agency has recently created a "Water Budget Tool," including a spreadsheet and associated analytic methods, to bring this analysis in landscape design into the mainstream.

as well as the spatial scale and physical attributes of a site, and volume of water relative to topography, surface porosity, vegetation, and built structures. The basic idea of water budget analysis, as Wescoat describes, is comprised of simple mass balance analysis of inputs (precipitation in various forms) minus outputs (evapotranspiration and runoff) plus change in storage (soil moisture recharge and discharge). This idea becomes more complex when applied over different time steps (e.g., daily, monthly, and decadal scales) and spatial scales (e.g., from weather station data at a point in space, to sites, regions, and global assessments). In that respect, water budget analysis today involves real-time monitoring of evapotranspiration and dynamic weather data via sensor instrumentation and online tools (Side Note 2), as well as irrigation design and scheduling that incorporates weather data and soil moisture irrigation control technologies. Approaching water budget analysis in this manner, Wescoat argues, defines it as a technology for water conserving design that links measurement, computation, and integrative analysis.

Yet, water budget analysis and water conserving design are also defined by age old practices that have been recently revived, ranging from rainwater and surface runoff capture in small to large reservoirs, the reuse of treated wastewater (often through bioremediation, for example using constructed wetlands), and the planting of native and drought-adapted species, also known as "xeriscaping" or "waterwise" planting.

This part's contributions provide examples for bridging the seasonal and annual gaps in water availability over a range of spatial and time scales. In the Wadi Hanifah case, hundreds of micro-catchment structures and planting swales were constructed throughout the floodplain to capture the scarce annual rainfall and enhance soil moisture, and thus increase the survival rates of plantings. In conjunction, check dams were constructed to attenuate flow, reduce erosion, retain sediment, and increase water infiltration to help establish vegetation. The Taragalte Ecolodge operates in a similar fashion on a much smaller scale; a series of cut-and-fill operations enable water capture for irrigation purposes during drought periods. Other examples for water collection methods are found in Part 1, while Part 2 provides examples for wastewater reuse, smart irrigation techniques, and appropriate plant selection.

Three themes emerge from this chapter's contributions in the context of water budget analysis and water conserving design.

The first concerns the adaptation of reference materials with input from local expertise and site-specific data. For instance, for the Mahtab Bagh conservation project, the California-based guidebook (known as Water Use Classifications of Landscape Species, WUCOLS) was used with input from Rajasthani horticulturalists for plant selection. The guidebook classifies plants as having high, medium, or low water requirements in different climatic regions of California, and it adjusts reference evapotranspiration by microclimate and planting density as well as species coefficients.

The second theme concerns the adaptation of historical concepts to modern water supply systems and the extension of water budget methods beyond the garden or site scale and into the city and surrounding region. For example, the proposed Residential Development at Al Ain in Abu Dhabi links traditional and modern water systems: *aflaj* irrigation systems tap hillslope aquifers and convey water by tunnels to the surface water distribution canals of an oasis and are linked to desalination and wastewater collection and reuse systems, as a joint strategy for a new urban development. The Taragalte Ecolodge was developed as a prototype for ecotourism that could be replicated in other locations as a broad anti-desertification strategy. In the Wadi Hanifah case study, the serial aggregation of micro-catchments and planting cells acts as a significant infrastructural component of the watershed management plan, specifically through mitigating the erosive forces of flash floods and conserving water used in irrigation.

Lastly, the third theme concerns the spatial implications and aesthetic potentials of water regulation. For example, site grading and a network of sunken courtyards or constructed open and covered reservoirs, in combination with planting geometries and materials selection, can reveal the fluctuating levels of water, whereby the seasonal transformation of space becomes its aesthetic expression. The Nagaur Mughal-Rajput Palace-Garden Project in Rajasthan, India, is a good example.

Mutually Supportive Systems

Modifying the presence of water offers vast possibilities for design and for shaping both social and ecological systems. Water can be detained on site or within a riverbed via reservoirs, check dams, micro-catchments, and inflatable dams (Side Note 3). Mechanical distribution via pumps and channels can be utilized to dissipate or attenuate water, and conversely, to intensify or concentrate water in specific areas.

What is most evident in this collection of essays and case studies is the aspiration to surpass the typical urban grid layout and planometric design approach, which often overlooks hydrological dynamics. In all of these projects, water systems serve as the framework around which urban development, public space, water-sanitation infrastructure, ecological systems, and agriculture are organized. With this approach, natural, social, and technological systems converge as multi-use spaces that operate in a mutually beneficial manner.

The proposed residential development in Al Ain, the Wadi Hanifah Restoration project, and the Jordan River Valley masterplan by Masoud (Chapter 2) provide excellent models for a closed-loop water management system, integrating hydrology and hydraulics as a means to rethink urban form and public landscape. The Wadi Hanifah bioremediation facility, which is in itself a hybrid of mechanical and biological processes, is nestled within a bioengineered riverbed and located in proximity of a massive highway interchange; it acts as an extension of the city in terms of wastewater management and public space. Masoud envisions the *wadi* as the spine for each neighborhood, where water collection, sanitation infrastructure, and public space converge; the relation between individual lots, street right-of-ways and open space are organized around surface water collection and effluent reuse. The Hiriya Landfill Park and Taragalte Ecolodge exemplify the same principle at a smaller scale and as strategies to unify architecture and landscape.

Bioremediation and bioengineering are key approaches to achieve multi-use and mutually supportive water-human systems. In some of the case studies in this chapter, such interventions are conceived as modern-day icons of progressive water management and open space design. Constructed wetlands, for example, are often designed as a food chain which supports habitat ranging from small organisms to fish to fowl, and as an interface between the terrestrial system (birds) and the aquatic system (fish, plants, invertebrates). Terrestrial and aquatic species not only provide nutrient removal function but also add value for public interest. Undoubtedly, bioremediation projects are successful in radically changing public perception of wastewater reuse and inhabiting water infrastructure.

3. See the Rio Besos project featured in Margolis and Robinson (2007).

REFERENCES

Abdelrahman, R. and Jägerskog, A. (2013) "A Last Ditch Effort to Save the Jordan River." *Waterfront* 1: 6–8. www.siwi.org/Resources/Water_Front_Articles/WF-1-2013_Cover%20_story_Jordan.pdf

Larson, E. K., Earl, S., Hagen, E. M., Hale, R., Hartnett, H., McCrackin, M., McHale, M., and Grimm, N. B. (2013). "Beyond Restoration and into Design: Hydrologic Alterations in Aridland Cities." in S.T.A. Pickett et al. (eds.), *Resilience in Ecology and Urban Design: Linking Theory and Practice for Sustainable Cities, Future City 3*. Springer Science+Business Media Dordrecht. 183–210.

Margolis, L. and Robinson, A. (2007) *Living Systems: Innovative Materials and Technologies for Landscape Architecture*. Birkhäuser.

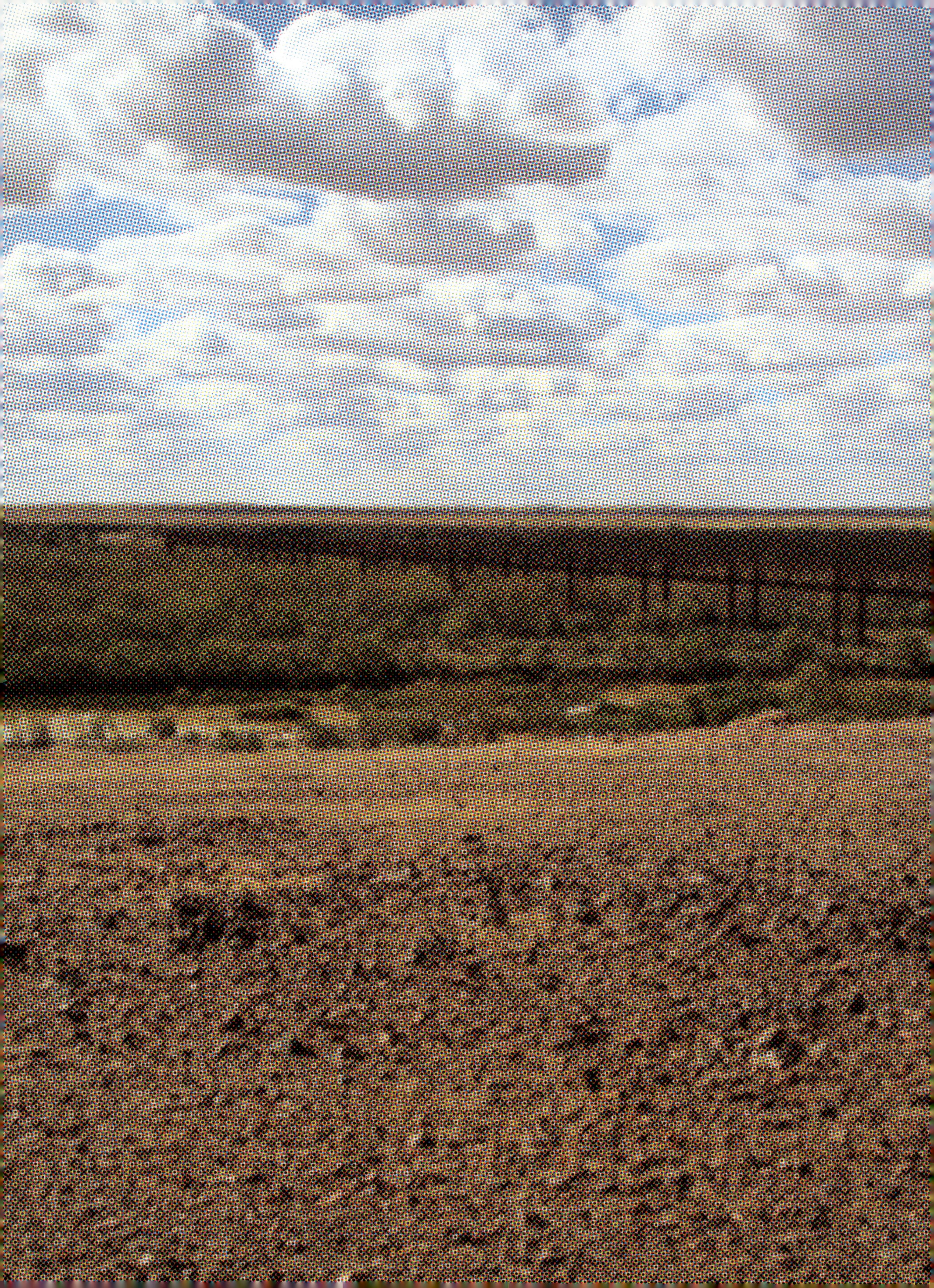

Micro-Urban Communities and Water-Made Landscapes: Critical Refugia, Technologies, and Coexistence in the Arid Lands

Gini Lee

Central Australia's landscapes are characterized by vast ephemeral water systems that shape the land and the settlements that they sustain. Critical *refugia* emerge in places supported by rare instances of permanent surface water and predominant access to subterranean water, promoting coexistence between the ecologies of aquatic, vegetative, and human populations. The Oodnadatta Track, in the arid lands of South Australia, traverses the now-marginal historical settlements that were established in the 19th century to aid in opening up the country's interior. Each micro-urban community, whether still inhabited or in ruination, tangibly demonstrates an affinity to the fluctuating presence of water. Water drawn from deep underground, collected during times of surface flow, or gathered from infrequent rains is stored and processed through a range of techniques designed for the irregularity of desert water supplies.

If we frame technology in terms of its etymological origins, the concepts of *techne* as a skill or craft and *logia* as knowledge of systems of organization can be used as critical theoretical constructs to aid in the understanding of continuing drylands occupation. In the small communities of the drylands, the presence of water is crucial to habitation, a magnet for humans in the landscape. Its total management—the provision of sufficient water for basic human needs—is essential for enduring occupation, and it appears as a cultural phenomenon for Aboriginal and non-indigenous peoples alike. Fieldwork informs this research, which examines the historical, cultural, interpretative, and environmental record on waterholes in ephemeral river systems in order to suggest implications for design-based management regimes that aim to enhance the viability of these micro-urban communities and their ecologies.

Figure 3: Algebuckina Bridge West (opposite)

Figure 1: Approaching Oodnadatta, hills, creeklines, floodplains, and township merge into an outback drylands 'scape (right)

Urbanism, Ecology, and Economies Framed by Water Presence and Absence

To spend time in the landscapes of the Neales River catchment in central South Australia is to become gradually aware of the diverse micro-communities of the arid lands. For many travelers, this barren country is devoid of much interest; for others, it is the elemental outback, replete with Aboriginal dreamtime stories, overlain with tragic accounts of the early explorers who perished in search of the fabled but absent inland sea. The 19th-century view of settlers and explorers of the inland as the "hideous blank" (Haynes, 2002, p. 10), as a place barren, alien, useless, and invested with horror, has been echoed over the years—for example, in a recent headline in the national newspaper announcing, "Lake at dead heart of the nation comes alive," after record-breaking rains filled inland waters and lakes with more water than had been seen for years (Schliebs and Edwards, 2011). Griffith Taylor's 1946 population maps of Australia are annotated with the terms "Useless, Empty Australia" and "Practically Uninhabited" (Head, 2000, p. 47).

These days, as one traverses the red dirt highways that undulate over dunescapes, ancient worn-down hills, and rolling floodplains, tree lines come into view. They herald the numerous creek crossings that bisect the main roadways linking the often marginal townships that are, nonetheless, the lifeblood of the outback. In the distance, the settlement of Oodnadatta, an outback micro-urban community, merges with the horizon (Figure 1). This cultural place is supported by arid ecological systems, in cohabitation with micro-urbanism that surpasses typical grid and infrastructure planning scenarios. This fluid eco-social interplay negotiates the imposition of imported regimes, as practiced by the early settlers, and the dynamics of contemporary coexistence in arid places.

The Lake Eyre Basin as Site for Interdisciplinary Collaboration
Critical Refugia Environments

Recent national attention has focused on the critical aspects of surface and groundwater systems in a drying refugia environment. This has spurred fieldwork that includes landscape assessment and landscape design methods, in order to scientifically survey the changing dynamics and health of water bodies in arid lands. In the western Neales River catchment, adjacent to the Lake Eyre Basin (LEB), research in knowledge gathering and subsequent management of these remote places is being sponsored by the South Australian Arid Lands Natural Resource Management Board (SAAL NRM).

The landscape component is part of a multi-disciplinary investigation into the following areas:

Hydrology: flows across the landscape over time and intensity

Aquatic ecology: recording and measuring native and pest fish in relation to water and waterhole quality

Ecology: identifying vegetation types and communities in relation to change

Geomorphology: tracing the mega-scale shifts in water and land systems over geological timescales

Practitioners of landscape architecture need to gain understanding of the mega-systems that flow towards the center of the continent, along with the very local conditions that impact upon waterholes, mound springs, and ephemeral creeks. The results of fieldwork concentrated around two of the identified micro-communities of the Neales catchment are outlined below: the Algebuckina Waterhole, a critical refugia micro-ecology; and the Oodnadatta Township, a critical micro-urban community.

The endorheic LEB system covers more than one million square kilometers of central Australia and is characterized by ephemeral rivers and creeks and vast, braided channels that all drain towards the central saline Lake Eyre (LEB, 2005; Figure 2). The Neales River catchment on the western rim contains rare permanent and semi-permanent waterholes, home to a number of competing and sometimes complementary land uses. Aboriginal association with the region has been demonstrated over tens of thousands of years, and their land use is linked to responsibility for Country—an Aboriginal concept for stewardship and familial occupation. In light of Australia's relatively newfound concerns for reconciliation and native title agreement, the importance of preserving and protecting ongoing cultural access to Country is increasingly recognized; water systems, and in particular waterholes, are almost always places of deep cultural significance.

Figure 2: Australia; The Lake Eyre Basin – the vast inland "sea"

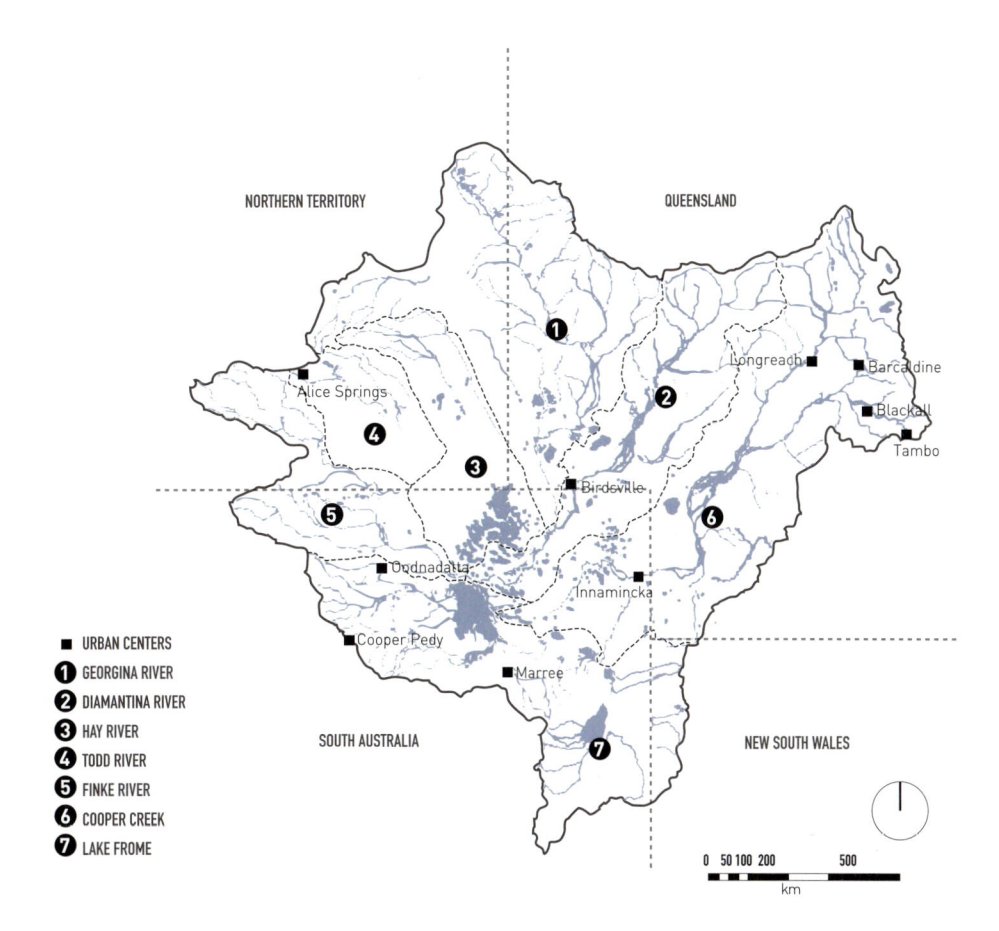

Pastoralism, in the form of sheep and cattle grazing, has been present from the mid-1800s, and continues to impact upon biodiversity to varying degrees. Generally, low stocking rates and scant use of chemicals suggest effective management, but it is clear that in times of scarce water, the presence of hoofed animals can seriously affect sensitive waterholes. Increasingly, mining and petroleum interests affect groundwater reserves, because of a substantial need for water extraction. Due to this and also to the effects of freely flowing pastoral bores, the water levels of geographically associated mound springs have fallen in recent years. Today, while almost all uncapped bores are no longer in use, due to the widely publicized natural, cultural, and spiritual significance of the LEB, a rise in outback cultural and eco-tourism has brought new demands for water potable to humans.

High concentrations of large and sophisticated off-road vehicles seeking remote and untouched natural places, preferably with water, have a heavy, though seasonal, impact on the riparian zones of creeks and waterholes. People prefer to camp right on the bank edge of creeks, if not in them. Increased pressure on remote services and infrastructure means that small urban settlements face considerable demand for water and waste disposal on an almost 24-hour basis. The consequent degradation of well-used places is a direct result of the truism that water is a magnet in the arid landscape—the mere sniff of water will bring humans, animals, and plant species to inhabit these special places, the critical micro-communities of the outback.

Micro-Concepts: Networks and Connectivity that Link Communities

The following are working characterizations of the micro-urban Oodnadatta community, the micro-ecology of the Algebuckina Waterhole, and the water points along the Oodnadatta Track as refugia communities, to assist in tracing their systematic interdependence.

Micro-communities and habitats: Examination of these can uncover the structural and symbiotic relationships between water, town spatial structures, and water extraction and containment.

Micro-urbanities: These areas manifest elements of major urban centers in miniature. Small communities can provide a lower base cost of living (excluding remote-area transport and operational levies, easy internal access, and a strong sense of neighborhood and community.

Micro-habitat: Ecologies of micro-habitats are specialized and discrete. The small-scale physical requirements of particular organisms or populations occupy niche spaces, for example, localized to a waterhole, or fragmented over many interconnected places.

The few inhabited townships along the Oodnadatta Track are interspersed by settlements, now long abandoned, which in times past were the central stopping points for rail and road travelers. These settlements were always located near waterholes or springs, from which water was extracted, piped, or carried by a range of robust and ingenious small-scale infrastructure.

Waterholes and other water bodies are magnets in the landscape for all communities, whether they are ecological, faunal, or human, and in times of extreme drought they become the critical refuges that sustain the last vestiges of the local ecosystem. The Australian government has recently nominated the Algebuckina Waterhole as the critical refugia site for the Neales catchment system. Critical refugia waterholes are essential water bodies that, due to their capacity to endure climatic or other changes that impact alternative habitats, provide remnant ecological habitats for relict species. Such critical refugia have tenuous and potentially doomed existences, as their distribution in arid areas is typically limited.

Typologies: Surface Water/Groundwater: Nature/Constructed Culture

Interdependent water systems form a spatial network, linking surface and deep underground waters, that connects and defines both ecological and urban/settler/explorer communities.

Waterhole: A fresh, semi-saline or saline surface water storage hole in the deeper and wider sections of an ephemeral river or creek's multiple channel systems. They are characterized by a range of bank and riparian conditions. They expand or contract according to the season and convey evidence of ephemeral occupation.

Dam: A constructed dam comprises deep, geometrically formed waters surrounded by extensive walls rising above the surrounding landscape. An outback dam stands either in drainage lines, to capture rain and overland flows, or in river channels, to capture floods. Dams are associated with water management infrastructure, such as windmills, as artificial incursions into the landscape.

Great Artesian Basin (GAB) spring: A naturally occurring saline water discharge from underground springs, contained within a shallow open pool. They are often confined by an encircling mound, or seeping into swales. Historically, these springs were the focus of explorer routes and remote outpost settlements.

GAB bore: A constructed water source. Artesian ground water is extracted under pressure by drilling into underlying rock layers, and tapped to provide managed water delivery. Untapped bores have a "tail" of Phragmites (common reeds), associated with water spilling over the landscape to follow natural or formed swales draining towards creek lines. Pastoral and/or mining infrastructure, such as yards, machinery, and tracks, is associated with bores.

Technology: *Techne* and *Logia* in Water-Driven Landscapes

An engagement with the etymological origins of the term "technology" allows the concepts of *techne*, skill or craft, and of *logia*, knowledge of systems of organization, to be used as theoretical constructs aiding understanding of continuing human drylands occupation. The importance of technology in remote arid places is evident in the design tactics revealed in everyday infrastructures and the humble, yet ingenious, solutions to the challenge of extracting enough water for survival employed by inhabitants. *Techne* is present in water drawn from deep underground, collected during times of surface flow, or gathered from infrequent rains to be processed and stored. Following the water trails, traces emerge of past uses and of adoption of seasonal and flexible lifestyles.

In Oodnadatta in the early 20th century, the Chinese market gardener Ned Chong made vegetable gardens on the banks of the ephemeral Hookeys Waterhole, using seasonal water in an ingenious irrigation system previously unpractised in the outback (Figure 3). His *logia*, brought from a wetter place, informed desert dwellers of micro-agricultures; before, the norm had been subsistence on seasonal hunting and gathering, or on scant supplies brought from far away.

Micro-urban communities tangibly demonstrate affinity with the fluctuating presence of water through association with mapped and culturally known ephemeral systems, visible in lines across the landscape that connect ecological systems and human systems. Yet rarely is water obviously present on the surface. People (and animals) learn to see the clues; the application of technology and local know-how—the cultural knowledge and skills embedded within a community—informs landscape use and spatial planning. The critical refugia project recognizes that in order to apply scientific knowledge about ecosystem health and survival, it is necessary to evaluate Aboriginal knowledge, historical settler practices, and contemporary communities' practices and diverse needs—to develop an understanding of the broader *techne* and *logia* systems.

Collaboration across Disciplines: Themes, Methods, and Processes

Landscape architecture and design thinking can contribute to scientific research projects even when those projects do not necessarily engage community or design outcomes. For landscape architecture to be relevant, recording multiple conditions informed by design methodologies is just the initial work. It is also necessary to find a language to translate design thinking across scientific and community methods and platforms, where a range of modes of expression and understanding are at play (Thompson and Steiner, 1997; Ndubisi, 2002).

The practices of noticing, recording, and conversing across disciplinary territories occur most effectively in the field. Around the waterhole, we sit down and talk about critical issues for arid landscapes, such as seasonal boom and bust, varying water quality, and ecosystem health and stress indicators. In these conversations, landscape architects can observe the presence of human-formed landscape detritus, ways of marking water points, and the crossing of water-shaping places, using an aesthetic and practiced perspective.

Out of our fieldwork discussions came the idea to develop intersecting ecological themes relevant to communities of practice, in order to allow overlapping perspectives on ecologies, landscape form and function, and processes of change to be captured. We first set down what each discipline regards as the critical aspects of our practices, prior to identifying our "universal" themes for these arid lands:

The way the river works—geomorphology. Assessing the big time-scale structures and dynamics that explain why the water works the way it does and, consequently, why communities settle where they do (Wakelin-King, 2011).

Refugia as fish recovery havens—aquatic ecology. Understanding how healthy fish and diverse populations indicate the health of the system (McNeil, 2011).

Flow events over time—hydrology. Understanding the dynamics of time-based water events and flow that contribute to where water is found and its quality (Costelloe, 2011).

Effects of change on riparian vegetation—ecology. Understanding the health of remote-area riparian systems in relation to water quality over time (Scholz, 2011).

Rivers and water holes as magnets in the landscape—landscape assessment and design. Understanding the character and coexistence of human and ecological systems, and the networks and structures that frame the landscape (Lee, 2011).

We then adopted seven themes highly relevant to our research practices as tools for classifying the features of the current situation. They needed to be robust enough to operate with the dynamics of future climatic, social, and economic change. Utilizing the concepts of Time, Landscape, Salt, Refugia, Pathways, Futures, and Vulnerability to support future strategies for planning and management, we now apply expanded disciplinary research methods to complex ecological and social factors in dryland river systems and their catchments.

FIGURE 4: Hookeys Waterhole: Fishing place and Mr. Ned Chong's garden, 1910 (top) and 2011 (bottom)

158

One outcome that arose from collaboration between the aquatic ecologists and the landscape architects was a Fish Day for Oodnadatta schoolchildren and their mothers and grandmothers at the women's waterhole, Hookeys Waterhole. This was a day for sharing knowledge of Aboriginal fishing practices and scientific ways of monitoring fish and waterhole health, and for observing landscape use, erosion, and management of riparian edges. The day included fishing, barbecuing what was caught, and drawing images of the landscape and ideas for the magic waterhole.

Field, Line, Point: Case Studies for the Arid Lands

To illustrate cross-disciplinary concepts viewed through a landscape lens, and to gain a landscape perspective on the vast catchment of the Neales River system, we have mapped the ecological and cultural networks spatially, while also developing a mechanism for understanding local dynamics in the context of external influences. Informed by landscape, architecture, and urban design methods (Allen, 1999) and cultural landscape frameworks (Lennon and Mathews, 1996; Fry, Tveit, Ode, and Velarde, 2009), the key findings are arranged into three spatial concepts: field, line, and point.

Field: Micro-Urban Communities and Ecologies

One field is Oodnadatta, the micro-urban place whose inconsistent urban condition stretches from town to river and encompasses the town common space in between. The watering places—the town pub and the waterhole—are magnets. For women and children, Hookeys Waterhole is not simply the main water supply, but rather the cultural center of town. Aboriginal desert people are fish people and, in stories, refer to the lakes and waters that used to be more abundant.

Line: The Oodnadatta Track

The line is the Oodnadatta track, where an itinerary reveals the tourist route and contextualizes exploration, transport systems, and European settlements, extant and ruined (Figure 5). All occupation exists due to present or past water, and the line traces an altered experience of the landscape and the micro-urban qualities encountered along the way (Austral Archaeology, 2001).

Point: Algebuckina Waterhole

At Algebuckina Waterhole, point and line converge within a new field operation, where design for management and interpretation is also a point for community interaction. Pastoralism, tourism, and fragile ecologies intersect at this critical refugium; it is a pinch point where ecologies and occupation reconcile and intensify. Here, contemporary landscape design can contribute to the conservation of ecological and social communities through landscape planning. For example, tourist infrastructure can draw from the *techne* and *logia* of land structures, water systems, and remnants of age-old occupation (Econsearch, 2008).

Conclusion

In the Neales River drylands, fieldwork planning considers geomorphology, ecology, and landscape sensibility to find the best spots for analysis and protection, and the right ways of accessing them. We negotiate across recognized *logia*—understanding of systems of organization drawn from experience and culture, including expert scientific, local, aboriginal, and outsider knowledge; and observed and practiced *techne*—the craft of working with the landscape, and the subtle requirements for developing micro-urban systems and support structures in remote and elemental landscapes.

The Neales catchment is a work in progress. Implementation will take many years of negotiation between researchers, planners, designers, and outback communities, supported by the financial and management input of government agencies and big business interests. It is clear that this is a multifaceted project, with many potential positive outcomes and follow-up projects for the ecosystems of arid Australia. Since collaboration across disciplines is essential in the long term, it is encouraging that concepts and language shared between science and design reveal normative practice in design to be relevant to new approaches to scientific research in the field, and vice versa. It is possible to embed design into the scientific lexicon.

Acknowledgements

The author would like to acknowledge the South Australian Arid Lands Natural Resources Management Board for their project management and funding support, and her fellow researchers Dale McNeil, Dave Schmarr, Gresley Wakelin-King, Justin Costelloe, Glen Scholz, and Brooke Madill for their collaboration in these journeys.

FIGURE 5: Moments along a 400km stretch of the Oodnadatta Track

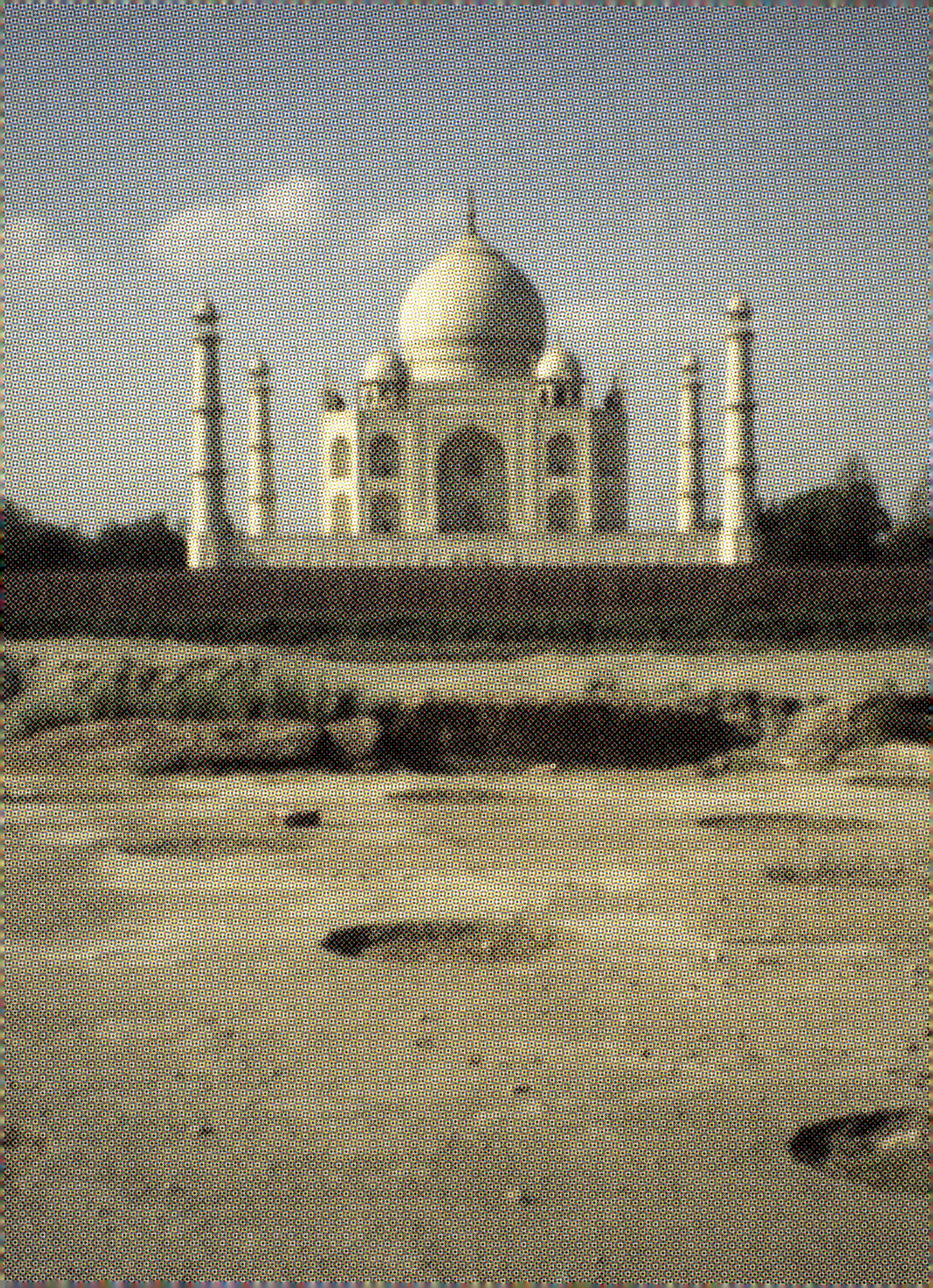

Water-Conserving Design Solutions: Contributions of Water Budget Analysis in Arid and Semi-Arid Regions

James L. Wescoat Jr.

Water budget analysis has made important contributions to water-conserving design in arid and semi-arid regions of South Asia, the Middle East, and North America. It is routinely employed in irrigation design and watershed planning. It developed from an initial emphasis on climate classification in the 1940s to irrigation, agronomic, and environmental planning applications in the later decades of the 20th century, culminating in ecological design, climate impact assessment, and adaptation planning in recent years.

Water budget analysis methods have expanded from empirical modeling and mass balance measurements at a point in space (e.g., with weighing lysimeters) to remote sensing technologies for regional analysis of soil moisture and evapotranspiration, and of water transport in soil, plant, and atmospheric systems, that draw upon advances in soil and weather sensor and controller technologies. Recent water budget analyses have sought to trace flows at the global scale, as well as the water footprints of industrial supply chains, and the water allocation and pricing institutions for urban and site scales. Adaptation of these ideas and methods across a range of scales, from the body to the site, city, region, and globe, represents an exciting frontier for arid zone design, and a valuable contribution to the broader field of water-conserving design. Here these prospects are explored in a series of case studies, from the garden complexes of Agra and Nagaur in India to a "new aflaj" system in Abu Dhabi.

The Expanding Scope of Water-Conserving Design

Water-conserving design is an exciting and vital frontier in landscape architecture, especially in arid regions. Emerging models of water-conserving design link the core problem of water use efficiency with the conservation of waterworks, livelihoods, experience, and meaning (Figure 1). My work in this field began with research on the water system of a Mughal garden, constructed just opposite the Taj Mahal on the Yamuna riverfront in 17th-century Agra. It expanded to include research on the conservation of a Mughal-Rajput palace-garden complex in Rajasthan, India; on the design of water supplies for a proposed settlement at Al Ain, Abu Dhabi; and on urban stormwater design studios in the U.S. (Wescoat, 2007a, 2007b, 2010).

This essay elaborates on one sphere of the water-conserving design model, known as "water resources conservation." It focuses on linkages between landscape design and water use efficiency, with some consideration of related aspects of water experience, values, and meanings (shown in blue on Figure 1). It does so by adapting the ideas and methods of water budget analysis, also known as water balance analysis, which have a fascinating history in fields ranging from irrigation design to river basin planning. The second part of the essay discusses the historical trajectory of water budget analysis and associated debates.

The basic idea involves simple mass balance analysis of inputs (precipitation in various forms) minus outputs (evapotranspiration and runoff) plus change in storage (soil moisture recharge and discharge). This idea becomes interesting when applied over different time steps (e.g., daily, monthly, and decadal scales) and spatial scales (e.g., from weather station data at a point in space, to sites, regions, and global assessments). In so doing, it becomes a technology for water-conserving design that links measurement, computation, and integrative analysis. The third section of the essay illustrates these advances through a set of increasingly complex landscape projects in South Asia and the Middle East.

Figure 4: Central pool and channel of the Mahtab Bagh complex in Agra, India

Water budget analysis can help answer fundamental questions in landscape architecture: How much water do native vegetation and undisturbed soils require under normal climatic conditions? How does landscape disturbance change these requirements? How do water requirements vary under different scenarios of climate and vegetation change? These questions have always been vital in arid and semi-arid regions, but they are increasingly recognized as important in all environments.

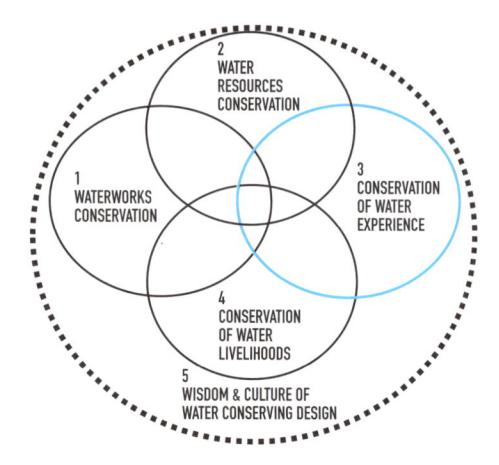

FIGURE 1: A model for water-conserving design

The Prospects for Water Budget Modeling in Design

Water budget analysis has a long history in landscape architecture and environmental planning: first in the field of irrigation design, in which the comparison of effective rainfall with potential evapotranspiration is central (Smith, 1996), second in the hillslope water balance model that receives a chapter in Dunne and Leopold's classic *Water in Environmental Planning* (1978, p. 236), and third in watershed management. Still, there are limits on the application of these ideas and methods in environmental design. Climate data are not always readily available. Estimating actual evapotranspiration rates for landscape plants and natural vegetation is difficult, since these have not received the same scientific attention as crop plants. To better understand these advances and limits in water budget analysis, the next section reviews its development in climatology, hydrology, and irrigation science, indicating how design and planning have drawn upon this research.

The Development of Water Budget Analysis in Hydroclimatology, Irrigation Science, and Landscape Planning

Concepts of hydrologic balance are ancient in water resources research (see Tuan, 1980). But an understanding of the balance among rainfall, infiltration, spring flow, and runoff did not develop in the West until the mid-18th century (see, e.g., Biswas, 1970).

Climatic water budgets that compare precipitation with evapotranspiration were developed still more recently, in the mid-20th century. The initial formulation in 1948, by climatologist Warren Thornthwaite, was for "a rational classification of climate." But the main research applications have been in the fields of agro-meteorology, agronomy, drought research, and irrigation science—not in the arid American West, as one might imagine, but in southern New Jersey, where Thornthwaite set up a Laboratory for Climatology, affiliated at various times with Johns Hopkins, the Drexel Institute, and the University of Delaware (Black, 2007; Field, 2005; Keim, 2010; Mather and Sanderson, 1995; Thornthwaite and Mather, 1957).

Scientists in the western U.S. developed comparable empirical formulas to estimate evapotranspiration. Empirical equations, such as the Blaney-Criddle formulas, were more commonly used in the West. All of the formulas produced errors when used in agricultural development projects that were not supported by weather records, weighing lysimeters and other micrometeorological instruments, and well-calibrated plant coefficients.

In the 1990s, the Penman-Monteith equation became more of an international standard for estimating reference evapotranspiration, disseminated by the UN FAO and other organizations (Allen, 1998; Brown, 2001). The underlying concept of water budget analysis lives on in irrigation design, scheduling and emerging controller technologies that incorporate rainfall data, more comprehensive weather data (temperature, wind, humidity, etc.), and soil moisture sensor inputs (Keim, 2010; U.S. Environmental Protection Agency, 2009). Online tools, such as the California Irrigation Management Information System (CIMIS), provide hourly, daily, monthly, and annual water budgets for user-specified time periods, weather stations, and regions (CIMIS, 2011). An online tool called WebWIMP (Web-Based Water-Budget Interactive Modeling Program) calculates water budgets globally at a half-degree grid cell resolution, and can incorporate variations in soil depth, infiltration rates, and climate change scenarios (Figure 2).

FIGURE 2: Water budget diagram for the Cambridge, Mass., USA, climate grid with soil depth and climate change variations

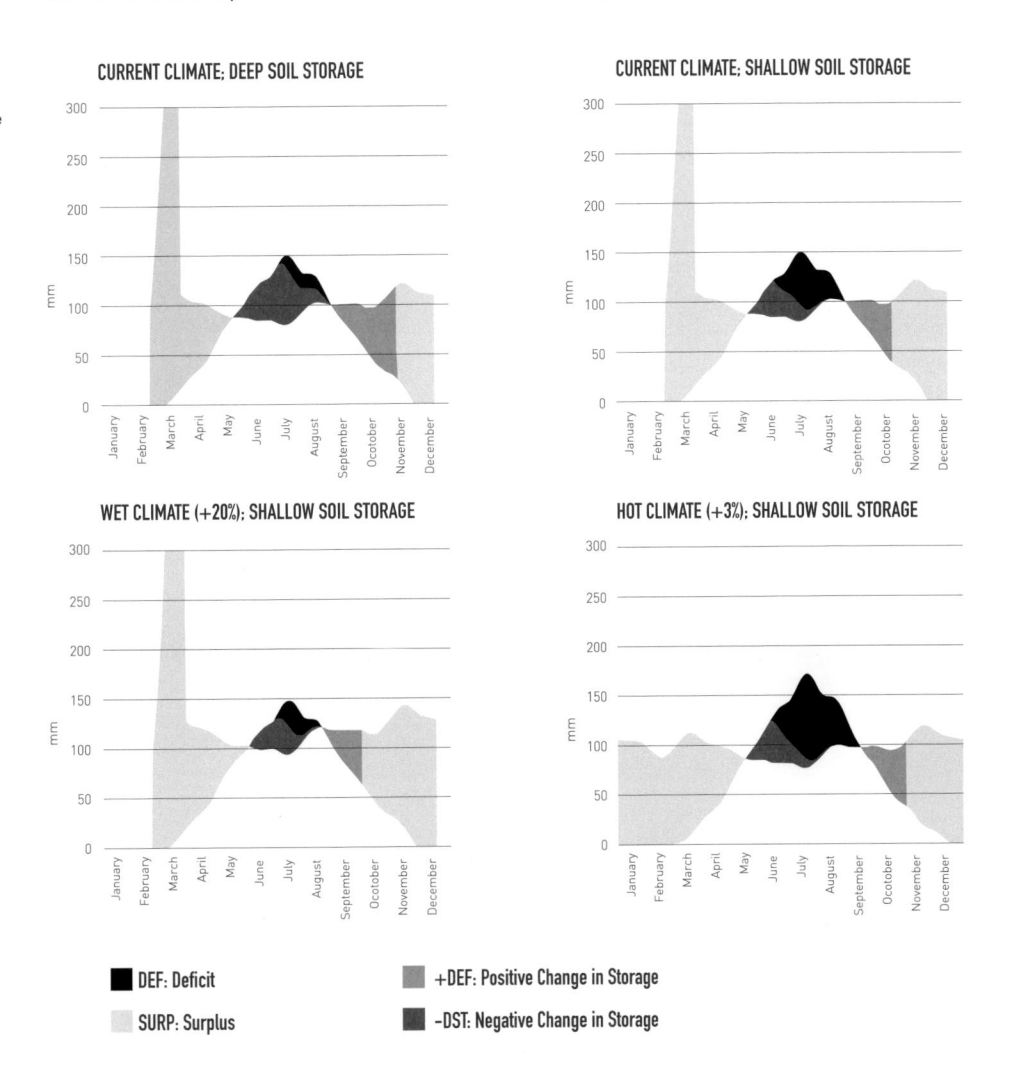

Applications in Landscape Architecture and Environmental Planning

Owing to its connection with irrigation, water budget analysis was incorporated in landscape architectural construction curricula that included irrigation design, although irrigation design later became a specialized field of landscape design consulting. Water budget analysis has contributed to the revival of native and drought-adapted planting design, also known as "xeric" or "waterwise" design, which stresses the grouping of plants with similar water requirements (e.g., Knopf, 1999). A large-scale application pioneered in Irvine, California, uses water budget analysis for conservation water rate policy, employing local weather data and water use software

(Ash and Lessick, 2002; DeOreo and Mayer, 2005; Hildebrand, Gaur, and Salt, 2009; Mayer, et al., 2008). The California Urban Water Conservation Council (CUWCC) developed methods for estimating evapotranspiration and water use budgeting in ornamental landscapes (Costello, Matheny, and Clark, 2000; CUWCC, 2011). The U.S. Environmental Protection Agency (2011) has recently created a "Water Budget Tool," including a spreadsheet and associated analytic methods, to bring this analysis in landscape design into the mainstream.

Water budget analysis has longstanding applications in environmental planning (Dunne and Leopold, 1978; Mather, 1978). It is often synonymous with water balance analysis, although the latter term may refer to an approach that gives somewhat greater attention to surface runoff, subsurface throughflow, and groundwater flux (e.g., Brooks and Ozay, 2000). The water budget and water balance are central concepts in hillslope hydrology, watershed hydrology, and wetland hydrology. By extension, they have been employed in research on slope stabilization, erosion, and land capability assessment (for a recent example, see Wang, Cresswell, Paydar, and Gallant, 2008).

Recent extensions include wetland design (Armstrong, 2007; Ayub, et al., 2010; Owen, 1995; Rayburg and Thom, 2009), brownfield and landfill reclamation (Dujardin, et al., 2011; Kostopoulou, Karagiannidis, Rakimbei, and Tsiouvaras, 2010; Nyhan, 2005), topsoil and soil amendment research (Pistocchi, Bouraoui, and Bittelli, 2008; Savabi, et al., 2003), rainwater harvesting (Briggs and Reidy, 2010), land application and wastewater reuse (Duan and Fedler, 2009; van Rooijen, Turral, and Biggs, 2005; Stannard, Paul, Laws, and Poeter, 2010), and urban hydrology (Claessens, Hopkinson, Rastetter, and Vallino, 2006; Gobel, et al., 2004; Mansell and Rollet, 2006; Mitchell, Cleugh, Grimmond, and Xu, 2008).

Myths, Pitfalls, and Research Frontiers

There are several important cautions about water budget analysis, particularly in groundwater management (Figure 3). Bredehoeft (1997, 2002) has underscored the pitfalls of using static mass balance models of groundwater recharge to estimate sustainable or safe yields. Aquifers must be modeled as dynamic systems, whose boundary conditions, transmissibility, and response to pumping are key factors influencing withdrawals. Some others agree, but give more emphasis to recharge rates and raise additional concerns about water quality variables in groundwater modeling (Alley, 2007; Devlin and Sophocleous, 2005; Sophocleous, 2004).

Water budget analysis is increasingly employed at all scales, from the field plot to the global hydrologic cycle under conditions of climate change, but it faces a number of questions (Abdulla, Eshtawi, and Assaf, 2009; Jorgenson and Al Tikriti, 2002). Which processes are scale-dependent and which are scale-invariant? How can the effects of heterogeneity in vegetation cover, soils, and hydrogeologic conditions be incorporated in the analysis? Which approaches for dealing with data constraints are sound? How can the uncertainties associated with these

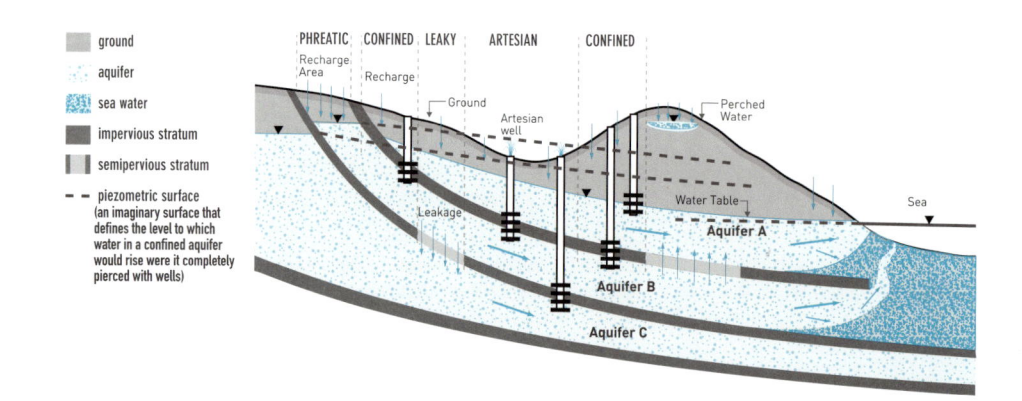

FIGURE 3: Cross-section of groundwater formations that complicate the hydroclimatic water budget analysis

processes be formally addressed in water budget analysis? These questions arise, in various forms, in every design project. The following trajectory of projects illustrates how they have contributed to advances in water-conserving design in arid and semi-arid regions.

Water Budget Contributions to Water-Conserving Design

Three case studies of water budget analysis in landscape research in South Asia and the Middle East are presented below to shed light on advances in the field. While focused on water use efficiency, they intersect with issues of infrastructure, economics, experience, and the culture of water in design (Figure 1).

The Mahtab Bagh (Moonlight Garden) Project in Agra, India

The Mahtab Bagh lies immediately opposite the Taj Mahal along the Yamuna River in Agra, India. For ages, tourist guides spun erroneous tales about an unbuilt "Black Taj" intended for the site. Mughal gardens had lined the Agra riverfront from the 16th through 18th centuries, but none had been excavated or analyzed in much detail. An international panel recommended scientific study of these historic gardens, and the Archaeological Survey of India and the Smithsonian Institution selected the Mahtab Bagh as a case to be studied in 1998–2000. They found that it had been a monumental pleasure garden, contemporary with, and probably part of, the Taj Mahal complex (Moynihan, 2000).

Previous research on Indo-Islamic gardens had focused on documenting physical aspects of garden waterworks (pools, channels, fountains, etc.) and interpreting their historical and cultural contexts (Wescoat, 2007a). The Mahtab Bagh study added a water budget analysis to these infrastructural and cultural aspects of garden research (Wescoat, 2000; Figure 4). It began with the question, "How much water would the garden require for its pools, fountains, and irrigated plantings?" Irrigation was by far the largest source of water demand, estimated through rough calculations of rainfall and the potential evapotranspiration components of the climatic water budget (Willmott, 1981; Figure 5).

The next question was, "How was that water supplied through a combination of monsoon rainfall, shallow alluvial wells, and short aqueducts along the river?" This question required an analysis of the garden water budget, which revealed how much water the irrigation system needed to provide, and in which months of the year. It also raised questions about the potential impact of groundwater pumping for garden restoration on the water supplies of surrounding villages. The main findings of this early study of a historical garden were that:

- irrigated plantings consumed by far the greatest volume of water;
- historical waterworks could be operated in ways that supplied those quantities of water; and
- reconstruction of historical water systems needs to address issues of equity and efficiency in the modern landscape.

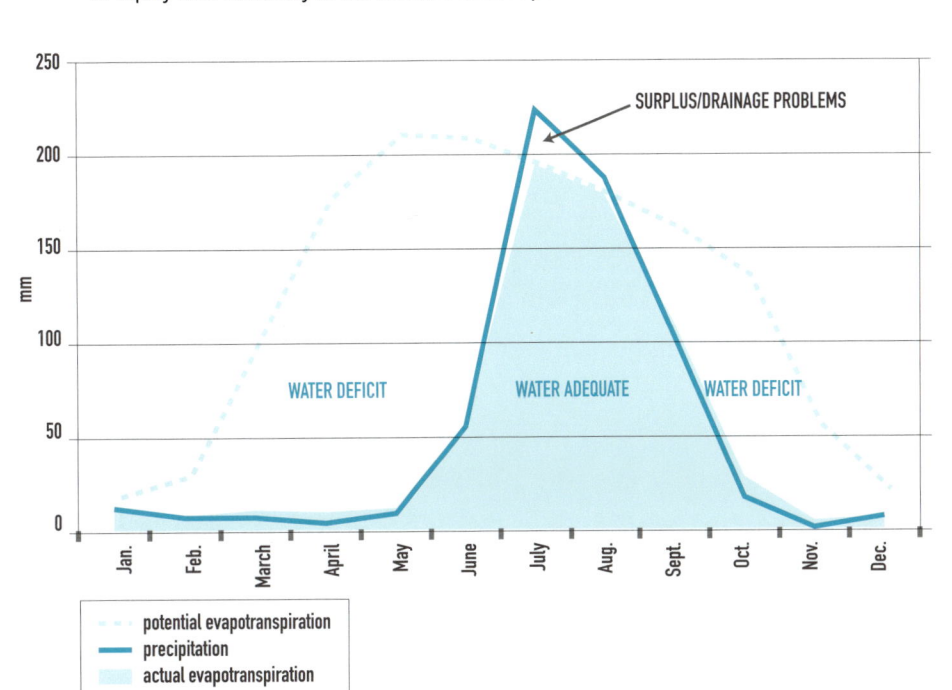

FIGURE 5: Monthly water budget diagram for the area of Agra, India

Nagaur Mughal-Rajput Palace-Garden Project in Rajasthan, India

A garden conservation project addressed these issues at the Ahhichatragarh Fort of Nagaur in the State of Rajasthan, India, owned by the Mehrangarh Museum Trust (Figure 6). A water budget diagram was prepared for the city of Jodhpur using the Willmott (1981) database, which revealed large hydroclimatic water deficits in every month of the year (Figure 7). These modern data were complemented by a review of paleoclimate research in Rajasthan, performance of different evapotranspiration formulae in the region, and climate change scenarios that could affect conservation proposals (Nandagiri and Kovoor, 2006; Wescoat, 2007d). The analysis went beyond the Mahtab Bagh project by incorporating water use efficiency coefficients, including adjustments for effective rainfall, irrigation conveyance losses, field efficiency, and different levels of gardener expertise.

FIGURE 6: Central cross-axial garden with shallow tanks, water lily pits, and irrigated plots in Nagaur Fort

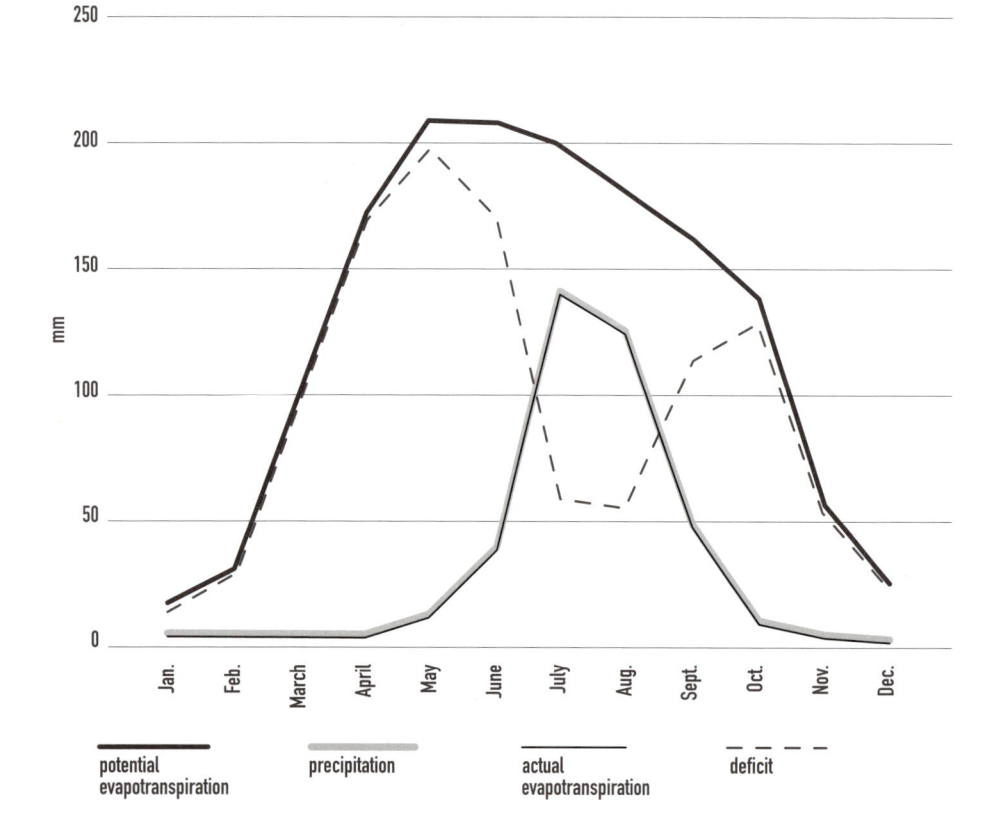

FIGURE 7: Monthly water budget diagram for the Nagaur climate grid, India

Conservation architect Minakshi Jain documented and analyzed historic rainwater harvesting surfaces, water pipes, and cisterns that collected and stored scarce monsoon rainfall in the Fort (see Wescoat, 2007c). Garden archaeologist Kathryn Gleason showed that soil profiles included porous sand substrate levels that held and conserved significant amounts of plant-accessible moisture (Figure 8).

Conservation landscape architect Priyaleen Singh based the planting design on contemporary Marwar paintings, and zoned the plantings according to common water use requirements (Figure 9). Small jewel-like gardens, similar to gardens in the paintings, were set within larger mesic and arid plantings (Wescoat, 2007d; Figure 10). Interestingly, this was accomplished by adapting landscape water budget methods from California (known as WUCOLS; Costello, 2000), with input from Rajasthani horticulturalists. The WUCOLS guidebook classifies plants as having high, medium, or low water requirements in different climatic regions of California, and it adjusts reference evapotranspiration by microclimate and planting density as well as species coefficients. Extensive areas of the Fort were planted with desert species that require only supplemental water for establishment. Water tanks were allowed to hold fluctuating elevations to reveal the aesthetics of seasonality in the garden (Wescoat, 2007a, 2010). Site grading helped restore large-scale rainwater harvesting and groundwater recharge systems.

FIGURE 8 : Excavated planting pit reveals porous sand substrate at Nagaur Fort, India (top);
FIGURE 9: Plantings zoned by water requirements in small irrigation basins (chiari) at Nagaur Fort, India (bottom)

FIGURE 10: Small, jewel-like garden plantings at Nagaur Fort, India (top);
FIGURE 11: Arid zone plantings at Nagaur Fort, India (bottom)

On an interim basis, the Fort relied on tanker trucks for its non-potable water needs. To analyze the benefits of water-conserving design, the design alternatives (xeric, mesic, and humid) were translated into increased tanker truck deliveries (up to 24 more tankers per day), tanker water costs (up to $40,000/year), and domestic water supplies that were not displaced (over 300 persons per year; Wescoat, 2007d). These extensions of water budget analysis helped support the case for water-conserving design alternatives.

Site-scale water budgets were complemented by urban and regional water budget studies that identified the components, though not the quantities, of the modern water supply system (Figure 11). There are further plans to extend these concepts beyond the garden walls, into the city of Nagaur and surrounding region. That larger regional perspective has implications for site-scale water budget planning and design, which are taken up in the final case study of Al Ain in Abu Dhabi.

Proposed Residential Development at Al Ain in Abu Dhabi, United Arab Emirates

Aflaj Al Foah is the name of a proposed residential development, located on the northern edge of a string of seven historical date palm oases and villages in Al Ain, Abu Dhabi, which were supplied by traditional aflaj water systems in southeastern Arabia (Brook, 2008; Figure 12).

Figure 12: Aflaj irrigated date farm at Al Ain oasis, Abu Dhabi

The project takes its name and inspiration from the aflaj irrigation systems that tapped hillslope aquifers and conveyed water by tunnel to the surface water distribution canals of an oasis (Beaumont, Bonine, and McLachlan, 1989; Costa, 1983; Lightfoot, 2000; Wilkinson, 1977). Although the project was not built, its conceptual design put forward interesting ideas for arid zone landscape planning.

The Al Foah project is a date farm that would include new residential development served by modern water systems. It is supplied by desalinated water from Al Fujairah about 100 km away, supplemented by very small amounts of local groundwater and occasional rainfall. Rather than view these traditional and modern water systems as separate approaches, this project sought to link them with one another through a progression of water budget analyses.

The climatic water budget of Al Ain underscores its aridity. Potential evapotranspiration is about 2500mm/year and precipitation only about 100mm/year (Figure 13). Annual precipitation variability is high, with a recorded minimum of 1mm and a maximum of 303mm. The extensive water budget of the region includes limited water supplies in shallow aquifers and wells that supported traveling Bedouins, herders, and native vegetation. The traditional aflaj system created a more intensive local water budget, and the modern Al Foah date farm further intensifies the water budget by using irrigation controllers and drip distribution lines.

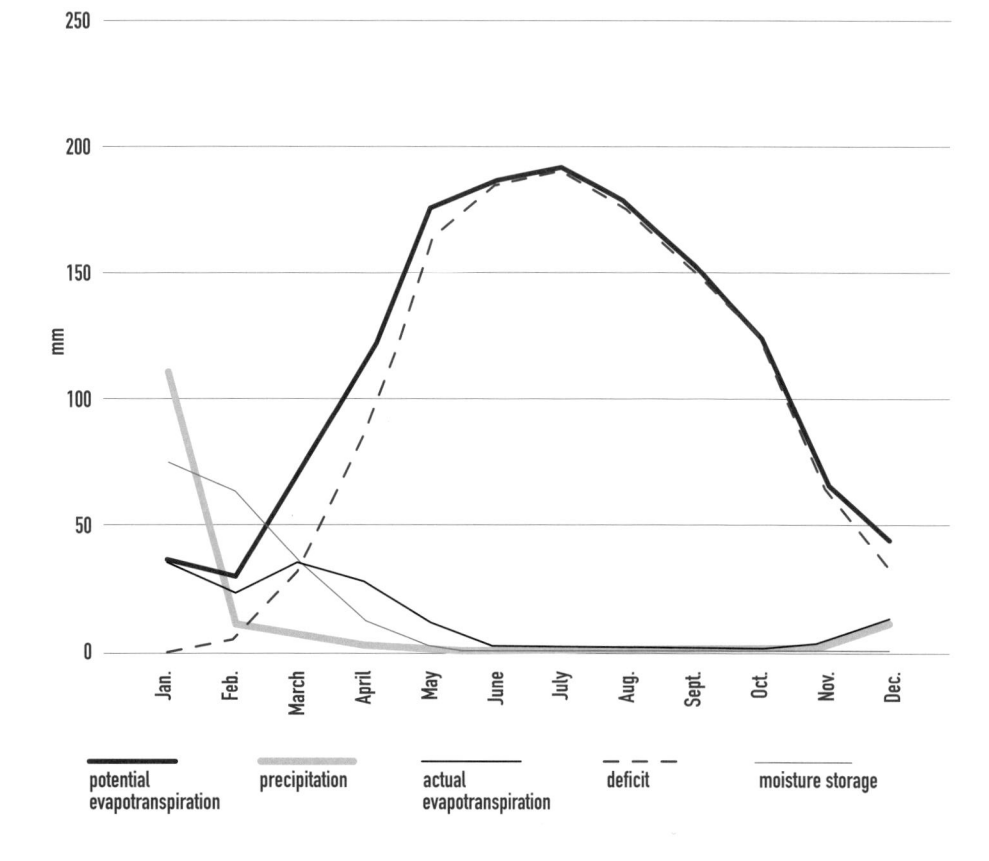

FIGURE 13: Monthly water budget diagram for the Al Ain climate grid, Abu Dhabi

The "new aflaj" concept would create a multi-use intensive water budget. In a traditional aflaj, seawater is tapped at a mother well, conveyed through a major tunnel to a shariati well, and distributed through a series of branching channels and institutions. The "new aflaj" is analogous: it taps seawater at a desalination plant and conveys it through a pipeline to a local water distribution plant, through a water distribution network, and finally through a wastewater collection and reuse system (which has on-site and off-site water reuse infrastructure). The key landscape analogies are elaborated below.

The water distribution plant, located where the desalination pipeline currently enters the site, would house a new Water Science Center. It would be a destination, rather than a conventional utility plant hidden in a corner of the site. Its landscape design would include water-conserving demonstration gardens. The Water Science Center would provide comprehensive water management for the project, including irrigation controllers based on evapotranspiration, soil moisture, and weather variation; scientific monitoring of water use and reuse; education programs for residents and schools; and research facilities for faculty and citizen-scientists interested in water. The Water Science Center would manage three types of water: date palm farm supply, potable household supply, and wastewater return flows from the municipality—the latter employing spatial separation, purple pipe, water quality monitoring, and so forth.

Just as traditional aflaj channels branched off from a main channel to secondary and lateral canals, the piped water distribution system at Aflaj Al Foah would follow the major circulation spine and neighborhood streets. The central spine would have tree plantings with bare earth (e.g., Salvadora persica for gnarled character, or Azadirachta indica for massing).

Unlike the traditional system, potable water mains would also run along the boundaries of the site and be connected to create a pressurized loop system. Al Foah wastewater would be discharged to the Al Ain Municipality Sewage Treatment Plant, which would supply treated sewage effluent for water-conserving irrigation in non-contact public spaces. Each neighborhood would thus know the source and sink of its water supply. As in traditional systems, but unlike modern utilities, each household would have tradable shares of potable water and treated sewage effluent, which it could allocate to establish different patterns of planting and water use.

Key neighborhood spaces and household gardens would have water distribution channels analogous to traditional aflaj, as a means of creating more lush vegetation and water experiences like those of historical oases (Figure 12). Irrigation channels that have negligible human contact would use treated effluent. Small courtyard pools and low fountain jets would have elegant narrow drainage channels that would water nearby planting beds. At each scale, the landscape water budget would weave together oasis, water-wise, and xeric plantings.

Each house would have an initial gross water budget allocation of approximately 375L per person per day, adjusted for seasonal demand. Residents would pay the full cost of building, operating, and maintaining the system for that amount as well as for their share of public water use. They would have interior water meters giving real-time readings of current and cumulative water use. If a household did not use its full water share, it would be able to rent it back to the development or to another buyer, which is a longstanding practice in the culture of traditional aflaj systems.

This water system provides a comprehensive approach that would draw inspiration from both traditional aflaj and innovations in water conservation science and technology. It would establish a water budget precedent for future settlement design in the Gulf region, and internationally.

New Directions in Water Budget Research and Design

As a review of the reference section for this essay indicates, only a small proportion of the research on plant-soil-atmosphere dynamics is currently being explicitly incorporated in environmental design. While this essay has focused on the supply side and touched upon connections with water infrastructure, experience, livelihoods, and meaning as depicted in water-conserving design (Figure 1), these linkages deserve much more research attention. The field is moving away from an historical emphasis on water supply towards a wider range of issues. For example, recent research is formally incorporating risk and uncertainty in water budget analysis (Bulygina and Gupta, 2009; Engeland, Xu, and Gottschalk, 2005; Faybishenko, 2010).

Finally, five other areas have special relevance for water-conserving design:

- Stormwater flows, infiltration, and Best Management Practices (BMPs) in the water budget
- Water quality parameters and treatment processes in the water budget
- Integrated assessment of multiple scales of water use and reuse
- Real-time water budget analysis in spatial decision support systems
- Incorporation of water budget analysis into environmental education and social learning and citizen science programs

These are several of the promising frontiers where water budget analysis can help expand the range of choice in water-conserving design.

Acknowledgements

The author would like to thank the case study sponsors, including the Archaeological Survey of India, the Smithsonian Institution, the Mehrangarh Museum Trust, Torti-Gallas and Partners, and the Al Foah Company.

HIRIYA LANDFILL RECYCLING PARK

Latz+Partners, Weinstein Vaadia Architects
Ayala Water & Ecology

Site: Tel Aviv, Israel
Longitude & Latitude: 32°01'N 34°49' E
Water Volume/Day: 40m³

Year: 2007
Status: Completed
Annual Precipitation: 530mm
Dimensions: 570m²

SITE PLAN

200m

LEGEND
1 subsurface wetland cells
2 visitor center
3 effluent storage
4 solid waste processing
5 Ayalon stream

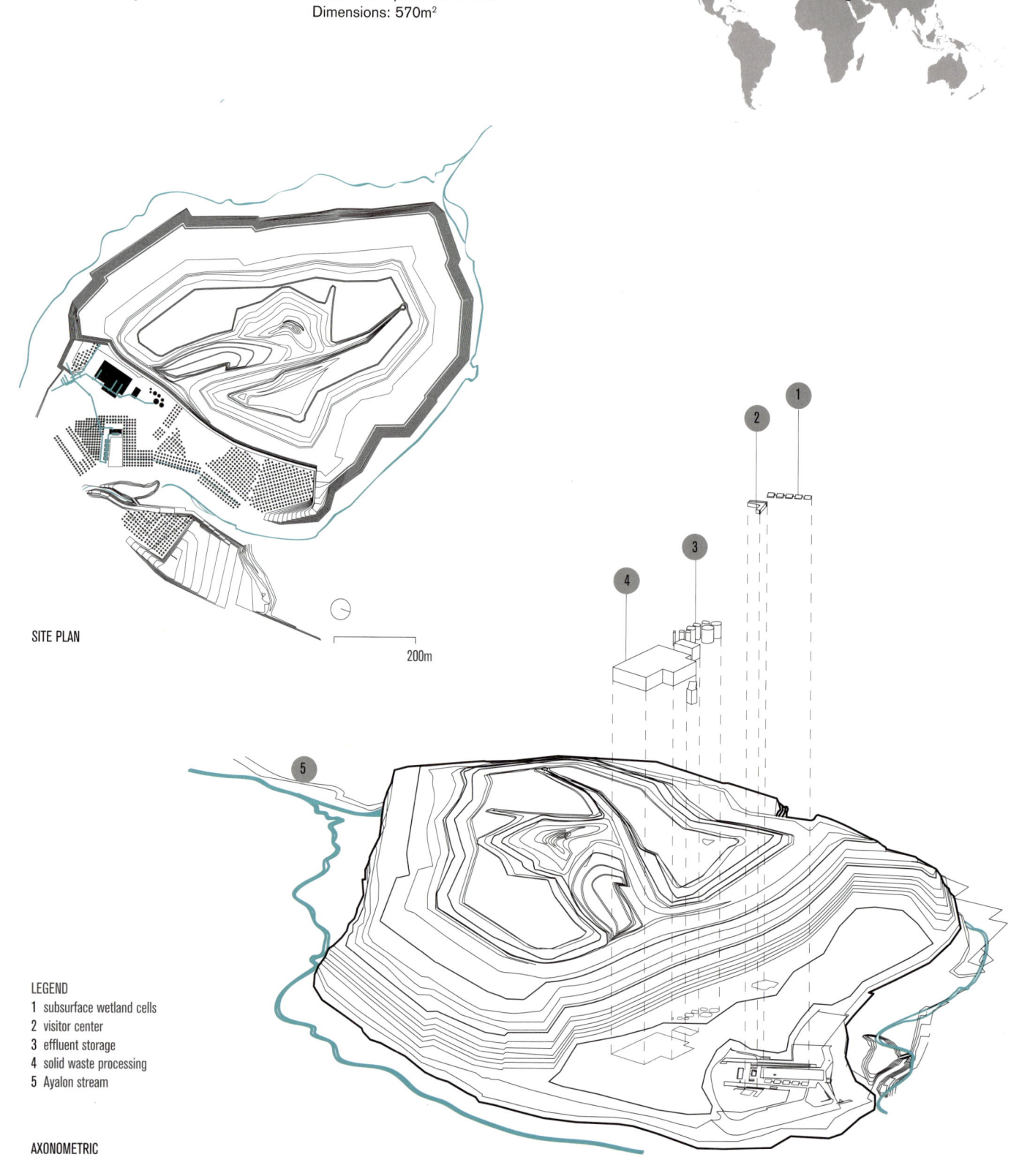

AXONOMETRIC

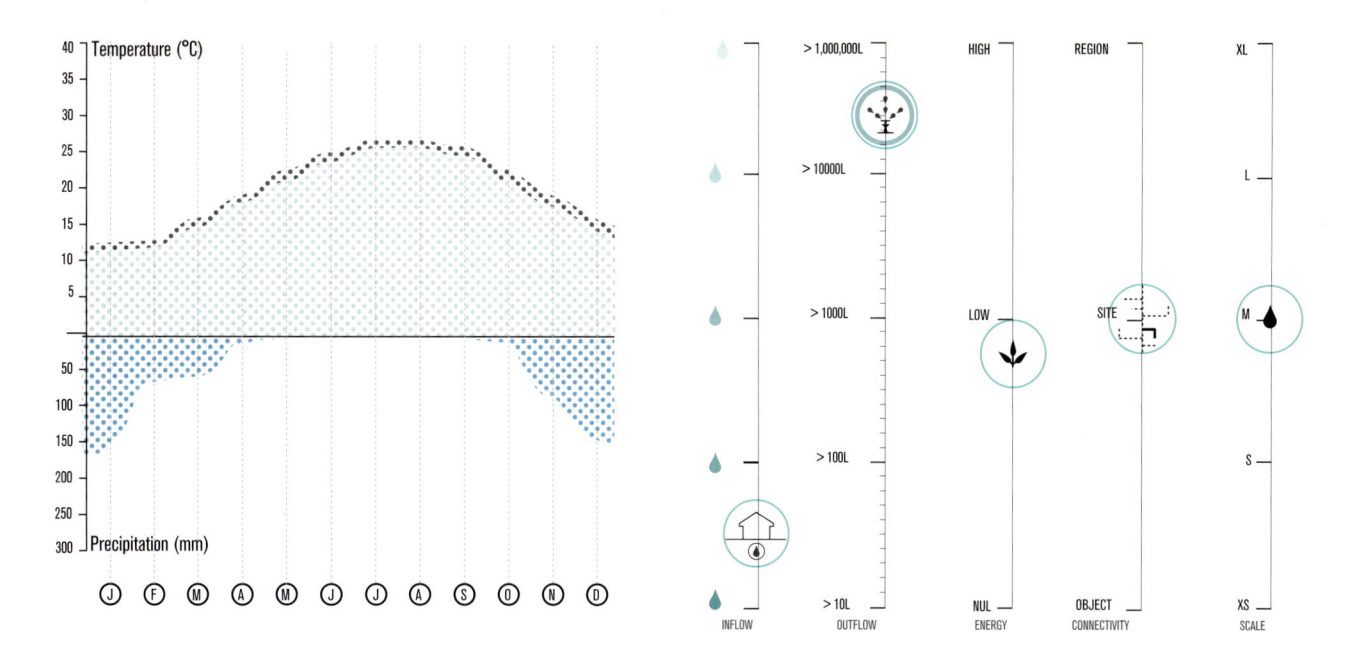

The Hiriya landfill served as the Tel Aviv Metropolitan Area's main disposal facility for municipal solid waste from 1954–1988. Its ongoing restoration consists of an 800ha public park, which includes a recycling facility and constructed wetlands for treating contaminated effluent on-site. The recycling facility processes municipal, construction, and yard waste and produces biogas. There are several sources of contaminated effluent at Hiriya, including landfill leachate, runoff from daily washing of garbage trucks, and effluent from the waste transfer's ArrowBio trash separation process, which accounts for 70,000t/year of separated organic and inorganic waste (Finstein, 2003). The 2004 winning masterplan for the Hiriya Park by Latz + Partners (with Weinstein Vadia and Ayala Water & Ecology) includes the design of 570m^2 of constructed wetland gardens with horizontal subsurface flow (SFW), designed to treat 40m^3 of effluent daily. Extending out from the visitors' center, the wetland garden serves as an emblem for Hiriya's Environmental Education Center.

Constructed wetlands (CW) are engineered systems that have been designed to utilize natural processes involving wetland vegetation, soil, and associated microbial assemblages to treat wastewater. These systems have been used for municipal or domestic wastewater treatment for more than 30 years. Today, municipal SFW systems also treat effluent from pharmaceuticals, oil refining, chemical production, pulp and paper production, tannery, textile manufacturing, abattoirs, food processing, and runoff from agriculture, airports, highways, and greenhouses, as well as landfill leachate (Vymazal, 2009).

SFW systems are particularly well suited for small to moderately-sized installations (Bulc, 2006). For example, in a domestic pilot project in central Mexico, treated water was suitable for irrigation purposes, alleviating local water scarcity (Belmont, et al., 2004). SFW systems can accommodate the diurnal flow pattern of domestic, municipal, and industrial wastewater. They are not suited for treatment of stormwater discharges, where peak flow may be much higher than the average, or agricultural runoff, with its intermittent peak events and high inorganic sediment loads (U.S. Environmental Protection Agency [EPA], 1993).

At Hiriya, the wetland garden consists of five rectangular SFW cells, arranged in a linear sequence along a 5% slope. Each is made of concrete, lined with a polymeric (ethylene propylene diene monomer) liner, and filled with aggregate and macrophytes that enable the removal of contaminants. These include Cyperus papyrus, Haspen, Cyperus alopecuroides, Thalia dealbata, Iris pseudacorus, Scirpus lacustris, Eleocharis geniculata, Cyperus gymnocaulos, and Canna generalis.

Aggregate size decreases incrementally from 50mm in the first cell to 5mm in the last. The effluent flows through settling chambers, and is then pumped into a mixing tank which regulates outflow in different seasons. From there it passively flows downward via gravitation through the SFW cells. Each cell includes a level spreader or weir to ensure uniform distribution of wastewater. The overall retention time is 3.5 days, and the treated water is used for on-site irrigation. The water surface remains unexposed below the media surface, eliminating odors and insect vectors, while keeping evaporation to a maximum of 3%.

The removal of organic and suspended solids and biochemical oxygen demand (BOD) through the long-term performance of SFW systems has been found to be effective. However, nitrogen and phosphorous are removed at lower rates (Vymazal, 2007, 2011; Verhoeven and Meuleman, 1999). The SFW systems are capable of achieving a reduction in fecal coliform, yet not enough to routinely satisfy discharge requirements (EPA, 1993). The removal of BOD is believed to occur through entrapment of particulate matter in the void spaces in the gravel media. BOD is removed by microbial growth on the media surfaces and attached to the plant roots and rhizomes penetrating the bed. Smaller rock sizes provide more surface area for treatment. This method's primary deficiency is the clogging of the void spaces either by the vegetation roots or by accumulation of suspended solids (EPA, 1993). A case study in Tanzania has demonstrated the capacity of Phragmites and Typha macrophyte species to remove 54% and 42.2% of nitrogen respectively (Senzia, Mashauri, and Mayo, 2003).

Baker (1998) notes that in arid regions where high-quality water is limited, wetlands that can treat nitrate could play an important role in the development of water resources. Similarly, Greenway (2005) discusses the potential of SFW for effluent polishing in subtropical and arid climates in Queensland, Australia, and adds that enhancing macrophyte diversity will maximize the removal of nutrients and pathogens. Kivaisi (2001) notes that wastewater reuse is an important strategy in countries that suffer from water shortage (e.g., Morocco, Tunisia, Egypt, Sudan, Namibia, India, and China). While nutrient content in wastewater is economically beneficial for its function as a fertilizer, there is a high risk of water-borne disease when raw, untreated sewage is used. While there is potential for the incorporation of low-cost constructed wetlands in small rural communities in developing countries due to ease of operation and maintenance, these systems have not found widespread use, due to lack of awareness of the technology and lack of local expertise in developing it (Kivaisi, 2001).

landfill leachate 3

garbage truck washing 2

waste transfer station effluent 1

subsurface bioremediation cells

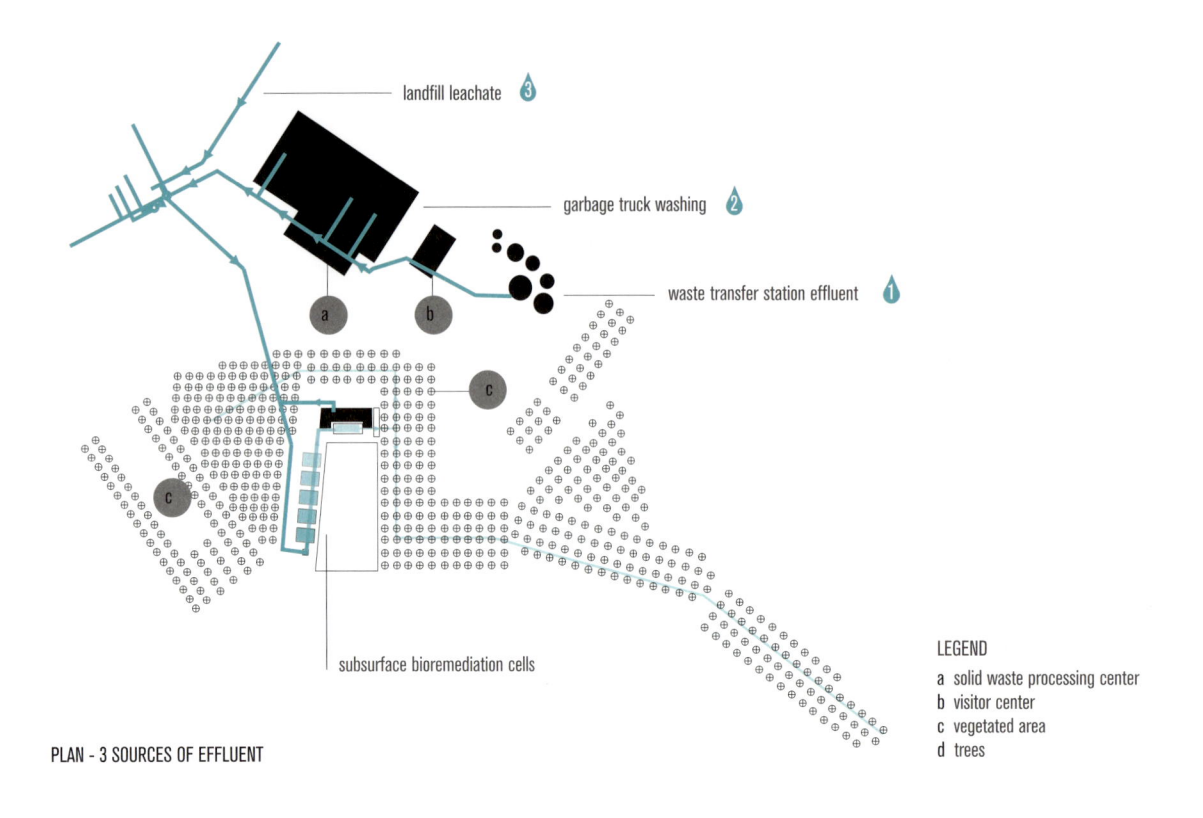

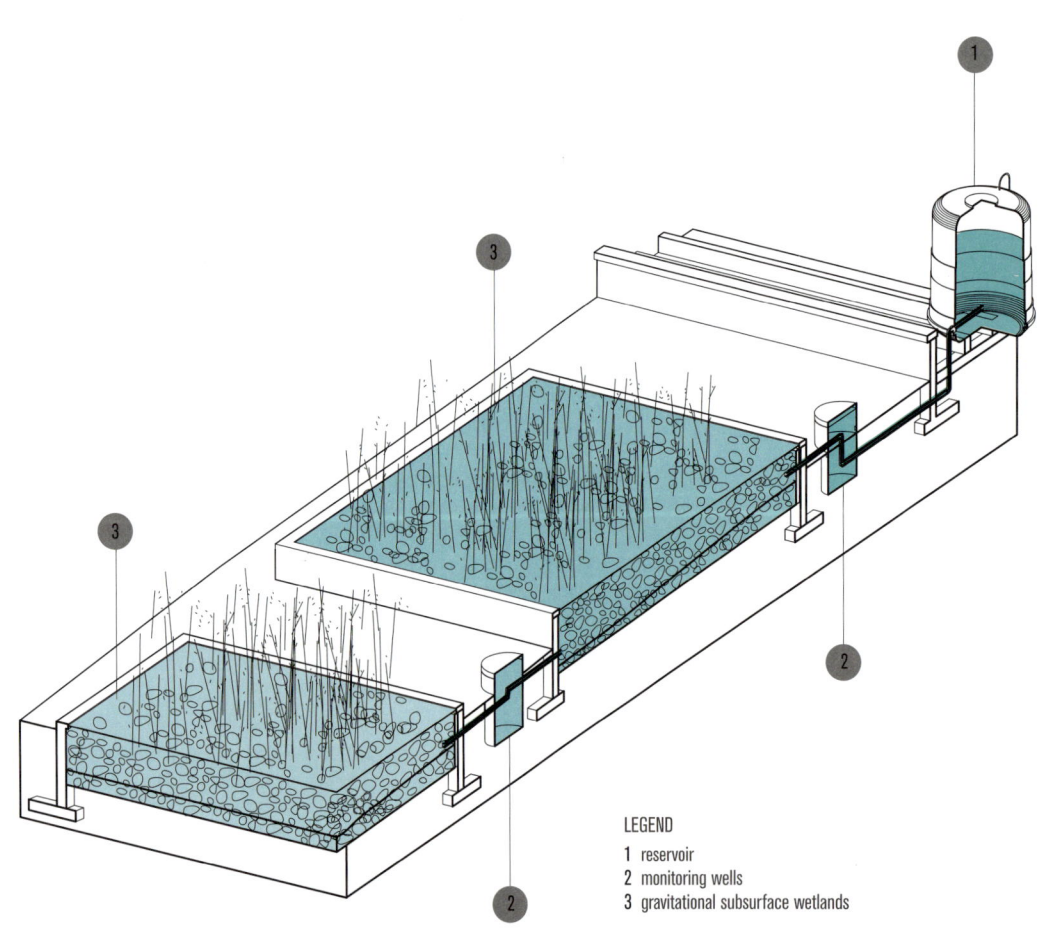

LEGEND
a solid waste processing center
b visitor center
c vegetated area
d trees

PLAN - 3 SOURCES OF EFFLUENT

LEGEND
1 reservoir
2 monitoring wells
3 gravitational subsurface wetlands

GRAVITATIONAL SUBSURFACE TREATMENT WETLAND AXONOMETRIC

176

LEGEND
1 reservoir
2 lawn
3 trees
4 concrete pathway
5 gravel
6 wood deck

polishing pond
100 m²

gravitational subsurface
wetlands 570 m²

PLAN

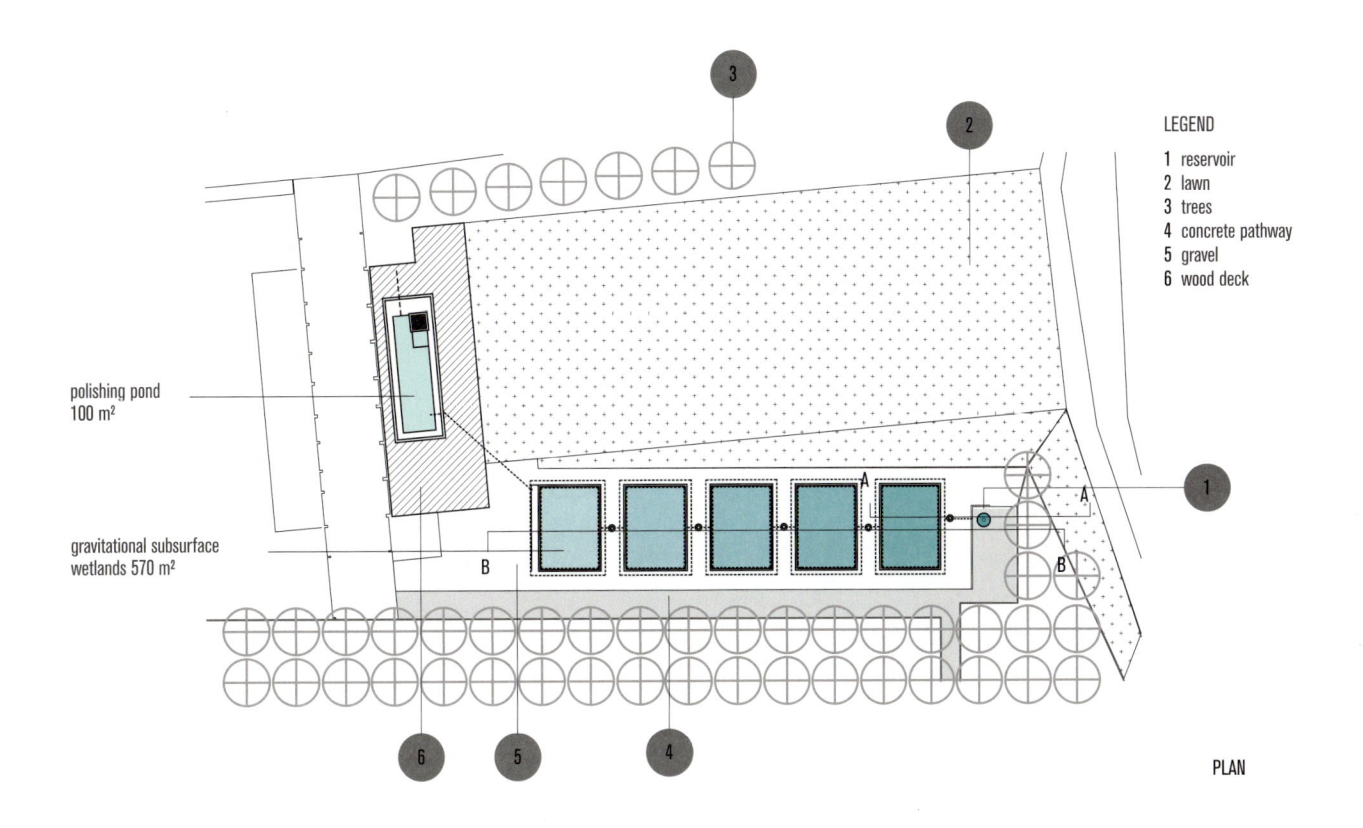

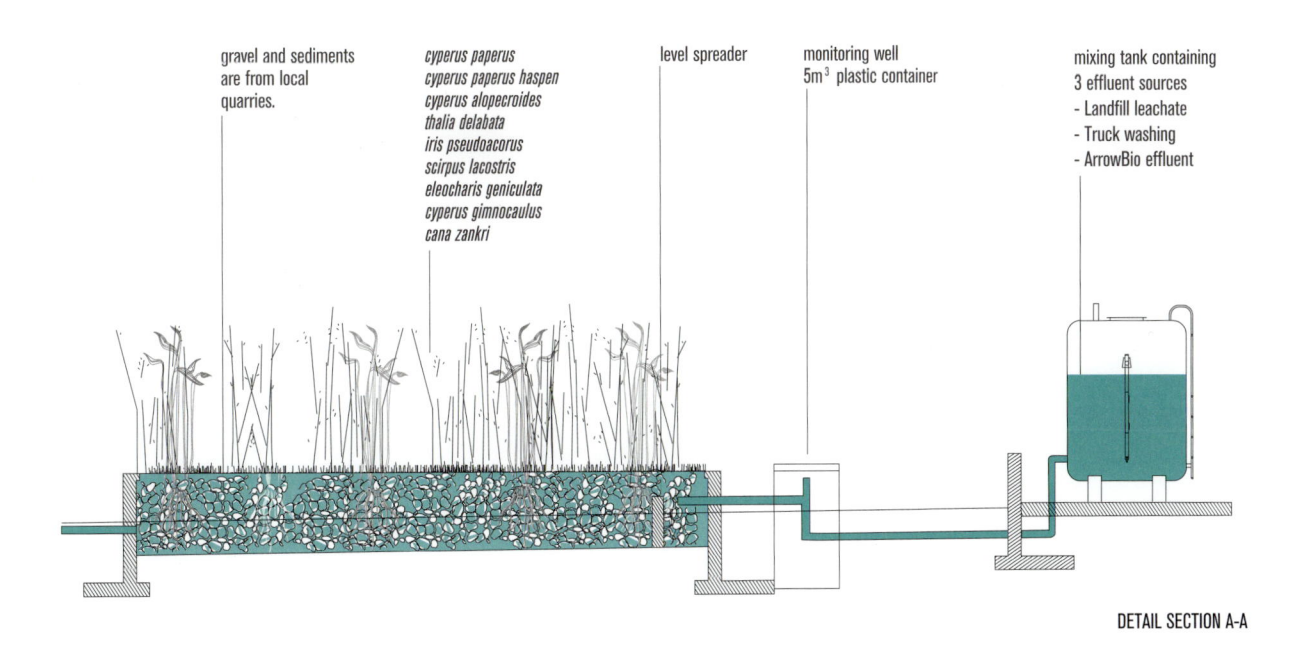

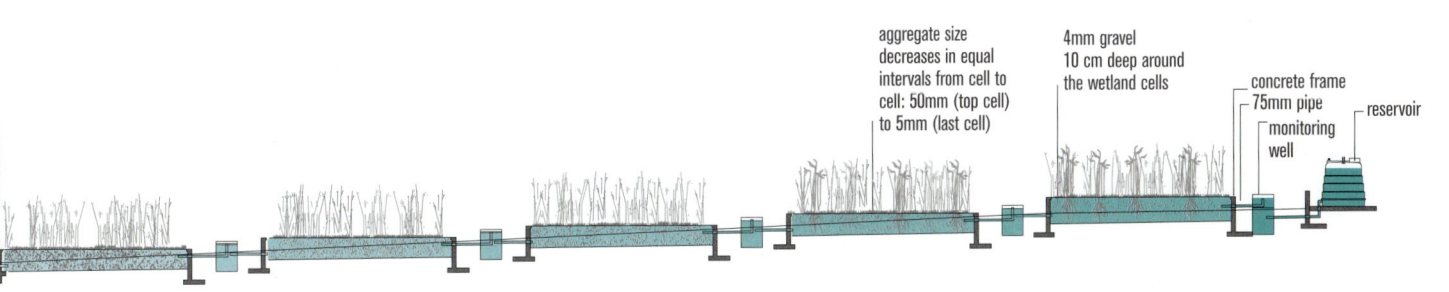

gravel and sediments
are from local
quarries.

cyperus paperus
cyperus paperus haspen
cyperus alopecroides
thalia delabata
iris pseudoacorus
scirpus lacostris
eleocharis geniculata
cyperus gimnocaulus
cana zankri

level spreader

monitoring well
5m³ plastic container

mixing tank containing
3 effluent sources
- Landfill leachate
- Truck washing
- ArrowBio effluent

DETAIL SECTION A-A

aggregate size
decreases in equal
intervals from cell to
cell: 50mm (top cell)
to 5mm (last cell)

4mm gravel
10 cm deep around
the wetland cells

concrete frame
75mm pipe
monitoring well
reservoir

SECTION B-B

177

TARAGALTE ECOLODGE
Bureau E.A.S.T. + Liat Margolis
Moroccan Ministry of Tourism, Butterfly Works

Site: M'hamid El Ghizlane, Morocco
Longitude & Latitude: 29°49'N 5°43'E
Annual Precipitation: 5mm

Year: 2008-present
Status: Under construction
Water Volume/Year: 130m³
Dimensions: 260m x 100m

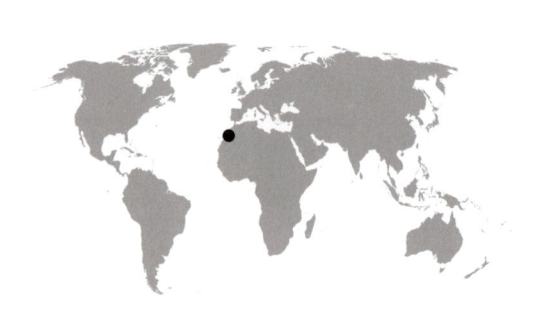

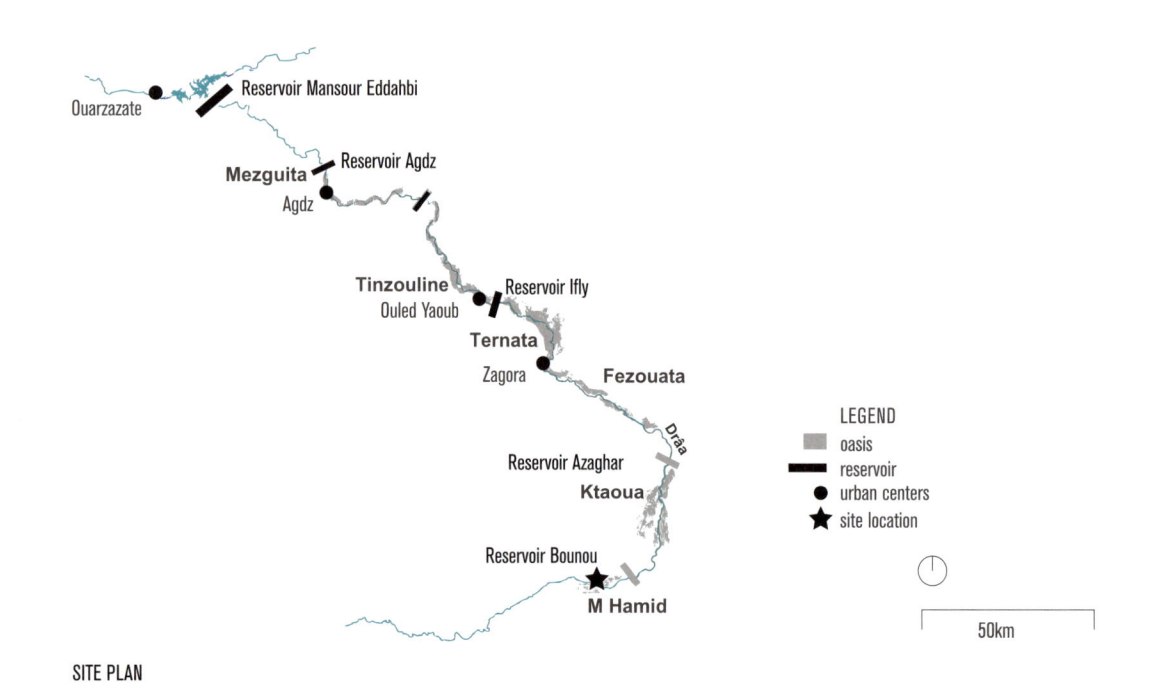

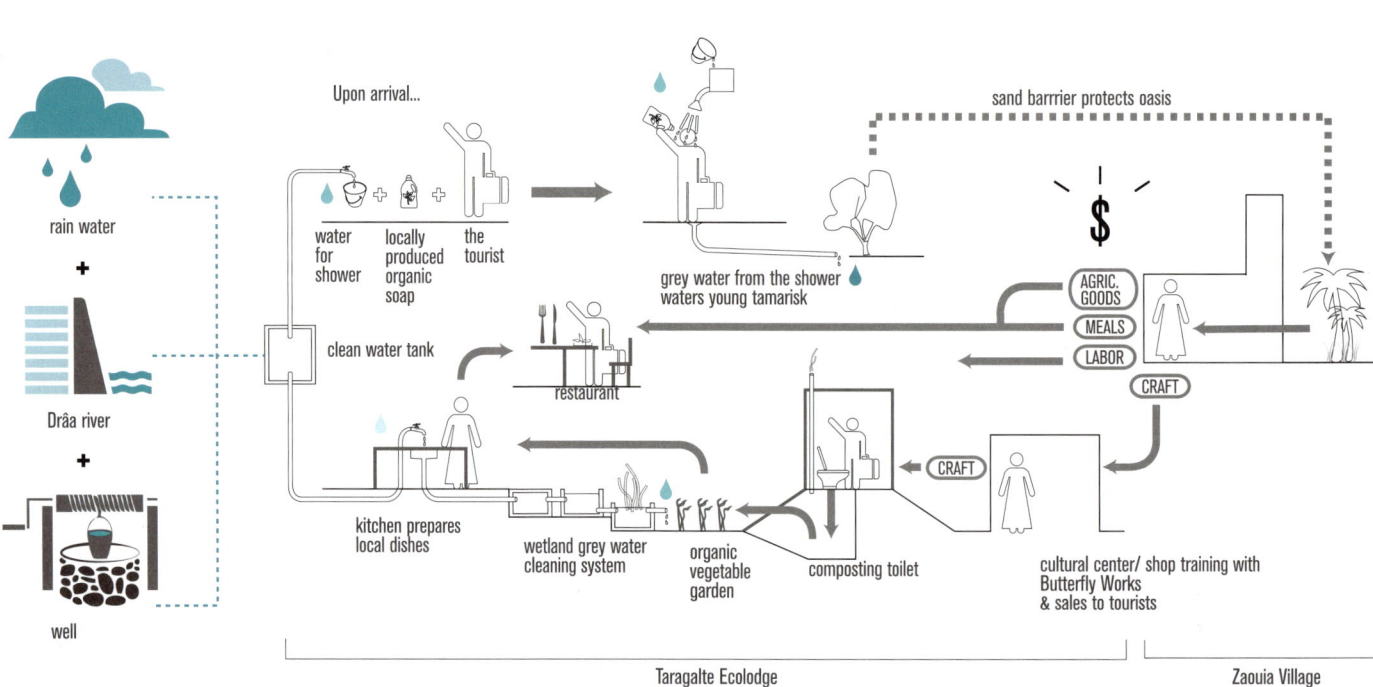

SITE PLAN

WATER FLOW DIAGRAM

178

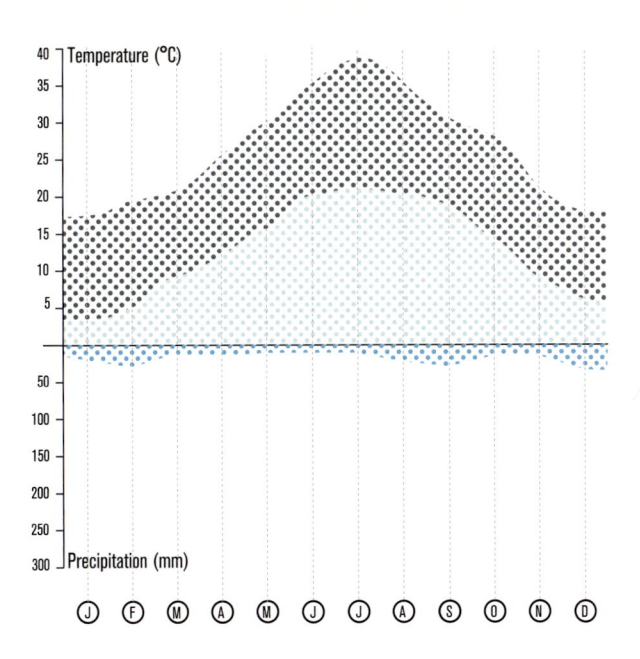

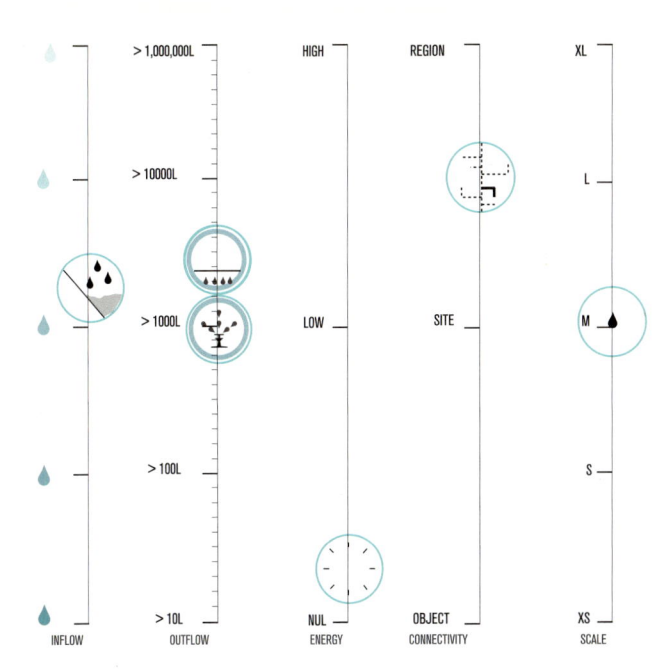

The Taragalte Ecolodge constitutes a node within an oasis-wide masterplan proposal that seeks to revitalize the oasis of M'Hamid el Ghizlane, integrating rainwater harvesting and sand retention strategies into its architecture and thereby developing a new typology of anti-desertification infrastructure for the oasis. The masterplan jointly addresses the derelict state of the agricultural landscape of the oasis, the advancement of sand dunes, ecologically damaging tourism practices, and deterioration of socio-economic conditions. In fact, the oasis of M'Hamid, located downstream from the Drâa Valley in sub-Saharan Morocco, was once a thriving agricultural center and a vibrant trading post along the salt and gold routes linking Mali to the Mediterranean shores. The oasis subsistence relied on a rigorous, communal water management system (Ouhajou, 1996) based on underground canals and the Drâa River, and on agricultural knowledge necessary to generate a micro-climate (see Chaouni, p. 113-127).

After Morocco gained independence in 1956, several factors contributed to M'Hamid's decline: the closing of borders and political tensions with nearby Algeria (Torres-Garcia, 2013); the disappearance of trade routes (Thomas, 1952); demographic decline (Ait Hamza, El Faskaoui, and Fermin, 2009); increased surface temperatures and weather variability caused by climate change, believed to be caused by changes in Northern Atlantic Oscillation and West African Monsoon activity (Hydrology for the Environment, Life and Policy, 2005); and most importantly, the construction of the Mansour Eddahbi dam upstream of the Drâa Valley (Sobczak, 2008). The dam's goals—flood control, hydroelectric generation, and continuous irrigation to downstream lands—had mixed results, mainly because the dam's episodic water regime was not accompanied by land consolidation, change in irrigation techniques, or crop rotation or water budgeting regulations (Heidecke, 2009).

Consequently, farmers either abandoned their lands or started to excessively pump water from the groundwater table, in turn leading to depletion of subsoil waters levels and soil salination. Without vegetation cover, desertification ensues, and the topsoil layer is exposed to the natural elements of wind and rain. Thus, erosion degrades the soil to barren rock or dry sheets of sand, and the sand dunes advance. Extensive and uncontrolled grazing has aggravated the situation (Ait Hamza, et al., 2009). Responses to this phenomenon in M'Hamid have included mechanical fixing of the sand dunes with woven palm tree leaf grids, which have proven to be effective only in the short term, and the planting of rows of drought-resistant tamarisk trees at the base of the sand dunes. The tamarisk roots bind the soil, which helps prevent erosion and sand displacement.

The masterplan for M'Hamid proposes addressing the desertification issues by an initiative to develop an oasis-wide buffer zone composed of sustainable hotels, or "ecolodges," which serve both as new sand dune retention systems and as socio-economic incubators.

The Taragalte Ecolodge illustrates this new typology. The ecolodge is located at the southern edge of the oasis, on loamy grounds that were formerly arable. The site holds a few clusters of palm trees and is surrounded and penetrated by 0.5–2m high barchans and transverse dunes, which move east-to-west and west-to-east. In order to stabilize the sand dunes, the ecolodge's design uses several strategies conjointly in order to form a multilayered, multifaceted sand fencing infrastructure. First, woven palm leaf grids are placed on the periphery of the site. Second, a series of tamarisk tree lines are located along the eastern and western edges of the site. Third, V-shaped berms, walls, and rooms are introduced along the eastern and western edges. By virtue of their shape and weight, these structures act not only as sand dune stabilizers but also as protectors of the tamarisk trees, which are very susceptible to sand storms and winds during their first year of growth. Finally, the ecolodge center is filled with a lush palm tree grove and vegetable garden, which acts as a dense tree fence.

To implement and sustain such an infrastructure, a series of rain-harvesting micro-catchments are created. In deserts, surface crusting, which develops when a sealed-over soil surface dries out after rainfall or irrigation, reduces infiltration and increases runoff. This runoff rarely reaches plants or the water table (Bull, Kirkby, Shannon, and Hooke, 2000). Micro-catchments can capture this local runoff, reduce transmission losses, and concentrate the runoff into the planted basins (Ali and Yazar, 2007). This method collects surface runoff from a contributing area (CA) over a flow distance of less than 100m and stores it for consumptive use in the root zone of an adjacent infiltration basin (IB; Boers and Ben-Asher, 1981). The key parameter in micro-catchment design is the CA/IB ratio, that is, the runoff production potential of micro-catchments and water storage capacity of the soil in the planted basins.

Because of reduced infiltration losses, the percentage of runoff increases with decreasing catchment size (Amerman and McGuinness, 1968). Hence, the whole ecolodge site's topography is sloped to better collect the natural southeastern runoff flow, and direct it towards the central depression of the palm tree grove. Moreover, small micro-catchments are placed behind the berms, rooms, and walls to foster the irrigation of the tamarisk trees.

The irrigation of the tamarisks and the date palms is complemented by grey water recycling and by water collected in a reservoir that comes from rainwater harvesting and from the Drâa River dam release. Highly variable precipitation in the region renders sole reliance on rain-harvesting micro-catchments a vulnerable approach. Similarly, sole reliance on the Drâa River's sporadic regime could place the ecolodge at high risk of water scarcity. Thus, the diverse anti-desertification infrastructure in the Taragalte Ecolodge project makes it resilient: if one system fails, others could continue to protect the oasis.

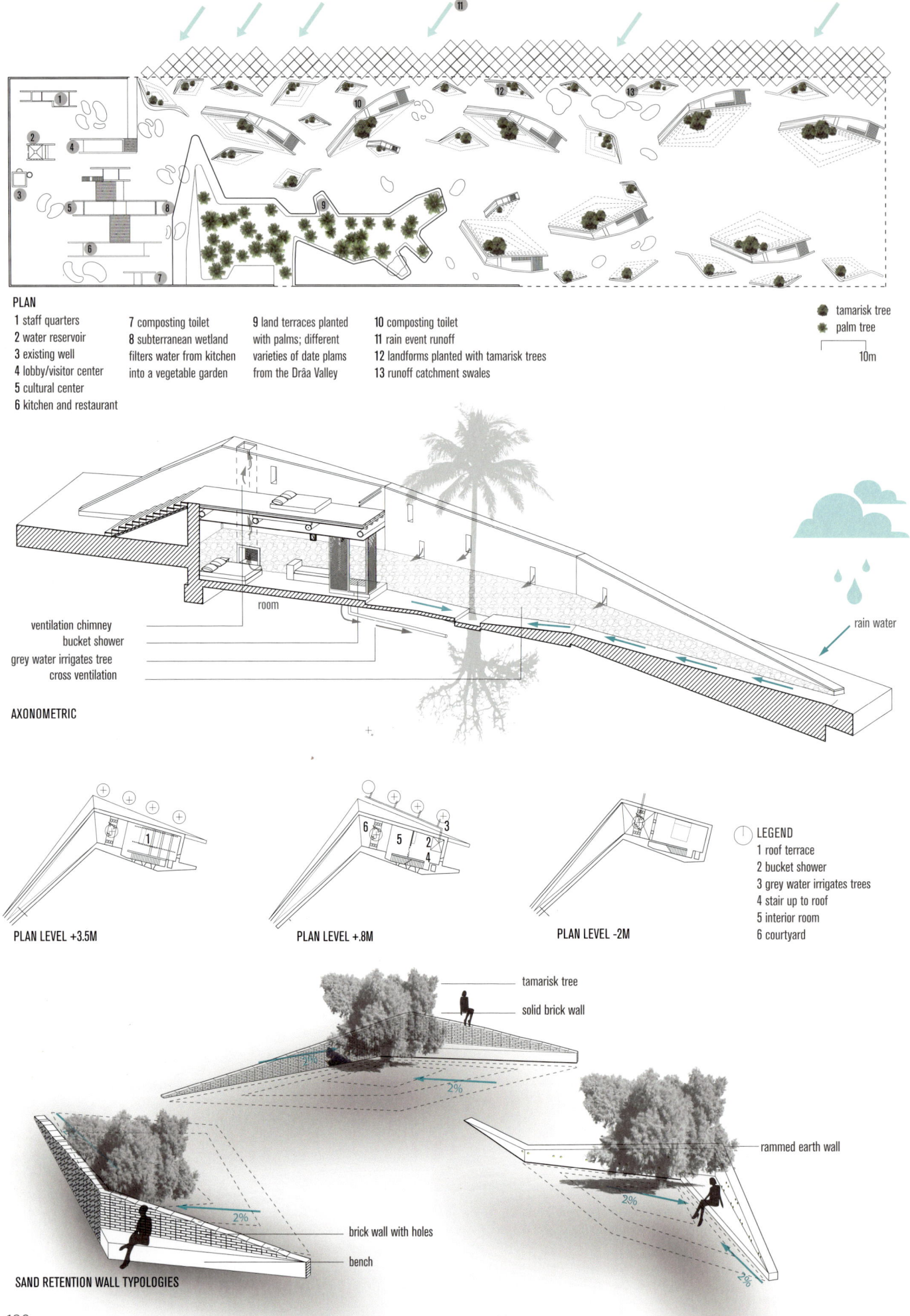

PLAN
1 staff quarters
2 water reservoir
3 existing well
4 lobby/visitor center
5 cultural center
6 kitchen and restaurant
7 composting toilet
8 subterranean wetland filters water from kitchen into a vegetable garden
9 land terraces planted with palms; different varieties of date plams from the Drâa Valley
10 composting toilet
11 rain event runoff
12 landforms planted with tamarisk trees
13 runoff catchment swales

● tamarisk tree
● palm tree
10m

AXONOMETRIC

ventilation chimney
bucket shower
grey water irrigates tree
cross ventilation

room

rain water

PLAN LEVEL +3.5M

PLAN LEVEL +.8M

PLAN LEVEL -2M

LEGEND
1 roof terrace
2 bucket shower
3 grey water irrigates trees
4 stair up to roof
5 interior room
6 courtyard

tamarisk tree
solid brick wall
rammed earth wall
brick wall with holes
bench

SAND RETENTION WALL TYPOLOGIES

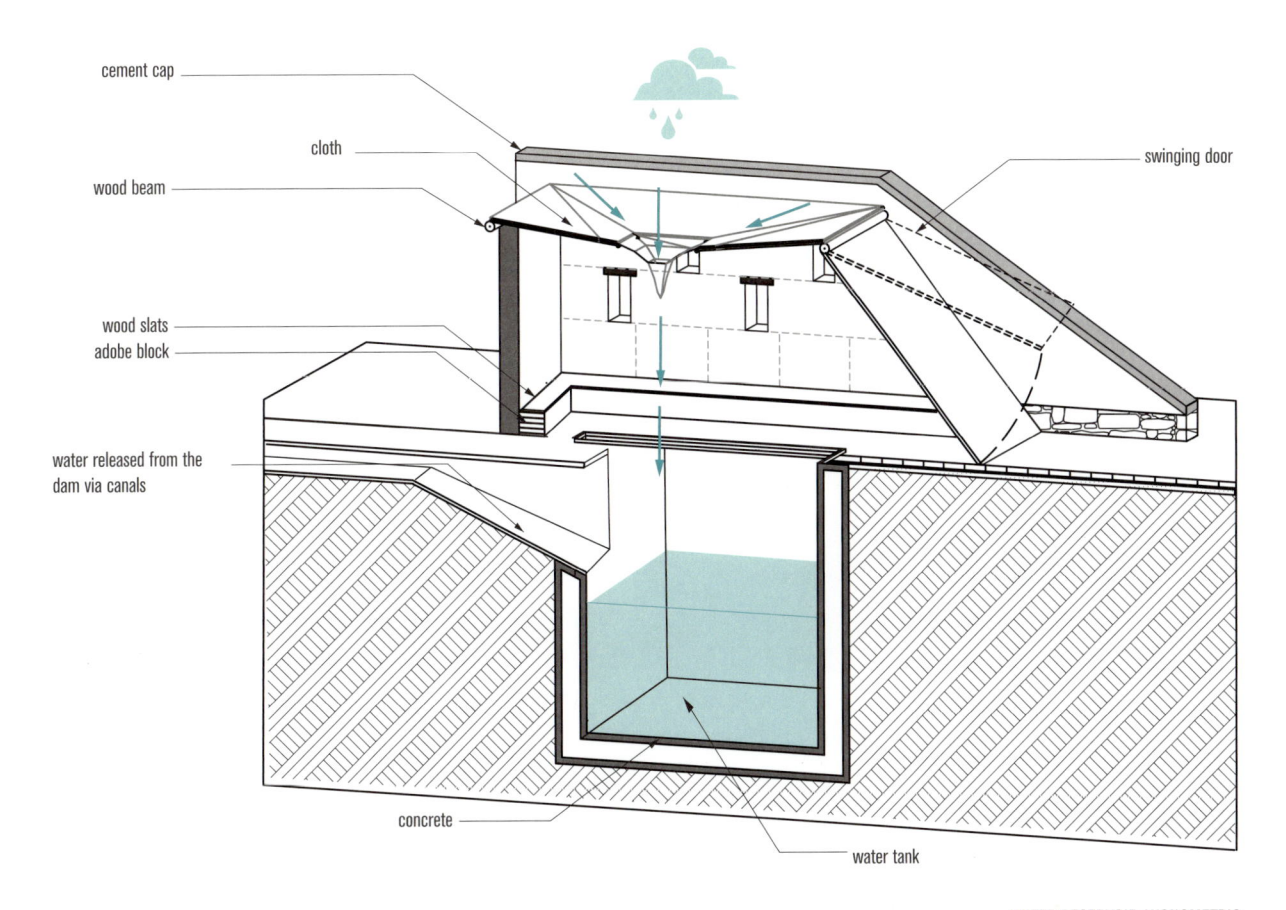

cement cap
cloth
wood beam
wood slats
adobe block
water released from the dam via canals
swinging door
concrete
water tank

WATER RESERVOIR AXONOMETRIC

LEGEND

ecolodge	new oasis limit	ecolodge labour (men)	tourist	supply paths	crafts	
village	well	population (women + children)	capital	economic drain	food	
road	water supply path	agricultural labour	camel	local labour		
seasonal riverbed				tourist activity		

200m

OASIS MASTERPLAN

181

WADI HANIFAH RESTORATION PROJECT
Moriyama & Teshima + Buro Happold

Site: Riyadh, Saudi Arabia
Longitude & Latitude: 24°39'N 46°42'E
Annual Precipitation: 100mm

Year: Masterplan 2001–2004; implementation 2004–2010
Status: Completed
Water Volume/Day: Varies
Dimensions: Varies

GROUND & SURFACE WATER HYDROLOGY

1. treated waste-water input from Manfuha sewage treatment plant for agricultural use
2. storm runoff
3. alluvial gravel, sands and silts
4. abstraction for small private supplies and agriculture
5. septic tank leakage
6. agricultural infiltration
7. groundwater level
8. regional groundwater flow direction
9. local groundwater abstraction
10. desalinated water supply from Jabal on the coast
11. main water supply
12. Manfuha STP treated sewage
13. control of groundwater pumping and drainage
14. Riyadh
15. shallow flows leaking from water pipes and sewers
16. high water table in wadi alluvium due to artificial discharges; shallow surface flows in evidence
17. high water table due to water mains, sewer leakage and rising groundwater
18. potential leakage from large-diameter sewage and treated wastewater pipes running in wadi alluvium
19. deep water aquifers: depth >1000m
20. other dry water flows
21. permanent surface water flows in wadi

evaporation

Jubala formation: massive limestone with fractures
Arriyadh formation: porous and fractured limestone
Arab formation/Sulaty formation
Kharj formation
Eastern alluvium

SITE PLAN

river

watershed + site

urban + municipal

aerial + site boundary

WATERSHED

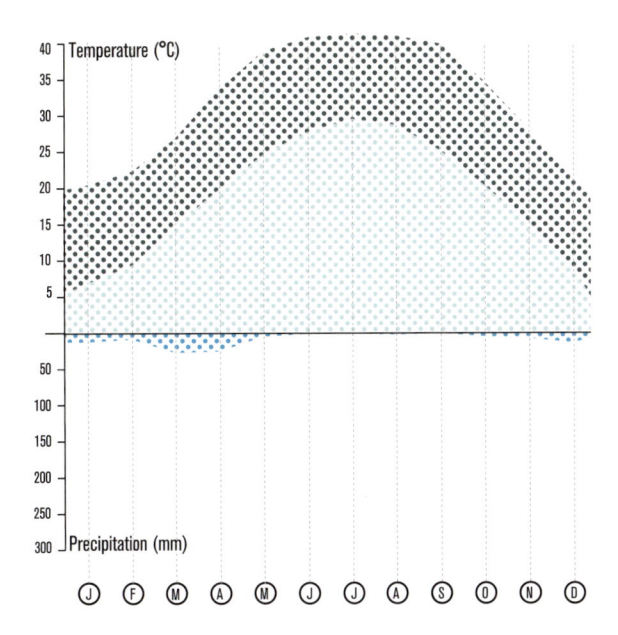

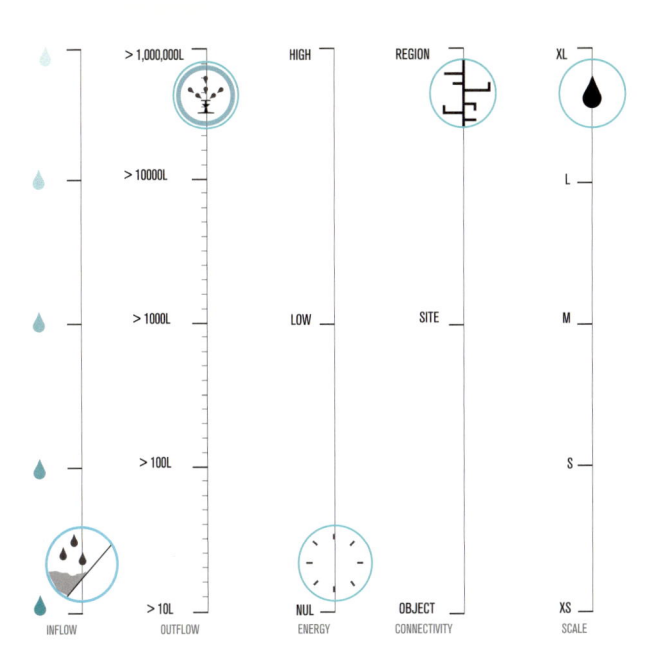

120km long, Wadi Hanifah and its tributaries form the most significant natural drainage system within central Saudi Arabia. Carved into the Najd Plateau, this desert watershed has a catchment area of 4,500km², traversing the western portion of Riyadh, Saudi Arabia's capital. Considered one of the fastest-growing cities in the world, Riyadh's population has exploded from 83,000 in 1950 to 4 million in 2001, and is expected to reach over 10 million by 2021 (Moriyama & Teshima, 2013). With this unprecedented growth and rapid urbanization, the regenerative capacity of the local environment has been severely eroded by competition for its resources and disruptions to its natural processes. Parts of Wadi Hanifah and its environs have been quarried and mined for construction materials to build the growing city, while other parts have been filled in to accommodate new subdivisions, roads, and infrastructure.

Rainfall in the region averages approximately 100mm/year and is characterized by intermittent and intense storm events. Unable to rely on seasonally recharged local aquifers to satisfy water demand, potable water is pumped uphill to Riyadh from desalination plants on the Gulf coast—nearly 500km away. This "new" source of water has not only transformed the lives of the Riyadh's inhabitants, but has also dramatically altered the local ecosystem. Wadi Hanifah has historically been dry except during the rainy season, but now contains surface flows that have been perennial since the 1980s, when rising levels of groundwater and urban discharges created a year-round river. Despite the increase in water supply, the quality of the water was very poor and Wadi Hanifah was thus generally perceived as a sewer until very recently.

The Wadi Hanifah Restoration Project Master Plan (2001–2004) was developed by Moriyama & Teshima and engineering firm Buro Happold, working with a team of international experts specializing in ecology, river hydrology, hydrogeology, hydraulics, infrastructure, transportation, landscape architecture, architecture, land use planning, urban management, economics, communications, and data management. The Master Plan consists of three interrelated and interdependent plans: the Environmental Plan, Water Resources Management Plan, and Land Use Plan. It creates connectivity between the city and Wadi, and identifies projects and programs that provide environmental gain as well as enhance people's quality of life, open new economic sectors such as tourism and create employment opportunities. The more the water quality of Wadi Hanifah is improved, the greater the potential for regaining the Wadi environment as the most significant open space in Riyadh. In order to meet the projected population growth, one of the main goals of the Master Plan is to make 1.2 million m³ of water available for reuse and multi-use by 2025.

Between 2004 and 2010, 1,000,000 m³ of dumped solid waste had been removed and 10 million m² of the wadi bed had been bioremediated through the naturalized channels. Among other accomplishments was the construction of 53km of roads, 7.4km of pedestrian promenades, 46.8km of recreational trails, nine major parks, and five lakes with a total area of 25.1ha. In addition, a bioremediation facility consisting of 134 biocells will treat 350,000m³ (2010) of urban wastewater per day for reuse (p. 186-189). Finally, 30,000 shade trees, 6,000 date palm trees, 2,000 large Acacia trees, and 50,000 shrubs were planted or transplanted. As a result of these developments, property values along the Wadi corridor have appreciated tenfold.

As part of the naturalized channels, hundreds of microcatchment structures and planting swales (each measuring 10–20m²) have been deployed through the floodplain to capture the scarce annual rainfall and enhance soil moisture in order to increase the survival rates of plantings. Those are implemented in conjunction with check dams, employed in riparian areas of the Wadi Hanifah and side wadis, with the purpose of attenuating flow and thus reducing erosion, retaining sediment, increasing water infiltration, and establishing vegetation. This method reduces soil evaporation and helps to develop an ecology of herbivorous species of insects, reptiles, birds, and mammals.

Microcatchments are earthen berm structures that continuously capture water during a rain event and allow for sediment as well as organic detritus to accrue. This process of accretion allows for a low-cost and low-maintenance re-vegetation technique to be implemented on a regional scale. The serial aggregation of the microcatchments and planting cells mitigates the erosive forces of flash floods and in turn conserves irrigation resources. Thus, they become a significant infrastructural component of the watershed management plan.

Microcatchment areas are planted with local genetic stock of indigenous vegetation to increase survival rates of self-propagating species and minimize maintenance. Planting strategies include transplanting whole plants or rootstocks, cuttings, and seed sowing. Locally available vegetation also provides appropriate habitat structure for native wildlife. In addition, shrubs and trees by the water's edge create attractive shaded areas for recreational use.

Once vegetation is established, the structure of the plant material will begin to entrap silts. If undisturbed, it will gradually expand to balance the sediment yield in the microcatchment for all but the most severe rain events.

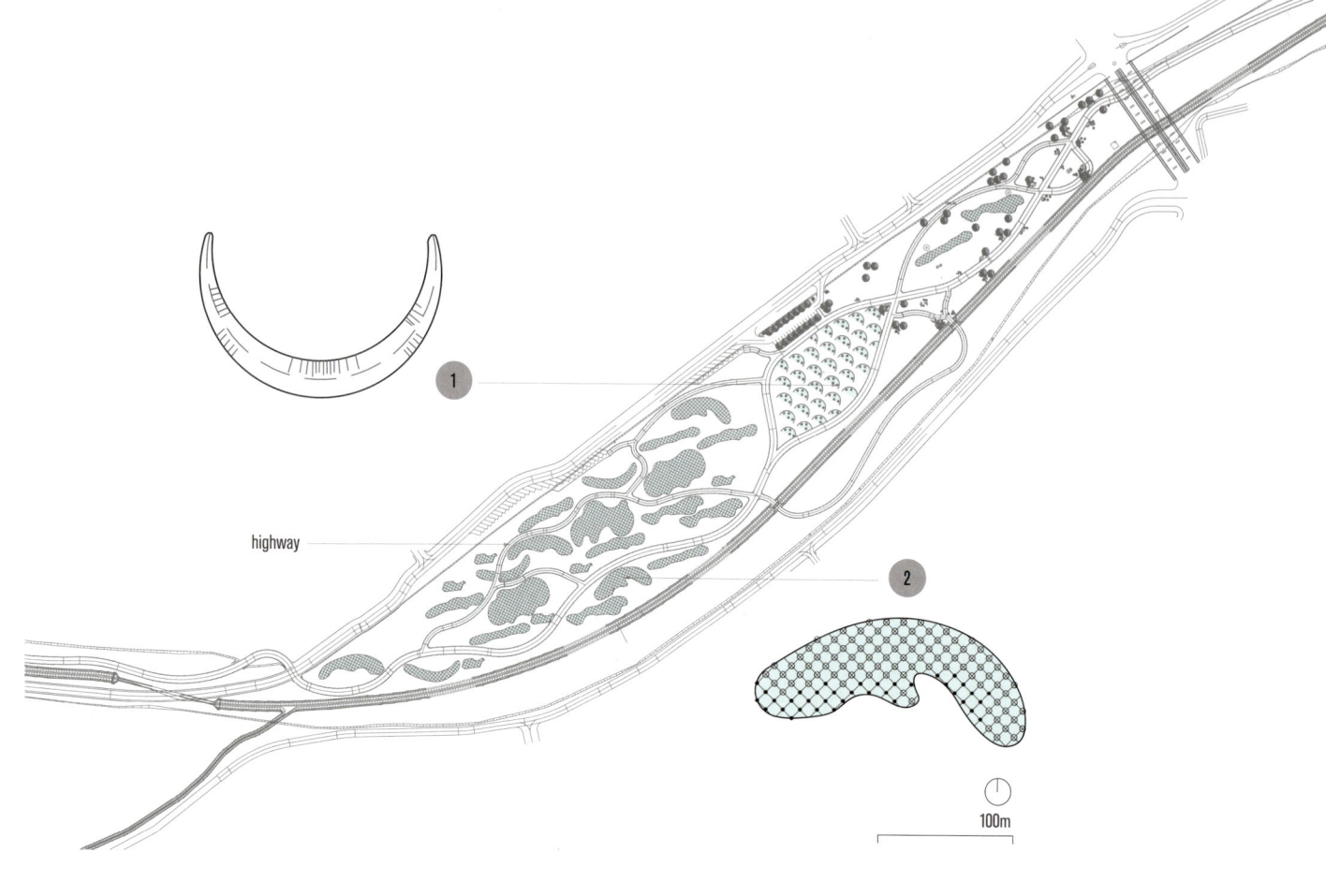

SITE PLAN

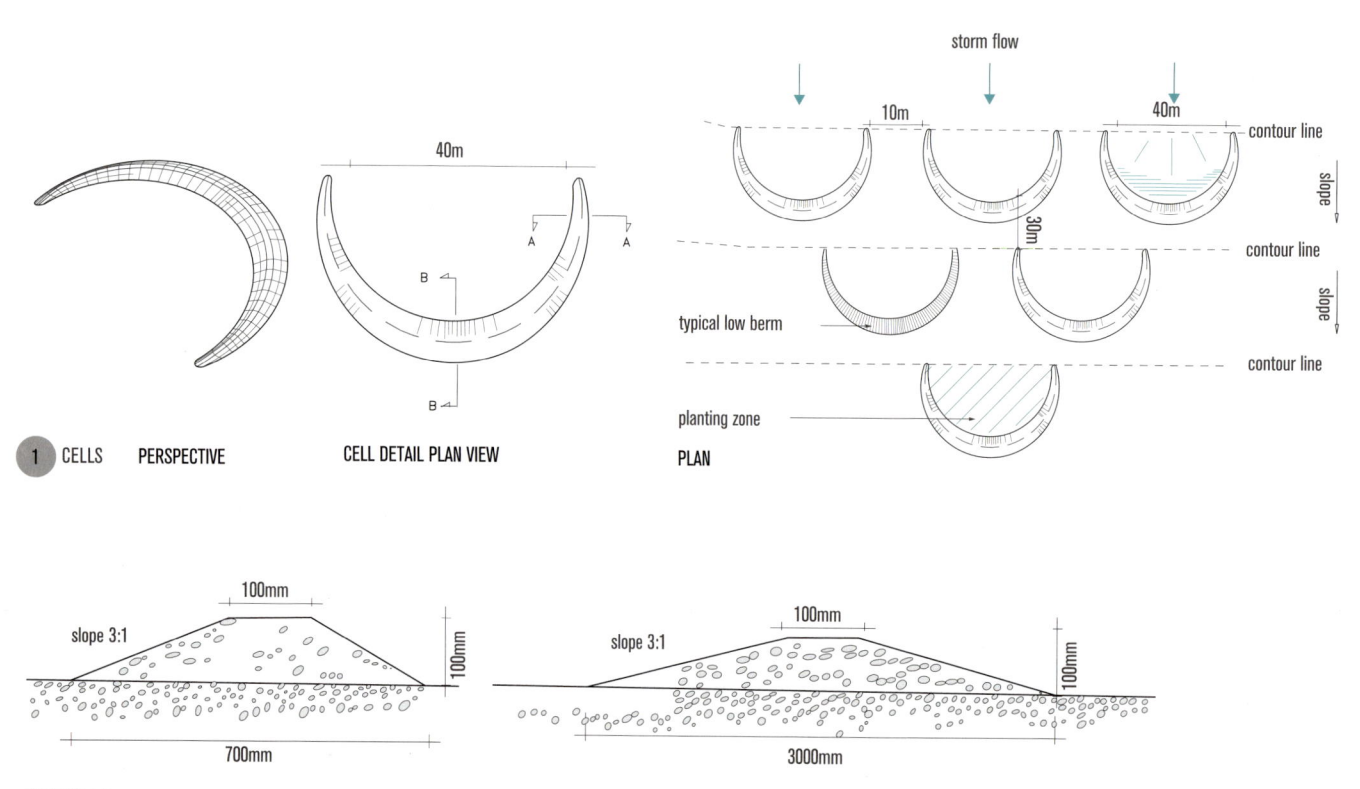

1 CELLS PERSPECTIVE   CELL DETAIL PLAN VIEW   PLAN

SECTION A-A   SECTION B-B

184

+0.00
+0.00
+0.00
-0.2m

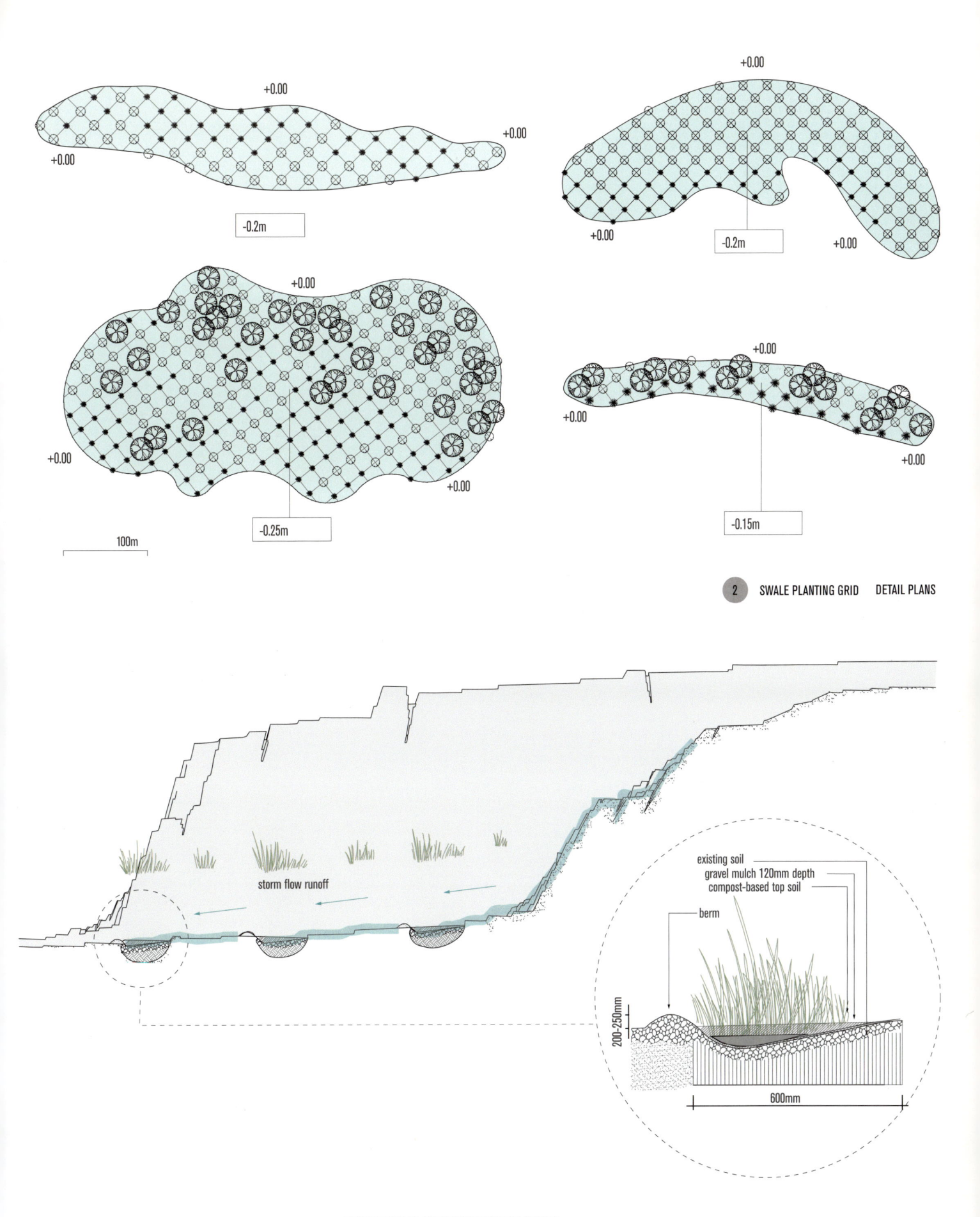

+0.00
+0.00
-0.2m
+0.00

+0.00
+0.00
-0.25m

+0.00
+0.00
+0.00
-0.15m

100m

2 SWALE PLANTING GRID   DETAIL PLANS

storm flow runoff

existing soil
gravel mulch 120mm depth
compost-based top soil
berm
200-250mm
600mm

SIDE WADI MICRO-CATCHMENT PLANTING SECTION

185

WADI HANIFAH BIOREMEDIATION FACILITY
Moriyama & Teshima + Buro Happold

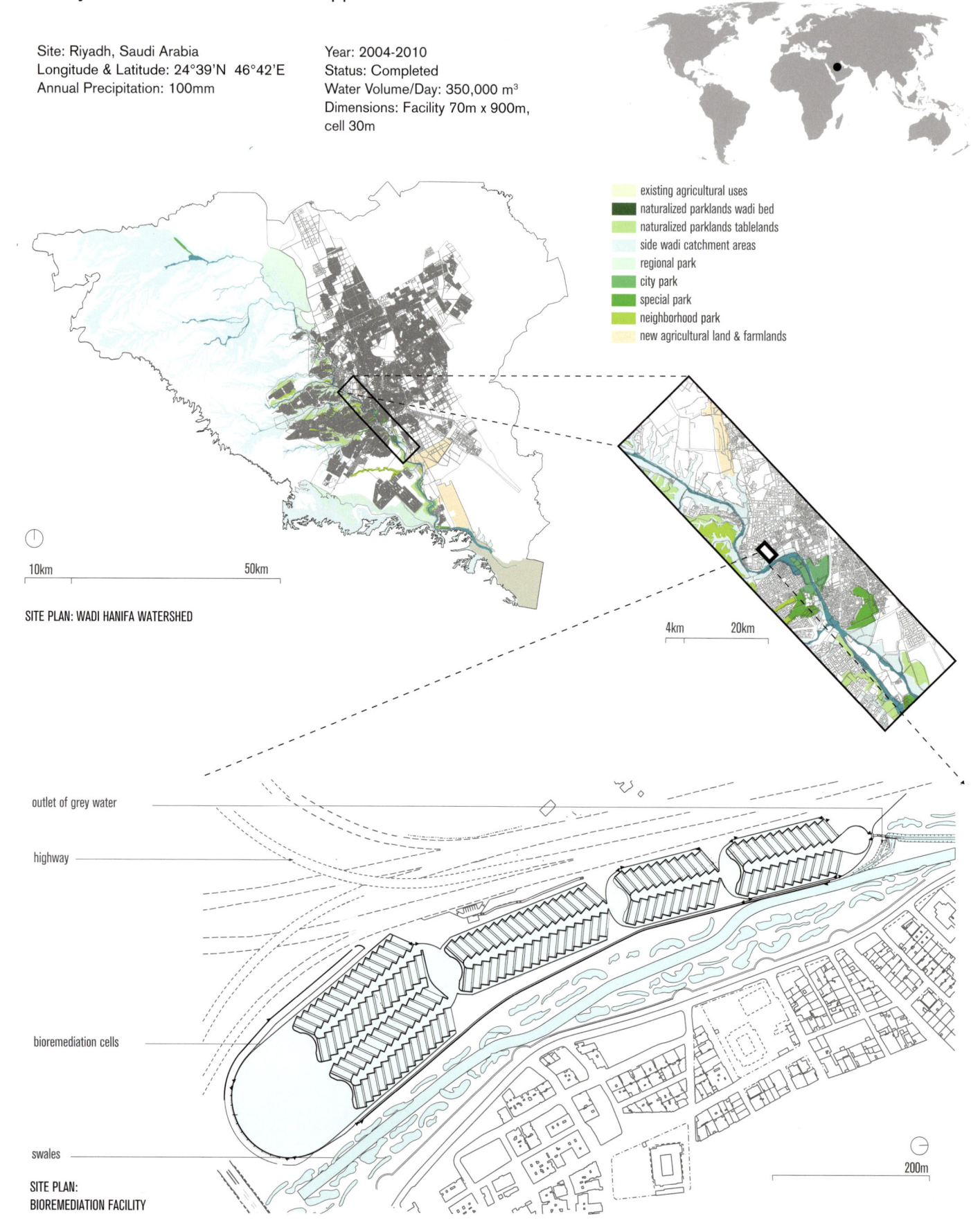

Site: Riyadh, Saudi Arabia
Longitude & Latitude: 24°39'N 46°42'E
Annual Precipitation: 100mm

Year: 2004-2010
Status: Completed
Water Volume/Day: 350,000 m³
Dimensions: Facility 70m x 900m, cell 30m

- existing agricultural uses
- naturalized parklands wadi bed
- naturalized parklands tablelands
- side wadi catchment areas
- regional park
- city park
- special park
- neighborhood park
- new agricultural land & farmlands

SITE PLAN: WADI HANIFA WATERSHED

outlet of grey water
highway
bioremediation cells
swales

SITE PLAN:
BIOREMEDIATION FACILITY

Designed and engineered by Moriyama & Teshima with Buro Happold, the Wadi Hanifah Bioremediation Facility, or Biocell, treats 350,000m³ of wastewater per day for non-potable uses including the irrigation of urban parks and agriculture. A massive undertaking, this project reduces the regional water deficit and environmental degradation that the Wadi Hanifah's 4,500km² watershed had incurred since the 1980s. The 900m long bioremediation facility is a key component of the Wadi Hanifah Restoration Project (p. 182-185) and the first biological wastewater treatment of its scale that successfully incorporates a public landscape within an urban context. Located north of the main highway interchange, the facility is a modern-day icon of the progressive regional water management to which the Arriyadh Development Authority has committed.

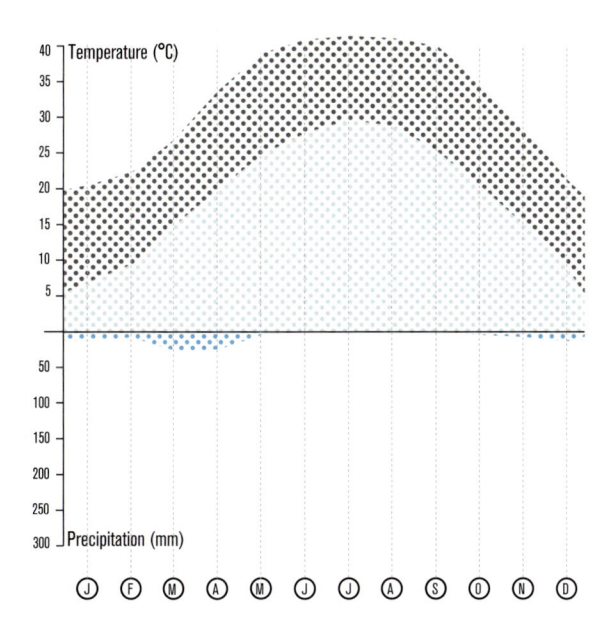

Bioremediation became the preferred methodology for cleaning the water because it enhanced the natural processes of the wadi ecology and was less costly than mechanical treatment. This has further contributed to environmental quality of the wadi, which in turn has greatly enhanced public perception and use. The project includes two levels of bioremediation. The first addresses year-round flow of contaminants from urban surface water and rural discharge into the watercourses, and includes grading and naturalizing channels (2.5 million m³ in reprofiling cut and fill). Rock-lined, stepped with weirs, and planted with streambed and stream-bank vegetation, the naturalized channels provide optimal conditions for neutralizing pathogens and absorbing excessive nutrients throughout the riparian corridor, while also creating attractive shaded areas for recreational use.

The bioremediation facility incorporates a series of weirs, riffles, pools, aerating pumps, bioremediation cells, artificial periphyton and benthic substrates (APBS), and riparian planting. Together, the elements of this design create the appropriate aquatic and riparian conditions to assimilate contaminants and further remediate the water through a community of natural organisms that aggregate to form a food web. The facility has been in operation since 2010 and has shown a mass reduction of harmful excess nutrients, including reductions in the following:

Fecal coliform bacteria—97%; Total coliform—87%; Ammonia—92%; Biological oxygen demand (BOD)—60%; Phosphorous—48%; Suspended solids—97%

Water entering the bioremediation facility is partially treated by the improvements made throughout the naturalized channel upstream. Each component performs a function in the bioremediation of the water.

The Head Pool provides habitat for a complex food web including an attached and floating microbial community, various algal species, and a diverse animal community including invertebrates and fish. APBS systems are installed in the Head Pools to maximize the nutrient assimilation into a periphyton community, provide habitat structure for benthic invertebrates and small fish feeding on the attached growth, and provide a spawning substrate for the fish.

The Inflow Channel distributes flow to each of the Biocells and achieves saturation oxygen levels in the water. It is 1m deep and has a rock-lined bottom. It was designed to distribute the water flow to the bio-cells evenly along its length on both sides. The Head Pool and Inflow Channel together increase the residency time of bacteria in the water to facilitate maximum exposure to the dissolved oxygen. To eliminate nighttime oxygen sag, which is due to the high respiration of the biological community, an aeration system is located in the supply channel and in each of the two pools to provide oxygen saturation levels in the water sufficient to be lethal to coliform bacteria.

The Biocell includes 134 units which function as the structural base for biofilm and periphyton growth and are responsible for the bulk of nutrient assimilation within the system. The cells consist of the following components:

The Biocell Head Pools (BHP) provide the major habitat for the assimilation of nutrients by the attached microbial and plant community. This function is enabled by the addition of APBS units, distributed through the BHP and including 371m² of growth surface for biofilm and periphyton. The rocky substrate provides a good habitat for a benthic community. However, the addition of APBS will increase the size of this habitat by up to two orders of magnitude due to the tremendous surface areas added to the system.

Fish will graze on the periphyton and prevent the nutrients from merely being released back into the water after these relatively short-lived organisms die. The fish will either swim downstream, or become a food source for humans or various animal species. The depth of the retention pools is 1m, which allows 150mm of space for potential sedimentation to occur and still permit the APBS units to function properly. An APBS unit can remove 1–2.6g of nitrogen per day depending on the specific conditions of the system. The number of units required is determined by calculating daily and seasonal fluctuations of effluent and ambient temperature.

The Central Marsh Channels (CMC) provide additional aquatic habitat and a major interface between the terrestrial system and the aquatic system. Birds such as herons, kingfishers, and waterfowl may utilize this habitat while feeding on small fish, plants, and invertebrates. These birds provide not only a nutrient removal function, but also add value for public use.

The Riffle Zone is the final compartment of the bioremediation facility, providing turbulence, oxygenation, and small organism habitat. The water is shallow enough to discourage downstream movement by the largest fish, but shallow enough to allow small fish passage.

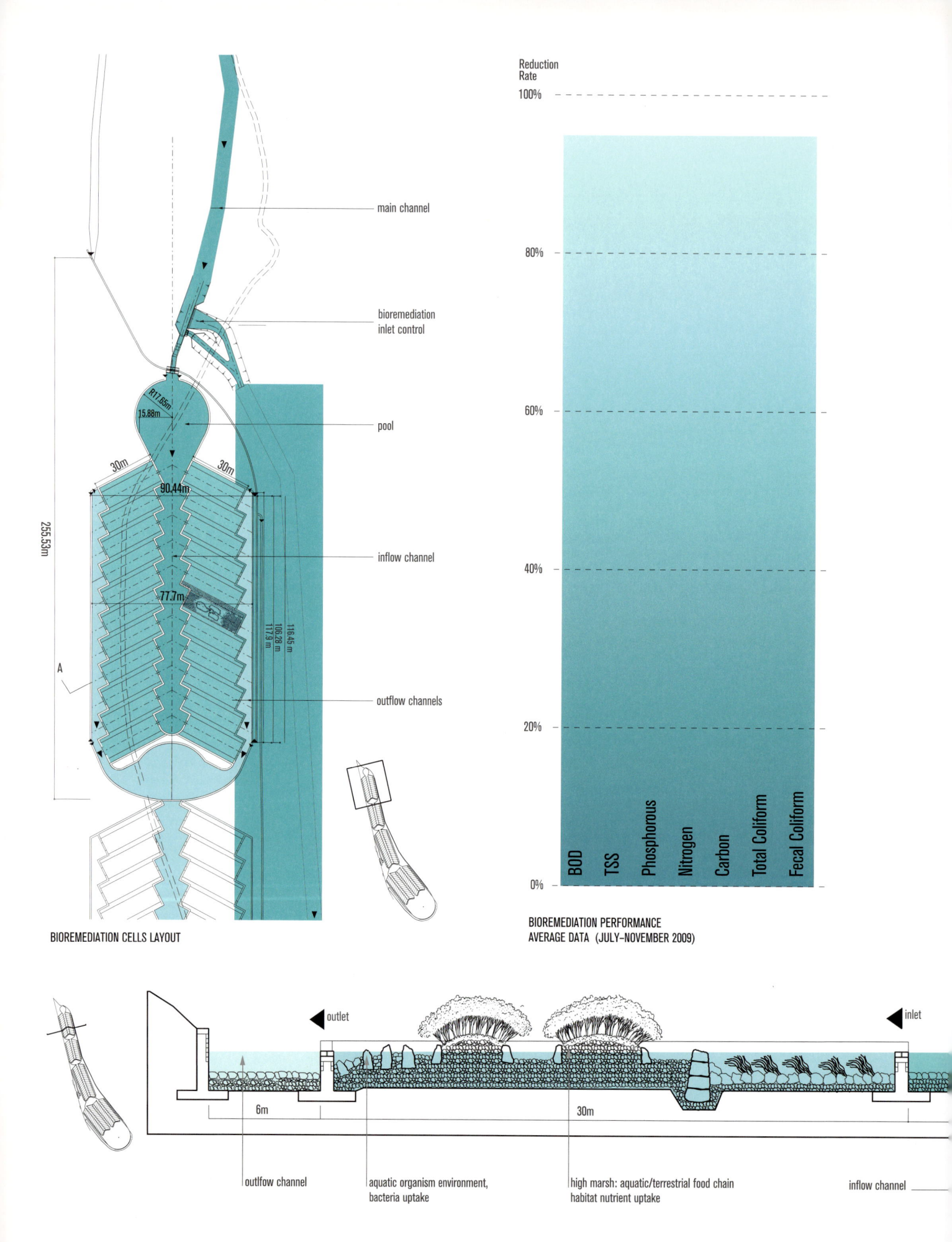

BIOREMEDIATION CELLS LAYOUT

BIOREMEDIATION PERFORMANCE
AVERAGE DATA (JULY–NOVEMBER 2009)

188

outflow channel

biocell

inflow channel

SECTIONAL PERSPECTIVE

small organism aquatic environment — high & low marshes — 150-200mm typ. — retention pond

stone capped concrete retaining wall, lime stone slab paving

◀ outlet

inlet ▶

emergent plant species

4m outlet crest weir ▶

◀ outlet

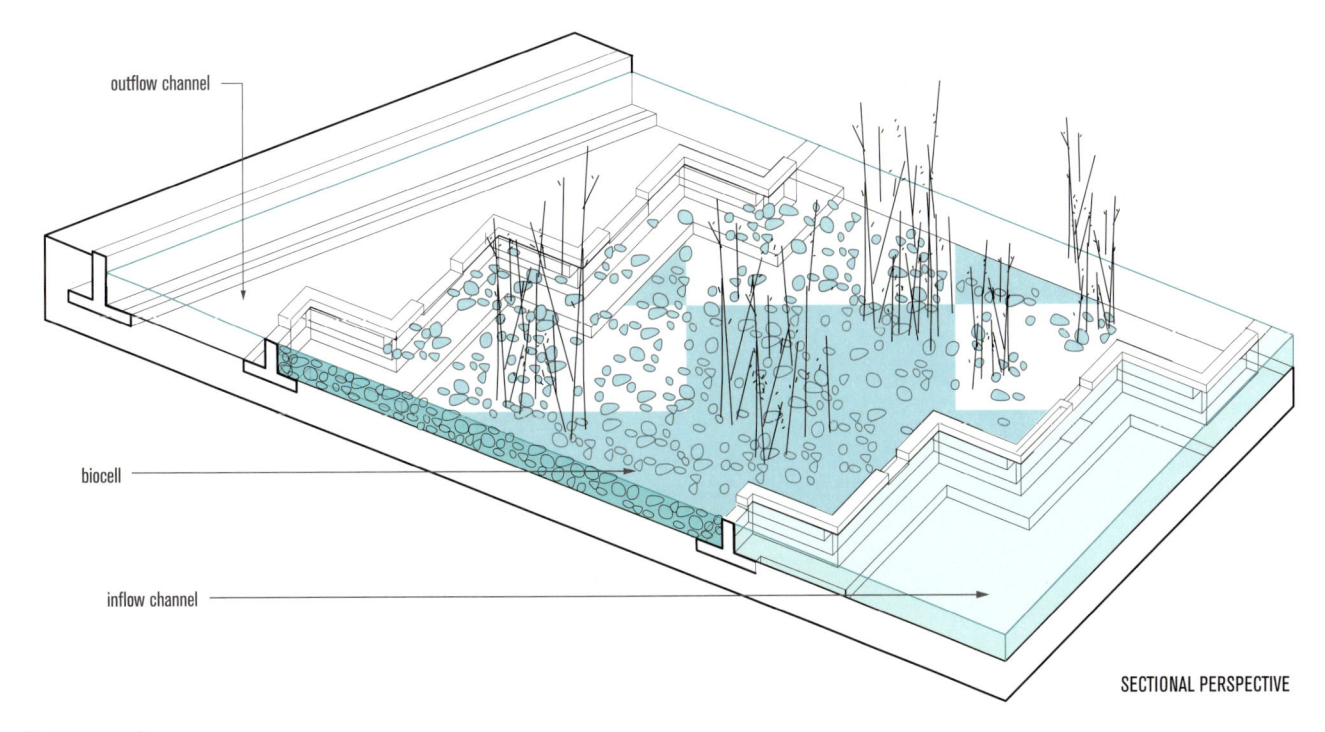

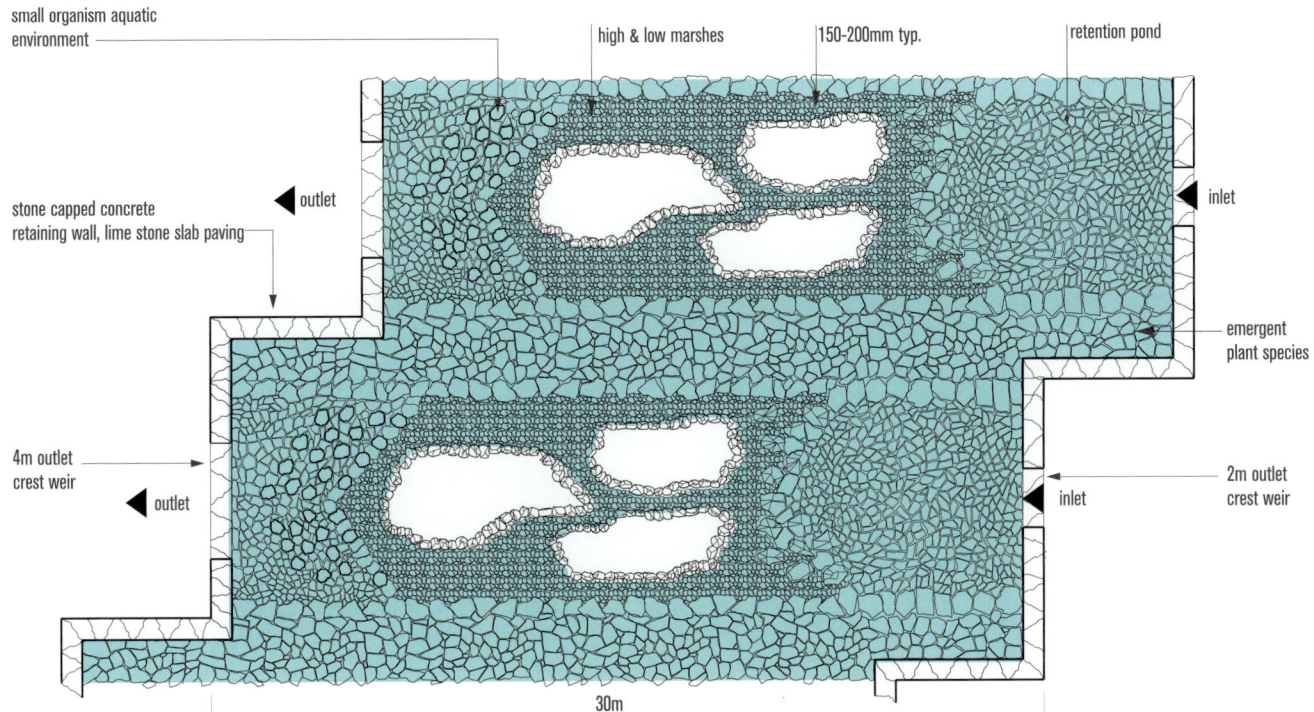

inlet ▶ 2m outlet crest weir

30m

INDIVIDUAL BIOREMEDIATION CELL DETAIL PLAN

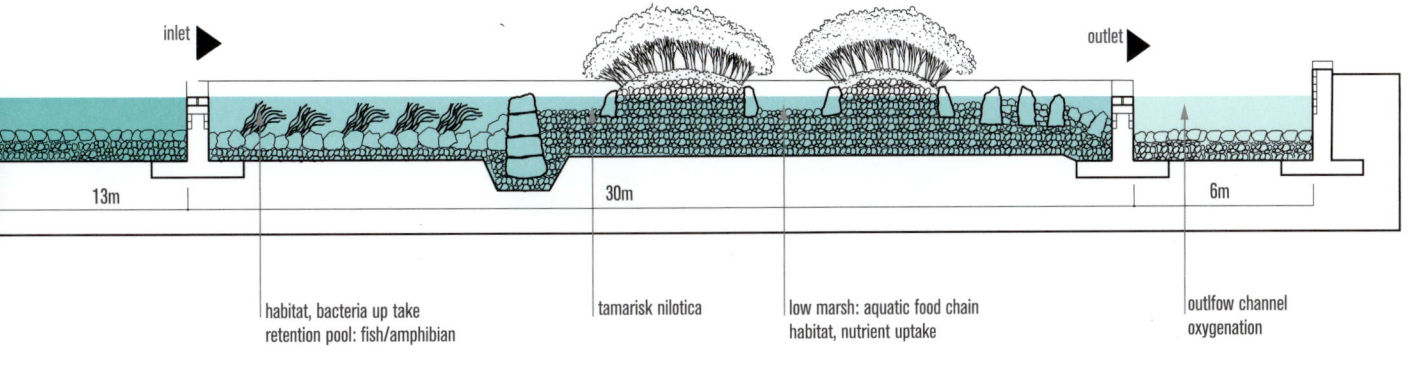

inlet ▶

outlet ▶

13m | 30m | 6m

habitat, bacteria up take retention pool: fish/amphibian

tamarisk nilotica

low marsh: aquatic food chain habitat, nutrient uptake

outlfow channel oxygenation

BIOREMEDIATION CROSS SECTION A-A

189

BIBLIOGRAPHY AND REFERENCES

ESSAYS

Alon Tal

"Desalination Back on the Agenda in Spain." (2004). *Global Water Intelligence* 5 (1).

Beltran, J. M., and Koo-Oshima, S., eds. (2006). *Water Desalination for Agricultural Applications.* Rome: FAO.

Braungart, M., and McDonough, W. (2002). *Cradle to Cradle.* New York: North Point Press.

Buros, O. K. (2000). *The Desalting ABC's, 2nd Edition.* Topsfield: International Desalination Association.

Dolnicar, S., and Schafer, A. I. (2006). "Public Perception of Desalinated Versus Recycled Water in Australia." *Proceedings of the AWWA Desalination Symposium.* http://ro.uow.edu.au/commpapers/138.

Dreizin, Y. (2004). "The Impact of Desalination: Israel and the Palestinian Authority." Presentation at the 2nd Israeli-Palestinian-International Conference on Water for Life in the Middle East, Antalya, Turkey, October 12, 2004.

Ehrlich, P. (1968). *The Population Bomb.* Cutchogue: Buccaneer Books.

European Commission (2006). *Water Desalination Market Acceleration, Environmental Technologies Action Plan.* Brussels: European Commission.

Garb, Y. (2010). "Desalination in Israel, Status, Prospects and Context." *Water Wisdom, a New Menu for Palestinian and Israeli Cooperation in Water Management*, edited by Tal, A. and Abed-Rabbo, A. New Brunswick: Rutgers University Press. 238–245.

Gleick, P. (2002). *The World's Water, Biennial Report on Freshwater Resources.* Washington: Island Press.

Haupert, J. S. (1964). "Development of Israel's Frontier Port of Eilat." *Harfur College* 16 (2): 13–16.

Homer-Dixon, T. (1999). *Environment, Scarcity and Violence.* Princeton: Princeton University Press.

Keely, G. (2008). "Drought Ignites Spain's 'Water War.'" *The Guardian*, April 6, 2008.

Knights, D., MacGill, I., and Passey, R. (2007). "The Sustainability of Desalination Plants in Australia: Is Renewable Energy the Answer?" *OzWater*, March 4–6, 2007.

Kronenberg, G. (2004). "The Largest SWRO Plant in the World: Ashkelon 100 million m^3/y BOT Project." *Desalination* 166: 457–463.

Lattemann, S., and Höpner, T. (2008). "Environmental Impact and Impact Assessment of Seawater Desalination." *Desalination* 220: 1–15.

Lavie, Z. R., and Gluekstern, P. (1974). "The MSF Desalination Units 1 and 2 in Elat Operational Experience from March 1, 1973 to November 30, 1974." *Seawater Desalination: Proceedings of the Eleventh National Symposium on Desalination, Oholo, March 19-20, 1975.* Jerusalem, Israel.

Lawhon Isler, P. (2010). "Is Desalination a Sensible Climate Adaptation Measure for Sydney's Water Supply?" Presentation at the NCCARF Workshop, Sydney, Australia, November, 2010.

Maestu, J., and Gomez, C. M. (2010). "Water Uses in Transition." *Water Policy in Spain,* edited by Garrido, L. London: Taylor and Francis.

Manero, A. (2008). "Desalination in California and Spain." *Comparative Water Management Practices in California and Spain,* Polytechnical University of Catelonia. http://upcommons.upc.edu/pfc/bitstream/2099.1/6053/11/10.pdf.

Martinez-Cortina, L. (2010). "Physical and Hydrological Characteristics." *Water Policy in Spain,* edited by Garrido, L. London: Taylor and Francis.

Myers, N. and Simon, J. (1994). *Scarcity or Abundance: A Debate on the Environment.* New York: W. W. Norton.

New South Wales (2004). *Meeting the Challenges—Securing Sydney's Water Future: The Metropolitan Water Plan.* Sydney: Government of New South Wales.

Nicol, K. (2009). "Work on Torrevieja's Desalination Plant Ceases for the Summer." www.torrevieja.com, June 16, 2009.

Nicoll, H.G. (2001). "Degremont Installs a Seawater Desalination Plant in Telde, Spain." *Water Conditioning and Purification Magazine,* September, 2000.

Onishi, N. (2010). "Arid Australia Sips Seawater, but at a Cost." *New York Times,* July 10, 2010.

Rassas, D. (2007). *Seawater Desalination in Israel, A Stakeholders' View of Agriculture and Environmental Implications.* Unpublished Master's Thesis. Be'er Sheva: Ben Gurion University.

Selby, J. (2003). *Water, Power and Politics in the Middle East.* London: I. B. Tauris & Co.

Shalhevet, J. (1993). "Using Water of Marginal Quality for Crop Production: Major Issues." *Agricultural Water Management* 25: 233–269.

Tal, A. (2006). "Seeking Sustainability: Israel's Evolving Water Management Strategy." *Science* 313: 1081–1084.

Tal, A. (2008). "Enduring Technological Optimism: Zionism's Environmental Ethic and Its Influence on Israel's Environmental History." *The Journal of Environmental History* 13: 275–305.

Tal, A., Ben-Gal, A., Lawhon, P., and Rassas, D. (2005). *Sustainable Water Management in the Drylands: Recent Israeli Experience.* Jerusalem: Israel Ministry of Foreign Affairs.

Tenne, A. (2011). Israel Water Authority. Personal Communication, March 17, 2011.

Wapner, P. (2010). "Sacrifice in an Age of Comfort." *The Environmental Politics of Sacrifice,* edited by Maniates, M. Cambridge: MIT Press.

Ward, D. (2002). *Water Wars: Drought, Flood, Folly and the Politics of Thirst.* London: Penguin.

Yermiyahu, U., Shamai, I., Peleg, R., Dudai, N., and Shtienberg, D. (2006). "Reduction of Botrytis Cinerea Sporulation in Sweet Basil by Altering the Concentrations of Nitrogen and Calcium in the Irrigation Solution." *Plant Pathology* 55: 544–552.

Yermiyahu, U., Tal, A., Ben-Gal, A., Bar-Tal, A., Tarchisky, J., and Lahav, O. (2007). "Rethinking Desalinated Water Quality and Agriculture." *Science* 318: 920–921.

Tommy Ka Kit Ngai and Camille Dow Baker

Bartram, J., and Cairncross, S. (2010). "Hygiene, Sanitation, and Water: Forgotten Foundations of Health." *PLOS Medicine* 7 (11): e1000367.

Hutton, G., Haller, L., and Bartram, J. (2007). "Global Cost-Benefit Analysis of Water Supply and Sanitation Interventions." *Journal of Water and Health* 5 (4): 481–502.

UN Millennium Project (2005). "Health, Dignity, and Development: What Will It Take?" *Task Force on Water and Sanitation.* London: Earthscan.

WHO (2008). *The Global Burden of Disease: 2004 Update.* Geneva: WHO. http://www.who.int/healthinfo/global_burden_disease/2004_report_update/en/index.html.

WHO and UNICEF (2008). *Joint Monitoring Programme for Water Supply and Sanitation: Progress on Drinking Water and Sanitation: Special Focus on Sanitation.* Geneva: WHO/UNICEF. http://www.wssinfo.org/en/40_MDG2008.html.

WHO and UNICEF (2012). *Progress on Sanitation and Drinking-Water: 2012 Update.* Geneva: WHO/UNICEF. http://www.unicef.org/media/files/JMPreport2012.pdf

Dov Pasternak and Lennart Woltering

"L'Habitat Rural Traditionnel des Oasis: Le Qsar, Problèmes de Rénovation" (2006). *Bulletin Economique et Social du Maroc* (BESM) 114: 83–107.

Burdon, D. J. (1985). "Groundwater Against Drought in Africa." *Hydrogeology in the Service of Man, Mémoires of the 18th Congress of the International Association of Hydrogeologists.* Cambridge: IAHS.

DGIRH (2001). *Etat des Lieux des Resources en Eau du Burkina Faso et de Leur Cadre de Gestion.* Ouagadougou, Burkina Faso: Direction Générale de l'Hydraulique, Ministère de l'Agriculture, de l'Hydraulique et des Ressources Halieutiques.

FAO (2005). *Irrigation in Africa in Figures.* Rome: FAO.

Gowda, C.L.L., Pasternak, D., Kumar, S., Nikiema, A., and Woltering, L. (2010). "Crop Diversification with Horticultural Crops for Enhancing Incomes and Improving Livelihoods of Poor Farmers in Dryland Areas." *Horticulture and Livelihood Security,* edited by Nath, P., and Gaddagimath, P. B. Rajasthan: Scientific Publishers. 269–279.

Intermediate Technology Consultants (2003). *Low-Cost Micro Irrigation Technologies for the Poor: Final Report to the UK Department for International Department, Knowledge and Research Programme (KAR) Project R7392.* Rugby: Intermediate Technology Consultants. www.itcltd.com/final_reports.htm.

Keller, J. (1990). *Irrigation Technologies for Small Holders.* Arlington: Winrock International. http://www.winrockwater.org/docs/Jack%20Keller_Irrigation%20Technologies%20(PDF).pdf.

Mahamadou, O. A. (2005). *Diffusion des Systèmes d'Irrigation Goutte-à-Goutte dans la Zone Péri-Urbaine de Niamey et dans la Région de Dosso au Niger.* L'Institut de formation et de Recherche appliquée IPR/IFRA de Katibougou, Mali.

Norman, W. R., and Walter, M. F. (1994). "Small Scale Irrigation in Traditional and Private Systems in Niger." *Applied Engineering in Agriculture* 10: 225–231.

Pasternak, D., and Bustan, A. (2003). "The African Market Garden." *Encyclopedia of Water Science,* edited by Stewart, B. A., and Howell, T. New York: Marcel Dekker Inc. 9–15.

Postel, S. L. (2011). "Getting More Crop per Drop." *State of the World 2011: Innovations that Nourish the Planet.* New York and London: W. W. Norton & Company Publishers. 39–48.

Weinberger, K., and Lumpkin, T.A. (2005). "Horticulture for Poverty Alleviation—The Unfunded Revolution." *AVRDC* 05-613: 20 (working paper 15).

Woltering, L., Pasternak, D., and Ndjeunga, J. (2011). "The African Market Garden: Development of a Low-Pressure Drip Irrigation System for Smallholder Producers in the Sudano-Sahel." *Irrigation and Drainage* 60 (5): 613–621. doi 10.1002/ird.610.

World Bank (2004). "Agriculture and Rural Development Discussion Paper 9—Extension Reform for Rural Development." *Privatization of Extension Systems Vol. 2,* edited by Rivera, W., and Alex, G.

World Bank (2008). *Development of Irrigation in Niger: Diagnostic and Strategical Options.* Agriculture and Rural Development AFTAR, African Region.

Aziza Chaouni

Ait Hamza, M., El Faskaoui, B., and Fermin, A. (2007). *Migration and Environmental Change in Morocco: The Case of Rural Oasis Villages in the Middle Drâa Valley.* Rotterdam: Erasmus University.

Bahani, A. (1994). *La Nouba d'Eau et son Évolution dans les Palmeraies du Drâa Moyen du Maroc: CERES.* Tunis: Les Oasis du Maghreb. 107–126.

Bauer, G., Hamburger, B., and Dethier, J. (1967). *Rénovation de l'Habitat de la Vallée du Drâa: Enquête et Propositions.* Rabat: CERF.

Cai, X., Ringler, C., and Rosegrant, M. W. (2006). *Modeling Water Resources Management at the Basin Level: Research Report No. 149.* Washington, D. C.: International Food Policy Research Institute.

Chang, H., Evans, B. M., and Easterling, D. R. (2001). "The Effects of Climate Change on Stream Flow and Nutrient Loading." *Journal of the American Water Resources Association* 37: 973–986.

Courlet, C. (2006). *Territoire et Développement Économique au Maroc: Le Cas des Systèmes.* Paris: L'Harmattan.

Cournoyer, C. (2004). "Le Paysage de l'Oasis dans le Sud du Maroc." Accessed on January 15, 2013. http://www.unesco-paysage.umontreal.ca/docs/projects/oasis_claude.pdf.

Dunne, T., and Leopold, L. (1978). *Water in Environmental Planning.* San Francisco: W. H. Freeman & Co.

Ferry, M., Bedrani, S., and Greiner, D., eds. (1999). *Agroéconomie des Oasis.* Cirad.

Gemma, M., and Tsur, Y. (2007): "The Stabilization Value of Groundwater and Conjunctive Water Management Under Uncertainty." *European Review of Agricultural Economics* 29 (3): 540–548.

Gurusamy, S., Prescott, M., and Theodoratos, N. (2012). *Future Cities Gazette* 12. Singapore: Future Cities Laboratory. Accessed on October 1, 2012. http://www.futurecities.ethz.ch/publications/gazette-12/.

Hammoudi, A. (1985). "Substance and Relation: Water Rights and Water Distribution in the Drâa Valley." *Property, Social Structure, and Law in the Modern Middle East,* edited by Mayer, A. E. New York: State University Press. 27–57.

Heidecke, C. (2009). *Economic Analysis of Water Use and Management in the Middle Drâa Valley in Morocco.* Dissertation. Bonn: University of Bonn.

Hensens, J. (1986). *Qsours et Casbas du Maroc, Réflexions sur l'Habitat Rural Traditionnel.* Morocco: Prix Agha Khan d'Architecture.

Hensens, J. (1989). "Le Nomade, la Ville, l'Aménagement Local." *Le Nomade, l'Oasis et la Ville.* Tours: URBAMA. 37–45.

Hensens, J. (1991). *Les Mutations de l'Architecture Paysanne au Maroc, la fin des Architectures de Base.* Roussillon: Université de Perpignan, Institut d'Économie et de Sociologie du Roussillon. 111–122.

Kölbl, O., Boussahl, M., and Hostettler, H. (2003). "Requirements in an Inventory on Cultural Heritage in Morocco and Reflections on the Presentation of the Information." *Proceedings of the XIXth International Symposium CIPA 2003: New Perspectives to Save Cultural Heritage.* Istanbul: CIPA. 25–28.

Kuhn, A., Schmidt, T., and Heidecke, C. (2005). "Economic Aspects of Water Management in the Drâa Region of Southeast Morocco." *Deutscher Tropentag 2005: Stuttgart-Hohenheim,* October 11–13, 2005. Stuttgart: University of Hohenheim.

Marino, M. (2001). *Conjunctive Management of Surface Water and Groundwater: Regional Management of Water Resources.* Proceedings of a symposium held during the Sixth IAHS Scientific Assembly at Maastricht, The Netherlands, July, 2001. IAHS Publ. no. 268.

Mostafavi, M., and Doherty, G. (2010). *Ecological Urbanism.* New York: Lars Müller Publishers.

Mouline, S. (1991). *Habitats des Qsour et Qasbas des Vallées Pré-Sahariennes.* Rabat: Ministère de l'Habitat.

Mouline, S., and Hensens, J. (1991). *Habitats des Qsour et Qasbas des Vallées Présahariennes.* Rabat: Royaume du Maroc, Ministère de l'Habitat.

Onno, E. (2003). *Les Resources et la Gestion en Eau en Milieu Aride : La Palmeraie du Fezouata de la Vallée du Drâa (Sud-Est Marocain).* Thesis. Université de Caen Basse -Normandie.

Ouhajou, L. (1996). *Espace Hydraulique et Société au Maroc: Cas des Systèmes d'Irrigation dans la Vallée du Drâa.* Thesis. Agadir, Morocco: Faculté des Lettres et des Sciences Humaines, Université Ibn Zohr.

Platt, S. (2006). IMPETUS Project: *Data of a Hotel Survey in Morocco in 2006.* Unpublished manuscript.

Praskievicz, S., and Chang, H. (2009). "A Review of Hydrological Modelling of Basin-Scale Climate Change and Urban Development Impacts." *Progress in Physical Geography* 33 (5): 650–671.

Préau, L. M. (2004). "Maroc, Vivre aux Portes du Sahara." *Terre Sauvage* 199: 14–36.

Rénovation de l'Habitat Traditionnel des Vallées Pré-Sahariennes (1968). Rabat: CERF.

Ringler, C. (2002). *Optimal Allocation and Use of Water Resources in the Mekong River Basin: Multi-Country and Intersectoral Analysis.* Frankfurt: Peter Lang.

La Roche, P. (1946). "L'Irrigation dans le Sud du Maroc." Summary presented for the Center of Hautes Études d'Administration Musulmane.

Roose, E., Sabir, M., and Laouina, A. (2010). *Gestion Durable des Eaux et des Sols au Maroc: Valorisation des Techniques Traditionnelles Méditerranéennes.* Marseille: IRD.

Roth., A. (2008). "Structure Agricole dans le Village Ouled Yaoub." *IMPETUS Atlas du Maroc.*

Sadeq, H. T. (2006). *Du Droit de l'Eau au Droit à l'Eau au Maroc et Ailleurs.* Casablanca: UNESCO.

Schulz, O., and Judex, M., eds. (2008). *IMPETUS Atlas Morocco: Research Results 2000–2007: 3rd Edition.* Bonn: University of Bonn Department of Geography.

Shoay, C. (1999). *L'Allegorie du Patrimoine.* Paris: Seuil.

Simon, S. (2011). "From Traditional to Modern Water Management Systems; Reflection on the Evolution of a 'Water Ethic' in Semi-Arid Morocco." *Current Issues of Water Management*, edited by Uhlig, U. InTech Publications. 229–258.

Spillmann, G. (1931). *Villes et Tribus du Maroc, Tome IX, Tribus berbères Tome II.* Paris: Districts et Tribus de la Haute Vallée du Drâa.

Steinitz, C., Anderson, R., Arias, H., Bassett, S., Cablk, M., Flaxman, M., Goode, T., Lozar, R., Maddock, T., Mouat, D., Rose, W., Peiser, R. and Shearer, A. (2000). *Summary Report: Alternative Futures for the Upper San Pedro River Basin Arizona, U.S.A. and Sonora, Mexico.* Cambridge: Harvard University, Graduate School of Design.

Steinitz, C., Arias, H., Bassett, S., Flaxman, M., Goode, T., Maddock T. III, Mouat, D., Peiser, R. and Shearer, A. (2003). *Alternative Futures for Changing Landscapes: The Upper San Pedro River Basin in Arizona and Sonora.* Washington, D. C.: Island Press.

Tsur, Y., and Graham-Tomasi, T. (1991): "The Buffer Value of Groundwater with Stochastic Surface Water Supplies." *Journal of Environmental Economics and Management* 21: 201–224.

Zainabi, A. (2003). *La Vallée du Dra: Développement Alternatif et Action Communautaire, 2001.* Background paper WDR 2003. World Bank.

Fadi Masoud

Assaf, S. A. (2007). "A Water for Peace Strategy for the Jordan River Basin by Shifting Cropping Patterns." *Water Resources in the Middle East. Israel-Palestinian Water Issues—From Conflict to Cooperation,* edited by Shuval, H., and Dweik, H. Berlin: Springer. 79–85.

Bromberg, G., Abu Faris, H., Faritz, G., Hoermann, S., and Turner, M. (2000). *Let the Dead Sea Live: Concept Document towards the Dead Sea Basin Biosphere Reserve and World Heritage Listings.* Amman, Bethlehem, Tel Aviv: EcoPeace/Friend of the Earth Middle East. http://foeme.org/www/?module=publications&project_id=21.

de Châtel, F. (2007). "Perceptions of Water in the Middle East: The Role of Religion, Politics and Technology in Concealing the Growing Water Scarcity." *Water Resources in the Middle East: Israel-Palestinian Water Issues—From Conflict to Cooperation*, edited by Shuval, H., and Dweik, H. Berlin: Springer. 53–60.

Fardous, A. N., and Al-Hadidi, L. (2007). "Waste Water Management and Reuse in Jordan." *Water Resources in the Middle East: Israel-Palestinian Water Issues—From Conflict to Cooperation*, edited by Shuval, H., and Dweik, H. Berlin: Springer. 399–408.

Levy, N., and Meyer, Y. (2007). "Feasibility Study for Cooperation in Wastewater Treatment Plants and Landfills for Israelis and Palestinians in the West Bank." *Water Resources in the Middle East: Israel-Palestinian Water Issues—From Conflict to Cooperation*, edited by Shuval, H., and Dweik, H. Berlin: Springer. 263–272.

Laster, R., Livney, D. (2010). "Managing the Jordan River Basin: An Israeli Perspective." Tal, A., and Rabbo, A. A., editors, *Water Wisdom: preparing the groundwork for cooperative and sustainable water management in the Middle East.* New Brunswick, N.J.: Rutgers University Press. 258-263.

Lipchin, C. (2003). "Water, Agriculture and Zionism: Exploring the Interface between Policy and Ideology." *Integrated Water Resources Management and Security in the Middle East*, edited by Lipchin, C., Pallant, E., Saranga, D., and Amster, A. Dordrecht: Springer. 251–268.

Lipchin, C. (2007). "A Future for the Dead Sea Basin: Water Culture among Israelis, Palestinians and Jordanians." *Water Resources in the Middle East: Israel-Palestinian Water Issues—From Conflict to Cooperation*, edited by Shuval, H., and Dweik, H. Berlin: Springer. 87–107.

Orthofer, R., Daoud, R., Isaac, J., and Shuval, H. (2007). "Options for a More Sustainable Water Management in the Lower Jordan Valley." *Water Resources in the Middle East: Israel-Palestinian Water Issues—From Conflict to Cooperation*, edited by Shuval, H., and Dweik, H. Berlin: Springer. 69–78.

Pahl-Wostl, C. (2007). "Transitions towards Adaptive Management of Water Facing Climate and Global Change." *Water Resource Management* 21: 49–62.

Rumman, N. (2010). "Managing the Jordan River Basin: A Palestinian Perspective." *Water Wisdom: Preparing the Groundwork for Cooperative and Sustainable Water Management in the Middle East,* edited by Tal, A., and Rabbo, A. A. New Brunswick: Rutgers University Press. 258–263.

Shuval, H. (2010). "Meeting Vital Human Needs: Equitable Resolution of Conflicts over Shared Water Resources of Israelis and Palestinians." *Water Resources in the Middle East: Israeli-Palestinian Water Issues—From Conflict to Cooperation,* edited by Shuval, H., and Dweik, H. Berlin: Springer. 3–16.

Tagar, Z. (2007). *Nature Agriculture and the Price of Water in Israel.* Amman, Bethlehem, Tel Aviv: EcoPeace/Friend of the Earth Middle East. http://foeme.org/www/?module=publications&project_id=23.

Tal, A., and Rabbo, A. A. (2010). "Desalination–Editor's Summary." *Water Wisdom: Preparing the Groundwork for Cooperative and Sustainable Water Management in the Middle East.* New Brunswick: Rutgers University Press. 246–247.

Turner, M., Nassar, K., and Khateeb, N. (2005). *Crossing the Jordan.* Amman, Bethlehem, Tel Aviv: EcoPeace/Friend of the Earth Middle East. http://foeme.org/www/?module=publications&project_id=23.

UNESCO (2008). *Operational Guidelines for the Implementation of the World Heritage Convention.* Paris: World Heritage Center.

Venot, J. P. (2003). *Farming Systems in the Jordan River Basin in Jordan: Agronomical and Economic Description.* International Water Management Institute (IWMI) Comprehensive Assessment Program, French Regional Mission for Water and Agriculture (MREA) French Embassy, and INA P-G Paris-Grignon National Institute of Agronomy.

Gini Lee

Austral Archaeology and Historical Research, Oodnadatta. *Track Heritage Survey 1998–2000.* denr.sa.gov.au/heritage/pdfs/surveys/Oodnadatta. Accessed on November 30, 2011.

Econsearch (2008). *Flinders Ranges and Outback SA Region Integrated Strategic Tourism Plan 2008–2014.* Adelaide: Urban & Regional Planning Solutions, Econsearch, Ecological Associates.

Fry, G.,Tveit, M.S., Ode, A., and Velarde, M.D. (2009). "The Ecology of Visual Landscapes: Exploring the Conceptual Common Ground of Visual and Ecological Landscape Indicators." *Ecological Indicators* 9 (5): 933–947.

Haynes, R. (2002). "Seeking the Centre: Pushing the Boundaries." http://escholarship.usyd.edu.au/journals/index.php/SSR/article/viewFile/606/580.

Head, L. (2000). *Second Nature: The History and Implications of Australia as Aboriginal Landscape.* Syracuse, New York: Syracuse University Press.

Lake Eyre Basin Coordinating Group (2005). "About the Basin." http://www.lakeeyrebasin.org.au/archive/pages/page03.html.

Lake Eyre Basin Coordinating Group (2005). "Land Use in the Basin." http://www.lakeeyrebasin.org.au/land_use?land_use.html.

Lee, G. (2011). *Cultural Landscape Assessment and Analysis of the Neales Catchment and Algebuckina Waterhole.* Port Augusta: Queensland University of Technology. http://www.saalnrm.sa.gov.au/Portals/8/Publications_Resources/Project_Reports/SAAL-Report_Water_nealescatchment_landscape_052011.pdf.

Ndubisi, F. (2002). *Ecological Planning: A Historical and Comparative Synthesis.* Baltimore: Johns Hopkins University Press.

Lennon, J., and Mathews, S. (1996). *Cultural Landscape Management: Guidelines for Identifying, Assessing and Managing Cultural Landscapes in the Australian Alps National Parks Report.* Canberra: Australian Alps Liaison Committee.

Schliebs, S., and Edwards, V. (2011). "Lake at Dead Heart of the Nation Comes Alive." *The Australian*, February 12, 2011. http://www.theaustralian.com.au/nationalaffairs/lake-at-dead-heart-of-the-nation-comes-alive.

Thompson, G. F., and Steiner, F.R., eds. (1997). *Ecological Design and Planning.* New York: John Wiley & Sons.

James L. Wescoat Jr.

Abdulla, F., Eshtawi, T., and Assaf, H. (2009). "Assessment of the Impact of Potential Climate Change on the Water Balance of a Semi-Arid Watershed." *Water Resources Management* 23 (10): 2051–2068.

Allen, R. G. (1998). *Crop Evapotranspiration: Guidelines for Computing Crop Water Requirements—Irrigation and Drainage Paper* 56. Rome: FAO.

Alley, W. M. (2007). "Another Water Budget Myth: The Significance of Recoverable Ground Water in Storage." *Ground Water* 45 (3): 251.

Armstrong, A. (2007). "Modelling the Water Balance of Wetlands for Ecological Management—Considerations of Scale." *Wetlands: Monitoring, Modelling and Management.* Leiden: Taylor & Francis. 249–254.

Ash, T., and Lessick, D. (2002). "Ten Years of Water Budget Tiered Rate Structure at the Irvine Ranch Water District." *2002 Water Sources Conference: Reuse, Resources, Conservation.* Las Vegas. 1–9.

Ayub, K. R., Zakaria, N. A., Rozi, A., and Ramli, R. (2010). "Water Balance: Case Study of a Constructed Wetland as Part of the Bio-Ecological Drainage System (BIOECODS)." *Water Science and Technology* 62 (8): 1931–1936.

Beaumont, P., Bonine, M., and McLachlan, K., eds. (1989). *Qanat, Kariz, and Khettara.* Wisbech, U.K.: Menas Press.

Biswas, A. K. (1970). *The History of Hydrology.* Amsterdam: North-Holland.

Black, P. E. (2007). "Revisiting the Thornthwaite and Mather Water Balance." *Journal of the American Water Resources Association* 43 (6): 1604–1605.

Bredehoeft, J. D. (1997). "Safe Yield and the Water Budget Myth." *Ground Water* 35 (6): 929.

Bredehoeft, J. D. (2002). "The Water Budget Myth Revisited: Why Hydrogeologists Model." *Ground Water* 40 (4): 340–345.

Briggs, J. F., and Reidy, P. C. (2010). "Advanced Water Budget Analysis for Rainwater and Related Harvesting Applications." *ASCE Conference Proceedings* 371: 53.

Brook, M. (2008). *Water Resources of Abu Dhabi Emirate.* Abu Dhabi: United Arab Emirates.

Brooks, D. B., and Ozay, M. (2000). *Water Balances in the Eastern Mediterranean.* Ottawa: IDRC.

Brown, P. W. (2001). "Penman Monteith Crop Coefficients for Use with Desert Turf Systems." *Crop Science* 41: 1197–1201.

Bulygina, N., and Gupta, H. (2009). "Estimating the Uncertain Mathematical Structure of a Water Balance Model via Bayesian Data Assimilation." *Water Resources Research* 45: W00B13.

California Urban Water Conservation Council (2011). Water Use Budgets. http://www.cuwcc.org.

Claessens, L., Hopkinson, C., Rastetter, E., and Vallino, J. (2006). "Effect of Historical Changes in Land Use and Climate on the Water Budget of an Urbanizing Watershed." *Water Resources Research* 42 (3).

Costa, P. (1983). "Notes on Traditional Hydraulics and Agriculture in Oman." *World Archaeology* 14 (3): 273–295.

Costello, L. R., Matheny, N. P., and Clark, J. R. (2000). *The Landscape Coefficient Method and WUCOLS III.* Sacramento: California Department of Water Resources. http://www.owue.water.ca.gov/docs/wucols00.pdf.

DeOreo, W. B., and Mayer, P. W. (2005). "Why the City of Boulder Chose a Water Budget Rate Structure, and Where They Go from Here." *Proceedings of the AWWA Annual Conference.* San Francisco: AWWA.

Devlin, J. F., and Sophocleous, M. (2005). "The Persistence of the Water Budget Myth and its Relationship to Sustainability." *Hydrogeology Journal* 13 (4), 549–554.

Duan, R. and Fedler, C. B. (2009). "Field Study of Water Mass Balance in a Wastewater Land Application System." *Irrigation Science* 27 (5): 409–416.

Dujardin, J., Batelaan, O., Canters, F., Boel, S., Anibas, C., and Bronders, J. (2011). "Improving Surface-Subsurface Water Budgeting Using High Resolution Satellite Imagery Applied on a Brownfield." *Science of the Total Environment*, 409 (4): 800–809.

Dunne, T., and Leopold, L. (1978). *Water in Environmental Planning.* San Francisco: W. H. Freeman & Co.

Engeland, K., Xu, C. Y., and Gottschalk, L. (2005). "Assessing Uncertainties in a Conceptual Water Balance Model Using Bayesian Methodology." *Hydrological Sciences Journal* 50: 45–63.

Faybishenko, B. (2010). "Fuzzy-Probabilistic Calculations of Water-Balance Uncertainty." *Stochastic Environmental Research and Risk Assessment* 24 (6): 939–952.

Field, R. T. (2005). "John Russell (Russ) Mather at the Laboratory of Climatology." *Physical Geography* 26 (6): 434–441.

Gobel, P., Stubbe, H., Weinert, M., Zimmermann, J., Fach, S., Dierkes, C., and Kories, H. (2004). "Near-Natural Stormwater Management and its Effects on the Water Budget and Groundwater Surface in Urban Areas Taking Account of the Hydrogeological Conditions." *Journal of Hydrology* 299 (3–4): 267–283.

Hildebrand, M., Gaur, S., and Salt, K. J. (2009). "Water Budgets and California Law." *Journal of the American Water Works Association* 101 (4): 85–89.

Jain, M. (2006). *Conservation Project Report C–Part Water System: 1998–2001. Ahhichatragarh Fort and Palace Complex, Nagaur, Rajasthan.* Jodhpur: Mehrangarh Museum Trust.

Jorgensen, D. G., and Al Tikriti, W. Y. (2002). "A Hydrologic and Archeological Study of Climate Change in Al Ain, United Arab Emirates." *Global and Planetary Change* 35: 37–49.

Keim, B. (2010). The Lasting Scientific Impact of the Thornthwaite Water-Balance Model. *Geographical Review* 100 (3): 295–300.

Knopf, J. (1999). *Waterwise Landscaping with Trees, Shrubs, and Vines: A Xeriscape Guide for the Rocky Mountain Region, California, and the Desert Southwest.* Albuquerque, New Mexico: Chamisa Press.

Kostopoulou, P., Karagiannidis, A., Rakimbei, P., and Tsiouvaras, K. (2010). "Simulating the Water Balance in an Old Non-Engineered Landfill for Optimizing Plant Cover Establishment in an Arid Environment." *Desalination* 250 (1): 373–377.

Lightfoot, D. R. (2000). "The Origin and Diffusion of Qanats in Arabia: New Evidence from the Northern and Southern Peninsula." *The Geographical Journal,* 166 (3): 215–226.

Mansell, M., and Rollet, F. (2006). "Water Balance and the Behaviour of Different Paving Surfaces." *Water and Environment Journal* 20 (1): 7–10.

Mather, J. R., (1978). *The Climatic Water Budget in Environmental Analysis.* Lexington, Massachusetts: D. C. Heath & Co.

Mather, J. R., and Sanderson, M. (1995). *The Genius of C. Warren Thornthwaite, Climatologist-Geographer.* Norman, Oklahoma: University of Oklahoma Press.

Matsuura, K. (2011). Web-Based Water-Budget Interactive Modeling Program. http://climate.geog.udel.edu/~wimp/.

Mayer, P., DeOreo W.B., Chesnutt, T., Pekelney, D., and Summers, L. (2008). *Water Budgets and Rate Structures: Innovative Management Tools.* http://www.iwaponline.com/wio/2008/09/wio200809AF91205F.htm.

Mitchell, V. G., Cleugh, H. A., Grimmond, C. S. B., and Xu, J. (2008). "Linking Urban Water Balance and Energy Balance Models to Analyse Urban Design Options." *Hydrological Processes* 22 (16): 2891–2900.

Moynihan, E. B., ed. (2000). *The Moonlight Garden: New Discoveries at the Taj Mahal.* Washington, D.C.: Freer and Sackler Galleries of Asian Art.

Nandagiri, L. and Kovoor, G. M. (2006). "Performance Evaluation of Reference Evapotranspiration Equations across a Range of Indian Climates." *Journal of Irrigation and Drainage Engineering* 132: 238–249.

Nyhan, J. W. (2005). "A Seven-Year Water Balance Study of an Evapotranspiration Landfill Cover Varying in Slope for Semiarid Regions." *Vadose Zone Journal* 4 (3): 466–480.

Owen, C. R. (1995). "Water-Budget and Flow Patterns in an Urban Wetland." *Journal of Hydrology* 169 (1–4): 171–187.

Pistocchi, A., Bouraoui, F., and Bittelli, M. (2008). "A Simplified Parameterization of the Monthly Topsoil Water Budget." *Water Resources Research* 44 (12): W12440.

Rayburg, S., and Thoms, M. (2009). "A Coupled Hydraulic-Hydrologic Modelling Approach to Deriving a Water Balance Model for a Complex Floodplain Wetland System." *Hydrology Research* 40 (4): 364–379.

Savabi, M. R., Shinde, D., Konomi, K., Nkedi-Kizza, P., and Jayachandran, K. (2003). "Modeling the Effect of Soil Amendments (Composts) on Water Balance and Water Quality." *Water Pollution VII–Modelling, Measuring and Prediction* 9: 57–66.

Smith, S.W. (1996). *Landscape Irrigation: Design and Management.* New York: Wiley.

Sophocleous, M. (2004). "Discussion of Bredehoeft's 'The Water Budget Myth Revisited: Why Hydrogeologists Model.'" *Ground Water* 42 (2): 618.

Stannard, D. I., Paul, W. T., Laws, R., and Poeter, E. P. (2010). "Consumptive Use and Resulting Leach-Field Water Budget of a Mountain Residence." *Journal of Hydrology* 388 (3–4): 335–349.

Thornthwaite, C. W. (1948). "An Approach Toward a Rational Classification of Climate." *Geographical Review* 38: 55–94.

Thornthwaite, C. W., and Mather, J. R. (1957). "The Water Balance." *Publications in Climatology VIII.* Centerton, New Jersey: Drexel Institute of Climatology.

Tuan, Y. F. (1980). *The Hydrologic Cycle and the Wisdom of God: A Theme in Geoteleology.* Toronto: University of Toronto Department of Geography.

U.S. EPA (2009). "Water Sense Water Budget Approach." Spreadsheet tool. www.epa.gov/watersense/excel/Waterbudget_tool_112509_Final.xls.

van Rooijen, D. J., Turral, H., and Biggs, T. W. (2005). "Sponge City: Water Balance of Mega-City Water Use and Wastewater Use in Hyderabad, India." *Irrigation and Drainage* 54 (4): S81–S91.

Wang, E., Cresswell, H., Paydar, Z., and Gallant, J. (2008). "Opportunities for Manipulating Catchment Water Balance by Changing Vegetation Type on a Topographic Sequence: A Simulation Study." *Hydrological Processes* 22 (6): 736–749.

Wescoat, J. L. Jr. (2000). "Waterworks and Landscape Design in the Mahtab Bagh." *The Moonlight Garden: New Discoveries at the Taj Mahal. Washington,* D. C.: Smithsonian Institution. 59–78.

Wescoat, J. L. Jr. (2007a). "Conserving Mughal Waterworks." Sir Bernard Feilden Lecture. New Delhi: INTACH.

Wescoat, J. L. Jr. (2007b). "Garden and Waterworks Conservation Workshop at Nagaur Fort, Rajasthan." *LA Journal of Landscape Architecture* 16: 16–17.

Wescoat, J. L. Jr. (2007c). "Waterworks Conservation at Nagaur Fort." Technical memo to the Mehrangarh Museum Trust, Jodhpur, India.

Wescoat, J. L. Jr. (2007d). "Nagaur Garden Conservation: Evaluating Plant Water Requirements And Conservation Alternatives." Technical memo to the Mehrangarh Museum Trust, Jodhpur, India.

Wescoat, J. L. Jr. (2010). "Wisdom in Water-Conserving Design." *The Ismaili* (India), July 20–27, 2010.

Wescoat, J. L. Jr. (2011). *Water and Waterworks in Garden Archaeology. Handbook of Garden Archaeology,* edited by Malek, A. In press.

Wilkinson, J.C. (1977). *Water and Tribal Settlement in South-East Arabia: A Study of the Aflaj of Oman.* Cambridge: Cambridge University Press.

Willmott, C. J., ed. (1981). *Average Monthly and Annual Surface Air Temperature and Precipitation Data for the World, Publications in Climatology.* Centerton: Laboratory of Climatology.

CASE STUDIES

Liquid Wrap

Byrne, J. A., Fernandez-Ibañez, P. A., Dunlop, P., Alrousan, D., and Hamilton, J. (2011). "Photocatalytic Enhancement for Solar Disinfection of Water: A Review." *International Journal of Photoenergy* 2011.

Bhutta, Z. A. (2009). "Solar Water Disinfection in Household Settings: Hype or Hope?" *PLOS Medicine* 6 (8).

Bovill, C. (1995). *Fractal Geometry in Architecture and Design.* Boston: Birkhäuser.

Peitgen, H. O., Jürgens. H., and Saupe, D. (1992). *Chaos and Fractals: New Frontiers of Science.* New York: Springer.

Kehoe, S. C., Joyce, T. M., Ibrahim, P., Gillespie, J. B., Shahar, R. A., McGuigan, K. G. (2001). "Effect of Agitation, Turbidity, Aluminium Foil Reflectors and Container Volume on the Inactivation Efficiency of Batch-Process Solar Disinfectors." *Water Research* 35: 1061–1065.

Mani, S. K., Kanjur, R., Bright Singh, I. S., and Reed, R. H. (2006). "Comparative Effectiveness of Solar Disinfection using Small-Scale Batch Reactors with Reflective, Absorptive and Transmissive Rear Surfaces." *Water Research* 40: 721–727.

Reed, R. H., Mani, S. K., and Meyer, V. (2000). "Solar Photo-Oxidative Disinfection of Drinking Water: Preliminary Field Observations." *Society for Applied Bacteriology: Letters in Applied Microbiology* 30: 432–436.

Lawand T. A., Alward, R., Odeyemi, O., Hahn, J., Kandpal, T. C., and Ayoub, J. (1988). "Solar Water Disinfection." *Proceedings of workshop held at the Brace Research Institute, Montreal, Canada,* August 15–17, 1988.

Feachem, R., Bradley, D., Garelick, M., and Mara, D. (1983). *Sanitation and Disease, Health Aspects of Excreta and Wastewater Management.* London: John Wiley & Sons.

Joyce, T. M., McGuigan, K. G., Elmore-Meegan, M., and Conroy, R. M. (1996). "Inactivation of Fecal Bacteria in Drinking Water by Solar Heating." *Applied Environmental Microbiology* 62: 399–402.

Downes, A., and Blunt, T. P. (1877). "Researches on the Effect of Light upon Bacteria and Other Organisms." *Proceedings of the Royal Society* 28: 488–500.

Acra, A., Jurdi, M., Mu'Allem, H., Karahagopian, Y., Raffoul, Z. (1989). "Sunlight as Disinfectant." *Lancet* 1: 280.

Acra, A., Karahagopian, Y., Raffoul, Z., and Dajani, R (1980). "Disinfection of Oral Rehydration Solutions by Sunlight." *Lancet* 2: 1257–1258.

Conroy, R. M., Elmore-Meegan, M., Joyce, T., McGuigan, K. G., and Barnes, J. (1996). "Solar Disinfection of Drinking Water and Diarrhoea in Maasai Children: A Controlled Field Trial." *Lancet* 348: 1695–1697.

Joyce, T., Kenny, V., McGuigan, K., and Barnes, J. (1992). Disinfection of Water by Sunlight. *Lancet* 340: 921.

Conroy, R. M., McGuigan, K. G., Joyce, T. M., Gillespie, J. B., and Elmore-Meegan, M. (1998). "Solar Disinfection of Drinking Water Contained in Transparent Plastic Bottles: Characterizing the Bacterial Inactivation Process." *Journal Applied Microbiology* 84: 1138–1148.

Wegelin, M., Canonica, S., Mechsner, K., Fleischmann, T., Pesaro, F., and Metzler, A. (1994). "Solar Water Disinfection: Scope of the Process and Analysis of Radiation Experiments." *Journal of Water Supply: Research and Technology* 43: 154–169.

SANDEC (2002). *Solar Water Disinfection: A Guide for the Application of SODIC.* Lausanne: EAWAG.

Conroy, R. M., McGuigan, K. G., Mosler, H. J., du Preez, M., Ubomba-Jaswa, E., Fernandez-Ibanez, P. (2012). "Solar Water Disinfection (SODIS): A Review From Bench-Top to Roof-Top." *Journal of Hazardous Materials* 235–236: 29–46.

Baker, M. N. (1949). *The Quest for Pure Water: The History of Water Purification from the Earliest Records to the Twentieth Century.* New York: American Water Works Association.

Kanchan Arsenic Filter

CAWST (2012). Household Water Treatment for Arsenic Removal Fact Sheet: Sorption. http://www.cawst.org/en/resources/pubs/education-materials/file/40-hwts-fact-sheetarsenic-removalpdfoct09.

Chiew, H., Sampson, M. L., Huch, S., Ken, S., and Bostick, B. C. (2009). "Effect of Groundwater Iron and Phosphate on the Efficacy of Arsenic Removal by Iron-Amended BioSand Filters." *Environmental Science and Technology* 43(16): 6295–6300.

Frazer, L. (2005). "Metal Attraction: An Ironclad Solution to Arsenic Contamination?" *Environmental Health Perspectives* 113 (6): A398–A401.

Mahin, T., and Ngai, T. (2008). "Bangladesh Technology Verification Application, Kanchan Arsenic Filter." Presented at the Centre for Affordable Water and Sanitation Technology (CAWST) Learning Exchange, Calgary, Canada, June, 2008.

Ngai, T., Murcott, S., Shrestha, R., Dangol, B., and Maharjan, M. (2006). "Development and Dissemination of Kanchan™ Arsenic Filter in Rural Nepal." *Water Science & Technology: Water Supply* 6: 137–146.

Ngai, T., Shrestha, R., Dangol, B., Maharjan, M. and Murcott, S. (2007). "Design for Sustainable Development—Household Drinking Water Filter for Arsenic and Pathogen Treatment in Nepal." *Journal of Environmental Science and Health* A42 (12): 1879–1888.

Hussain, M. D., Haque, M. A., Islam, M. M., and Hossen, M. A. (2001). "Approaches for Removal of Arsenic from Tubewell Water for Drinking Purpose." *Technologies for Arsenic Removal from Drinking Water,* edited by Ahmed, M. F., Ali, M. A., and Adeel, Z. Tokyo, Dhaka: The United Nations University/Bangladesh University of Engineering and Technology. http://archive.unu.edu/env/Arsenic/Hussain.pdf.

Huisman, L., and Wood, W. E. (1974). *Slow Sand Filtration.* Geneva: World Health Organization.

Robins, R. G., Nishimura, T., and Singh, P. (2001). "Removal of Arsenic from Drinking Water by Precipitation, Adsorption or Cementation." *Technologies for Arsenic Removal from Drinking Water,* edited by Ahmed, M. F., Ali, M. A., and Adeel, Z. Tokyo, Dhaka: The United Nations University/Bangladesh University of Engineering and Technology. http://archive.unu.edu/env/Arsenic/Robins.pdf.

MIT (2008). "Kanchan™ Arsenic Filter Project for Rural Nepal." *Safe Water for 1 Billion People.* http://web.mit.edu/watsan/tech_hwts_chemical_kanchanarsenicfilter.html.

Vena

Hanby, V., Loveday, D., and Al-Ajmi, F. (2005). "The Optimal Design for a Ground Cooling Tube in a Hot, Arid Climate." *Building Services Engineering Research and Technology* 26: 1–10.

Kidron, G. (1999) "Altitude Dependent Dew and Fog in the Negev Desert, Israel." *Agricultural and Forest Meteorology* 96: 1–8.

Gandhidasan, P., and Abualhamayel, H. I. (2005). "Modeling and Testing of a Dew Collection System." *Desalination* 180: 47–51.

Kogan, B., and Trahtman, A. (2003). "The Moisture from the Air as Water Resource in Arid Region: Hopes, Doubts and Fact." *Journal of Arid Environments* 53: 231–240.

Lekouch, I., Muselli, M., Kabbachi, B., Ouazzani, J., Melnytchouk-Milimouk, I., Beysens, D. (2011). "Dew, Fog, and Rain as Supplementary Sources of Water in South-Western Morocco." *Energy* 36, 2257–2265.

Ore Design + Technology (2011). "Vena." http://oredesign.org/projects/vena.html.

Isla Urbana

Abdulla, F. A., and Al-Shareef, A. W. (2009). "Roof Rainwater Harvesting Systems for Household Water Supply in Jordan." *Desalination* 243: 195–207.

Domènech, L., and Saurí, D. (2011). "A Comparative Appraisal of the Use of Rainwater Harvesting in Single and Multifamily Buildings of the Metropolitan Area of Barcelona (Spain): Social Experience, Drinking Water Savings and Economic Costs." *Journal of Cleaner Production* 19: 598–608.

Tortajada, C., and Castelán, E. (2003) "Water Management for a Megacity: Mexico City Metropolitan Area." *Ambio* 32 (2): 124–129.

Grillo, I. (2009). "Dry Taps in Mexico City: A Water Crisis Gets Worse." *Time*, April 11, 2009. http://www.time.com/time/world/article/0,8599,1890623,00.html.

Vaes, G., and Berlamont, J. (1999). "The Impact of Rainwater Reuse on CSO Emissions." *Water Science and Technology* 39 (5): 57–64.

Fewkes, A. (1999). "Modelling the Performance of Rainwater Collection Systems: Towards a Generalised Approach." *Urban Water* 1: 323–333.

Leggett, D. J., Brown, R., Brewer, D., Stanfield, G. and Holliday, E. (2001) *Rainwater and Greywater Use in Buildings: Best Practice Guidance.* London: Construction Industry Research and Information Association.

Down to Earth

Boers, T. M., and Ben-Asher, J. (1982). "A Review of Rainwater Harvesting." *Agricultural Water Management* 5: 145–158.

Cowan, M. K. (2008). "Harvesting RAIN." *The Ecologist* 38 (5): 40–43.

Evaneri, M., Shanan, L., and Tadmor, N. H. (1968). "'Runoff Farming' in the Desert. I. Experimental Layout." *Agronomy Journal* 60: 29–32.

Lightfoot, D. R. (1997). "Qanats in the Levant: Hydraulic Technology at the Periphery of Early Empires." *Technology and Culture* 38 (2): 432.

Lüttge, U. (2010). "Runoff-Rainwater for Sustainable Desert Farming." *Desert Plants*, edited by Ramawat, K. G. Berlin: Springer-Verlag. doi 10.1007/978-3-642-02550-1_21.

Prinz, D. (2002). "The Role of Water Harvesting in Alleviating Water Scarcity in Arid Areas." *Proceedings, International Conference on Water Resources Management in Arid Regions 23-27 March, 2002, Vol. III.* Kuwait: Kuwait Institute for Scientific Research. 107–122.

Rice, W. E. (2004). "Desertwater Harvesting to Benefit Wildlife: A Simple, Cheap, and Durable Sub-Surfacewater Harvester for Remote Locations." *Environmental Monitoring and Assessment* 99: 251–257.

Rubin, R. (1988). "Water Conservation Methods in Israel's Negev Desert in Late Antiquity." *Journal of Historical Geography* 14 (3): 229–244.

Zhu, K., Zhang, L., Hart, W., Liu, M., and Chen, H. (2004). "Quality Issues in Harvested Rainwater in Arid and Semi-Arid Loess Plateau of Northern China." *Journal of Arid Environments* 57, 487–505.

Gafni, A. (2010). "KKL-JNF Reservoirs Provide Priceless Benefits." *The Jerusalem Post*, November 1, 2010. http://www.jpost.com/GreenIsrael/WATERFORISRAEL/Article.aspx?id=120270.

Mekorot (2013). "Wastewater Treatment and Reclamation." http://www.mekorot.co.il/Eng/Activities/Pages/WastewaterTreatmentandReclamation.aspx.

Mekorot (2007a). "Israel is a World Leader in Recycling Treated Wastewater." http://www.mekorot.co.il/Eng/NewsEvents/Pages/23102007-1.aspx.

Mekorot (2007b). "Wastewater Treatment and Reclamation." http://www.mekorot.co.il/Eng/Activities/Documents/Wastewater%20Treatment%20and%20Reclamation-%20WATEC%202007.pdf.

Juanico, M., and Friedler, E. (1999). "Wastewater Reuse for River Recovery in Semi-Arid Israel." *Water Science and Technology* 40 (4–5): 43–50.

Friedler, E. (2001). "Water Reuse—An Integral Part of Water Resources Management: Israel as a Case Study." *Water Policy* 3: 29–39.

Friedler, E. (1999). "The Jezreel Valley Project for Wastewater Reclamation and Reuse, Israel." *Water Science and Technology* 40 (4–5): 347–354

Tahal (2013). "Kishon Integrated Multi-Source Water Supply Scheme." http://www.tahal.co.il/projects_item.aspx?FolderID=96&docID=347.

Hiriya Landfill Park

Baker, L. A. (1998). "Design Considerations and Applications for Wetland Treatment of High-Nitrate Waters." *Water Science Technology* 38: 389–395.

Belmont, M. A., Cantellano, E., Thompson, S., Williamson, M., Sanchez, A., and Metcalfe, C. D. (2004). "Treatment of Domestic Wastewater in a Pilot-Scale Natural Treatment System in Central Mexico." *Ecological Engineering* 23: 299–311.

Bulc, T. G. (2006). "Long Term Performance of a Constructed Wetland for Landfill Leachate Treatment." *Ecological Engineering* 26: 365–374.

EPA (1993). *Subsurface Flow Constructed Wetlands for Waste-Water Treatment, a Technology Assessment.* EPA 832-R-93-008. http://water.epa.gov/type/wetlands/restore/upload/2003_07_01_wetlands_pdf_sub.pdf.

Finstein, M. S. (2003). *ArrowBio Process for Municipal Solid Waste: Recovery of Material and Energy Resources in a Single System.* http://www.dnrec.delaware.gov/SWMTWG/Documents/8e02fb1254f2476f8d3e50ec6fd24ceeGenericDescriptionArrowBio.pdf.

Greenway, M. (2005). "The Role of Constructed Wetlands in Secondary Effluent Treatment and Water Reuse in Subtropical and Arid Australia." *Ecological Engineering* 25 (5): 501–509.

Kivaisi, A. K. (2001). "The Potential for Constructed Wetlands for Wastewater Treatment and Reuse in Developing Countries: A Review." *Ecological Engineering* 16: 545–560.

Senzia, M. A., Mashauri, D. A., and Mayo, A. W. (2003). "Suitability of Constructed Wetlands and Waste Stabilization Ponds in Wastewater Treatment: Nitrogen Transformation and Removal." *Physics and Chemistry of the Earth* 28: 1117–1124.

Vymazal, J., (2007). "Removal of Nutrients in Various Types of Constructed Wetlands." *Science of the Total Environment* 380: 48–65.

Vymazal, J. (2009). The Use of Constructed Wetlands with Horizontal Sub-Surface Flow for Various Types of Wastewater. *Ecological Engineering* 35: 1–17.

Vymazal, J. (2011). "Long-Term Performance of Constructed Wetlands with Horizontal Sub-Surface Flow: Ten Case Studies from the Czech Republic." *Ecological Engineering* 37: 54–63.

Verhoeven, J.T.A., Meuleman, A.F.M. (1999). "Wetlands for Wastewater Treatment: Opportunities and Limitations." *Ecological Engineering* 12: 5–12.

Taragalte

Bull, L. J., Kirkby, M. J., Shannon, J., and Hooke, J. M. (2000). "The Variation in Estimated Discharge in Relation to the Location of Storm Cells in South East Spain." *Catena* 38 (3): 191–209.

Amerman, C. R., and McGuinness, J. L. (1968). "Plot and Small Watershed Runoff: Its Relation to Larger Areas." *Transactions of the ASAE* 10 (4): 464–466.

Ali, A., and Yazar, A. (2007). "Effect of Micro-Catchment Water Harvesting on Soil-Water Storage and Shrub Establishment in the Arid Environment." *International Journal of Agriculture & Biology* 9 (2).

Ait Hamza, M., El Faskaoui, B., and Fermin, A. (2009). *Migration and Environmental Change in Morocco: The Case of Rural Oasis Villages in the Middle Drâa Valley*. Rotterdam: Erasmus University Rotterdam.

Torres-Garcia, A. (2013). "U.S. Diplomacy and the North African 'War of the Sands' (1963)." *The Journal of North African Studies* 18 (2): 324–348.

Boers, T. M., and Ben-Asher, J. (1982). "A Review of Rainwater Harvesting." *Agricultural Water Management* 5 (2): 145–158.

Sobczak, K. (2008). "Changes in the Environment and Migration in Southern Morocco—Example of the M'Hamid Oasis." *Miscellanea Geographica* 13: 239–250.

Thomas, B. E. (1952). "Trans-Saharan Routes." *Geographical Review* 42 (2): 267–282.

UNESCO (2005). "Drâa (Morocco)." *HELP, Hydrology for the Environment, Life and Policy.* UNESCO, the International Hydrological Programme.

Ouhajou, L. (1996). *Espace Hydraulique et Société au Maroc: Cas des Systèmes d'Irrigation dans la Vallée du Drâa*. Agadir: Faculté des Lettres et des Sciences Humaines, Université Ibn Zohr.

Heidecke, C. (2009). *Economic Analysis of Water Use and Management in the Middle Drâa Valley in Morocco*. Dissertation. Bonn: University of Bonn.

Wadi Hanifah Restoration Project

Moriyama & Teshima Planners. "MEDSTAR City Planning Study." Accessed on April 1, 2013. http://www.mtplanners.com/

ILLUSTRATION CREDITS

All case study drawings and diagrams are based on original material provided by the respective case study authors.

Preface
Figure 1: John Howarth
Figure 2: David Fletcher, Fletcher Studio Landscape Architecture + Urban Design
Figure 3: Andrew Kudless, Matsys
Figure 4: Carol Moukheiber and Christos Marcopoulos, Studio N-1; Robert Wright; Don Shillingburg
Figure 5: Jimenez Lai, Bureau Spectacular

Introduction
Figures 1–3: ArRiyadh Development Authority and Moriyama & Teshima Planners
Figure 4a: Amit Geron
Figure 4b: Weinstein-Vaadia Architects
Figures 5a–5c: Kristin S. Malone, Jason O. Vollen, and Anna H. Dyson, Center for Architecture Science and Ecology (CASE), Rensselaer Polytechnic Institute
Figure 6: Matthias Schuler, Kai Babetzki, and Hendrik Hasert, Transsolar Energietechnik GmbH

Antoine Picon
Figure 1: Les Archives du Canal du Mid
Figure 2: Musée National des Châteaux de Versailles et de Trianon
Figure 3: Gauthey, E. M., and Navier, C.L.M.H. (1809). *Oeuvres de M. Gauthey.* Paris: Firmin Didot
Figure 4: Abraham-Louis-Rodolphe Ducros, Musée Cantonal des Beaux-Arts de Lausanne
Figure 5: Ecole Nationale des Ponts et Chaussées
Figure 6: Musée Carnavalet
Figure 7: Elliott (1992). *Technics and Architecture: The Development of Materials and Systems for Buildings.* Cambridge, Massachusetts: MIT Press, p. 225

WATER FOR DOMESTIC USE

Alon Tal
Figure 1: U.S. Geological Survey for the Middle East Water Data Banks Project
Figure 2a and 2b: Israel Water Authority (2008)
Figure 3: Sabine Lattemann and Thomas Höpner (2008)
Figures 4a and 4b: Israel Water Authority
Figures 5 and 6: IDE Technologies Ltd.
Figure 7: *The Australian* (January 23, 2010)
Figure 8: *Technology Review* (2008)

Baker and Ngai
Figures 1–8: Centre for Affordable Water and Sanitation Technology (CAWST)

Kanchan Arsenic Filter
Massachusetts Institute of Technology Global Water & Sanitation (WatSan), Nepal Environment and Public Health Organization (ENPHO), and Rural Water Supply and Sanitation Support Programme (RWSSSP)
CAWST. (2012). *Biosand Filter Construction Manual: A CAWST Participant Manual*
CAWST. (2012). *Household Water Treatment for Arsenic Removal, Fact Sheet: Sorption/ Kanchan Arsenic Filter*

Liquid Wrap
Mark Collins and Toru Hasegawa, Proxy Design Studio

Vena Water Condenser:
Thomas Kosbau, ORE Design + Technology

Isla Urbana:
Isla Urbana

Down to Earth:
Ruth Kedar

WATER FOR AGRICULTURAL PRODUCTION

Eilon Adar
Figures 1–5: Eilon Adar
Figures 6a and 6b: Albatross Aerial Photography
Figure 7: Kibbutz Yotvata archive

Pasternak and Woltering
Figures 1–3, 5: Dov Pasternak and Lennart Woltering
Figure 4: Woltering, L., Pasternak, D., and Ndjeunga, J. (2011). "The African Market Garden: Development of a Low-Pressure Drip Irrigation System for Smallholder Producers in the Sudano-Sahel." *Irrigation and Drainage* 60 (5): 613-621

Aziza Chaouni
Figures 1, 2, 10, 11b: Aziza Chaouni
Figures 3–5: Schulz, O., and Judex, M., eds. (2008). IMPETUS *Atlas Morocco: Research Results 2000–2007, 3rd edition.* Bonn: University of Bonn Department of Geography.
Figure 6: Direction Générale de l'Hydrologie, Rabat
Figures 7, 11a: Heidecke, C. (2009). *Economic Analysis of Water Use and Management in the Middle Drâa Valley in Morocco.* Dissertation. Bonn: University of Bonn.
Figure 8: Office Régional de Mise en Valeur Agricole de Ouarzazate (ORMVAO), Société Générale d'Etudes et de Travaux d'Irrigation au Maroc (SOGETIM)
Figure 9: La Roche, P. "L'Irrigation dans le Sud du Maroc." Summary presented for the Centre des Hautes Études d'Administration Musulmane
Figure 12: Prodanovic, P., and Simonovic, S. P. (2006). "Systems Approach to Assessment of Climatic Change." *Small River Basins, Proceedings of the 23rd Conference of the Danubian Countries on the Hydrological Forecasting and Hydrological Bases of Water Management, Belgrade, Republic of Serbia, 28–31 August 2006.*
Figures 13a, 13b: Aziza Chaouni Projects

Fadi Massoud
Figures 1, 2, 4–10: Fadi Massoud
Figure 3: Fadi Masoud
Based on material from:
S. A. Assaf (2010). "A Water for Peace Strategy for the Jordan River Basin by Shifting Cropping Patterns." In H. Shuval and H. Dweik (Eds.), *Water Resources in the Middle East: Israel-Palestinian Water Issues—From Conflict to Cooperation*. Berlin: Springer. 79–85
Phillips, D.J.H., Attili, S., McCaffrey, S., and Murray, J. S. (2007). "The Jordan River Basin: 2. Potential Future Allocations to the Co-riparians." *Water International* 32: 39–62.
Orthofer, R., Daoud, R., Isaac, J., and Shuval, H. (2010). "Options for a More Sustainable Water Management in the Lower Jordan Valley." *Water Resources in the Middle East: Israel-Palestinian Water Issues—From Conflict to Cooperation*. Berlin: Springer. 69–78
Mimi, Z. A., and Sawalhi, B. I. (2003). "A Decision Tool for Allocating the Waters of the Jordan River Basin between all Riparian Parties." *Water Resources Management* 17: 447–461.

Wastewater Treatment and Reclamation in Israel
All figures p. 142: Adapted from diagrams by Tawab Hlimi
All figures p. 144: Friedler, E. (2001). "Water Reuse: An Integral Part of Water Resources Management: Israel as a Case Study." *Water Policy* 3: 29–39
All figures p. 145: Mekorot

WATER FOR ECOSYSTEM SERVICES

Gini Lee
Figures 1, 3–5: Gini Lee
Figure 2: Google Earth and Terra Metrics. (2010). Lake Eyre Basin, South Australia, https://www.google.ca/maps/place/Kati+Thanda-Lake+Eyre,+South+Australia,+Australia/@-27.0991256,140.8911437,1583423m/data=!3m1!1e3!4m2!3m1!1s0x6a8588dcbf6a7371:0x2a033654a8627350

James L. Wescoat Jr.
All figures: James L. Wescoat Jr.
Figures 3, 5: James L. Wescoat Jr.
Based on material from: Willmott, C. J., Mather, J. R., and Rowe, C. M. (1981). "Average Monthly and Annual Surface Air Temperature and Precipitation Data for the World." Centerton: C. W. Thornthwaite Associates Laboratory of Climatology

Hiriya Landfill Recycling Park
Latz + Partner, Weinstein Vaadia Architects, and Ayala Water & Ecology

Taragalte Ecolodge
Aziza Chaouni and Takako Tajima, Bureau E.A.S.T.; Liat Margolis

Wadi Hanifah Restoration Project
Moriyama & Teshima and Buro Happold

Wadi Hanifa Bioremediation Facility
Moriyama & Teshima and Buro Happold

ABOUT THE AUTHORS

Eilon Adar is Director of the Zuckerberg Institute for Water Research and Associate Professor in the Department of Environmental Hydrology and Microbiology at the Jacob Blaustein Institutes for Desert Research, Ben-Gurion University of the Negev in Israel. Adar's main research activities are associated with quantitative assessment of groundwater flow systems and sources of recharge in complex arid basins with puzzling geology and scarce hydrological information. Adar has developed the novel transient Mixing Cell Model (MCMtr) which has been developed to define groundwater flow patterns in multiple-aquifer flow systems by environmental tracers. The model has been applied in several hydrological basins worldwide, from the Kalahari Desert (Namibia), Jezreel, Bessor basins (Israel), Arava Basin (Jordan-Israel) to the Ili basin in Kazakhstan. Other research activities include: (1) the role of water reservoirs and shallow groundwater on top-soil salinization; (2) the effects of forestation over sand-dune terrain on local groundwater reservoirs; (3) the dynamics of flow and pollutant transport in a fractured chalk aquitard; (4) identification and quantification of pollutant sources into ephemeral rivers from anthropogenic activities; (5) the effect of industrial effluents on the hydraulic properties of a fractured chalk aquitard; (6) identification of irregular salinization processes in the coastal aquifer of Israel; (7) salinization and deterioration of topsoil water quality due to anthropogenic activities; (8) soil and groundwater contamination in the coastal aquifer of Israel by organic industrial pollutants and (9) hydrological aspects of management and policy associated with transboundary water resources in Israel and the Middle East. Adar holds a Bachelor of Science in Geography, Geology, and Climatology, and a Master in Physical Geography and Hydrology both from the Hebrew University of Jerusalem, and a PhD in Hydrology from the University of Arizona, Tucson, Arizona.

Camille Dow Baker is Co-Founder of the Centre for Affordable Water and Sanitation Technology (CAWST) and was its volunteer President and CEO for its first 10 years. CAWST is a Canadian non-governmental organization (NGO) and charity that focuses on providing training and expert consulting services in water and sanitation for organizations that serve the poor in developing countries. Baker has more than 30 years experience as a professional engineer. Prior to founding CAWST, Baker enjoyed a very successful 20-year career in the petroleum industry in various leadership positions at significant Canadian energy corporations. She left the oil and gas industry in 1998 to earn a graduate degree from the University of Calgary in environmental design, with a focus on water and sanitation in developing countries. CAWST was founded in 2001. Baker has been President of the Board of Directors for the YWCA of Calgary, a long standing Calgary NGO, as well as a member of the board of the Alberta Oil Sands Technical Research Authority, a provincial government agency. She has been awarded an honorary Doctor of Laws degree honoris causa from the University of Calgary and an honorary Bachelor of Business Administration in Non-Profit Studies from Mount Royal University. She is also a recipient of the Alberta Centennial Medal, Global Woman of Vision Award, the National GRIOT Award for science and technology, and a Rotary Integrity Award.

Aziza Chaouni is Assistant Professor of Architecture at the University of Toronto, John H. Daniels Faculty of Architecture, Landscape, and Design and the Founding Principal of the design practice Aziza Chaouni Projects (ACP) with offices in Fez, Morocco, and Toronto. She is also the Director of the Designing Ecological Tourism Research platform at the Daniels faculty. She is also the Director of the Designing Ecological Tourism Research platform at the Daniels faculty which has received funding from the Royal Society of Conservation of Nature in Jordan, the Cook Foundation, the Moroccan Ministry of Tourism, and the Latin American and Caribbean Region Grant. DET design and research projects has received a Progressive Architecture Citation Award and a ASCA Collaboration Award. Chaouni's practice, research, and teaching focus on sustainable design and construction in the developing world. She is also interested in the integration of architecture and landscape, particularly through the implementation of sustainable technologies in arid climates. Her work at both ACP and her previous office Bureau E.A.S.T with partner Takako Tajima has been recognized with top awards for both the Global and Regional Africa and the Middle East competition from the Holcim Foundation for Sustainable Construction; the Architectural League of New York Young Architects Award; the Environmental Design Research Association Great Places Award; the American Society of Landscape Architects Design Awards, among others. Her work has been published and exhibited internationally, including the International Architecture Biennale in Rotterdam; INDEX: Design to Improve Life in Copenhagen; the United Nations Human Settlements Programme (UN HABITAT) World Urban Forum; the Venice Architecture Biennale; and the Louisiana Museum of Modern Art in Copenhagen. Chaouni holds a Masters of Architecture with distinction from the Harvard University Graduate School of Design and a Bachelor of Science with Honors in Civil Engineering from Columbia University.

Herbert Dreiseitl is an urban designer, landscape architect, water artist, interdisciplinary planner, and Professor in Praxis. He is an expert in creating Liveable Cities around the world, with a special hallmark of his work on the inspiring and innovative use of water to solve urban environmental challenges by connecting technology with aesthetics and encouraging people to take care of and ownership for places. He has realized projects in the fields of urban design, urban hydrology, water art, stormwater management, planning, and landscape architecture. Dreiseitl is the Director of the Liveable Cities Lab, a think tank at the Rambøll Group, and founder of Atelier Dreiseitl, a globally integrated design studio with more than 35-year history of excellence in urban design, landscape architecture, and ecological waterscapes.
He explores the potentials and conditions for Liveable Cities through a collaborative network and as Harvard GSD Loeb Fellow and Visiting Professor at National University of Singapore (NUS). He lectures worldwide and has authored many publications, including three editions of *Waterscapes. Planning, Building and Designing with Water*.

Gini Lee is a landscape architect and interior designer and holds the Elisabeth Murdoch Chair of Landscape Architecture at the University of Melbourne, where she teaches and researches landscape design studio and theory that engages with the curation and postproduction of complex landscapes. Prior to this she was Professor of Landscape Architecture at Queensland University of Technology (2008-2011) and Head of School at the University of South Australia (1999-2004) as a researcher and lecturer in cultural and critical landscape architecture studies and spatial interior design. She is Past Head of School at the University of South Australia. Her PhD entitled "The Intention to Notice: the collection, the tour and ordinary landscapes", investigated ways in which designed landscapes are incorporated into the cultural understandings of individuals and communities. Focusing on the arid environments of Australia, her multidisciplinary research into water landscapes of remote territories contributes to the scientific, cultural, and indigenous understanding and management strategies for fragile landscapes. Her recent curatorial practice is an experiment with Deep Mapping methods to investigate the landscapes of remote and rural Australia. Deep Mapping for the Stony Rises is a contributor to the Stony Rises project for the volcanic country of southwestern Victoria. Lee's work derives from aspects of country encountered while travelling over the stony ground of dissimilar landscapes. She is a registered landscape architect.

Liat Margolis is Assistant Professor of Landscape Architecture at the University of Toronto, John H. Daniels Faculty of Architecture, Landscape, and Design. Her research interests are in green building technologies and green infrastructure. Margolis is co-Founder and Director of the Green Roof Innovation Testing Laboratory (GRIT Lab)—an interdisciplinary research collaborative dedicated to the study of green roofs, green walls, and solar photovoltaic systems. Using sensor technologies and real-time data acquisition, her research team focuses on analyzing the environmental performance metrics of green building technologies in relation to urban water management, thermal cooling, energy production, as well as biodiversity and habitat creation. For her work on GRIT Lab, Margolis received the 2013 American Society of Landscape Architects (ASLA) Excellence in Research Award. The GRIT Lab is supported by over a dozen industry partners as well as grants from the City of Toronto Environment Office, Connaught Fund, Landscape Architecture Canada Foundation, MITACS, Natural Sciences and Engineering Research Council of Canada, Ontario Centres of Excellence, and RCI Foundation. Prior to joining the Daniels Faculty, Margolis worked as a landscape architect for Hargreaves Associates and had a primary role in the design of a three-mile post-industrial waterfront in Knoxville, TN. She was also co-Founder and Director of Research at the Harvard University Graduate School of Design's Material Collection and before that, Director of Research at Material ConneXion, Inc. in New York. Her 2007 book *Living Systems: Innovative Materials and Technologies for Landscape Architecture* demonstrates how urban landscapes can work in concert with the dynamics of environmental systems. The book is widely used as a reference for architectural design instruction and professional practice. Margolis holds a Bachelor of Fine Arts in Industrial Design from the Rhode Island School of Design and a Masters of Landscape Architecture from the Harvard Graduate School of Design.

Fadi Masoud is Lecturer in Landscape Architecture and Urban Design at the Massachusetts Institute of Technology's School of Architecture + Planning and an affiliate faculty with the Center for Advanced Urbanism. He held appointments at the Harvard Graduate School of Design and at the University of Toronto, where he taught design studios and courses on landscape, urbanism, and visual representation. Masoud holds a Bachelor of Environmental Studies from the University of Waterloo's School of Planning, a Masters of Landscape Architecture from the University of Toronto, and a Post-Professional Master in Landscape Architecture II from Harvard University's Graduate School of Design, where he graduated with distinction. Masoud is the recipient of several awards including the Fulbright Fellowship, the Heather M. Reisman Gold Medal in Design, and the Jacob Weidenman Prize, and has practiced as a landscape architect and a planner at several leading firms. Masoud's work focuses on establishing nascent relationships between landscape and planning principles and models. His work has been recognized through several international competitions and exhibitions, and has been published in several venues including *Topos, Landscape World Journal, MASS Context Journal, Conservation of Architecture Journal, Design for Flooding, and New Geographies Journal*.

Tommy Ka Kit Ngai is the Director of Research Learning at the Centre for Affordable Water and Sanitation Technology (CAWST), a Canadian non-governmental organization and charity that focuses on providing training and expert consulting services in water and sanitation for organizations that serve the poor in developing countries. Ngai mentors practitioners to implement Water, Sanitation and Hygiene (WASH) programs using the best available research knowledge, and supports academics to conduct research relevant to the practitioners' needs. He has traveled to Peru, Zambia, Ghana, India, Nepal, Bangladesh, Cambodia, and Laos to assist CAWST clients to conduct research projects which lead to evidence-based recommendations. His other key role at CAWST is to measure, analyze, and report the organization's performance, according to best practice in monitoring and evaluation. His research focuses on the complexity in designing appropriate WASH technologies, including the Kanchan Arsenic Filter, and formulating sustainable WASH program policies. Ngai was Lecturer and Research Affiliate at the Massachusetts Institute of Technology (MIT). Ngai holds a Bachelor of Applied Science in Chemical Engineering from the University of Toronto, a Master of Engineering in Environmental Engineering from MIT, and PhD in Engineering for Sustainable Development from the University of Cambridge.

Dov Pasternak is Principal Scientist for Systems and Crops Diversification at ICRISAT (International Crops Research Institute for the Semi-Arid Tropics) Sahelian Center-Niger since 2001 and Director of the International Program for Arid Land Crops (IPALAC) since 1997. He was former Head of the Institute for Agriculture & Applied Biology at the Ben-Gurion University of the Negev from 1976-2001. Working for IPALAC, an Israeli initiative designed to share relevant aspects of the Israeli experience in combating desertification, Pasternak has developed a pilot project in Africa which uses his expertise on arid land agriculture and the Israeli invention—the low pressure drip irrigation systems (LPDI)—to help farmers grow crops. The Israel Ministry of Foreign Affairs international development organization—MASHAV—has recently appointed Pasternak as the Israeli representative for Western Africa. Among Pasternak's achievements, he has pioneered the practice of using saline water for irrigation, has developed novel "solar" greenhouses and systems that produce crops without chemical sprays, and co-developed a system that allows farmers to supervise agricultural operations remotely. His work follows a theme: research and systems that help farmers reclaim degraded land. In addition to the technologies and research Pasternak is giving to Africa, he is currently developing a new education program for village primary schools that he calls "Farmers of the Future."

Antoine Picon is Professor of the History of Architecture and Technology and Co-Director of Doctoral Programs at the Harvard Graduate School of Design. Trained as an engineer, architect, and historian, Picon works on the history of architectural and urban technologies from the 18th century to the present. His *French Architects and Engineers in the Age of Enlightenment* (1988; English translation, 1992) is a synthetic study of the disciplinary "deep structures" of architecture, garden design, and engineering in the eighteenth century, and their transformations as new issues of territorial management and infrastructure-systems planning were confronted. Whereas *Claude Perrault (1613-1688) ou la Curiosité d'un classique (1988)* traces the origin of these changes at the end of the 17th century, *L'Invention de l'Ingénieur Moderne, L'Ecole des Ponts et Chaussées 1747-1851* (1992) envisages their full development from the mid-18th century to the 1850s. Picon has also worked on the relations between society, technology, and utopia. This is in particular the theme of *Les Saint-Simoniens: Raison, Imaginaire, et Utopie* (2002), a detailed study of the Saint-Simonian movement that played a seminal role in the emergence of industrial modernity. Picon's more recent book, *Digital Culture in Architecture: An Introduction for the Design Professions* (2010) offers a comprehensive overview and discussion of the changes brought by the computer to the theory and practice of architecture. Picon has received a number of awards for his writings, including the Médaille de la Ville de Paris and twice the Prix du Livre d'Architecture de la Ville de Briey, a well as the Georges Sarton Medal of the University of Gand. In 2010, he was elected a member of the French Académie des Technologies. He is Chevalier des Arts et Lettres since 2014. Picon received engineering degrees from the Ecole Polytechnique and from the Ecole Nationale des Ponts et Chaussées, an architecture degree from the Ecole d'Architecture de Paris-Villemin, and a doctorate in history from the Ecole des Hautes Etudes en Sciences Sociales.

Alon Tal is an Associate Professor at the Jacob Blaustein Institutes for Desert Research at Ben-Gurion University of the Negev. He has held faculty appointments at Tel Aviv and Hebrew Universities in Israel, at the University of Otago in New Zealand and between 1990 and 1999 was an adjunct faculty member at Harvard University. He was also the founding director of Adam Teva V'din (The Israel Union for Environmental Defense) in 1990, today Israel's leading environmental advocacy organization. Tal served as chairman of Life and Environment, an umbrella group for 110 environmental organizations in Israel, from 1998-2004. In 1996, Tal founded the Arava Institute for Environmental Studies, a graduate studies center in which Israeli, Jordanian, and Palestinian students join environmentalists from around the world in an advanced interdisciplinary research program. In 2011 he was elected chairman of the Green Movement, Israel's green party. Tal is author of numerous books and articles, including *Water Wisdom, a New Menu for Palestinian and Israeli Cooperation in Water Management* (2010), *Environment in Israel: Natural Resources, Crises, Campaigns and Policy from the Advent of Zionism until Twenty-first Century* (2006), and *Pollution in a Promised Land – An Environmental History of Israel* (2002). Tal holds a Bachelor degree in Political Science from the University of North Carolina, Chapel Hill, a Criminal and International Law degree from the Hebrew University Law faculty, a Master of Science and Policy in Environmental Science and Law and a Doctorate in Health Policy from the Harvard School of Public Health.

James L. Wescoat, Jr. is Aga Khan Professor of Architecture at the School of Architecture + Planning at Massachusetts Institute of Technology. His research focuses on water systems in South Asia and the US, from site scale to international river basin scales. At the site scale, Wescoat focuses on historical waterworks of Indo-Islamic gardens and cities, including a Smithsonian Institution project on "Garden, City, and Empire: The Historical Geography of Mughal Lahore" in Pakistan; and water systems in Agra, Champaner-Pavagadh, Delhi, and Nagaur in India. At the regional scale, his work has addressed water policy issues in the Colorado, Indus, Ganges, and Great Lakes basins. Current work includes three projects on water-conserving and disaster resilient design in the Indus basin. His publications include *Water for Life: Water Management and Environmental Policy* (2003) with geographer Gilbert F. White; *Political Economies of Landscape Change: Places of Integrative Power* (2007) with Douglas Johnston; and essays in *Sustainable Design in Arid Climates* (1996), published by the Aga Khan Trust for Culture and Dumbarton Oaks. Wescoat earned his Bachelor of Landscape Architecture degree at Louisiana State University and a Masters degree in Geography at the University of Chicago with an emphasis on water resources.

Lennart Woltering is Water Management Specialist for the GFA Consulting Group in Hamburg, Germany, in the Agricultural and Rural Development department. His major task is to set up projects in Africa and to find the right pool of experts for the assignment. From 2005-2010 he acted as water management specialist in the Agro-Ecosystems team at the International Crops Research Institute for the Semi-Arid Tropics (ICRISAT) in Niger. He was responsible for the research and dissemination of the African Market Garden (AMG) technology, an integrated horticultural production package based on low-pressure drip irrigation. His research focused on the economic evaluation of the African Market Garden versus traditional irrigation methods through farmer monitoring and on-station experiments. He was responsible for the planning, implementation, and management of AMG projects in West Africa using energy sources like solar pumps, artesian wells, and natural elevations. Woltering has a Master of Science in Water Resources Management and Hydrology from the Delft University of Technology.

PROJECT INDEX

The index includes the texts and captions; it does not include the drawings, references, and bibliography.

Aflaj Al Foah Residential Development at Al Ain *149, 150, 170-173*

African Market Garden (AMG) *93, 105-111*

Age of Waste, Los Angeles *8, 11*

Agronica *130*

Ahhichatragarh Fort of Nagaur *168*

Al Ain Municipality Sewage Treatment Plant *173*

Ashkelon Desalination Plant *46, 51, 52, 53*

Ashdod Desalination Plant *50, 51*

Barrage du Sautet *36*

Broadacre City *130*

Cairo Nilometer *31*

Canal du Midi *28, 30*

Centre Pompidou *21*

Ciliwung River Watershed study *113*

Corduan Noria *31*

Desert House, Erfoud *124, 127*

Duisburg-Nord Landscape Park *21*

Down to Earth, Negev Desert *24, 86-89*

Drâa Oasis Valley *9, 113-126, 147, 148, 178, 179, 180*

Eilat RO facility *51*

Emscher Landscape Park *21*

Erie Canal *34*

Hadera Desalination Plant *51, 52*

Hiriya Landfill Recycling Park *18, 20, 21, 24, 148, 150, 174-177*

Hoover Dam *36*

IMPETUS model, Drâa Valley *114, 116, 122, 123*

Isla Urbana, Mexico City *17, 24, 82-85*

Jordan Red Sea project *134*

Jordan River Valley masterplan *150*

Kanchan Arsenic Filter, Biratnagar *18, 24, 42, 60, 65, 67, 70-73, 83*

Kurnel Desalination Plant *54, 55, 56*

Liquid Wrap, Za'atari Refugee Camp, Jordan *24, 42, 74-77*

Mahtab Bagh conservation project *149, 162, 167, 168*

Marly Hydraulic Engine, Paris *30*

Modèle intégré de la vallée du Drâa (MIDAV) *116, 122, 123, 124, 126*

Nagaur Mughal-Rajput Palace-garden Project, Rajasthan *149, 163, 168, 169, 170*

New Regional Pattern (Hilberseimer) *130*

Oodnadatta Track *153-160*

Ourcq Canal *36*

Out-House *10*

"Out of Water" exhibition *8, 9, 11*

Palmachim Desalination Plant *51, 52*

Parc des Buttes-Chaumont, Paris *32*

Pontcysyllte Aqueduct *34*

Red Sea–Dead Sea Canal *131*

Rio Besos project *150*

Rouse Hill Recycled Water Network System Plan *43*

San Pedro River project *113*

Shafdan Desalination Plant *50*

Sietch Nevada *10, 11*

Solar Enclosures for Water Reuse (SEWR) *21, 22, 44*

Strategic Master Plan for the Dead Sea *133*

Super Earth *10, 11*

Taj Mahal, Agra *167*

Taragalte Ecolodge, M'Hamid El Ghizlane *18, 24, 126, 148, 149, 150, 178-181*

Three Gorges Dam *36*

Timna Mine water reservoir *96*

Torrevieja desalination project *56*

Vena Water Condenser, Sana'a *18, 24, 42, 78-81*

Victoria Desalination Project *43*

Wadi Hanifah Bioremediation Facility, Riyadh *14, 186-189*

Wadi Hanifah Restoration Project, Riyadh *14, 16, 17, 18, 21, 24, 147, 148, 149, 150, 182-185, 186-189*

Warragamba Dam *54*

Wastewater Treatment and Reclamation in Israel *18, 19, 142-147, 148*

Water Management in the Jordan River Basin *129-141, 150*

Water out of Air Device (WOA) *21, 23, 44*

Wonthaggi desalination plant *56*

Zayed National Museum *44*

ACKNOWLEDGEMENTS

We thank our book editor Andreas Müller for his invaluable insight and editorial feedback throughout the development of this book. We are grateful to the Daniels' Faculty Deans George Baird and Richard Sommer for their unwavering support. The research and development of drawings and diagrams for the case studies and essays would not have been possible without the dedicated efforts of research assistants: John Bautista, Matthew Brown, Tawab Hlimi, You-Been Kim, Fadi Masoud, Vjosana Shkurti, Hannah Tabatabae, Danny Tseng, Matthew Wong, Kaegan Walsh, Shannon Wiley, and Yi Zhou. The design of the "Out of Water" exhibition was undertaken in collaboration with Takako Tajima, and the installation was executed by Scott Powers. We thank all the participants of the "Out of Water" conference: Eilon Adar, Hadley Arnold, Kai Babetzki, Camille Dow Baker, Felipe Correa, Farid Esmaeil, Walter H. Kehm, Gini Lee, Kristin Malone, Fadi Masoud, Antoine Picon, Virginie Picon-Lefebvre, Byron Stigge, Alon Tal, Alan Travers, Anthony M. Watanabe, Drew Wensley, James L. Wescoat, Lennart Woltering, as well as session moderators: Robert Levit, Mary Lou Lobsinger, Alissa North, Ted Kesik, Jane Wolff, and Robert Wright. The following students and staff were instrumental in the development and management of the "Out of Water" conference: Nene Brode, Jacqueline Raaflaub, Zita da Silva D'Alessandro, Johnny Bui, John Howarth, Mahan Javadi, Nicole Napoleone, Martha Sparrow, Stefan Marc Kuuskne, Caitlin Blundell, Melissa Cao, Amanda Chong, Bridget Kane, Scott Rosin, Utako Tanabe, Samar Zarifa, Fred Thwainy, and Annie Wang. Finally, we acknowledge SSHRC (Social Sciences Humanities Research Council) of Canada, Holcim (Canada) Inc., The University of Toronto Connaught New Researcher Award, OALA (Ontario Association of Landscape Architects), LACF (Landscape Architecture Canada Foundation), and the John H. Daniels Faculty of Architecture, Landscape, and Design for funding support.